Counselling Adolescents

4th Edition

Counselling Adolescents

The Proactive Approach for Young People

Kathryn Geldard, David Geldard and **Rebecca Yin Foo**

$SAGE

Los Angeles | London | New Delhi
Singapore | Washington DC

Los Angeles | London | New Delhi
Singapore | Washington DC

SAGE Publications Ltd
1 Oliver's Yard
55 City Road
London EC1Y 1SP

SAGE Publications Inc.
2455 Teller Road
Thousand Oaks, California 91320

SAGE Publications India Pvt Ltd
B 1/I 1 Mohan Cooperative Industrial Area
Mathura Road
New Delhi 110 044

SAGE Publications Asia-Pacific Pte Ltd
3 Church Street
#10-04 Samsung Hub
Singapore 049483

Editor: Susannah Trefgarne
Assistant editor: Laura Walmsley
Production editor: Rachel Burrows
Marketing manager: Tamara Navaratnam
Cover design: Lisa Harper-Wells
Typeset by: C&M Digitals (P) Ltd, Chennai, India
Printed and bound in Great Britain by Ashford
Colour Press Ltd

First edition published 1998. Reprinted 1999, 2000, 2002, 2003
(twice)
Second edition published 2004. Reprinted 2005 (twice), 2006,
2007
Third edition published 2010. Reprinted 2011, 2012, 2013, 2014.
This fourth edition published 2016

Library of Congress Control Number: 2014957076

British Library Cataloguing in Publication data

A catalogue record for this book is available from
the British Library

ISBN 978-1-4462-7603-7
ISBN 978-1-4462-7604-4 (pbk)

At SAGE we take sustainability seriously. Most of our products are printed in the UK using FSC papers and boards.
When we print overseas we ensure sustainable papers are used as measured by the Egmont grading system.
We undertake an annual audit to monitor our sustainability.

Contents

List of Figures and Tables

Figures

Tables

About the Authors

Dr Kathryn Geldard is adjunct senior lecturer in counselling in the faculty of Arts and Business at the University of the Sunshine Coast (USC), Australia. Her academic career includes program leadership of the Counselling program at USC as well as development of the postgraduate Master of Counselling degrees. Her research interests include adolescent peer counselling, and counsellor training, assessment and effectiveness. Additionally, Kathryn conducted research with Australian Aboriginal adolescents with regard to developing a culturally sensitive peer support programme in a regional community. She is the author of a number of textbooks founded on her extensive clinical counselling background with children, young people and their families and has several years' experience in supervising and training counsellors.

David Geldard has extensive experience in working as a counselling psychologist with troubled children and their families. He has worked in mental health and community health settings, and also in private practice. Together with his wife Kathryn he has been heavily involved in training counsellors, social workers and psychologists, in ways to use media and activity when counselling children. Additionally he has shown a keen interest in training workers in the use of experiential counselling methods and in family therapy. He and his wife Kathryn are the authors of several counselling texts published internationally and translated into several languages.

Rebecca Yin Foo is an Educational and Developmental Psychologist who is experienced in providing psychological support for children with developmental disabilities and their families at the Cerebral Palsy League. Her work has led her to take a high level of practical and academic interest in ways of working with children to promote optimal positive outcomes. She currently works in private practice in Brisbane, Australia. Prior to obtaining her honours degree in Psychology and Masters degree in Educational and Developmental Psychology she completed a Bachelor of Medical Engineering. She has published a number of journal articles and presented conference papers nationally and internationally in relation to her studies in both Engineering and Psychology. She is the third author of the book, *Counselling Children: A Practical Introduction*.

Preface to the Fourth Edition

I have known Kathryn for seven years now; we met during my Honours year in psychology at the Queensland University of Technology (QUT). It was an honour to work with Kathryn on my Honours and Masters theses and an absolute delight to join with Kathryn and David to complete the revisions for the fourth edition of their book *Counselling Children: A Practical Introduction.* I am equally as excited to now be writing the preface to the newly revised *Counselling Adolescents: The Proactive Approach for Young People.* This revision has been a significant one, with two new chapters, updated information in existing chapters and the inclusion of more learning resources.

The context in which young people of today find themselves has changed significantly in recent times. A range of new opportunities, and challenges, are present that didn't exist when the first edition of *Counselling Adolescents* was published in 1999. Consequently, we have written a new chapter, Chapter 5, on the contemporary context of adolescence. We have drawn on systems theory in Chapter 5 in order to provide you with an overview of the systems influencing, either directly or indirectly, the young people of today. We have particularly spent some time focusing on the technological landscape that now makes up a significant part of life for young people. This leads us into the next new chapter, Chapter 18, which focuses on using technology within the counselling process itself. In light of the high rate of adaption of technology among young people, and the advances in technology suited to the counselling process, we felt it was important to provide you, the reader, with an overview of the technology currently being used when counselling young people. We have included references to a number of counselling resources in this chapter that you can access on the Internet (please see Table 18.1).

In addition to the two new chapters we have also updated information in a number of the existing chapters to reflect more recent understandings and literature. We have added case studies to Chapters 14 to 18 to help readers apply the strategies introduced in these chapters to their practice. We have also added an extra section to the end of each chapter entitled 'Further Resources' in order to link the reader with up-to-date information and resources which supplement the book content and are freely available on the Internet.

We sincerely hope that you, the reader, find these additions useful and that *Counselling Adolescents* is a helpful support in your work counselling young people – an often challenging but very rewarding undertaking!

Rebecca

The Companion Website

Visit https://study.sagepub.com/geldardadolescents to find a range of additional resources for lecturers, to aid study and support teaching.

Instructor resources

Twelve-Session Training Programme based on the on three key themes:

- Skills
- Values and Self Discovery
- Role and Ethics

The training programme is adapted from the authors' adolescent peer counsellor training program (Adolescent Peer Support Program) which was developed as a result of research conducted with participants in a denominational co-educational high school.

   Printouts of a selection of the figures and tables from the book are available to download for use in your own sessions.

Part 1

Understanding the Young Person

1

The Nature of Adolescence

There are many professional counsellors who work exclusively with young people and gain success and satisfaction from their work. However, there are many other counsellors who are reluctant to work with them. This may be because they find young people difficult to work with or are discouraged by outcomes. Although some young people are difficult to work with, counselling them can be exciting, challenging and effective, provided that some basic principles are understood and respected. The principles and practices required for counselling young people are not complicated or difficult but are in many ways significantly different from those required for counselling either children or adults. It is only by recognizing the different approach required that satisfaction and success are likely to be achieved.

In order to help young people effectively it is important to understand the nature of their stage in life and the developmental processes that are involved. Once we have this understanding, we can use a counselling approach that is specifically designed to parallel their developmental process and to take account of normal communication processes used by young people. By doing this, there is synchrony between the counselling process and the adolescent's own experiences. This enables the counsellor to join appropriately with the young person to achieve a mutually beneficial working relationship.

In Part 1 of this book we will discuss the developmental processes that occur in young people and will consider the impact of a variety of internal and external stimuli on their development. We will begin the discussion in this chapter by considering the question 'What is the stage called adolescence?'.

This book is not intended to be primarily a theoretical treatise, but a practical guide for counsellors who wish to work with young people. It is a companion book to *Counselling Children: A Practical Introduction* (Geldard et al., 2013). Those readers who wish to review the theory related to the development of young people in more depth may wish to refer to Dacey et al. (2006) who provide discussion of the contributions of a number of important theorists, including G. Stanley Hall, Sigmund Freud, Ruth Benedict, Margaret Mead, Albert Bandura, Robert Havighurst, Abraham Maslow, Erik Erikson and Richard Lerner.

What is adolescence?

The question 'What is adolescence?' is one of definition, and the precise nature of the definition is likely to vary from culture to culture. In this book we will consider adolescence to be the stage in a person's life between childhood and adulthood. It is the period of human development during which a young person must move from dependency to independence, autonomy and maturity. The young person moves from being part of a family group to being part of a peer group and to standing alone as an adult (Call et al., 2002).

Generally, in Western society, movement from childhood to adulthood involves much more than a linear progression of change. It is multi-dimensional, involving a gradual transformation or metamorphosis of the person as a child into a new person as an adult. It is important to note, however, that the required changes in a young person during adolescence differ with culture. For example, in some cultures some of the roles played by children and adults are similar. Children may be expected to perform work-like tasks for the welfare of the family while quite young. Also, in some cultures the number of years spent in being educated before working is short. In such cultures the transition from childhood to adulthood is likely to be less challenging (Mead, 1975).

> ❝Culture influences the way young people develop❞

Adolescence involves a process that extends over a significant period of a person's life. However, there are individual differences, with some young people moving through adolescence much more quickly than others. Adolescence presents many challenges as physiological, biological, psychological and social changes are confronted. Important processes of change need to occur within the young person if these challenges are to be confronted adaptively and with success. When a young person is unable to confront and deal with a developmental challenge successfully there are likely to be unhelpful psychological, emotional and behavioural consequences. It is in dealing with these that counselling may be useful, with the counsellor helping the young person to find new ways to proceed adaptively along the required developmental journey.

As will be discussed more fully in Chapter 6, some young people are more successful than others at confronting and dealing with the challenges they meet; they are more resilient and have better coping strategies. This may be partly related to personality traits and partly to past history and the current environment. The development of young people can be considered in terms of the following challenges that inevitably occur:

- biological challenges
- cognitive challenges
- psychological challenges

- social challenges
- moral and spiritual challenges.

Biological challenges

Adolescence begins with the well-defined maturation event called *puberty*. Puberty refers to the biological events which surround the first menstruation in girls and the first ejaculation in boys. These events signal the beginning of a process of profound physical change (Colarusso, 1992). Although this is a normal maturation process it can cause difficulties for the individual. This may particularly be the case where a young person is precocious in puberty or if puberty is significantly delayed. In these situations the young person may experience an uncomfortable level of stress. Consequences may be a lowering of self-esteem and self-concept, with the person feeling awkward and lacking self-confidence. The biological changes of adolescence result in physiological changes, sexual changes and emotional changes.

Physiological changes

During adolescence major physiological changes take place. The young person grows in height, weight and strength, develops sexually, and changes in appearance. Girls develop breasts, boys' voices break, body hair grows, and changes occur in sexual organs. These physiological changes occur over a period of time. They happen at different ages and different rates for different young people. Consequently, there may be issues for a young person who may feel embarrassed, self-conscious, awkward and out of step with peers who are developing at a different rate. It is therefore not surprising that many young people become very anxious about their appearance.

Each young person is a unique individual

Sexual changes

Significant and important increases in the production of sexual hormones occur during puberty. These result not only in changes to the body as described above, but also trigger an increase in sexual arousal, desire and urge in both males and females. These changes are likely to cause discomfort for a young person. As sexual drive rises, they are confronted with issues of personal sexuality and sexual identity. These issues will influence their decisions with regard to relationships. In early adolescence, young people tend to form close relationships with friends of the same sex because they feel secure with them (Blos, 1979). Additionally, this is a part of their process of movement away from dependence on their parents and family. During this time, some will become involved in sexual experimentation with their friends. However, for others the sexual feelings of early adolescence are managed through the use of fantasy and masturbation. The early stage of adolescence typically extends from the age of 11 to 14 years. From this stage the young person gradually moves into the later stage of adolescence, which occurs typically from 15 to 18 years. The early stage and the later stage are distinguished by differences in cognitive, moral and social thinking (Dacey et al., 2006).

By late adolescence, with the acceptance of the new physically and sexually mature body, there is a gradual move, in most young people, toward heterosexual relationships. According to Colarusso (1992), by late adolescence many young people are psychologically ready for an active sexual life, which includes intercourse. Some young people may at this stage begin to explore their sexual orientation and discover an attraction to homosexual relationships. Because many in society tend to be homophobic, such explorations may be a source of anxiety, particularly if the decision is to choose a partner of the same sex (Mabey and Sorensen, 1995).

With regard to sexual development, some young people have difficulty progressing from the early stages of adolescence through to the later stages. This may be because they are unable to separate their own sexuality from their parents'. As a consequence they may engage in unhelpful sexual fantasies that fail to direct them to appropriate non-incestuous partners (Colarusso, 1992). When assessing sexual development it is important to recognize that early sexual experience is not an indicator of rapid developmental progression. Indeed, it may be an indicator of childhood sexual trauma.

Emotional changes

During adolescence, the rise in sexual hormones may influence the young person's emotional state. It would, however, be a mistake to assume that hormones act in isolation and that they alone are the cause of mood changes. They act in conjunction with other major changes that are impacting on the young person, such as changes in social relationships, changes in beliefs and attitudes, and changes in self-perception.

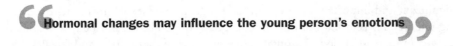

Hormonal changes may influence the young person's emotions

Biological changes clearly present the young person with major challenges. They have to cope with body changes that may be disturbing and worrying, and with the emergence of sexual urges that drive them into the exploration of new relationships which produce new social challenges.

Cognitive challenges

While biological changes are occurring in the young person, cognitive changes are also taking place. The young person develops a capacity for abstract thinking, discovers how to think about relationship issues, discerns new ways of processing information and learns to think creatively and critically.

Development of abstract thinking

According to Piaget (1948/1966), during early adolescence young people typically make the transition from 'concrete operations' to the 'formal operations' stage. That is, they move from the limitations of concrete thinking to being able to deal cognitively with ideas, concepts and abstract theories. They are able to become passionately interested in abstract concepts and notions and are therefore able to discern what is real from what is ideal.

Flavell and colleagues (2002) suggested a number of ways in which a young person's thinking progresses beyond that of childhood. Included among these were the ability to:

- imagine possible and impossible events
- think of a number of possible outcomes from a single choice
- think of the ramifications of combinations of propositions
- understand information and act on that understanding
- solve problems involving hypothesis and deduction
- problem solve in a wider variety of situations and with greater skill than in childhood.

The young person is challenged both in the development of these cognitive skills and in their use. As confidence is gained in using such skills, it is likely that they will be tried out in new situations, but not always with success.

Egocentric thinking

Young people are egocentric. This trait starts in early adolescence and develops more fully in mid-to-late adolescence. They may have the idea that everyone is watching them as though they were on stage. Sometimes they will deliberately 'parade' themselves in front of others, exhibiting particular poses or behaviours to invite attention to themselves. Young people frequently make up stories about themselves, which Dacey et al. (2006) refer to as *personal fables*. They may have dreams of success and may start to believe that these are true. They may have the idea that they are both unique and invulnerable (Elkind, 1967). They may at times feel omnipotent, all-powerful and that they cannot be hurt. This is all part of the complex process of becoming a separate unique individual on a journey that will lead to adulthood. Unfortunately, these beliefs, and in particular the sense of uniqueness, make it difficult for young people to believe that anyone else is capable of understanding them or how they are feeling. This has important implications for counsellors.

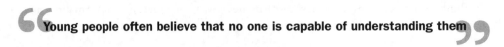

Young people often believe that no one is capable of understanding them

The ability to think about other people

Along with the sense of uniqueness or individuation comes the ability to think critically about other people and interpersonal issues. Young people learn how, from their own perspectives, to understand or 'make sense of' other people. This enables them to make decisions about how to interact with others.

New ways of processing information

During adolescence the ability of young people to perceive, comprehend and retain information seems to improve with age (Knight et al., 1985). Additionally, they progressively develop the ability to make better use of memory strategies and are more able to detect contradictions (Keil and Batterman, 1984). Thus older young people tend to have a greater ability than those who are younger for dealing with complex social and ethical issues. They have a more complex level of information processing. However, this information-processing ability is dependent on intelligence because, as described by Jensen et al. (1989), the ability to process information quickly is directly related to higher levels of intellectual functioning.

The ability to think critically

Young people develop the ability to think logically and to use their capacity for logical thinking to make judgements and decisions for themselves. They are able to recognize and define problems, gather information, form tentative conclusions and evaluate these to make decisions. Of particular importance to counsellors is that several studies suggest that young people can be taught to improve their capacity for critical thinking (Pierce et al., 1988). Thus, part of a counsellor's role may be to help a young person to find ways to do this.

It can be useful to help a young person develop critical thinking

The ability to think creatively

Creative thinking involves divergent thinking, flexibility, originality, the consideration of remote possibilities and the ability to consider a variety of solutions to the same problem. During adolescence young people develop the ability to think creatively and are consequently better able to understand and use metaphor (Dacey et al., 2006). This latter ability can be particularly useful in a counselling situation where metaphor can be a powerful tool for producing change.

Psychological challenges

The biological and cognitive changes that have been described not only present challenges directly, but also have a significant impact on psychological functioning. Additionally, there are major psychological challenges for the young person with regard to a central feature of adolescence which involves the formation of a new identity. The young person is no longer a child; a new person is emerging.

Forming a new identity

Perhaps the most important psychological task for a young person is the formation of a personal identity. Failure to achieve a satisfying personal identity is almost certain to have negative psychological implications. This is supported by Waterman (1992), who conducted an extensive review of research which showed a strong link between ego identity and effective psychological functioning. As discussed by Kroger (2005), major theorists including Erikson, Blos, Kohlberg, Loevinger and Kegan have written about the development of identity in adolescence using terms which are individual to themselves, such as 'self', 'ego', 'I' and so on. Although they have used individual terms, they all seem to agree that 'personal identity', as we will call it, should be defined in terms of what is taken to be 'self' in contrast to what is considered to be 'other'. The means by which we differentiate ourselves from others is central to our experience of personal identity. A young person has the task of forming a personal identity that is unique and individual. However, during the process in which a conscious sense of individual identity develops there will also be an unconscious striving for continuity of the individual's personal character (Erikson, 1968). As personal identity develops, over time, maturation occurs, moving the young person towards adulthood.

Young people strive for a personal identity

Functions of personal identity

Adams and Marshall (1996), drawing on numerous analyses and studies of the self and identity, suggest the following as the five most commonly recorded functions of personal identity:

1. Providing the structure for understanding who one is.
2. Providing meaning and direction through commitment, values and goals.
3. Providing a sense of personal control and free will.
4. Enabling consistency, coherence and harmony between values, beliefs and commitments.
5. Enabling the recognition of potential through a sense of future possibilities and alternative choices.

Adams and Marshall (1996) believe that the search for identity is a continuing process which is not just restricted to adolescence. They indicate that personal identity can be altered through heightened self-awareness, and that there are sensitive points along the life-cycle, one of which is adolescence, where self-focusing and identity formation are heightened. Even though we agree that the search for identity is a process that continues throughout life, our observations of young people indicate that such self-focusing and identity formation are more pronounced in adolescence and are central characteristics of adolescence.

Individuation

Whereas a child is joined with parents and family, a young person moves away into a separate space, becoming a separate individual. In other words, *individuation* occurs. The process of individuation involves the development of relative independence from family relationships, the weakening of ties to objects which were previously important to the young person when a child, and an increased capacity to assume a functional role as a member of adult society (Archer, 2005). The processes of establishing a personal identity and achieving individuation have implications socially. The young person can only construct concepts of self within the context of relations with others, yet is also seeking to establish separateness through boundaries. Thus their process of socialization is based on a balance between individuation together with the formation of personal identity, on the one hand, and integration with society on the other (Adams and Marshall, 1996). Unless this balance is achieved, there are likely to be personal crises that may result in the need for counselling. For example, if a young person seeks a very high degree of individuation the consequence may be that relationships with peers are damaged. This may result in them being marginalized. In this situation they will sometimes seek the company of other marginalized peers. Even so, there are likely to be consequences as their sense of being valued by others may be reduced (Schlossberg, 1989).

Rather than seek a high degree of individuation, some young people do the opposite and seek extreme connectedness with others. This can leave young people prone to difficulties in adapting to new circumstances where they need to deal with situations on their own (Josselson, 1987).

Emotional responses

As young people progress on their journey of self-discovery, they are continually having to adjust to new experiences, encounters and situations, while at the same time adjusting to biological, cognitive and psychological changes. This is both stressful and anxiety-provoking for them. It is not surprising, therefore, that young people demonstrate a decreased ability to tolerate, assimilate and accommodate change (Shave and Shave, 1989). The developmental stage of adolescence is therefore characterized by emotional reactivity and a high intensity of emotional response. This makes it difficult for young people to control and modulate their behavioural responses, which at times may be inappropriately extreme. Stimuli of relatively minor significance for most adults may result in significant mood swings for a young person who may respond with unexpectedly high levels of emotion, including excitement, anger, sadness, depression and embarrassment. Young people clearly have a difficult time dealing with the heightened intensity of their emotions and reactions.

> **Young people commonly experience mood swings**

A major disruptive emotion of early adolescence is shame (Shave and Shave, 1989). Young people frequently experience feelings of ridicule, humiliation and embarrassment, and feel disgusted and ashamed of themselves. It is therefore understandable that they tend to develop strong defence mechanisms that may include disavowal, denial, projection and regression. These defence mechanisms play an important role in the way young people in early adolescence react to situations and interact with others. Inappropriate behaviour may often be a consequence of these internal ego-defending mechanisms.

Ethnic identity and psychological adjustment

For young people who belong to ethnic minority groups there are special problems with regard to establishing personal identity. An important part of their personal identity is likely to involve their ethnic identity. Waterman (1984) has suggested a model of ethnic identity formation. In the first stage of ethnic identity development, minority young people accept the values and attitudes of the majority culture. This often includes internalizing negative views of their own group. Waterman (1984) believes that this first stage of ethnic identity development continues until individuals have an experience of racism or prejudice which forces them to see themselves as members of a minority group. This awareness then leads them to a personal ethnic identity search. The search involves efforts to learn about their own culture and is often likely to be highly emotional. In this stage, emotions such as anger and outrage may be directed towards the majority society. A satisfactory outcome of this ethnic identity process can then be achieved with individuals developing a deeper sense of belonging to a group.

Career identity

Another important aspect of personal identity that young people are exploring is that of career. Career identity involves the young person exploring work options in order to develop their identity as a worker and determine what work role might suit them best. Such exploration generally occurs during secondary school as students are already making decisions regarding their future careers, for example, by the subjects they choose. Working towards a well-developed career identity in adolescence has been found to support well-being and the transition to adulthood (Malanchuk et al., 2010).

Social challenges

A major challenge for young people is concerned with their need to find their place in society and to gain a sense of fitting in that place. This is a process of socialization involving the young person's integration with society. This process occurs at the same time as the search for personal identity. In fact, the socialization process and the search for personal identity are strongly interrelated and interdependent. Socialization enhances the sense of personal identity, and the development of personal identity helps the young person to deal with society's expectations and standards.

The wider society, parents, families and peer groups all have expectations regarding young people. These expectations are based on the appropriate assumption that the maturing individual is now becoming capable of behaving differently. The combined expectations of society, parents and peers, together with newly acquired psychological and cognitive changes, challenge young people to make changes in their social behaviour.

Society's expectations

Society's expectations pose a challenge for young people and are valuable in helping them to progress along the path to adulthood. In communities where adults express consistent values and expectations, young people tend to develop a positive sense of self (Ianni, 1989). In contrast, in communities where family, school and community fail to offer consistent direction and positive goals, young people drift towards undesirable behaviours, tend to become confused and cynical and to experience a generally diffused sense of self.

A young person can only construct a personal identity in the context of relationships with others. Having relationships with others unquestionably involves respecting and responding appropriately to their expectations. Society in general has expectations about how young people should behave and these will often conflict with a young person's expectations. Hence, the need to achieve individuation provides a conflictual challenge for the young person who is striving for personal identity and is, at the same time, exploring new ways of fitting into society. Consequently, there is likely to be marked ambivalence in many young people concerning issues of independence versus dependence, and with regard to expressing attitudinal and behavioural changes while maintaining social relationships (Archer, 2005).

Many of the tasks of adolescence involve strong social expectations. Havighurst (1972) believed that the mastery of the nine developmental tasks listed below were critical to adaptive adolescent adjustment:

1. Accepting one's physique and sexual role.
2. Establishing new peer relationships with both sexes.
3. Achieving emotional independence of parents.
4. Selecting and preparing for an occupation.
5. Developing intellectual skills and concepts necessary for civic competence.
6. Achieving assurance of economic independence.
7. Acquiring socially responsible behaviour patterns.
8. Preparing for marriage and family life.
9. Building conscious values that are harmonious with one's environment.

This list of tasks might seem daunting for many young people. Some will find the challenges overwhelming and will feel alienated from society because they are unable to achieve society's expectations.

> " **Young people are commonly pressured by society's expectations** "

As young people grow, they start to look like young adults and are able to communicate more maturely and effectively than children. Consequently, it is understandable that many adults expect that the behaviour of young people ought to reflect the norms of adult behaviour. The expectation that they will be responsible and will conscientiously set out to meet the developmental tasks of adolescence is unrealistic. They are in a process of growth and are dealing with new and previously unmet challenges, so are unlikely to stay focused on particular tasks and are sure to make mistakes. Young people who are overwhelmed by society's expectations may revert to anti-social behaviour, becoming involved in behaviours ranging from low-level delinquency to serious crime. Some will find ways of satisfying their needs through membership of delinquent gangs. By being in a gang they may experience the feelings of belonging that they need, along with expectations that they can meet.

The impact of society's stereotypical expectations for young people of both sexes has been clearly identified in the relevant literature (Schrof, 1995). In spite of the influence of feminism, girls may get messages that their primary role in life is to marry, have children and become good wives and mothers. This may play havoc with their selection of long-term goals and be damaging to some girls' self-esteem. Similarly, the ideas that teenage boys have about being an adult male can be psychologically destructive when they try to live up to them. For both girls and boys, problems ranging from addiction to violence may often have their roots in a young person's inability to cope with the demands of the socialization process.

Parental expectations

Most parents do not know what is normal and realistic with regard to their expectations of their children as they progress through adolescence. Many parents become worried, and at times distressed, by behaviours that are normal for young people. Rutter (1995) believes that most young people are not particularly difficult or troublesome but the problem, in Western society, is how parents respond to them. She argues that the parents' response may create negative feelings and catapult the young person into anti-social behaviour. In her discussion of the issues she draws on research by Steinberg (1990).

Steinberg's (1990) hypothesis is that when children reach puberty the combination of the adolescent phase of development and the behaviour and emotions of parents produces tremendous changes in the parents, with parents becoming increasingly distressed. This may often be accompanied by a decline in marital satisfaction, regret for missed childhood opportunities, recognition of the ageing process, emotional rejection and isolation from a young person who is becoming independent, increasing criticism from a challenging teenager, decline in respect for previously accepted authority and guidance, powerlessness, loss of youthful appearance and doubt about their own sexuality. These changes, Steinberg and Steinberg (1994) believe, often result in parents disengaging from their young people at a time when they need continuing guidance and support. It is understandable, although unfortunate, that some parents withdraw from appropriate contact with their children as they progress through adolescence. Young people need to withdraw because becoming independent is central to their role. Unfortunately this does lead to many parents feeling dismayed and abandoning them at a time when they need special care and attention because of the transitions they are making.

Even when there are tensions in family life, the family remains one of the most effective vehicles for promoting values in adolescence, enabling young people to be successful at school and to have confidence in peer relationships. Steinberg and Steinberg (1994) find that the common link between successful young people is that they generally have positive relationships with their parents. Thus an important challenge for young people is to maintain positive relationships with their parents while achieving their developmental goals, one of which, somewhat paradoxically, is to separate and detach from their parents. Clearly, this is hard to achieve.

Most children begin to detach from their parents at an age of about 14. Although this may sometimes be the result of family dysfunction, it must also be recognized as part of the normal process for young people. There are gender differences: boys generally seem to spend less time with their families than girls. Also girls are more likely to talk about personal issues with parents than are boys.

It can be difficult for parents to adjust to a young person's individuation

Many parents become distressed because in adolescence their children do not want to discuss personal issues with them. However, because young people are seeking independence they are more likely to talk to parents at a time that suits them rather than responding to parental enquiries at other times. Further, they are more likely to continue talking if they are allowed to take the lead. These traits of young people have significance for counsellors.

Adolescent expectations

A question of importance for counsellors is what young people themselves believe are their major challenges. Young people believe that their major challenges revolve around relationship issues with peers and others and performance issues within society, school or college (Youniss and Smollar, 1985). There are some differences here with regard to age. School pressures have been identified by young people in early adolescence as being the most problematic, whereas for young people of 14 years and older, parent–adolescent conflicts were identified as being the most problematic.

Issues concerning peer relationships were universally considered to present problems, although more so for the young person in late adolescence (Spirito et al., 1991). Along with forming close relationships and friendships, most young people are interested in belonging to a group whose members share common attitudes and interests. Within these groups they have strong expectations that their friends will be trustworthy and loyal to them. They tend to be intolerant of disrespectful acts, moodiness, stubbornness, conceit, drinking too much and bragging. Such behaviours are most likely to cause conflict (Youniss and Smollar, 1985).

Moral and spiritual challenges

Important to the processes of social development and the formation of a personal identity are issues relating to moral and spiritual development.

Moral development

During adolescence the young person is confronted and challenged by a wide range of moral decisions. There are a number of differing views concerning the process of moral development. Important contributors to theory in this field are Kohlberg (1984) and Gilligan (1983). Kohlberg (1968, 1984) suggests a model that outlines stages of moral development based on ways of thinking about moral matters. His stages of moral development are:

- *Stage one*: pre-conventional morality (aged 4–10 years). In this stage the child will do good or avoid wrong with a motive of either avoiding punishment or receiving a reward.
- *Stage two*: conventional morality (aged 10–13 years). During this stage the child or young person learns to conform to the society in which they live. The motives for doing good or avoiding wrong depend on the approval of older people. Additionally, there is an emphasis on conforming with law and order.

- *Stage three*: post-conventional morality (aged 13 years onwards). During this stage the individual develops a sense of human rights and starts to develop a conscience. Being aware of human rights may involve thinking about changes in the law to strive for more acceptable conditions. Additionally, at this stage young people develop clear ideas about what they believe in and what they are prepared to stand up for. No longer does the individual act merely out of fear or the need for approval. Instead, moral principles are integrated within, and owned by, the individual.

Kohlberg (1984) is conscious that not all young people reach stage three. For some young people, morality and motives may be at a stage-one level. For them, morality is tied up with rewards or with not 'getting caught'.

Gilligan (1983) believes that Kohlberg's theory does not truly represent the moral development of females, and it must be acknowledged that much of Kohlberg's research was based on male subjects. Gilligan suggests that there are three distinct levels of female development:

- *Level one*: individual survival is the driving force for moral reasoning. The female is limited strictly by concern for herself.
- *Level two*: the young person moves to a position of self-sacrifice and social conformity.
- *Level three*: moral decisions in this stage are characterized by consideration for the woman's individual needs as well as those of others. There is an emphasis on not hurting others.

Moral development is subject to gender differences

Gilligan (1983) believes that women often use the ethic of care in making decisions about their lives. She suggests that the ethic of care comes from the attachment of children to their mothers, and that through their mothers girls learn about the 'give-and-take' nature of relationships in which moral decisions are made. Comparison of Gilligan's and Kohlberg's theories of moral development suggests that there are differences between males and females in the development of moral decision making. The development of moral reasoning may also be heavily influenced by the context in which a young person lives and is largely dependent on intellectual development which also occurs at this time (Lovat, 1991).

Spiritual development

As young people seek to establish their personal identity, they attempt to find meaning in their lives. They look within themselves to examine thoughts and feelings, and to reason about them. This leads many young people to seek answers to questions of a spiritual nature (Elkind, 1980). Conventional religious beliefs and participation in organized religious practices demonstrate aspects of spirituality. However, adolescent spirituality is often demonstrated in a more fundamental way through the young person's search for meaning in life's daily experiences.

Fowler (1981) believes that spirituality can develop only within the scope of the intellectual and emotional growth of the individual. He sees the spiritual beliefs of children from the ages of 5 and 6 as relying heavily on the verification of facts from authority figures such as parents and teachers. In early adolescence, the emphasis is on symbolism rather than knowing factual truth. Later in adolescence, personal experiences, symbols and rituals may play a major part in the development of spiritual beliefs. At this stage the young person is likely to recognize that other people might have different and equally valid ways of understanding and expressing their spirituality. Some young people find conventional religious systems problematic and inconsistent with their need to achieve some level of separation from their family's traditions and values. Those young people who are struggling with identity formation, and are striving to find their place in society, may be attracted to unorthodox religious cults and practices in order to explore their spiritual beliefs and values. Some young people will look to such cults to provide them with a deeper sense of the meaning of life. Unfortunately, they may then become involved in religious practices that are unacceptable in conventional society. This may lead to a young person being marginalized.

Involvement in Satanism is an example of an unorthodox way in which young people may seek to explore their spirituality. Tucker (1989) suggests that young people are deeply fascinated by the kind of experience found in the practice of Satanism. Unfortunately, Satanism can seem attractive for a number of reasons. It provides a sense of group identity and bonding, the opportunity to develop a self-perceived 'charismatic' personality, power because it engenders fear in others and freedom from the restrictions of conventional belief systems. It also offers the opportunity to reject mainstream religion openly. It is not surprising that some young people are attracted to this belief system.

In summary

Clearly, adolescence is a time of change and crisis that may be adaptively encountered by some but for others presents the possibility of undesirable psychological, social and emotional consequences. The primary goal of adolescence is to make the transition from childhood to adulthood. Young people need to do this while dealing with biological, psychological and social challenges. Further, reaching adulthood successfully and unscathed will be influenced by the childhood experiences, environmental stresses and environmental hazards discussed in Chapters 2, 3 and 4.

KEY POINTS

- in adolescence a young person individuates and moves from being part of a family group to being part of a peer group
- young people face biological, cognitive, psychological, social, moral and spiritual challenges during adolescence
- biological challenges experienced by young people relate to physical, sexual and emotional changes
- cognitive challenges include new ways of processing information, and the ability to think critically and creatively
- psychological challenges include individuation, forming a new personal identity, ethnic identity and career identity
- social challenges include parental, family and society's expectations
- as a consequence of moral and spiritual development, young people are confronted by new challenges

FURTHER RESOURCES

Further information and resources about the developmental stage of adolescence is available from the 'Child Development Institute'.

- childdevelopmentinfo.com

2

The Influence of Childhood Experiences

In Chapter 1 we explored the biological, cognitive, psychological and social challenges which young people need to negotiate and overcome. These developmental challenges may be daunting and overwhelming for some. However, many young people are ready and keen to accomplish the tasks confronting them. In favourable circumstances, given support from loving parents, from understanding teachers and from the wider society, the transition through adolescence can be managed with relative ease, the outcome being a well-adjusted mature adult. Unfortunately, in reality, many young people will not experience a smooth, untroubled journey through adolescence. Difficulty may be attributed to a variety of factors, the most important of which may be the young person's personality and ability to cope. Other factors include the influence of early childhood experiences, external or environmental stresses, and current social conditions. All of these may interfere, at times, with the ability of the young person to proceed along the developmental journey towards maturity and adulthood.

In this chapter we will examine the influence of childhood experiences which may, if not resolved, interfere with a young person's ability to deal adaptively with the tasks of adolescence. We will discuss the effects of unresolved childhood issues related to each of the following:

- early attachment problems
- the influence of unhelpful parental behaviour
- the effects of abuse
- the effects of trauma
- genetic effects
- the impact of educational experiences.

Early attachment problems

The word *attachment*, as used in developmental psychology literature, describes the tendency of a child to repeatedly seek closeness with a specific person, usually the mother, in order to reduce internal tension. Bowlby (1969) is a major contributor to the relevant theory. He believed that attachment is an enduring affectionate bond which has a vital biological function indispensable for survival, and that the relationship between a child and the attachment figure provides a secure base from which the child can explore and master the world.

Some children do not have the opportunity to form a secure attachment to one person. They may have neglectful or abusive parents, be subjected to hospitalization which separates them from a parent, lose their parents through illness, accident or war, or be subjected to other repeated traumatizing events which prevent a secure attachment from forming. As a consequence, these children are likely to suffer from what is known as an *attachment disorder* which can have quite serious consequences for them.

The kind of attachment that a child develops with the primary caregiver may impact on that child's development throughout life. Young people who have relatively secure attachments experience fewer and less stressful events related to school, and less strain during college years, than those with less secure attachments. They also exhibit higher academic performance (Burge et al., 1997). Attachment to parents is also found to have a strong effect on self-image, particularly with regard to aspects that gain prominence during adolescence such as body image, vocational goals and sexuality (O'Koon, 1997).

> **Early attachment can affect a young person's ability to cope**

Early attachment with primary caregivers seems to have an effect on much of a young person's later experiences and to influence the way in which the young person deals with stressful situations. Insecure or unsatisfactory attachments during childhood have been linked, in young people, with later substance abuse (Gerevich and Bacskai, 1996; Burge et al., 1997), eating disorders (Burge et al., 1997; Salzman, 1997), early sexual activity and high-risk sexual behaviour (Smith, 1997) and poor self-image (O'Koon, 1997). It has been found that anxiety disorders were more likely to occur in young people who had anxious attachments to their mothers as infants when compared with those who had secure attachments (Warren et al., 1997).

Clearly, it is important for counsellors who work with young people to recognize that some maladaptive behaviours may be partly the result of poor attachment relationships with primary figures during childhood.

The influence of unhelpful parental behaviour

The family is the primary provider of the emotional, intellectual and physical environment in which a child lives. This environment will impact on that child's views of the world later in life and on the child's ability to cope with future challenges. Thus, family connectedness and structure will impact on a young person's adjustment. Clearly, the ability of a family to function healthily will depend on the parent or parents.

It is both obvious and trite to say that parents have a major influence over child and young person development. Even so, we need to recognize that although many children who have competent parents grow up to confront the challenges of adolescence successfully, others do not. It is also important to recognize that when parents give their own needs priority without adequate regard for the needs of their children, family systems become dysfunctional (Neumark-Sztainer et al., 1997) and as a consequence children will be affected in a variety of ways, as described in this chapter. Because this book is about counselling we will often be considering those factors that lead to problems for young people, so that these problems can be understood by the counsellor when devising proactive counselling strategies.

Parents need to address unacceptable behaviours in their children and to encourage the development of socially appropriate behaviours. If they do not do this, there will be consequences, either in childhood or when the child reaches adolescence, with regard to social relationships. There is generally a developmental sequence in which anti-social and aggressive behaviours develop. Such behaviours often begin in early childhood and include arguing, bragging and demanding attention. Unless these behaviours are addressed appropriately by parents they are likely to develop in middle childhood into behaviours such as being cruel, fighting, lying and cheating, with consequent poor peer relationships. Destructiveness and stealing in the home may then begin to emerge. Anti-social and aggressive behaviours thus start in mild forms of unacceptable behaviour in children and develop in intensity, frequency and form as the child gets older.

> " Anti-social and aggressive behaviours often begin in early childhood "

Some parents engage in behaviours which are unacceptable to society, with consequent damage to their children. Unfortunately, when parents engage in anti-social and maladaptive behaviours they increase the possibility of their children doing the same (Kazdin, 1985). It has been consistently demonstrated that both criminal behaviour and alcoholism in parents, particularly in fathers, is related to young person anti-social behaviour (West, 1982). Thus, irresponsible behaviour by parents may result in anti-social and aggressive behaviours being passed down within a family to successive generations.

The effects of abuse

When children are abused there will be psychological and emotional consequences for them at the time that the abuse occurs, and also later when they reach adolescence.

The psychological and emotional effects of abuse will almost certainly result in the development of maladaptive behaviours unless the child or young person is able to resolve related troubling issues satisfactorily. In considering the effects of abuse we will discuss:

- neglect
- emotional abuse
- physical abuse
- sexual abuse.

Often the effects of different types of abuse overlap. In addition, the young person's responses may be affected by underlying factors such as genetic predisposition, poor early attachment relationships and dysfunctional family patterns of behaviour, as previously discussed.

Neglect

The impact of neglect on children has been the focus of numerous studies. Many children at risk of neglect come from low socio-economic environments and underprivileged or culturally deprived minority groups. Others come from dysfunctional families where there are psychological problems, alcohol and/or drug abuse or financial problems (Swanson, 1991). Neglect can result in behaviour problems, poor school attendance, weak academic grades and low achievement generally. Children who have been neglected demonstrate a higher risk of having a diagnosis later in life of anti-social personality disorder (Luntz and Widom, 1994).

When a young person has had a history of childhood neglect, the young person may carry angry feelings towards the neglectful carers, and is likely to have problems with regard to such matters as personal safety, the provision of essential needs, equity, fairness, trust and responsibility.

Emotional abuse

Emotional abuse is often combined with other types of abuse. McGee et al. (1997) examined young people's perceptions of maltreatment experiences, including emotional abuse, physical abuse, sexual abuse, neglect and exposure to family violence. Of these various types of abuse, the young people in the study reported emotional maltreatment as the most potent type of maltreatment.

Some parents put their own needs first at times when their children and/or young people need assistance, affirmation and reinforcement for positive behaviour. By doing this, these parents absent themselves emotionally from their children. This is abusive. When these children reach adolescence they are likely to have unresolved issues with regard to their emotional needs. Consequently, it is highly likely that they will seek out new ways to meet these needs. They may, for example, become involved in substance abuse or join up with peers who are engaged in 'exciting' risk-taking delinquent behaviours.

> **" Emotional abuse can have far-reaching consequences for a young person "**

Similarly, in families where substance abuse and/or chemical dependence is occurring, there may be a lack of communication between parents and children, inadequate and inconsistent discipline within the family, and an absence of close emotional support and attachment (Garcia, 1992). Children growing up in these families are likely to carry emotional scarring into adolescence and will consequently be prone to develop dysfunctional behaviours.

Young people who have experienced emotional abuse as children may often present in counselling with behaviour problems. It is the proactive counsellor's task to identify the underlying emotional issues and to help the young person to find resolution.

Physical abuse

Children who have been subjected to physical abuse are certain to carry psychological scars with them into adolescence. In many cases, they not only need to deal with painful experiences from their past, but also may have to deal with continuing abuse in the present. An important dynamic in physical abuse is the issue of power and control. Consequently, young people who have been abused as children are likely to have strong unresolved emotional feelings around the issues of power and control.

Abusive parents tend to have common characteristics such as not taking responsibility for their behaviour, blaming the child, being incongruent, saying one thing and doing another, needing to have power over the child, distrusting their children, being selfish and being over-concerned with their own needs. They tend to repeat their abusive behaviour compulsively (McEvoy and Erickson, 1990).

Often, physical abusers of children have developed strong beliefs about parenting and the use of physical control and corporal punishment of children as a way of shaping behaviour. They should not be confused with parents who are authoritative, rely on non–abusive methods of behaviour management and use adaptive communication strategies. Unfortunately, parents who rely solely on power approaches such as using force, physical punishment and threats to deal with their children are less likely to be successful with regard to developing their children's moral values (Hoffman, 1988). Parents who rely on praise, social isolation and withdrawal of affection for punishment seem to produce children with high levels of conscience development because their children internalize parental standards and values (Baumrind, 1971). Authoritative parents are most successful in producing children who are socially competent and responsible.

It has been found that children and young people exposed to physical abuse may develop symptoms similar to those of post-traumatic stress disorder (Glod and Teicher, 1996). These authors also observed that children who had been physically abused had activity profiles similar to those of children diagnosed with attention deficit hyperactivity disorder (ADHD). This could be confusing for counsellors and is of considerable importance to them. It would be easy to make incorrect assessments because of the similarities in presentation of physically abused and children and young people with ADHD.

Parents need to develop new skills if they are to make the transition from parenting a child to appropriate parenting of a young person. Making this transition is stressful for some parents. Consequently, young people from drug and chemically dependent families and alcoholic families may be at risk of physical abuse because their parents may become frustrated by their changing behaviour. In addition, many chemically dependent and alcoholic parents have poor anger-management skills.

Young people who have been physically abused as children and suffer abuse which continues into adolescence commonly respond to such abuse in one of two ways: they may express their feelings by acting out in anti-social ways with high levels of aggression, or they may hold back and internalize their feelings with the consequent development of depression and suicidal ideation. Those who internalize their feelings may also withdraw and disengage from mainstream young person social contacts and become marginalized in socially disconnected peer groups (Schmidt, 1991).

A further problem for those young people who internalize their feelings and experience powerlessness as a consequence of childhood and/or continuing physical abuse is the risk of suicide. Suicide and suicide attempts are increasingly recognized as options by young people with poor coping strategies. Kaplan et al. (1997) found that the rate of suicide attempts increased in adolescents who had been physically abused as compared to young people who had not been abused. These young people were also different from the non-abused peers in that they demonstrated significantly greater risk factors for suicide; for example, depression, substance abuse and disruptive behaviour.

Physically abused youngsters are at increased risk of developing unhelpful behaviours

Sexual abuse

Sexual abuse occurring during childhood has been widely documented as contributing to later young person and adult adjustment problems. Further, sexual victimization prior to adolescence contributes to the risk of delinquency in young people (Widon, 1994). Studies examining the short-term effects of childhood sexual abuse indicate that symptoms of depression and anxiety are common. The victims may also suffer from other sequelae which may continue through adolescence, including sexualized behaviours, nightmares, social withdrawal, isolation, sleep difficulties, anger, acting-out behaviours, somatic problems and schooling difficulties.

Studies of the long-term effects of childhood sexual abuse reveal that, as adults, victims of such abuse tend to have a high level of mental health problems, including depression, anxiety disorder, substance abuse, sexual dysfunction and interpersonal difficulties (Browne and Finkelhor, 1986). Further, sexual abuse during childhood and adolescence has been documented as contributing to suicidal gestures and attempts (VanderMay and Meff, 1982; Bagley et al., 1997).

Garnefski and Diekstra (1996) noticed that sexually abused boys had considerably more emotional and behavioural problems, including suicidal behaviour, than their female counterparts. Their research suggests that there may be gender differences in the ways that young people respond to sexual abuse. Sexually victimized young females often have feelings of inferiority or disgust about their femininity and sexuality. This may lead to concern about their body weight, shape and size (Oppenheimer et al., 1985). It is not surprising, therefore, that many sexually abused young people report disturbances in body image, seeing themselves as fat, ugly and unworthy. They may then develop eating disorders (Hall et al., 1989). Clearly, sexual abuse in childhood and body-image disturbance are related. Welch et al. (1997) discovered that young people who were diagnosed with bulimia nervosa reported previous life events, such as sexual abuse, which involved a threat to their sense of bodily integrity and safety. Additionally, Casper and Lyubomirsky (1997) showed bulimic eating behaviour to be significantly related to sexual abuse.

It is common for children to be sexually abused by someone they know and trust. Such abuse may last for several years and often continues into adolescence. According to Alexander and Kempe (1984), the most serious type of sexual abuse is incest between father and daughter. There is also a high incidence of sexual abuse between stepfathers and stepdaughters. Often a daughter will be manipulated into wrongly believing that the abuse is all her fault. In addition, she may be warned that if she talks to anyone about the abuse she will be seen as a bad person and may also be arrested and jailed. Sadly, the outcome of such a situation is often for the young person to withdraw socially or run away from the family. The young person may engage in truancy, sexual promiscuity and have difficulty with future relationships (Alexander and Kempe, 1984). Some will move towards prostitution. Unfortunately, young people with a history of childhood sexual abuse not only feel victimized, but also are at risk of victimizing others and of sexual offending themselves (McClellan et al., 1997).

Sexual abuse can often be found in the histories of young people with severe mental health disturbances. Atlas et al. (1997) document the presence of features of dissociative identity disorder in young people with a history of sexual abuse. Sanders and Giolas (1991) also suggest that dissociative symptoms are associated with traumatic sexual abuse experiences in adolescence. Dissociative symptoms appear to be related to very frightening sexual abuse that leaves the young person highly fearful. A behavioural analysis of situations in which the child 'spaces out', loses track of time or appears unresponsive to external stimuli is essential in such cases.

The effects of trauma

Most of the research on post-traumatic stress disorder has looked at the treatment of symptoms in adults rather than children. Reports of children's responses to traumatic events suggest that they bear a close resemblance to those symptoms of post-traumatic stress disorder in adults. Some recent studies of the disorder in children have examined children exposed to natural disaster (Frederick, 1985; Earls et al., 1988), man-made disasters (Handford et al., 1986), war-related trauma (Arroyo and Eth, 1985), violent crimes (Nader et al., 1990) and traumas related to medical procedures (Stoddard et al., 1989). Findings from these studies support the validity of the existence of post-traumatic stress disorder in children where the traumatic events have resulted in physical harm to the child or injury or death of a significant other.

One of the most common forms of trauma experienced by children today is domestic violence. Typically, when domestic violence occurs there will be injury and sometimes death of adults, young people or children in the home. Even if children are not personally involved as victims, they will be traumatized by witnessing the violence and will suffer from post-traumatic stress.

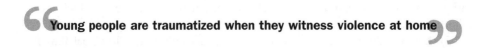

Young people are traumatized when they witness violence at home

As a result of post-traumatic stress, the traumatic event may be persistently re-experienced by the young person through recurrent and intrusive memories and/or dreams. They may experience dissociative flashback episodes where they find themselves acting or feeling as if the event was actually reoccurring. They may experience intense distress when internal or external cues that resemble an aspect of the traumatic event trigger off memories. They may persistently avoid stimuli associated with the trauma and may experience a general unresponsiveness or numbing. Numbing involves attempts to avoid thoughts or feelings associated with the trauma, an inability to recall and report aspects of the trauma, marked disinterest in or lack of participation in activities, and feelings of being detached. They may also have a restricted range of emotional affect (for example, be unable to have loving feelings). Sometimes they may have persistent feelings of arousal, hyper-vigilance, irritability and difficulty in concentrating (American Psychiatric Association, 2013).

Exposure to severe violence is highly associated with psychiatric disorders, specifically post-traumatic stress disorder (PTSD). In a study by Steiner et al. (1997) the prevalence of PTSD in incarcerated juvenile delinquents was assessed. One half of the subjects described witnessing interpersonal violence as their traumatizing event. Of those subjects diagnosed with PTSD, all showed elevated distress, anxiety, depression and lowered restraint, impulse control and suppression of aggression. They had high levels of immature defences such as projection, somatization, conversion, dissociation and withdrawal.

Unfortunately, just as with sexual abuse where the victim may become an abuser, children subjected to, or witnessing, domestic violence are likely to become violent themselves. As evidence of this, strikingly high levels of severe violence, such as shooting or stabbing, have been found to be perpetrated by inner-city youths who witnessed severe violence themselves (Singer et al., 1995).

There are also long-term effects of trauma in adolescence. Desivilya et al. (1996) examined the long-term psychological symptoms and behavioural changes resulting from exposure to a terrorist attack during adolescence. Consequences included difficulties in intrapersonal and interpersonal relationships, significantly high levels of mental health problems, greater vulnerability to psychological difficulties triggered by war-like events, lower levels of intimacy with spouses, as well as a more unstable employment history than young people who had not been exposed.

Loss

Children and young people are frequently traumatized by loss. They may lose peers such as boyfriends and girlfriends through relocation, rejection, death or suicide. They may also experience loss of parents through rejection, abandonment, divorce or death. For homeless children there are a number of losses, a critical one being denial of an education (Eddowes and Hranitz, 1989).

Where children experience loss, the grieving process may extend into adolescence and may influence their emotional state and behaviours. It is becoming increasingly recognized as important for young people to work through the grieving process so that their developmental journey is not impeded by their grief. While depression during bereavement is normal, it is important to consider when depression becomes pathological. Young people suffering the loss of a friend who has committed suicide appear to be more likely to experience a major depression occurring as a complication of the bereavement (Brent et al., 1993). Young people may also develop an increased risk of suicide themselves after someone they loved has completed suicide. As youth suicide is becoming more prevalent in Western society, it has been noticed that bereavement after suicide is more complicated. Guilt plays a greater role in bereavement when death has been by suicide as compared with death by natural causes (Peters and Weller, 1994).

Young people who suffered the loss of a parent by death reported intense shock, disbelief and a sense of loss. These experiences were found to be more intense than those of adults who lost parents through death. Young people also reported more anger at the deceased, sleep disturbances, dream activity and irritability than the adults (Meshot and Leitner, 1993).

The impact of educational experiences

Children spend a great deal of their time at school. While for many children the school experience is positive, there are multiple challenges that the educational system can present. In some cases, these challenges can have lasting effects on a young person's well-being. One of the challenges that children may face at school is with their peers; a child may feel excluded (as discussed in more detail in Chapter 3) or be actively bullied. In fact, about one in three children report being bullied at school (Cross et al., 2009). Bullying can have both short- and long-term impacts for the recipient of the bullying and for those who bully. For example, children who were bullied were found, as adults, to have more mental health, social and economic concerns (Takizawa et al., 2014).

Other children may find the academic aspects of school challenging. This is particularly true for children who have a diagnosis of Intellectual Impairment, Learning Disability or other disability or mental health concern that impacts on their ability to learn. Children who find it difficult to 'fit' into the educational system can, unfortunately, be given a label. Labelling is one way in which humans create order and meaning; labels provide information in a concise way about our world and the people in it. Some labels have positive connotations, such as 'smart' or 'well behaved', others bring with them quite negative assumptions, such as 'dumb' or 'troublemaker' (Asher, 2001). Other labels are more formal; indeed, we have used some of these formal labels in this very paragraph (Intellectual Impairment and Learning Disability). Both formal and informal labels can be difficult to remove once put in place, leaving the child in a 'box' that may overlook their true abilities and potential. Labels can have a lasting impact due to the way they become part of a child's lived experience, therefore part of their identity (Hudak, 2001).

Genetic effects

When counselling young people we need to recognize that, in addition to the effect of life experiences, there may also be genetic predispositions to psychological and behavioural disorders in adolescence. Comings (1997) reviewed evidence to support the concept that many childhood and young person disruptive behaviours, including ADHD, Tourette's syndrome, learning disabilities, substance abuse, oppositional defiant disorder and conduct disorder are part of a spectrum of interrelated behaviours and have a strong genetic component. Comings (1997) also suggests that the genetic components of these disorders have a number of genes in common which affect dopamine, seratonin and other neuro-transmitters.

In summary

In this chapter we have considered various factors relating to unresolved childhood issues which impact on the young person. It is essential that, when counselling young people, we examine the impact of their early childhood experiences on their ability to negotiate the developmental tasks of adolescence.

KEY POINTS

- childhood experiences such as attachment problems, parental behaviour, abuse and trauma, may interfere with a young person's ability to respond adaptively
- abuse may include neglect, emotional, physical and/or sexual abuse
- parents need to develop new skills to make the transition from parenting a child to appropriately parenting a young person
- there are gender differences in the way that young people respond to sexual abuse
- children and young people are traumatized when they witness violence in the home
- experiences at school can have a lasting impact on children and young people
- life experiences and/or genetic predispositions have an influence on the development of psychological and behavioural disorders in young people

FURTHER RESOURCES

For more information on the range of childhood experiences that can have a continuing impact on young people, readers are encouraged to explore the 'Raising Children Network', 'Kids Matter' and 'Centre on the Developing Child' websites. These websites are designed to provide parents, schools and professionals with information and strategies to support children with a range of challenges and make a wonderful resource for counsellors.

- raisingchildren.net.au
- www.kidsmatter.edu.au
- developingchild.harvard.edu

3

Young People's Environments

Adolescence is a time of change where the young person faces new experiences. The various environments in which they move are likely to present new and unexpected situations and events which require responses which may never have been previously used. Dealing with the unexpected and being required to use new, untested responses is certain to raise anxiety and cause stress.

There are wide differences in the ways in which young people respond to stress (see Chapter 6). Some young people are particularly resilient and have high-level coping strategies, whereas others have difficulty attending to the requirements of the developmental process in which they are engaged. The following are a number of environments and situations which have an inherent potential for raising stress in young people:

- the family environment
- the educational environment
- the work environment
- changing relationships
- exposure to sexuality issues
- socio-economic pressures and unemployment.

Clearly, a young person is unable to escape exposure to these environments because being exposed to them is an inevitable part of living. Moreover, this exposure is needed as part of the process that enables them to make the transition from childhood to adulthood.

The family environment

There are a number of factors within the family environment that have the potential to cause stress for the young person. These include:

- the family's style of functioning
- parenting style

- the parental relationship
- separation and divorce
- blended family issues
- having an alcoholic parent
- domestic violence
- cultural issues.

A young person clearly has no control over any of these factors. However, they make up an important part of the environment in which the young person has to learn new behaviours in moving from childhood to adulthood. Although the quality of the environment may have an influence on a young person's potential for successful movement towards adulthood, it is the individual's personal responses to the environment that will finally determine the extent of that success.

Each young person has their own unique way of responding

The family's style of functioning

As described by the McMaster model of family functioning (Epstein et al., 1980), families vary along different dimensions. Some families are very rigid and others laissez-faire; some families are very enmeshed and others are disengaged. In rigid families rules are clear and inflexible, with definite and specific consequences if they are broken. There is a strong commitment to maintain the status quo, and a low threshold for the tolerance of disagreement. Naturally, these families have great difficulty in times where change and growth are necessary. Consequently, they may find that experimentation by a young person in the family with new behaviours is unacceptable to the family and causes conflict and disharmony. Also, since disagreement is not permitted, there is likely to be a lack of conflict resolution where there can be explicit negotiation of differences (Garralda, 1992).

Other families are laissez-faire, with very free and easy rules. These families may have fewer problems as the young person changes. However, young people from these families may experience difficulties adjusting in wider society and the workplace where different rules and expectations may apply. There could also be other difficulties for them: because of the absence of external control by parents they will need to rely almost entirely on their internal locus of control to avoid self-destructive behaviours which may seem attractive in adolescence.

In enmeshed families a young person may find the home environment overprotective and family members unwilling to accept their need to seek a level of separation and individuation. Thus, the young person's development of autonomy and independence may be retarded. Similarly, families where there is a high level of warmth and affection may find that it is hard to allow a young person to move away from the family to establish the necessary and required independence.

Young people from disengaged families may have some advantages in seeking independence because family members already have high levels of independent functioning within clear individual boundaries. However, these young people may not receive the family support they need during the transition to adulthood.

It is clear from this discussion that, whatever the family style of interaction, there may be some problems for a young person. Adjusting to the changes of adolescence is difficult, regardless of the family environment. However, some families do provide helpful environments for growth and development. The emotional climate within a family is certain to have some influence on the ability of the young person to develop adaptively and with a minimum of stress.

Optimum conditions for young people exist in families where the environment is harmonious, where there is a genuine level of warmth and caring, where there is acceptance of difference, a respect for others' needs, good communication and the ability to resolve conflict. It is to be expected that in families where the environment is coloured by discord and disharmony, where communication is poor, tolerance of others' behaviours is low, and conflict-resolution skills are absent that the young person may be subjected to levels of stress and anxiety which will make adaptive progression to adulthood more difficult.

Harmonious families provide the best conditions for personal growth

Parenting style

Young people have little option but to cope with whatever style of parenting their parents choose to use. If the parenting style is one that inhibits change and tries to maintain the same structure that applied when the young person was a child, then the young person will struggle to make the changes which are required to move towards adulthood. They may respond with compliance, in which case normal adolescent development will be inhibited. Alternatively, there may be confrontation, in which case a high level of stress and conflict will be inevitable.

Although parents need continually to provide a young person with opportunities for change, they need to continue to exert a level of parental control, remembering that the young person is not yet an adult. This requirement is supported by Baumrind's (1991b) research. Baumrind suggests that young people tend to be higher in competence and self-esteem in families where the parents are supportive, encourage positive rational and interactive communication while they use firm and constant discipline. In other words, the parents are authoritative. The advantage in having such parents may be because the transition into adolescence is one that requires autonomy while avoiding self-destructive behaviour during an inherently demanding process of individuation (Searight et al., 1995).

Clearly, parenting communication styles are very important. Those parents who are able to communicate with their adolescent offspring effectively, and to do this in a two-way process so that both they and the young person get the opportunity to state their points of view, are more likely to enable the young person to develop adaptively.

Parental expectations are also important. Most parents have expectations of their adolescent children with regard to behaviours, beliefs, attitudes, values and choice of friends. Their expectations may also extend to academic or employment performance. Clearly, these expectations will impact on the young person and may either be helpful in promoting development or may be an impediment.

The parental relationship

The quality of the parental relationship, whether the parents are together, separated or divorced, is of major importance to a young person. Grossman and Rowat (1995) examined a number of families where the parents were married and living together, were separated or divorced. They found that low life satisfaction, a diminished sense of the future and high anxiety were related to the quality of the parental relationship, and not to the separated, divorced or married status of the family. Even so, it might be expected that young people will benefit from being in families where there are stable and adaptively functioning parental relationships. Such an environment is likely to provide the young person with feelings of security and safety during a period in life when much is changing. Additionally, a well-functioning parental relationship can provide modelling of suitable ways of relating in couple relationships for the young person.

Separation and divorce

At a time when a young person is trying to establish independence it can be very disturbing for the family to break up. Ideally, young people need to be able to determine their own independence without being concerned about the safety and security of their families. Unfortunately, where there is parental disharmony there are likely to be problems for the young person, as discussed, whether separation occurs or not.

There is a demonstrated association between parental divorce and young person depression (Aseltine, 1996). Additionally, separation and divorce create numerous secondary problems as a result of the altered life situation.

Blended family issues

Some people have the view that divorce and subsequent remarriage involving the blending of two families adversely affects the development of young people. Certainly, there are issues for young people when parents separate and divorce, and there will also be issues when their parents join up with new partners. One of the challenges faced by new blended families is the fact that boundaries and role expectations may not be clearly defined leading to role ambiguity. This role ambiguity may lead to conflict between family members regarding role expectations. Conflict may also arise over resources (possessions, space, time, and finances), children's behaviour, parenting, visitation arrangements, and household rules (Coleman et al., 2001; Golish, 2003). Inability to resolve these challenges and adjust to a newly formed family can increase the risk for a number of negative outcomes for young people, for example, emotional problems, decreased social competence and pro-social behaviour, decreased academic functioning and increased behavioural problems (Martinez and Forgatch, 2002). Challenging blended family transitions can also have a significant impact on relationship quality between the young person and the non-residential parent, residential parent and stepparent (Dunn et al., 2000; Warshak, 2000). However, divorce and remarriage do not necessarily relate to difficulties in young person adjustment. What is more important is that young person adjustment is found to relate to the level of perceived family conflict. If harmony prevails, then the effect on the young person is likely to be diminished (Borrine et al., 1991). Indeed, most stepfamilies face the challenges of transitioning into a blended family well, building positive relationships with time (Taanila et al., 2002).

Having an alcoholic parent

Parental alcoholism affects the way a family functions. Alcoholic parents tend to be emotionally detached from their children, and are often not available to them as a consequence of their drinking patterns. Alcohol abuse may also lead to other forms of dysfunctional behaviour such as physical and sexual abuse. Roles of family members often become rigid and set in families where there are alcoholic parents. Vernon (2009) describes a number of dysfunctional roles that evolve in alcoholic or chemically dependent families. Three of these roles are particularly relevant for young people:

1. *The enabler*: this family member is usually the partner of the alcoholic person, but may be a son or daughter in late adolescence. This person's role is to soften the negative effects of alcoholism by covering up the alcoholic's drinking.
2. *The hero*: this is usually the oldest child in the family. The role is to provide hope and pride to the family through activities such as excelling in school.
3. *The scapegoat*: the scapegoat tends to get recognition from peers by engaging in acting-out behaviours. Typically, in adolescence, these young people develop at-risk behaviours such as early substance abuse.

An understanding of these roles, and others described by Vernon (2009), may be useful to the counsellor in helping young people from alcoholic families.

Research by Tomori (1994) suggested that young people with alcoholic parents have high levels of anxiety. However, although this anxiety may be partly due to being in an alcoholic family, it may also be related to a personality trait. Parental alcoholism is associated with a heightened incidence of child and adolescent symptoms of psychopathology. However, it is not true that a major portion of the population of children and young people from alcoholic homes will develop psychological disorder (West and Prinz, 1988). Chassin and Barrera (1993) discovered that adolescent children of alcoholics whose alcoholic fathers had discontinued drinking tended to understand the need for self-control in limiting drinking, recognized the risk of future drug problems and could see the negative effects of alcohol in others. They suggested that these young people might be deterred from substance abuse because of their beliefs.

Domestic violence

Domestic violence has a significant impact on the development of young people. Where they have witnessed either parent–child violence or violence between parents there are negative effects on adjustment, with consequent externalizing and internalizing behavioural problems (O'Keefe, 1996). Additionally, when young people witness violence in the home, they may come to accept this as a normal and acceptable part of family life.

Cultural issues

As contemporary Western society becomes increasingly multi-cultural we need to recognize the special problems of young people who belong to ethnic minority groups. There are likely to be problems for those young people who grow up in a society where their own family cultural background differs from the major cultural influences of their environment. Friedman (1993) argues that the meaning of adolescent social development differs with culture. He notes that different meanings for particular cultures are affected by the changing social environment, differing cultural patterns of social development in puberty and marriage, and issues of health and health promotion.

Problems arise when family and societal cultures are different

Major problems for young people growing up in cultures different from that of their families is stress due to conflicts in culturally determined social and moral values and exposure to conflicting beliefs, attitudes and behaviours. Young people in this situation not only have to cope with their normal developmentally changing beliefs, attitudes, values and behaviours, but also have to consider how these fit within the present and future cultural contexts of their lives.

The educational environment

Young people find the pressures of school, college and university stressful. Both the risk and experience of failure, in an educational setting, are sources of psychosocial stress. These stresses are likely to be intensified when there is conflict with parents. As a consequence, poor school performance is made worse when conflict occurs with parents about issues concerning scholastic achievement and educational plans (Hurrelman et al., 1992).

There are also other concerns for the young person at school or college. Generally, in educational environments, the student has little power or authority and those teaching the student have considerable power and authority. For a young person, issues of power and authority are very salient. If they are to learn to take responsibility in the way that adults do, then they need to be able to have some level of control over what they do and how they do it. Educational environments may therefore be stressful for young people because they can be disempowering.

School refusal

Some young people either refuse to go to school or truant. These young people are responding, in the best way they know how, to particular stressors. Although there can be many different reasons for school refusal, problematic family relationships have often been cited as the underlying cause of such behaviour. Kearney and Silverman (1995) have suggested that there are three different types of families where young people refuse to go to school:

1. *The enmeshed family*: the focus is on over-involved parent–child/young person relationships, particularly mother–child relationships, where an affectionate but overprotective attachment has been fostered.
2. *The disengaged family*: members are not sufficiently involved with one another's activities to attend to one another's thoughts and needs. Parents within these families may not be particularly vigilant about their child's activities or problems until they are readily apparent or severe.
3. *The isolated family*: characterized by little extra-familial contact, they tend to shun activities outside the home.

Unfortunately, school refusal among young people may lead to severe long-term dysfunction if left untreated.

Social inclusion at school

One important aspect of a young person's school experience is the level of inclusion they encounter. The degree of inclusion, or exclusion, experienced within the school environment has been linked to adolescents' levels of substance use, behaviour and academic achievement. Indeed, supporting a school's degree of social inclusion has been found to decrease behaviours such as substance use and anti-social behaviours (Patton et al., 2006). The effects of social inclusion can be long-lasting, for example, connection to school via non-academic or extracurricular activities has been found to influence adolescents' tertiary educational goals (Uno et al., 2010).

The work environment

Many young people find part-time employment while still studying at school, college or university; others leave school to go into full-time employment. The employment environment is one in which adult behaviours are generally required. Consequently, experience in the workplace may impact on a young person's developmental process.

In the workplace, young people learn to take responsibility for the completion of tasks assigned by supervisors, generally experience some level of autonomy, have to deal with conformity issues regarding workplace expectations and are subjected to a variety of relationship issues (Safyer et al., 1995). They are exposed to relationships with peers, with adults and with those in authority, in an environment that has structure and expectations. Clearly, such a situation provides opportunities for personal growth and movement towards adulthood. It also presents challenges which may result in stress for the young person.

The workplace may provide an opportunity for personal growth

Changing relationships

Young people continually face issues that are likely to be stressful for them concerning changes in relationships. As they mature, relationships with parents, siblings, peers and those in positions of authority will all undergo change. Additionally, there are likely to be romantic attachments involving sexual attraction and these relationships may well be temporary, unstable and vulnerable to change because young people are in a stage of exploration and experimentation. Most young people experience powerful feelings of romantic love. Consequently, they may suffer in self-esteem when rejected by the person they love and may feel confused if their feelings change and they become attracted to someone else.

The young person's relationship with parents needs to change as the young person assumes more responsibility and parents start to hand over responsibility. Many parents struggle with the issue of handing over responsibility and may, either consciously or subconsciously, wish to retain control of their children because of their own attachment to them, coupled with fear that relinquishing control might lead to disaster. Typically a struggle will develop with the young person wanting more control over life decisions and the parents being reluctant to allow this to occur at a pace acceptable to the young person. When such a struggle occurs, communication between the young person and their parents is clearly of paramount importance if conflict is to be avoided.

White (1996) discusses problems that arise when communication with parents is not satisfactory. Unfortunately, when young people perceive communication with their parents as less than satisfactory, they may be forced into the company of others who are more accepting of their views and opinions. If this happens, parental influence will be diminished.

Exposure to sexuality issues

Dusek (1996) points out that there are wide differences between cultures with regard to the sexual behaviours expected of young people. At one extreme, there are cultures where children and young people are expected to refrain from engaging in sex until married and adult. At the other end of the continuum, there are societies where sexual behaviour develops more gradually and may be allowed or even encouraged in young people with few restrictions. In contemporary Western society there are clearly wide individual differences in attitudes and behaviours, both culturally and because of belief systems. The young person may therefore be faced with difficult choices which need to be made on the basis of information coming from a variety of sources which offer differing opinions about what is appropriate.

Most importantly, Dusek (1996) draws on research findings to confirm that parental influences on the sexual behaviour of young people are minimal. Young people whose parents discuss sex with them or whose parents keep a tight rein on their activities are no more or less likely to engage in premarital sex (although some evidence indicates that greater maternal monitoring of activities is associated with reduced *unprotected* sex for females). Young people who have sexually active friends or believe their friends are sexually active are more likely to be sexually active themselves. These factors are stronger for older rather than younger young people, and also for females rather than males. Risks associated with sexual activity for young people will be discussed in Chapter 4.

Socio-economic pressures and unemployment

In today's society, with television and the print media, there are high pressures placed on young people in terms of socio-economic expectations. The media continually display role models where those who are attractive seem to have a high level of material possessions (for example clothes). This is particularly unfortunate in a society where many young people find it difficult to obtain employment.

Research convincingly demonstrates that unemployed young people tend to suffer from a number of serious problems. Being unemployed is generally a negative experience for young people, whereas gaining employment is a positive experience (Patton and Noller, 1990). Moreover, unemployed youth report significantly more depression, negative mood and loss of behavioural and emotional control than the employed (Winefield and Tiggemann, 1990; Heubeck et al., 1995). Additionally, a number of studies show that unemployment is associated with increasing risks of psychological disorder among young people (Hammarstrom, 1994; Fergusson et al., 1997a; Meeus et al., 1997).

> **Unemployment can have significant negative consequences for young people**

There is an association between unemployment and juvenile crime. In particular, being unemployed after leaving school may be associated with increased risks of juvenile offending. However, much of the association between unemployment and juvenile crime is likely to reflect common life-course processes and factors that make young people vulnerable to both unemployment and criminal offending (Fergusson et al., 1997b).

Although poverty tends to have a negative influence on the development and behaviour of young people, these effects have been found to be mediated by the organizational structure and cultural features of the neighbourhood (Elliot et al., 1996). It is clear that much depends on the local social system and the controls and influence which this has on the young person. We discuss the multiple and interacting systems that impact on the young person in more depth in Chapter 5.

In summary

In this chapter we have considered the effects of a number of environmental stresses on young people. In Chapter 4 we will discuss specific challenges. During the normal developmental process the young person will be confronted by both environmental stresses and challenges. Some young people will cope with these adaptively; others will not, and they may seek counselling. It is essential for a counsellor to recognize the significance of those situations, events and stimuli which present difficult challenges for a young person and to be able to find ways to enable the young person to deal with these effectively.

KEY POINTS

- environmental stresses relate to family, educational and work environments, relationships, sexuality and socio-economic pressures
- a family's style of functioning can have a significant impact on a young person's growth and development
- a young person faces particular challenges where their family culture is different from the culture of their wider social environment
- challenges in school and work environments may provide an opportunity for personal growth by the young person
- sexuality issues present young people with difficult choices as information from different sources may offer differing opinions about what is appropriate

FURTHER RESOURCES

The 'Teens Health' website is a great resource for counsellors and young people alike. It provides information on a range of challenges that young people may encounter in their environments, in addition to suggestions on how to face such challenges.

- kidshealth.org/teen

4

Challenges for Young People

In Chapter 3 we dealt with some of the environmental stresses which impact on young people. There are also a number of specific challenges that are likely to confront them. During childhood, most young people live in an environment which is protected and structured and where parents or other adult carers are in control. During adolescence, young people tend to have less dependence on the protection of the family as they make new relationships and enter into situations which they have not previously encountered. Dealing with these new situations is part of the growing-up process. Because young people have not previously experienced similar situations, they have to devise ways of responding to them and this can be challenging.

Adolescence is a time of experimentation and of trying out new behaviours in response to new situations. This is risky. Unfortunately, young people are inherently susceptible to engaging in excessive and unchecked risk-taking because they often have the egocentric belief that they are almost indestructible. In this chapter we will consider some of the challenges confronting young people. In particular we will discuss:

- the influence of parents and peers
- peer groups and gangs
- smoking, sniffing, alcohol and other drugs
- sexual behaviour
- risk-taking involving anti-social behaviour
- weight control.

The influence of parents and peers

During adolescence, parental influence should be expected to reduce and the influence of peers to increase. However, both the influence of parents and the influence of peers will be impacting on the young person. At times these influences will conflict, and when they do they will inevitably create an internal struggle for the young person, who may have a difficult time trying to work out how to respond.

The influence of parents

Even though parental control generally diminishes during adolescence, most parents continue to exert a significant influence in their children's lives, and this will have an effect on the way in which the young person deals with the challenges that present themselves.

The process of adolescence requires the young person to strive for autonomy, and, ideally, in doing this to avoid self-destructive behaviours. This is difficult to achieve in what is an inherently demanding process of individuation. It is here that parents can help. Research suggests that supportive parents who encourage positive, rational and interactive communication while they use firm and consistent discipline (that is, authoritative parents) have adolescent children who are higher in competence and self-esteem and are better equipped to deal with hazardous life events (Baumrind, 1991a, 1991b).

Supportive authoritative parenting can be beneficial

Young people test limits and boundaries, and this is what they need to do so that they can gain a clear sense of how to respond to the world in which they will live as adults. During this testing period it is advantageous if parents provide boundaries for support, so that the young person has some sense of containment to foster the development of security at a time when there will be inner turmoil. What is best is for parents to set clear, consistent, non-punitive limits and boundaries, which also respect the young person's boundaries (Gaoni et al., 1994).

In order to feel good, young people need to believe that they have the approval of their families. Research confirms that both males and females have higher self-esteem in early adolescence if they perceive that they have approval and support from their families. However, there are gender differences, with young females being much more dependent on family approval and support than young males (Eskilson and Wiley, 1987).

The struggle between peer pressure and parental pressure

It is easy to understand how there may be tension between the expectations of a peer group and the expectations of parents. Young people are striving for individuation with some sense of separation from their families, while at the same time having a need for acceptance. This need for acceptance drives young people to join with peers and it is desirable that they should do so. Failure to develop good peer relationships can have unfortunate consequences with regard to behavioural and scholastic problems (Connor, 1994). In attempting to join with peers, there may be strong pressure to participate in undesired or undesirable activities as the price of acceptance. Those young people with high self-esteem and self-confidence are better able to resist negative peer pressure because they are more easily able to form and maintain friendships and to be accepted by others.

The struggle between family pressure and peer pressure will be influenced by the qualities of the family system. Where a family atmosphere is supportive of independence and does not press for achievement, young people in early adolescence tend to use their peer group as a source of emotional support without a strong need to conform to group pressure. This is in contrast to early adolescent young people whose family life is characterized by conflict, emphasis on achievement and lack of support for individual development. In these families, the young person is likely to become more conformist to group pressure (Shulman et al., 1995).

The influence of peer pressure

Peers clearly do exert pressure on young people and this is often most noticeable in terms of the way in which young people present themselves. This can be disconcerting for many parents who become anxious when their adolescent children make changes to their personal appearance in ways that are not easily acceptable to them. They may correctly blame peer influences. However, it is important to recognize that such changes, although due to the influence of peer pressure and a need for acceptance by peers, are also consistent with the young person's search for individuation and identity. In the personal search for identity, young people may choose hair styles and make-up which reflect contemporary teenage standards, they may wear unconventional clothes which are fashionable for their peer group, engage in body piercing and have tattoos. All of these ways of presenting themselves are subject to fad and are directed towards both the achievement of individuation and peer group affiliation.

Some behaviours may be seen as a demonstration of emerging individuation

Many adults tend to interpret the way in which many contemporary teenagers present themselves as anti-establishment, destructive and as having negative connotations. However, the way they present themselves can be viewed as an indicator of their search for personal identity in ways which may be constructive for them. As Martin (1997) points out, what is seen by an adult as mutilative or destructive may, from the young person's point of view, be decorative.

Peer groups and gangs

During adolescence the formation of peer groups is normal developmentally. The tendency to form such groups starts in childhood. Playmates, school friends, boy and girl scout groups are examples of the natural inclination of young people to form group attachments which provide a social outlet.

Gangs formed by young people are in essence peer groups. However, they are groups whose behaviours are perceived negatively by the majority in society. Gangs are generally considered to be socially pathological and the result of infiltration of peer groups by individuals with violent and/or other anti-social tendencies (for example, drug dealers). Gangs tend to develop mostly in urban areas and may exert undesirable influences on impressionable young people (Sigler, 1995).

It is quite understandable how gangs can become a part of young person behaviour. Unfortunately, research indicates that for females as well as males involvement with gangs is associated with increased levels of delinquency, substance abuse and sexual activity. Further, female gang members have low expectations of completing school (Bjerregaard and Smith, 1993). Similarly, research results indicate that high-school students who are members of gangs have significantly lower self-esteem than students who are not gang members (Wang, 1994).

Because of the negative concept which many adults have of gangs and the destructive impact that they can have on society, traditional school programmes generally consider gang membership anti-social. As a result, schools tend to outlaw gang presence by banning symbols of gang membership. Even so, it needs to be recognized that gangs do serve a purpose for many young people. In particular, where young people are members of minority groups, belonging to a gang can help them in retaining their own culture. The downside of this is that assimilation with the majority culture is then less likely to occur (Calabrese and Noboa, 1995).

A major problem for both female and male gang members is the possibility of abuse. Gang members generally, but especially females, can become victimized by other gang members and subjected to physical, sexual and psychological abuse (Molidor, 1996). Clearly, young people in peer groups or gangs will generally be subjected to strong social pressures to conform to group behaviours. Where these behaviours are self-destructive or anti-social there are likely to be negative consequences for the young person. In addition, young people in groups tend to compete for status and attention. Consequently there is likely to be strong pressure to participate in life-threatening risk-taking behaviours.

A detailed description of issues related to gang membership by young people together with evidence-based recommendations of ways to work with them are provided by Hallsworth and Young (2009).

Smoking, sniffing, alcohol and other drugs

Many, if not most, young people in contemporary Western society are confronted with the dilemmas of deciding whether to use, and to what extent to use, available addictive substances. Some of these are legal for adults and others are not, although most are illegal for young people below certain ages in most states and/or countries. Addictive substances include cigarettes, volatile substances which can be inhaled, marijuana, a variety of chemical substances such as amphetamines, including ecstasy, ice, psychotropic substances such as fantasy, 'magic mushrooms', datura, LSD and hard drugs, including cocaine and heroin.

> **The natural tendency of young people to explore and experiment puts them at risk**

Part of young person development is to explore, find out and experiment. Young people are curious; they want to know more about the world in which they are progressively having more freedom to make their own decisions. Consequently, they are likely to consider experimenting with the use of addictive substances. However, experimentation with addictive substances will depend on a number of factors, including availability of the substance, family and peer influences.

Several research studies on young people have investigated the effects of family and peer influences. These studies make it clear that both family and peer influences are important. Webster et al. (1994) found that whereas peer influences are exerted predominantly through modelling behaviour, parental influence is exerted predominantly through perceived normative standards. Frauenglass et al. (1997) found that deviant peer modelling was strongly associated with levels of use of tobacco, alcohol and marijuana by young people, but family support of the young person reduced that influence with regard to tobacco and marijuana use. Robin and Johnson (1996) also identified the importance of peer pressure regarding use of alcohol, cigarettes and drugs by young people. They found that both peer approval and disapproval were important. The greater the peer pressure against use, the less frequent the use. Bauman and Ennett (1996) claim that the magnitude of peer influence in drug behaviour by young people has been over-estimated by some authorities in the area, and correctly make the point that the individual is able to make a personal decision within the context of peer influence. However, the evidence demonstrating the importance of peer influence is strong.

Smoking

Exposure to smoking is a hazard which some children face in childhood. However, in adolescence, because of the developmental issues of adolescence, it presents a real challenge even though it is publicly acknowledged that smoking is a health hazard. Peer influences are particularly important with regard to smoking. Hu et al. (1995) found that even though there are differences in the reasons young people smoke, in general the influence of friends' smoking is more important than the influence of parents who smoke. Further, Wang et al. (1997) found that the smoking behaviour of best friends was the only consistent and significant social factor in predicting young person smoking.

Michell and West (1996) were interested in what causes a young person to start smoking. They noted that previous research had suggested that smokers persuaded others to smoke through coercion, teasing, bullying or rejection from a desired group. However, their own research suggested that the process was complex and included strong elements of self-determined behaviour by the young person. This suggests that individuals may play a more active role in starting to smoke than has previously been acknowledged and that social pressures other than peer pressure need to be taken into account. This fits with the theory of adolescent development where the young person, although wanting to be part of a peer group for acceptance, is also making strong moves towards individuation and the establishment of a personal identity.

It is interesting to note from a community health perspective that data on ciga-rette smoking show that smoking uptake usually occurs during adolescence through a gradual process of change from non-smoking to susceptibility, experi-mentation and then adoption of regular use. Consequently, from a public health point of view, it is important to address the cigarette-smoking issue during adolescence (Wills et al., 1996).

Sniffing volatile substances

Some young people seek to achieve an altered state of consciousness by sniffing volatile substances such as glue solvents, petrol, butane gas and the fumes from aerosol cans. Substances used for sniffing are easy to obtain and are inexpensive. For example, in most countries a young person can walk into a craft shop and buy a tube of glue without raising suspicion. Unfortunately, sniffing is highly dangerous and can cause brain dam-age and/or death.

Ives (1994) examined the use of volatile substances in England, Scotland and the USA. He identified the importance of a number of factors which are helpful in reduc-ing sniffing behaviour. These include parental involvement, the promotion of decision-making skills, peer involvement in treatment, and self-esteem. These factors are clearly important for consideration when counselling a young sniffer.

If as a reader you are interested in working with young people who sniff volatile substances, we suggest that you read the chapter written by Ives (2009) in which he describes suitable evidence-based practical interventions.

Alcohol, marijuana and other drugs

A major factor in the use of drugs by young people is connected with sensation-seeking and risk-taking tendencies (Perry and Mandell, 1995). These tendencies are part of the normal developmental process for young people. Young people are in the stage of their lives where they experiment and look for new experiences. Young people want to try things out for themselves rather than relying on information provided by others. This sets them up to be vulnerable to the temptation to experiment with alcohol and other drugs.

❝Peer pressure is an important influence in alcohol and drug use❞

Young people tend to justify their use of alcohol and other drugs by statements such as 'It's cool' or 'Everyone else drinks alcohol (or uses drugs)'. As might be expected, peer use and peer pressure are major factors for introducing young people to the use of alcohol and other drugs, such as marijuana and ecstasy, or hard drugs such as heroin and cocaine. Several research studies support this. Dupre et al. (1995) found that 55 per cent of young people in their study were first given alcohol or drugs by a friend. Jenkins (1996) found that the strongest correlate with starting to use drugs was affiliation with drug-using friends. Similarly, Yarnold and Patterson (1995) found that young person crack users tend to have friends who use crack. The relationship between drug use and peers who use is not surprising, for two reasons. First, young people are seeking acceptance by their peers. Second, those who socialize with friends who are users are likely to have easier access to the substance concerned.

Not surprisingly, abstainers from alcohol, marijuana and other drugs tend to come from families that are less likely to use drugs. These young people are also less likely to have friends who use drugs, and are not as likely to have psychosocial or school problems as are users of alcohol, marijuana and other drugs (McBroom, 1994). With regard to school problems, Jenkins (1996) found, as might be expected, that level of academic performance is inversely related to drug use.

If you, the reader, are involved in helping young people with problems such as those just described, you may wish to read the evidence-based strategies suggested by Levingston and Melrose (2009) with regard to alcohol use, and by Schaeffer et al. (2009) with regard to illicit drug use.

Sexual behaviour

It is natural and appropriate that in adolescence the young person will experiment with adult behaviours, and this is almost certain to include some level of sexual behaviour. Unfortunately, because young people are inexperienced they are likely to engage in sexual activity without fully understanding the social, psychological and physical consequences of this behaviour.

Among young people there is a significantly high and disconcerting frequency of self-reported risk-taking sexual behaviour (Downey and Landry, 1997). Interestingly, once young people have experienced sexual intercourse, they tend to engage in it relatively persistently rather than sporadically (Tubman et al., 1996). This may be because they enjoy sex and see sexual behaviour as a sign of maturity and adulthood.

Clearly, there are significant risks in sexual behaviour. There are risks of pregnancy and disease, and there are likely to be risks to self-image if sexual activity is undertaken in the absence of a context of respect and caring. Because males do not run the risk of pregnancy, the consequences of risky sexual behaviour are less salient for males than for females (Word, 1996). Females naturally see teen parenthood as more of a problem than do males and are more likely to believe that sexual urges can be controlled (DeGaston et al., 1996). Clearly, there are gender differences with regard to sexual issues for young people. DeGaston et al. found that, in early adolescence, females, as compared with males, saw sexual activity as more detrimental to them with regard to their future goal attainment. Although young females viewed parents as less approving of their sexual behaviour, they were more likely than young males to discuss sex and their dating practices with them.

The discussion so far has related to heterosexual behaviour. However, we also need to take account of homosexual behaviour in young people. Although a number of young people in early adolescence engage in homosexual exploratory behaviour, as they grow older the majority engage exclusively in heterosexual behaviour. Unfortunately, lesbian, gay, bisexual and transgender (LGBT) young people who recognize their homosexuality may experience intense conflicts with their social environments, particularly at school. In addition, there may be deleterious effects on family life, peer relationships and the development of close relationships with others (Anderson, 1993). Consequently, LGBT young people may have diminished ability to achieve a sense of identity and self-esteem because of social stigmatization (Radkowski and Siegel, 1997), and are thus susceptible to loneliness, isolation and depression. Further, Sussman and Duffy (1996) suggest that there is a need for more research on the sexual practices of gay males (aged 13–19 years) so that fact-based preventative interventions can be devised to combat the growing number of AIDS cases among this group throughout the world.

Sexuality is an essential part of adolescent development

We need to remember that sexuality is a major and positive dimension of human development. It is important that young people come to terms with their sexuality in ways which are positive. Unfortunately, the unintended consequences of a narrow focus on fear and disease may lead to increased rates of sexual inadequacy and interpersonal problems (Ehrhardt, 1996). Counsellors therefore need to achieve a sensible balance when providing information for young people about protective behaviours.

As a reader you may be interested in the evidence-based interventions for helping young people with sexual health related problems provided by Moore (2009) and with regard to sexual behaviour problems by Lambie (2009).

Risk-taking involving anti-social behaviour

Experimentation by young people may involve a significant amount of risk-taking behaviour. Many of them like to have fun and excitement and to do things that their parents have not allowed them to do. This predisposes them to consider engaging in anti-social behaviours. They may be tempted to do things such as:

- shoplifting
- vandalism
- driving cars at high speed
- fire-lighting
- listening to loud and/or aggressive music.

All of these things may be done for fun and thrills and with the influence of peer modelling and/or pressure.

Shoplifting

It has been found that the tendency for teenagers to shoplift is not related to socio-economic variables, but is related to fun, thrills and peer pressure (Lo, 1994). Shoplifting is strongly influenced by friends' shoplifting behaviour, but may be moderated by young people's attachment to their parents and their own beliefs regarding this behaviour (Cox et al., 1993).

Vandalism

Many young people feel a sense of powerlessness and a lack of respect by society in general and consequently become frustrated and/or angry. These feelings may be acted out by vandalism. Similarly, some will express their feelings through the use of graffiti. Usually, graffiti has to be created clandestinely, and the risk factor is appealing to many young people. Graffiti can be artistically creative and satisfying, and can be used to convey messages and express ideas. Peters (1990) observed that for some young people graffiti could express a concern for belonging and identity, and for others it might emphasize popular values taken to the extreme.

Driving cars at high speed

Young people are tempted to drive cars recklessly. As previously mentioned, they often have the impression that they are indestructible. They are looking for an identity of which they can be proud. They therefore like to test their skills in difficult situations. High-speed driving raises their level of adrenaline, is risky, exciting, fun and gives them an opportunity to show off in front of their peers.

Fire-lighting

Although serious addiction to fire-lighting is an indication of psychiatric disorder, some young people like the thrill involved in lighting fires and enjoy watching things burn. Fires present risk, excitement and challenge, exactly what the young person may be seeking. It is also easy to light fires.

Practical evidence-based interventions for helping young people who are involved in five-lighting are provided by Sharp et al. (2009).

Listening to loud and/or aggressive music

Young people want to explore every facet of their existence and this includes exposure to sensation. Loud music, especially of the hard rock or heavy metal variety, provides a high level of auditory and somatic stimulation (Arnett, 1992). In discos, high noise levels seem to change the state of consciousness of the participants so that they become engulfed by the music and transported from the pressures of their daily lives. Additionally, the lyrics of popular teenage music often hook into the young person's current emotional frustrations and experiences.

Unfortunately, there are dangers in listening to loud music. Bronzaft and Dobrow (1988) raise concerns not only about young people listening to loud music at discos, but also playing electronic games. Excessive noise can be intrusive to others and damage relationships and, more importantly – concerning the long-term well-being of the young person – it can and does result in deafness.

Weight control

There are clearly hazards for young people with regard to body-weight control. A study by Grigg et al. (1996), involving 14- to 16-year-old female students, showed that over one-third of the subjects had used at least one extreme dieting method in the previous month, such as crash dieting, fasting, slimming tablets, diuretics, laxatives and/or cigarettes to lose weight.

Young people are particularly vulnerable to modelling by others

Unfortunately, the problem for young people is in their search for identity, which makes them particularly vulnerable to modelling by others. They are subjected to heavy modelling in the print media and on television where underweight female models are portrayed as beautiful and desirable and slightly overweight males and females are seen as unattractive and worthy of derision. Female young people tend to be more susceptible to pressure from friends regarding the importance of thinness and the desirability of engaging in weight-loss strategies. Peer pressure may involve modelling of dieting behaviour, and taunting and teasing. Taunting and teasing are also problems for males who are either under- or overweight.

Weight problems include not only the extreme cases of anorexia nervosa and bulimia but also obesity. Although the incidence of both anorexia nervosa and bulimia is low in males compared with females, there are males who suffer from those conditions. Obesity is a problem for some young people of both sexes. A number of research papers show that there are some cultural differences with regard to problems associated with teenage weight control (Raich et al., 1992; Wardle et al., 1993; Story et al., 1995).

Practical evidence-based interventions for helping young people address eating problems are provided by Hoste and le Grange (2009).

In summary

In this chapter we have dealt with some of the challenges of adolescence. Confronting these challenges can be harmful for those who are unable to respond adaptively. However, confronting challenges is an essential part of the young person's journey towards adulthood. As an adult, the individual has to take responsibility for dealing with whatever situations and events present themselves. Learning how to do this is one of the young person's developmental tasks.

Young people often seek help from counsellors at times when they are unable to deal adaptively with particular challenges. It is the counsellor's task to enable young people to find satisfactory methods for overcoming hazards so that they can move forward along the required developmental path. In this connection it may be helpful for readers to refer to the book *Practical Interventions for Young People at Risk* edited by Kathryn (Geldard, 2009).

KEY POINTS

- challenges for young people include the influence of peers, gangs, smoking, sniffing, use of alcohol and other drugs, sexual behaviour, risk-taking involving anti-social behaviour, and weight control
- it is advantageous for young people to have supportive and authoritative parents
- behaviours by young people that may be negatively described by adults are often an indicator of the young person's search for personal identity
- peer involvement and peer pressure are major factors for introducing young people to the use of alcohol and other drugs, introduction to sexual behaviour, and introduction to other risky behaviours
- it is preferable to use evidence-based practical interventions when addressing specific problem behaviours of young people

FURTHER RESOURCES

For young people facing challenges in their lives, it can be useful for them to connect with other young people facing similar challenges. 'Reach Out' and 'Kooth' provide online forums to support young people to connect with other young people. They also provide information and suggestions for young people seeking help.

- reachout.com
- kooth.com

5

The Contemporary Context of Adolescence

So far in Part 1 we have focused on experiences and factors that may impact on an individual throughout the period of adolescence. Now we take a step back in order to consider the systems in which young people of today live. Indeed, to connect with young people it is important to have some understanding of their context; a context which we will explore within the framework of Bronfenbrenner's (1977) ecology of human development. A summary of the major systems comprising the context of

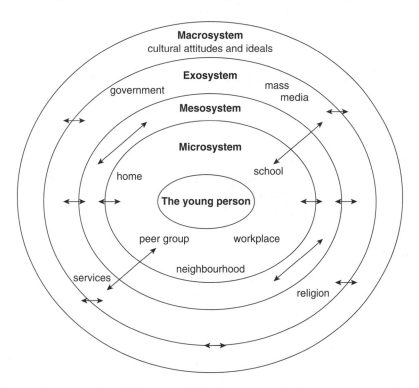

FIGURE 5.1   *The context of adolescence within the framework of Bronfenbrenner's (1977) ecology of human developments*

adolescence is presented in Figure 5.1. For the reader interested in a more comprehensive overview, the *Journal of Research on Adolescence* devoted an entire issue in 2002 on the modern experiences of young people (Volume 12, Issue 1).

Macrosystem

The macrosystem is the overarching cultural attitudes and ideals that guide the structures and relations within the other systems of Bronfenbrenner's model. Here we will consider Western cultural beliefs about adolescence. Indeed, adolescence itself is a Western cultural invention of the late nineteenth and early twentieth centuries. This new developmental stage was in response to a number of changes during this time, particularly urbanization and the emergence of secondary education and later entry into the workforce. The result is a lengthening of the preparation for adulthood in order to meet the increasing demands and complexity that the adult life brings (Larson, 2002). In the Western world, adolescence is seen as a period of increasing independence and responsibility (moving away from their family and into a widening circle of influence) and exploration of their identity (related to increased experimentation and risk-taking behaviours) (Call et al., 2002; Larson, 2002). This Western view of adolescence is, however, continually in flux as a number of trends, such as globalization and increased cultural diversity, impact upon the values and beliefs held by Western society (Larson, 2002).

The period of adolescence is a Western invention

Exosystem

The exosystem consists of the formal and informal social structures that impact indirectly upon the young person and their immediate environment. The exosystem includes mass media, government and the services they provide (transportation, communication, health, and so on) and religious institutions.

Mass media

Mass media is a pervasive influence for today's young people. Modern technology means that the media's messages can be accessed almost anywhere and at any time (Larson, 2002). A complex and overwhelming array of information is presented in the media today. Here we will focus on the impact of three common themes in the media: consumerism, sexuality and violence.

A strong message of consumerism exists within Western media (Larson, 2002). We are continually bombarded with advertisements across multiple types of media. It is certainly hard to avoid the message to buy. However, shopping can provide opportunities for the development of important skills, such as identity exploration (in terms of peer group belonging and related shopping preferences), skill development (such as time and money management) and social bonding. On the other side of the coin, shopping can present risk factors, for example, preoccupation with shopping and having the 'right' brands. Furthermore, peer ridicule may be experienced by those who cannot afford to keep up with the trends, and therefore maintain social norms and values around consumption (Shim et al., 2011).

Sex is also strongly presented in the media, prompting concerns regarding its influence on the development of sexuality in young people. A recent review confirmed the high level of sexual content in media accessed by young people. However, there is a lack of research with respect to the impact this high level of sexual content has on the young person. In saying this, there are some studies which suggest that the high content of sexuality in TV shows is linked to a faster development of sexuality, for example, young people entering into sexual relationships earlier (Escobar-Chaves et al., 2005). It is important to remember that the relationship between media access and influence on young people is complex, with multiple factors, such as individual characteristics (personality, learning styles, gender), developmental stage and social environment (including peers and family), determining the impact of the media's message. Interestingly, while parents express significant concern about the level of sexuality expressed in the media, young people don't share their concern (Werner-Wilson et al., 2004).

Increased access to violent media is also concerning (Call et al., 2002). While the occurrence of violent or aggressive behaviour is complex, with multiple risk factors involved, from biological to environmental, exposure to violent media is recognized as one of these risk factors (Boxer et al., 2009).

Sexual and violent content in media can influence young people's attitudes and behaviour

Government

The government has a significant influence on the environment in which young people find themselves. A government determines the level of stability of a country and access to services and support. The provision of stability and services directly impacts on opportunities the young person has and the level of protection they enjoy, for example in the event of aggressive acts (such as terrorism) or natural disasters (Larson, 2002). The provision of services also has more everyday influences. We explore the impact of transportation, communication and health services below.

Services

Social activities are a key developmental activity for young people in light of the growing importance of friendship groups during the adolescent period. One factor that may facilitate, or hinder, access to social activities is the transportation services provided by the government. Young people have greater access to social activities when they have greater access to public transport. Adequate public transport also affords easier access to school, work and other significant events.

Communication technology is another service that can impact directly on a young person's social connections. There is a diversity of modes of communication now available, including mobile phones (calls and text messaging) and the Internet (chat rooms, email, social networking sites, instant messaging and more). The use of technology for communication presents both risk and protective factors. Due to the high accessibility of communication technologies, young people are at a higher risk of viewing uncensored content, for example, pornography or aggressive messages, or engaging in unhealthy interactions, such as cyberbullying or sexting (Larson, 2002; Underwood et al., 2013). Exposure to concerning content or interactions may lead to new anxieties or feed into old anxieties, for example, heightening feelings of low self-worth through comparison or feeling unable to protect oneself from bullying. Another consequence of highly accessible technologies is the difficulty of 'switching off', possibly leading to excessive use with outcomes similar to withdrawal symptoms (Graham, 2011), including decreased participation in other areas of life (Baker and White, 2011). Indeed, using the Internet for chatting, socializing or game playing has been found to be associated with poorer academic performance. However, this relationship is reversed if Internet time is task-focused, for example, searching for information for schoolwork. Hence, access to the Internet presents both opportunities and distraction with respect to academic achievement (Chen and Fu, 2009).

There are also many other benefits to using technology to communicate, such as the ability to connect with peers, and hence develop social skills and access support (Call et al., 2002; Underwood et al., 2013). Indeed, there is growing research showing that using the Internet to communicate with existing friends strengthens social connectedness and well-being, and supports socially anxious young people to connect with peers (Valkenburg and Jochen, 2009; Bonetti et al., 2010). Technology also facilitates self-expression, hence identity formation (Baker and White, 2011), an important development task during adolescence. Another developmental task supported by communication technology is that of separating from parents and fostering independence (Underwood et al., 2013).

> **Communication technology presents both risk and protective factors for the young person**

During the twentieth century, the World Health Organization (WHO) became a major advocate for ensuring good health, which was seen by governments as a fundamental human right. Subsequently, great gains have been made by developed nations in both treatment and preventative health care and public health initiatives (Irvine et al., 2006). Despite these gains, there still exists some inequality regarding access to good health, which may make the developmental period a challenge for those young people who need, but don't have adequate access to, health care.

Religious institutions

Unfortunately, there is a lack of research of the impact of religion on young people. This is a shame as religion does play an important role in many young people's lives as they explore their identity (Larson, 2002). However, one recent study suggests that young people of today participate in very little exploration before making decisions about their ideological beliefs, which includes religious (as well as political) values. This suggests that young people may be more passive with respect to the development of their religious identity and possibly highly influenced by parental belief (Bartoszuk and Pittman, 2010). This is an interesting finding in an age of growing opportunity for religious exploration in light of the increased cultural diversity in many Western nations.

Microsystem and mesosystem

The microsystem incorporates the immediate settings of the individual, including home, school, peer group, the workplace and neighbourhood. These individual settings interact within the mesosystem.

Home

Family systems are now more diverse and transitional. Families are smaller: couples are having fewer children later in life (or no children); there is a trend towards nuclear, rather than extended, families; and single-parent families are more common, particularly female-headed households. As a result of these trends, there are fewer adults, particularly male role models, to provide support and guidance to young people. However, families are also becoming more intergenerational, for example, many young people have connections with their grandparents and even great-grandparents. There are also changes in parenting style, with more responsive approaches and increased investment of money, emotions and time. Ties between the family and community are no longer as strong but they are more diverse, for example, increased maternal employment increases social connections to the wider community (Larson et al., 2002). Maternal employment may also provide an increased diversity of role models and access to social capital. There is also an increased generational gap between family members due to significant cultural changes over time that can lead to conflict when traditional and modern worlds collide (Call et al., 2002).

School

With the lengthening of secondary education, school is an important setting for most young people. School is not just about learning but also about construction of identity through both learning processes and peer socialization (Volman and ten Dam, 2007). Unfortunately, some young people lack motivation to participate in school. One potential reason for this is that the approaches to teaching do not match learning styles, interests or developmental stages (Moula et al., 2009). Other young people may find a lack of clear connections between school and work, and therefore feel that school is not preparing them well for their work life. The limited relevance of school can lead to either early drop out or extensive tertiary education in an attempt to gain more relevant training (Shanahan et al., 2002). Increasingly, secondary schools are attempting to address this lack of connection to the work environment by offering flexible learning options such as apprenticeships and links with universities and colleges. Furthermore, transition-to-work programmes to assist young people who have dropped out of school are becoming more common and provide services such as 'education, training, employment, counseling and social services' (Bloom, 2010: 92–93). This is an important support option as many young people who drop out of high school come from low-income families and, without higher education, continue in low-paying jobs or remain unemployed, therefore making the transition to adulthood more challenging (Bloom, 2010).

Peer group

Peers become increasingly important during adolescence. This importance is reflected in the amount of time young people spend with their peers both at school and outside school. As we discussed earlier, young people today connect with their peers both in face-to-face interactions and via communication technology. As online relationship networks can be large and transitory, potentially having less depth, it is important for young people to work at forming close bonds. Strong peer relationships in adolescence are linked with well-being through provision of social support and a sense of meaning (Valkenburg and Jochen, 2009). On the flip side, time with peers can also lead to increased conflict and bullying.

The increased focus on time with peers also allows for the development of romantic relationships, which are entered into at earlier and earlier ages. This may be a result of earlier puberty and the increased presentation of sex and romantic relationships in the media, as we discussed earlier. There is also increased acceptance of diversity, for example, different sexual identities, within peer groups today. This acceptance of difference is also reflected in peer groups by the higher diversity of cultural backgrounds from which young people come (Larson et al., 2002).

66 **Young people connect with their peers face-to-face and via communication technology** 99

Workplace

There are two aspects of the workplace that we will consider: part-time work, which many young people engage in while at school, and preparation for the adult world of work. Part-time work, in moderation, can have beneficial effects with respect to a young person's future work and doesn't have to impinge on other activities, such as homework, social activities, household chores and so on (Shanahan et al., 2002).

With respect to preparing for the adult world of work, we have already touched on the inability of school to fully prepare some young people for work. Hence, there is a trend for later entry into the workforce while young people seek out further training (at universities or training colleges), or experience by engaging in transitory work. Transition programmes such as work shadowing or internships can also help to foster ties with the adult work world while protecting young people from the full gamut of adult responsibilities and potential abuses (Shanahan et al., 2002).

Neighbourhood

There is great diversity between neighbourhoods in which young people live. For example, there is a growing gulf between rich and poor neighbourhoods, with poorer neighbourhoods being linked with an increased risk of failing at school, early pregnancy, substance use and delinquency (Call et al., 2002). On the other hand, neighbourhoods that are rich in 'social and emotional resources' are protective, supporting adolescents' resilience (Call et al., 2002: 85).

As a result of globalization and increasing ethnic diversity, there is an increase in cultural change within neighbourhoods, which in turn impacts on values and beliefs. This cultural diversity and change may result in either conflict or increased relations and ties between ethnic and cultural groups. There are also differences in population growth, resulting in diversity in access to resources and opportunities across neighbourhoods. One factor that seems to be growing is urbanization, meaning that more young people are living in cities rather than in rural areas (Larson, 2002).

In summary

The context in which young people find themselves today is a complex one. There are many diverse settings and structures which all impact on a young person's experiences either directly (micro- and mesosystems) or indirectly (macro- and exosystems), presenting a mix of risk and protective factors. Having a sense of this complexity will help when providing support to young people.

KEY POINTS

- there are multiple systems that interact to create the context in which young people today live.
- the overarching cultural beliefs of the modern Western world are represented by the macrosystem.
- the exosystem is composed of the social structures that indirectly influence the young person and include mass media, government (and the services they provide) and religious institutions.
- the immediate settings of the young person (home, school, peer group, workplace and neighbourhood) are represented by the microsystem and mesosystem (in which the individual settings interact).

FURTHER RESOURCES

For a short video outlining more information about Bronfenbrenner's (1977) ecology of human development, readers are encouraged to check out the 'Education Portal' website.

- education-portal.com/academy/lesson/bronfenbrenners-ecological-systems-theory-of-development-definition-examples.html#lesson

6

The Development of Mental Health Problems

In this chapter we will discuss the ability of young people to cope and the development of pathology in those who are unable to cope adaptively. We will also describe some of the more common mental health problems which affect young people. Although this book is not intended to be used as a treatment guide for those who manage young people with mental health problems, it is hoped that mental health workers will find the proactive counselling approach useful as part of an overall treatment plan for many troubled young people. Our assumption is that many counsellors who read this book will be working in settings where their role is to help troubled young people who have not developed serious mental health problems. However, it is important for all counsellors to be able to recognize the early signs of the development of mental health problems. By recognizing these early signs, appropriate referrals to specialist professionals or mental health services can be made.

Referral

Assisting those young people who have not been able to develop successful coping strategies and resources is quite obviously an important function for a counsellor. However, it is essential that counsellors recognize their personal and professional limitations with regard to treating young people who are demonstrating signs of developing pathology. It is important to recognize these limits and be open with clients regarding them.

We are firm in our belief that all counsellors need to have experienced and qualified supervisors with whom they can discuss both personal issues and client-related matters. Where there are indications that a young person is developing pathology, counsellors need to consult with their supervisors and to make decisions with regard to continuing treatment or referral to specialists.

The correct diagnosis of the onset of pathology can be complicated, particularly when the client is a young person. Miller (1983) cautions counsellors not to over-interpret typical and perhaps seemingly bizarre behaviour, thoughts or feelings of young people as necessarily being indicative of severe psychopathology. They may be indicative of the young person's developmentally appropriate response to the environment. However, the flip-side is that the consequences of incorrectly disregarding symptoms as typical young person behaviour can be serious and may deprive young clients of much-needed psychiatric help. We therefore believe that it is wise and ethically necessary to err on the side of caution by ensuring that specialist assessments are made where there are possible indications of developing psychopathology.

Certainly, when a young person is consistently using dysfunctional or maladaptive coping strategies and where counselling interventions have failed, there is a strong indication that referral may be necessary. Such young people need assessment by an experienced mental health worker who can devise an appropriate treatment plan, which may include the use of medication in conjunction with psychotherapy.

Ability to cope with the challenges of adolescence

There are remarkable differences in the abilities of young people to cope with the challenges that confront them. Some young people have great difficulty in dealing with problems which for others would be minor. Because these young people are not able to cope with stresses in an adaptive manner they may develop problem behaviours and are at risk of developing mental health problems. Other young people with major problems seem to be able to emerge from stressful encounters not only successfully but also with increased abilities and resources (Seiffge-Krenke, 1995). For them, dealing with stressful situations stimulates personal growth and helps them to move along the adolescent developmental path towards adulthood.

Some young people are more resilient than others

Differences in the ways in which young people cope and respond to the challenges that confront them raise the question of why these differences occur. In order to understand why they occur, we first need to understand what it is that young people find stressful.

What do young people find stressful?

Young people consider an event to be stressful when they make an appraisal that the event has negative implications for their own well-being. Sandler et al. (1997) suggest that they ask themselves three questions:

1. Should I care?
2. Is this positive or negative?
3. In what way am I or my goals or commitments involved?

If the answers to these questions are 'Yes, I should care', 'This has negative implications for me' and 'My goals or commitments may be compromised', then the young person is likely to appraise the situation as stressful. In making this appraisal, the young person may also take into account whether the event has occurred previously, once or on a number of occasions, and the extent to which the event is perceived as controllable. They may also take into consideration their own perception of their ability to deal with the stressor. Once an event is appraised as stressful, the young person's coping resources will be called into play.

The young person's coping resources

A young person's personal coping resources are relatively stable characteristics of the individual. These resources influence how they cope in specific situations. Most importantly, coping resources include temperamental and personality characteristics. They also include beliefs about self and about the world. When a young person perceives themself as a competent person who copes, and believes that the environment is basically friendly or at least benign, the likelihood of successful coping strategies being used is increased. Clearly, a young person's coping resources will be related to the individual's self-esteem, locus of control, optimism and skills and knowledge of problem-solving techniques (Sandler et al., 1997).

Individuals who cope most successfully are those who make the best use of their own personal coping resources and also make use of other resources that may be available and of value. For example, a young person might use a friend, parents or a counsellor as a resource at times when their own resources are being stretched. Similarly, they might use an environmental resource, such as a peaceful place in which to relax, think and make decisions.

The young person's coping style

The ability to make use of available resources, including personal coping resources, has little to do with the nature of specific problems or childhood history or the current environmental situation in which the young person lives; instead, it has more to do with the personal qualities of the individual concerned. Each individual will have a personal coping style. This may be influenced by cultural factors, gender, socio-economic status and current environmental factors. Frydenberg and Lewis (1993) suggest three styles of coping that can broadly be described as follows:

1. *Solving the problem*: behaviours such as seeking social support, focusing on finding a solution, seeking a relaxing diversion, investing in close friends, seeking to belong, working hard to achieve and being positive. In this style of coping the individual works on the problem while remaining optimistic, fit, relaxed and socially connected.
2. *Reference to others*: turning to others, such as peers or professionals, for social and spiritual support.
3. *Non-productive coping*: worrying, seeking to belong, wishful thinking, not coping, ignoring the problem, keeping things to oneself and self-blame.

"Active coping strategies are preferable to passive strategies"

The first two styles of coping listed above involve an active process, whereas the third style is a passive process. In an active process, the individual takes action to deal with the stress and the stressor. In the passive process, no positive attempt is made to address these. It has been suggested that the use of active coping strategies tends to decrease with declining socio-economic status, and that the more passive coping of lower socio-economic groups is dysfunctional because it leads to problems for the individual (Jackson and Bosma, 1990). If this is correct, it is particularly unfortunate for people from these groups as it may tend to prevent them from attempting to change their current socio-economic status. Clearly, helping a young person to move from a passive coping style to an active one can be an important goal for a counsellor.

The use of cognition in coping

Cognitive functions can have an important role in coping with stressful events. By thinking things through, the coping process can be goal-directed and flexible while still allowing an appropriate level of emotional expression. It is therefore useful for counsellors to help young people to learn cognitive strategies for assessing stressful events and for working out ways of responding that might have positive outcomes.

The need to respond to stress promptly

The most adaptive way for individuals to deal with stress is for them to deal with the emotional and psychological outcomes as soon as possible after a stressful event has occurred. Where young people are unable to deal effectively with stressful events themselves, help from counsellors is most effective if it is offered at the earliest available time. The truth of this is supported by research regarding the short- and long-term consequences of stressful events which clearly indicates that counselling interventions should take place immediately after an event has occurred in order to promote positive coping behaviours (Seiffge-Krenke, 1995).

Maladaptive coping strategies

As highlighted above, there are multiple ways in which young people cope with challenges in their lives. Unfortunately, some young people use coping strategies that may ease their stress in the short term but can have ongoing long-term effects. Here we touch on two common maladaptive coping strategies: substance use and self-harm.

Experimenting with substances is not uncommon in adolescence (Gilvarry and McArdie, 2007) and some young people may choose to use drugs or alcohol to help cope with the challenges they face. For some young people, using substances as a coping strategy may have long-term consequences in the form of substance misuse, abuse or dependence. Consequently, substance misuse can interfere with an individual's education, work and relationships (American Psychiatric Association, 2013). There are a number of factors that increase the likelihood that a young person will develop a dependency on substance use, including environmental influences (for example, cultural norms around drug and alcohol use and lower socio-economic status), social aspects (for example, exposure to family or peer substance use, family difficulties and experiences of adverse advents such as abuse) and individual characteristics (for example, genetic predisposition, the presence of a mental health disorder and personality traits such as sensation-seeking) (Gilvarry and McArdie, 2007).

There are also multiple factors that can increase the likelihood that a young person will choose self-harm as a coping strategy. These factors include genetic/biological predispositions (for example, serotonin imbalances), psychological makeup (for example, personality traits such as perfectionism and impulsivity, cognitive styles such as challenges with social problem solving and presence of a mental health disorder), social (especially exposure to negative life events and friends and/or family members who also self-harm) and cultural influences (Hawton et al., 2012). Young people who self-harm often report a decrease in negative emotions and an increase in feelings of relief when self-harming, reflecting the effectiveness of self-harm as a short-term coping strategy. However, there are side effects of self-harm, for example, increased feelings of shame or disgust with themselves for participating in self-harm (Laye-Gindhu and Schonert-Reichl, 2005). There is also the potential for serious injury or even death, with an increased likelihood of suicidal ideation and attempts (Skegg, 2005).

In addition to being used as coping strategies, substance use and self-harm can be more common when young people are diagnosed with a mental health condition.

Development of psychological disorder as a response to stress

Simeonsson (1994) cites many studies which estimate that between 15 and 18 per cent of children and young people present with behavioural disorders that are psychological in origin. These disorders can broadly be divided into *internalizing* or *externalizing* disorders. Internalizing disorders are characterized by social withdrawal and feelings of loneliness, depression and anxiety. In contrast, externalizing disorders are characterized by behaviours such as disruptive acting-out, aggression, hyperactivity and other behaviours that are typical of conduct disorders.

Where young people are not able to deal adaptively with stressors, pathology is likely to develop. It is therefore important for counsellors to be able to distinguish between young people who are making use of adaptive coping processes and young people who are making inappropriate use of defence mechanisms to avoid facing stressors. It needs to be recognized that defence mechanisms do serve a purpose in enabling individuals to deal with the shock of the initial intense stage of trauma.

For example, when someone first discovers that they are dying, they may hold on to a belief in a miracle cure until they are able to accept and deal with reality. The initial use of the defence mechanism of denial can cushion the person's response, enabling them to gather the emotional strength to move forward. However, using defence mechanisms clearly distorts the individual's perceptions of reality, and if their use persists, then the result will be inappropriate behaviour and inappropriate emotional responses.

> ## Inability to respond adaptively to stress may result in pathology

In severe cases where young people are unable to cope adaptively with stressors, they may present with a wide variety of pathological reactions, such as the development of somatic symptoms, panic attacks, obsessive-compulsive behaviour, or a process of fragmentation with behaviour becoming automatic, ritualized and irrational. Instead of responding adaptively, some young people subjected to stress switch into pathology (Haan, 1977).

While this is not a mental health textbook, we believe that it is important to consider a number of psychological disorders experienced by young people and will consider the following:

- depression
- anxiety disorders
- suicidal ideation and behaviours
- early signs of developing psychosis
- post-traumatic stress disorder
- attention-deficit hyperactivity disorder
- autism spectrum disorder.

We will discuss each of the above because they are conditions which all counsellors who work with young people need to recognize. First, depression and anxiety are the most common internalizing disorders that are recognized as psychiatric conditions. Second, it is essential for counsellors to be able to recognize and respond appropriately when young people are suicidal or are showing signs of possible early symptoms of psychosis. Third, counsellors are frequently confronted by young people who have experienced trauma. Therefore, counsellors need to be able to recognize the symptoms of post-traumatic stress disorder so that the necessary management and treatment are offered. Finally, it is important for counsellors to be aware of developmental disorders generally diagnosed in childhood, such as attention-deficit hyperactivity disorder and autism spectrum disorder, which continue to influence how young people face challenges in their lives.

Depression

Depression is characterized by significantly impaired mood with a loss of interest or pleasure in activities that are normally enjoyable. Depression may be mild, moderate or severe, as described below (World Health Organization, 1994):

- *Mild depression*: effort is required to do normal daily tasks.
- *Moderate depression*: involves occupational and social impairment. Depression prevents the individual from doing things that need to be done.
- *Severe depression*: involves marked social and occupational impairment and may include psychotic symptoms such as hallucinations or delusions.

Most people experience depression from time to time. However, psychiatric illness involving a major depressive episode can be distinguished from normal depression by its severity, persistence and duration (World Health Organization, 1997).

Dysthymia, a milder but more persistent form of depression, involves long periods, of at least two years, during which time the individual experiences depressed mood, loss of interest and energy, social withdrawal, poor concentration and memory, feelings of inadequacy, low self-esteem, guilt, anger, hopelessness, irritability and despair. Dysthymia does interfere with social and occupational functioning, and some individuals with dysthymia experience major depressive episodes during the course of their dysthymic disorder.

Children demonstrate a relatively low incidence of depression. However, during adolescence most young people experience depression from time to time as part of their normal life, and they consequently have a risk of the development of depression at troubling levels. Often, loneliness and social withdrawal are antecedents to depressive disorders in young people (Simeonsson, 1994).

Depression in adolescence may result from a wide variety of situations or stimuli such as:

- a succession of loss experiences
- a history of parental separation and/or divorce
- a series of moves, perhaps including moving away from trusted friends
- death of a loved one, friend or pet
- receiving low levels of positive reinforcement
- being unable to escape from punishment.

Depression may also result from negative thoughts. These thoughts might include negative views of self, negative interpretations of one's experiences and negative views of the future.

Young people respond to depression in a variety of ways. Some young people run away from home. Some, particularly boys, express their feelings through externalizing behaviours and may act out aggressively. Girls more often express depression by internalizing it, worrying and/or becoming anxious.

Anxiety disorders

Everyone is anxious at times, and being anxious can be useful. Relatively high levels of anxiety can be helpful when they are consistent with the demands of a situation. For example, during a game of football, an exam or a job interview anxiety may help to increase alertness and performance. Unfortunately, too high a level of anxiety may reduce performance.

" Anxiety can be motivating or disabling "

Suffering from an anxiety disorder is not just a matter of being too anxious. Individuals with anxiety disorders suffer levels of anxiety which are more pervasive than the anxiety generally experienced in normal life. The disorder will usually have social consequences for the person, with relationships being impaired.

Four common types of anxiety disorder in young people, as described in *DSM–5* (American Psychiatric Association, 2013), are generalized anxiety disorder, social phobia, specific phobia and obsessive-compulsive disorder.

Generalized anxiety disorder is characterized by long periods of persistent and excessive anxiety and worry, the source of which is non-specific. Young people experiencing generalized anxiety disorder may present with symptoms of nervousness, restlessness, trouble falling or staying asleep, poor concentration, frequent urination, irritable mood, depressed mood, light-headedness, dizziness, muscular tension or becoming easily fatigued. Young people with generalized anxiety disorder often exhibit an additional anxiety disorder such as social or specific phobia.

Social phobia is characterized by significant anxiety when exposed to certain types of social or performance situations. This disorder often leads to avoidance behaviours. *Specific phobia* is characterized by a persistent and irrational fear of a particular object or situation, and can also lead to avoidance behaviours.

With *obsessive-compulsive disorder* individuals may experience unpleasant and intrusive thoughts that are difficult to control. For example, they may be obsessively concerned about contaminating or harming themselves or their family. The obsessional thoughts often lead to uncontrollable compulsive rituals; for example, repetitively cleaning, checking or counting.

Counsellors working with young people need to recognize that young people exhibiting behavioural problems and symptoms of anxiety may also be experiencing depression, because the symptoms of anxiety and depression often overlap. Both anxiety and depression can sometimes be difficult to diagnose because they can be masked by observable behaviours that do not directly suggest these conditions.

Suicidal ideation and behaviours

Many individuals experience some level of suicidal ideation at some point during adolescence. Stress, anxiety and depression in young people are increasing in Western society, resulting in suicidal ideation, attempted suicide and completed suicide (Dacey et al., 2006). Whether a young person thinks of suicide as an option, and/or chooses it, will depend on their personal coping resources and style. Particularly vulnerable to suicide are those young people who suffer from a depressive illness. They are more likely to commit suicide than young people with other psychiatric or medical illnesses (World Health Organization, 1997).

Young people who choose suicide as their option for coping are obviously seriously psychologically disturbed. For many, this may be a result of stress, anxiety and depression. For others, it may be related to psychotic illness or a result of substance abuse. Young people who attempt suicide often exhibit some of the following characteristics:

- They tend to over-invest themselves in very few but very intense interpersonal relationships.
- They tend to express troubled feelings through behaviour rather than verbal communication.
- They perceive themselves as unable to control their environment and are more at risk of attempting suicide than young people who feel in control of their environment.
- They express high levels of hopelessness and the belief that things will not get better.
- They tend to overreact to situations and may be hypersensitive.

Young people who attempt and complete suicide often have more stressful lives, fewer coping skills and are under-achieving, with poor school performance (Dacey et al., 2006). Quite often suicide is related to problems such as:

- family problems, particularly those which threaten family stability
- serious impairment of communication between parents and the young person
- peer relationship problems
- not having any friends and not belonging to a group
- inability to live up to parents' or others' expectations.

The availability and accessibility of firearms can heighten suicidal risks in young people. Recent research also suggests that well-publicized suicides bring out latent suicidal tendencies in young people (Dusek, 1996). Clearly, counsellors need to be able to recognize and appropriately deal with suicidal thinking and behaviour to prevent tragedies from occurring. They also need to recognize the limits of their competence: counsellors working with suicidal clients need to work under close supervision and refer to other specialist helpers.

Early signs of developing psychosis

Psychosis involves a loss of ego boundaries with gross impairment of reality testing. Symptoms include hallucinations and/or delusions. Where hallucinations are in evidence they occur in the absence of insight by the individual, according to *DSM–5* (American Psychiatric Association, 2013).

66 Vigilance is required in identifying the early signs of psychosis 99

There is evidence that genetic factors play a role in the development of psychotic ill-nesses. However, psychosocial factors involving stress or substance abuse are likely to act as triggers that bring about the initial and subsequent episodes in vulnerable people. During an acute episode of psychosis young people are particularly at risk of self-harm. They may have hallucinations which command them to harm or kill themselves. The strength of these thoughts and the individual's ability to act on them need to be assessed by a mental health professional.

One of the most common psychotic illnesses is schizophrenia, and this can develop during adolescence. Psychosis resulting from substance abuse, such as the use of cocaine, amphetamines, alcohol or marijuana, shares many of the symptoms of schizophrenia, including hallucinations, delusions and abnormal speech.

Schizophrenia can be divided into three phases: the prodromal phase, the active phase and the residual phase. Clearly, it is in the best interests of clients if counsellors are able to recognize symptoms during the prodromal phase so that treatment can be provided at this early stage.

1. *The prodromal phase*: This phase occurs in the weeks or months preceding the first onset of the typical symptoms of schizophrenia. During this phase, it is common for a number of non-specific symptoms to be in evidence, particularly in young people. These symptoms include a general loss of interest, avoidance of social interaction, avoidance of work or study (for example, dropping out of school or college), being irritable and over-sensitive, having odd beliefs (for example, superstitious or magical beliefs) and engaging in strange behaviours (for example, talking to oneself in public). It needs to be recognized that many normal young people display some of the described symptoms of prodromal schizophrenia, and this can make accurate assessment difficult. However, it is important that counsellors are alert to the possibility of schizophrenia in young people and when in doubt refer clients for mental health assessment.
2. *The active phase*: During the active phase of schizophrenia, psychotic symptoms such as delusions, odd behaviours and hallucinations are prominent and are often accompanied by the expression of strong emotions such as distress, anxiety, depression and fear. If untreated, the active phase may resolve spontaneously or may continue indefinitely.
3. *The residual phase*: The active phase of the illness is usually followed by a residual phase. The residual phase is similar to the prodromal phase where psychotic symptoms are less likely to be accompanied by the expression of strong emotions.

Another type of psychotic disorder which may present in adolescence is *acute and transient psychotic disorder*. The symptoms are usually associated with acute psychological stress and occur over a matter of days, resolving within two or three weeks (World Health Organization, 1997).

Post-traumatic stress disorder

The precursors and symptoms of post-traumatic stress disorder (PTSD) were discussed in Chapter 2. This psychological disorder occurs following acute or ongoing trauma. If PTSD is left untreated it can develop into a severe incapacitating disorder which will impact on the young person's social and occupational functioning. Additionally, many of the symptoms of PTSD can be confused with some of the other major psychological disturbances previously mentioned; for example, depression, generalized anxiety disorder and psychosis. The latter is due to the possibility of symptoms of dissociative hallucinosis in PTSD.

Untreated PTSD can have serious consequences

Attention-deficit hyperactivity disorder

Attention–deficit hyperactivity disorder (ADHD, as defined by *DSM-5*) or hyperkinetic disorder (as defined by the World Health Organization) is characterized by challenges in maintaining attention (for example, lacking in persistence and moving frequently between activities) and impulsive and excessive activity. While considered a disorder of childhood, the latest edition of the *DSM* acknowledges that symptoms of ADHD can persist throughout adolescence and into adulthood (American Psychiatric Association, 2013). Symptoms of ADHD can have a lasting impact across multiple domains of a young person's life, including school, work, family and peers. ADHD has also been found to increase the likelihood of other mental health and substance use disorders (Biederman and Faraone, 2005).

For a comprehensive overview of appropriate assessment used to explore a potential diagnosis of ADHD please refer to Sattler (2014). If signs of ADHD are present, it is important to refer the young person to a paediatrician or psychiatrist who is experienced in diagnosing ADHD. This is particularly important as support for young people with ADHD can include medication (Biederman and Faraone, 2005).

Autism spectrum disorder

Individuals with an autism spectrum disorder (ASD) present with challenges within the social and communication domain. In addition, individuals with ASD do not have as wide a base of interests compared to their peers (World Health Organization, 1994; American Psychiatric Association, 2013). There is significant variation in the degree to which ASD impacts on a young person's life. Some individuals with ASD require support with many aspects of their life; they may have developmental delay, an Intellectual Impairment or may not be able to communicate verbally. On the other end of the spectrum, many young people with ASD lead largely independent lives; there is little evidence of developmental delay and they present with typical or superior intelligence. In addition to the defining characteristics of ASD, it is common for individuals also to live with anxiety and depression (Mazurek and Kanne, 2010). Sattler (2014) provides a summary of the assessment procedures available to investigate a possible ASD diagnosis. As with ADHD, it is important to refer a young person presenting with behaviours typical of ASD to a paediatrician or psychiatrist for accurate diagnosis and intervention planning.

In summary

Where young people are demonstrating symptoms of mental health problems they should be referred to mental health services or psychiatrists who can assess and treat their condition. Mental health disorders can usually be managed through the use of appropriate medication and psychotherapy. Without medication, many individuals suffering from these disorders will continue to feel overwhelmed, distressed and worried by intrusive thoughts and uncontrollable behaviours.

KEY POINTS

- where the possibility of psychopathology is identified counsellors should consult with their supervisors regarding possible referral to specialists
- some young people are more successful than others in coping with stress
- active coping responses to stress tend to be more successful than passive ones
- young people may turn to maladaptive coping strategies, such as substance abuse and self-harm, in response to the challenges they may face
- common problems encountered by counsellors when working with young people include depression, anxiety, suicidal ideation and behaviour, early signs of developing psychosis, post-traumatic stress disorder, attention-deficit hyperactivity disorder and autism spectrum disorder
- it is useful for counsellors to be aware of the symptoms of psychological disorder so that they can recognize these and refer to specialists when necessary

FURTHER RESOURCES

'MindEd' is an e-learning portal designed to support individuals working with young people. It provides a wealth of information about a range of mental health concerns that may be experienced by children and young people. For more information about diagnostic criteria for mental health concerns, readers are encouraged to explore the webpages of the ICD-10 and *DSM-5*.

- www.minded.org.uk
- apps.who.int/classifications/icd10
- www.dsm5.org

Part 2

Proactive Counselling for Young People

7

Making Counselling Relevant for Young People

Although some counsellors specialize in working only with young people, many counsellors see clients of all ages including children and adults. It has long been recognized that counselling children is very different from counselling adults. When working with children, counsellors not only need to use specific counselling skills, as they do with adults, but also need to involve the child in the counselling process through the use of media and activity. Just as there are differences between counselling children and counselling adults, there are also important differences between counselling young people and counselling either children or adults.

Differences involved in counselling young people

Counselling young people is different from counselling children and adults in the following ways:

1. If young people are to be encouraged to use counselling, we need to offer a special type of client–counsellor relationship which is appropriate for them (see Chapter 8).
2. The process of counselling young people needs to be different from the processes used when counselling children or adults (see Chapters 8 and 9).
3. Particular skills and strategies which enhance the counselling conversation with a young person are required (see Chapter 11).

Even though counselling young people involves the above differences, there are some features that are common to counselling children, young people and adults (for example, many of the micro-skills used and some of the counsellor attributes). For most counsellors, those common features make it easier to move from counselling one age group to counselling another. However, it is the differences which, when ignored, may result in disappointing outcomes.

Counselling children

Counsellors working with children need to be able to select and make use of relevant media and activities as described by Geldard et al. (2013). They need to pay particular attention to the child's developmental age and consequent ability to resolve issues. Additionally, they need to recognize that the child's capacity for self-reflection may be limited because it is a developmental skill which comes through maturation, social experiences and the development of communication skills.

Children cannot usually leave their families. They are dependent on them, and their families generally provide the main social system within which they grow and develop. It is from within the family that the child develops ideas about their own personal value, abilities and aspirations (Downey, 2003). Unfortunately, many children have little power or influence on their families. As children's problems are often related to their family environment, counsellors working with children often need to work with the child's family in order to enable the family to make the necessary changes for the well-being of the child.

Differences between counselling young people and counselling children

There are three major differences that are relevant when counselling young people as compared with counselling children. These are:

1. Unlike children, young people have less dependence on their families. For most young people, their social system involves peer relationships, together with other relationships developed within the educational system and/or at work. Their relationship with their family is changing as they seek more independence. Counsellors therefore need to recognize and respect that some young people will not want to have their families involved in the counselling process in any way, because this might compromise their growing individuation. This may create difficulties for a counsellor who is working with a young person whose parents are experiencing problems in accepting the changes of adolescence, as they may want to be included in the counselling process. However, some young people are willing to have their families involved in the counselling process. For them, a combination of family therapy and individual counselling may be an option. Sometimes it can be useful for counsellors to act as advocates for young people in negotiations with their families or parents.

"Many young people are reluctant to disclose their problems to their families"

2. Young people have more complex cognitive processes and more advanced cognitive skills than children. This more mature level of functioning allows the counsellor to

choose more advanced cognitive intervention strategies which usually cannot be used when counselling children. Although sometimes it is useful when counselling a young person to make use of media and activity (see Chapters 14 and 15), care must be taken to respect the maturity and self-image of the client.

3. The counselling relationship needs to respect the developmental needs of the young person, which includes respect for them as an individual who is neither a child nor an adult. The counselling relationship must give the young person the right to make decisions with regard to their involvement in the counselling process and must allow them to have a genuine sense of personal responsibility for counselling outcomes.

Differences between counselling young people and counselling adults

Counselling young people also differs significantly from counselling adults. The adult is generally relatively free to make decisions and choices without excessive influence from family or others. Consequently, counselling with adults is based on the assumption that adults have personal autonomy and have choice regarding their actions as individuals (Downey, 2003). Although most young people achieve a level of cognitive independence, this does not usually free them from what may be considerable influences of their families and social environments. As a result, most young people do not have a full sense of personal autonomy and are not certain about the extent to which they can make choices for themselves because they are not yet adults. They are in a developmental process of identity formation and individuation, and being in this process tends to inhibit them from believing that they can have considerably more control over their lives than they did when they were children. Consequently, counsellors have to respect the young person's developmental dilemma regarding the extent of their personal ability to choose for themselves and take responsibility for their own lives.

Another difference relates to the normal developmental tasks that are appropriate for young people and tasks that are appropriate for adults. For example, a young person is striving for personal identity, individuation, sexual identity and new relationships with peers, whereas most adults are striving for goals such as stability, continuity, raising a family and success at work. Clearly, the issues that need to be addressed when counselling young people will generally be different from those that are relevant when counselling adults.

Counselling young people needs a specific approach

It is clear from the above discussion that young people are a special group because of their developmental stage and the special challenges this presents. If we try to act as counsellors for them using strategies and techniques which are suitable for either children or adults, it is unlikely that we will have a high level of success. We need to remember that young people are not children and they are not adults: they are in transition. We therefore need to tailor our counselling approaches to engage the young person directly and actively and to use strategies that will specifically address their needs in ways which are acceptable to them.

> ❝The counselling process needs to be acceptable to the young person❞

The whole of the counselling process must take account of the young person's developmental process. As counsellors of young people, we need to deliberately strive to ensure that each of the following fits with that developmental process:

• the young person–counsellor relationship
• the counselling skills needed for successful outcomes
• the strategies to be used to address particular problems.

The proactive approach described in this book is designed to achieve the required fit between the young person's developmental processes and the counselling process.

It is widely recognized that individual counselling with young people is not the only way to help young people manage emotional, psychological and behavioural problems. Family therapy, group therapy and self-help support groups, or a combination of these, may all be useful in helping young people deal with troubling issues.

Differences between individual counselling and family therapy

Family therapy primarily addresses interpersonal relationship issues within the family. It does not directly address a young person's internal emotional and psychological needs. These intrapersonal needs are best addressed through individual counselling in a private and confidential situation where the focus can be on the young person's unique personality, developmental process and personal distress. In the individual counselling setting, the therapeutic approach and strategies used can be formulated to address the young person's individual needs specifically (Vernon, 2009).

Combining individual counselling with family therapy

We have noticed that in the past there have been two differing traditions with regard to counselling young people. One tradition involves individual counselling of the young person, whereas the other involves family therapy.

Many counsellors who belong to the individual counselling tradition believe that it is sufficient to work with the young person alone in helping them to address and resolve troubling issues. Similarly, many counsellors who are committed to the family therapy tradition believe that family therapy alone is sufficient.

Some family therapists argue that working individually with a young person is undesirable because they become scapegoated, stigmatized and pathologized. On the other hand, some counsellors who work with young people individually believe that family therapy does not provide an opportunity for the young person to address intensely personal and sensitive troubling issues. We certainly agree with the latter position as we have noticed that when we work with an young person individually they will be likely to reveal personal information which would have been too difficult to disclose in the context of the whole family. However, we have found that once troubling information has been disclosed by a young person in an individual counselling session, subsequently they are often able to share this information with their family or parents. If family therapy alone is used this information is unlikely to surface, with the consequence that the young person's troubling issues are likely to persist. For this reason we believe that if we are to actively facilitate change quickly, we are likely to be more successful if we integrate individual work with the young person with family therapy. Readers who are interested in combining individual counselling for young people with family therapy might like to read our book *Relationship Counselling for Children, Young People and Families* (Geldard and Geldard, 2009). The approach described is based on our own integrative relationship counselling model (the CACHO model) and is applicable to both young people and children. The CACHO model is grounded in the Gestalt therapy theory of change and stands for *Communication* in order to raise *Awareness* so that opportunities for *CHoice* arise leading to an *Outcome* for the family system. The book *Relationship Counselling for Children, Young People and Families* outlines in detail how the CACHO model can be applied to support change both within the family system and for the young person.

"Individual counselling with family therapy can be advantageous"

The relationship between the young person's world and the counselling environment

Figure 7.1 illustrates systemically the position that the counselling environment occupies in the young person's world. In this figure the young person's journey from child to adult is demonstrated as a move from the secure base of the family to the rather less secure base of the peer environment. The family is shown with a solid boundary to represent a place where containment, nurturing and healthy growth are fostered. Not all young people have the opportunity to develop in environments like this. For many young people the family boundary is fragmented so that they are deprived of some of the benefits they might otherwise have. The environment into which the young person is moving (the peer environment) is depicted as having a broken boundary because it is open to outside influences and also allows movement into and out of the environment by the young person so that individuation can develop.

Peer groups do not meet all the needs of the young person. In Figure 7.1, the young person is depicted as having both an inner and an outer boundary. The inner boundary holds the young person's personality, past history and accumulated skills, while the outer boundary is broken and open to outside influences. The outer boundary represents the young person's newly emerging sense of self. This sense of self will consolidate as the young person moves through the journey to adulthood. As this boundary strengthens it will allow the young person to exist in the peer environment more comfortably and with more freedom to make individual decisions and choices. The consolidating boundary allows a sense of self-containment to develop within the open peer environment, with the consequence that adjustments to peer relationships will need to be negotiated. As young people move out from the family circle they develop a different relationship with their families and with individual family members. This is possible because of the newly developing sense of self.

Although the counselling environment is located in the young person's world, it is separate from the family and peer environments. The counselling boundary, as shown in Figure 7.1, is solid, to depict a place of safety, security, dependability and consistency. However, it has an opening for easy access and departure. Positive experiences within this environment will encourage young people to return when their own internal and external boundaries become fragile and/or overwhelming. In addition, the young person is subjected to a wide variety of external influences as illustrated in Figure 7.1.

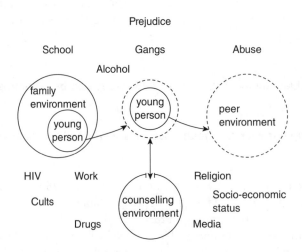

FIGURE 7.1   *The young person's world and the counselling environment*

Why do young people seek counselling?

It is well documented that young people generally prefer to seek help from their peers in the first instance rather than from parents or other adults (Buhrmester and Prager, 1995; Gibson-Cline, 1996; Turner, 1999).

Research has shown that young people repeatedly suggest that strong positive relationships with potential helpers are very important in influencing them to seek help from either peers or adults (Wilson and Dean, 2001). Also they are more amenable to receiving help from a helper who they perceive to have 'gone through the same sort of thing' and can describe how they went about resolving their problem. This situation is most likely to occur when young people talk with other young people who are experiencing, or have experienced, similar troubles.

> ❝ **Young people prefer to seek help from other young people** ❞

In looking at why young people seek counselling, we need to recognize that the word 'counselling' when applied to young people has a wide range of meanings. Counselling for young people, as generally understood by the community and young people themselves, can involve any of the following:

1. Giving advice, where reaching the right decision is seen as very important.
2. Guidance, where the young person is experiencing difficulties because of immaturity and/or behaviours, and would like some directive help.
3. Psychotherapy, where the focus is on psychological and emotional distress. The expectation is that counselling will result in changes in attitudes and patterns of behaviour so that the young person feels more comfortable.

Counselling may involve a combination of all of these (Tyler, 1978), although we believe that generally, although not always, advice-giving is not helpful for young people who need to start taking responsibility for their own decisions. It is, however, appropriate for counsellors to provide useful and correct information that the young person may need in order to make sensible decisions. Naturally, many young people consult with counsellors in order to receive advice. This may be because they need to make difficult decisions and may recognize that they do not have the necessary experience which can provide them with the information they need in order to reach a decision. Others seek counselling because they are emotionally distressed.

When young people do come for counselling help they generally have the belief that they will get help to solve problems or will receive directions or advice. They expect that the counsellor will be knowledgeable, that is, experienced in life, and will have knowledge regarding their specific problem. They also expect that the counsellor will be a person who will have concern for others, be understanding, caring and supportive (Gibson-Cline, 1996). Counsellor characteristics will be discussed more fully in Chapter 8.

Young people seek professional help generally when life has become very difficult because of serious problems where previous attempts at resolution have failed.

Unfortunately, though, many young people will not seek help for problems on their own. This is particularly the case for young people in early adolescence who have more immature cognitive patterns than their older counterparts. These young people may have to rely on their parents to recognize when they might need help and to find out where they can get that help.

Parents are most likely to seek professional counselling for their adolescent children when the young person's behaviour is posing problems for the parents themselves or, alternatively, when the young person's problems have become serious (Raviv and Maddy-Weitzman, 1992). In the latter case, parental assistance will depend very much on the parents' own ability to recognize and identify problematic and dysfunctional behaviour in their children. Not all parents are able to do this. Consequently, young people are often referred for counselling by other community systems such as schools, statutory organizations, the juvenile justice system, self-help groups and community organizations.

Many young people go through adolescence without consulting with a counsellor. Research suggests that those young people who are better adjusted tend to use their own resources or to seek help and advice from others in their immediate social environ-ment (Billings and Moos, 1981; Lazarus and Folkman, 1984; Compas et al., 1988; Ebata and Moos, 1991; Frydenberg, 1999). However, some young people feel unable to use the resources in their own environment, so will directly seek help from counsellors. Several authors have contributed to the growing literature on help-seeking behaviour in young people and have identified factors such as the age and gender of the young person, racial and ethnic differences, seriousness of the problem, low socio-economic status and locus of control as variables which influence the likelihood of a young person seeking counselling. A comprehensive summary of research in this area is provided by Schonert-Reichl and Muller (1996). Unfortunately, for some young people there is a stigma connected with the need to use counselling services. This is particularly so for those who may be suffering from the emerging symptoms of psychosis because they may additionally be concerned about negative stereotypes of mental illness, and may have negative ideas about the type of service which they may receive. As a consequence they may delay seeking help (Lincoln and McGorry, 1995).

The risk of stigmatization discourages young people from seeking counseling

Self-disclosure and confidentiality

Self-disclosure will usually only occur where there is a strong sense of privacy. Of par-ticular interest to counsellors is the research finding that whether or not a young person seeks help depends on the perceived benefits of seeking help and also the perceived threat of negative consequences which might result from seeking help. For example, in substance-abusing young people, fear of police and statutory involvement has been found to be a deterrent with regard to seeking help (Darke et al., 1996). Clearly, seeking counselling help can be threatening for many young people because counselling requires self-disclosure about personal feelings, thoughts and problems. Counsellors therefore need to be aware of issues that might arise for the young person regarding confidentiality, privacy and the sharing of information with others (see Chapter 8).

KEY POINTS

- counselling young people requires a particular client–counsellor relationship, different processes from those used when counselling children or adults, and particular skills and strategies to enhance the counselling conversation
- young people are moving from strong involvement in their family into a new social system involving peer relationships
- a proactive process enables the counsellor to adjust the counselling process to fit the young person's developmental needs
- there can be significant advantages in combining individual counselling with family therapy
- young people are reluctant to seek help from adults and are more likely to consult with their peers in the first instance

FURTHER RESOURCES

'Kids Help Line' regularly releases overviews of the services they provide, including information about why young people access their telephone and online counselling services. Readers are encouraged to access the 'Kids Help Line' website to find out more about the reasons young people seek help.

- kidshelp.com.au

8

Foundations of the Proactive Approach

From the discussion in Chapter 7 it is clear that for young people to be engaged in counselling with optimum success, the counselling process needs to be tailored specifically to meet their needs. When counselling young people, we recommend what we will call a *proactive approach*. This is an approach to counselling which enables the counsellor to meet young person needs, as described in Part 1, by using a range of counselling skills and strategies in ways which will be described in this and subsequent chapters.

The proactive process for counselling young people will be described in the next chapter (Chapter 9), but first, in this chapter, we will describe the underlying philosophies and counsellor and relationship characteristics that combine to create a foundation for the proactive approach. These are:

- an existentialist philosophy
- constructivist thinking
- personal qualities of the counsellor
- particular qualities of the relationship between the young person and the counsellor.

Figure 8.1 illustrates the way in which the proactive approach is supported by the four elements listed above, with each new element sitting on a foundation created by the ones below. Thus, proactive counselling has as its primary foundation existentialism, upon which is seated constructivism. The other elements are then supported by this base to create a foundation for the proactive counselling approach for young people.

By utilizing the underlying philosophical orientations of existentialism and constructivism as a base to support the other elements of proactive counselling, it will be seen that we are able to tailor the counselling process so that it parallels and fits with the young person's own developmental processes.

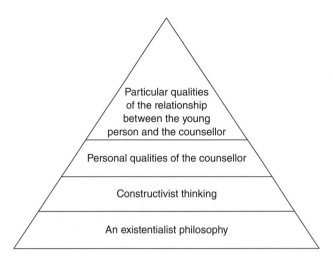

FIGURE 8.1   *Foundations of the proactive counselling approach for young people*

Existentialism

Existentialism is concerned with the human search for the meaning of life. The existentialist view is that the only way human beings can make sense of their existence is through their personal experiences. The existentialist philosophy fits closely with a young person's own developmental processes because making sense of life through their own personal experiences is precisely what young people are trying to do.

The existentialist approach emphasizes that human beings are free to choose and are therefore responsible for their choices and actions. However, these choices are not limitless but lie within situational boundaries. We are not free to choose whatever we want; rather, we are free to choose how to respond to unavoidable and unpredictable 'stimuli' which our world presents to us (Spinelli, 2003).

The assumption of freedom of choice in existential philosophy matches a young person's newfound sense of freedom. Young people generally have the opportunity to make choices and decisions about life, but only within the limits of the boundaries inherent in their social environments. Emphasizing freedom to choose within the inevitable constraints of the real world helps a young person to focus on acceptance of personal responsibility.

Existential philosophy does not focus on psychopathology, which stresses deficits rather than strengths. The philosophy promotes a growth-oriented model that is focused on the future, on the goals that provide direction in life and on the ability of young people to create their own destiny. This approach respects the individual for exploring new aspects of behaviour.

Existential philosophy places emphasis on the search for meaning in life, on freedom and responsibility, on creating one's personal identity, and establishing meaningful relationships with others. Additionally, existentialism places emphasis on anxiety as a condition of living, with awareness of death as a major cause of that anxiety (Corey, 2013). All of these ideas fit very closely with the fundamental tasks and condition of adolescence.

Consequently, an existential counselling philosophy is very appropriate when counselling young people as it parallels much adolescent thinking, encourages the client to accept anxiety as a reality and moves them towards taking responsibility for making decisions within a realistic sense of freedom.

The relationship is more important than the strategies used

The existential approach stresses that the counsellor's techniques are far less important than the quality of the therapeutic client–counsellor relationship and emphasizes the relationship as the major factor that leads to constructive personal change (Corey, 2013). Existential therapists invite clients to grow by modelling authentic behaviour. The existentialist counsellor has the task of encouraging clients to examine their personal experiences to make sense of them and of life, and to explore their options so that they can create a meaningful existence. Thus, the counselling relationship can be likened to that of mentor and student. Mentors encourage young people to go in a direction determined by themselves and dictated by their conscience. This will inevitably bring a realization of responsibility towards one's self and towards others. Experiences of success and defeat will be seen as a normal part of life.

Constructivist thinking

The proactive counselling approach makes use of a constructivist philosophy which is superimposed on an existential foundation. It is important to understand that constructivism is not a theory of counselling. It is a theory that can be useful in helping explain how we set about trying to make sense of the world in which we live (Fransella and Dalton, 2000). As described in existentialism, in trying to make sense of the world in which they live, human beings use their personal experiences of the world to conceptualize and develop ideas or beliefs about the world. In other words, using constructivist terminology, they form constructs that encapsulate their concepts about the world in which they live. These constructs or personal interpretations of the world will not be fixed, but will be revised and replaced as new information becomes available to the individual concerned. Thus, personal construct theory is based upon the philosophical assumption that all of our present interpretations of the universe are subject to revision or replacement (Kelly, 1955). Each of us behaves like a scientist, formulating hypotheses, using our experiences to test them out and if necessary revising them (Winter, 2003). This is precisely what young people do.

The young person is in a stage of development which involves a high level of exploration, so that new, previously unmet experiences challenge the young person to revise and replace inappropriate and/or inadequate constructs with new ones. As Kelly (1955) pointed out, constructions can be reconstructed at any time and reconstruction usually occurs when constructs are invalidated by experience.

Constructivists believe that people actively and proactively construct their worlds so that personal identity and personal equilibrium are maintained. Individuals have some core constructs and these are particularly resistant to change because they are tied in to the person's own sense of personal identity. To change them may be threatening and may cause guilt or anxiety. Individuals adopt different strategies to avoid such anxiety or guilt. Some may tighten constructs so that the world becomes more predictable, whereas others loosen constructs to avoid the possibility of them being invalidated.

When counselling young people, we need to stay in touch with ways of thinking that are similar to theirs. The principles of constructivism fit with adolescent development, so counsellors working with young people will find it useful to use constructivist ideas as a frame of reference.

Implications for counselling

Some counsellors use a construct counselling model as described by Fransella and Dalton (2000). Briefly, this involves determining the clients' constructs, using them to hypothesize about the reasons for their problems, and enabling them to revise their constructs. The proactive approach does not rely on this model. It merely uses the constructivist philosophy as a frame of reference.

By using constructivist philosophy, the counsellor can engage with the young person in an assessment procedure which encourages the client to express their view of the world and explore this view in their own terms, using their own constructs rather than those of the counsellor. The constructivist assessment process is consistent with the young person's need to be believed at a time of internal and external change. The counsellor's primary interest is in understanding and exploring the young person's story and associated constructs.

It is important to respect the young person's constructs

Clearly, constructivism demands that the counsellor actively listens to the young person's personal and individual narrative, and explores, understands and respects the constructs on which the narrative is based. Such an assessment process provides an opportunity for the counsellor to select therapeutic strategies and techniques that fit with the young person's personal constructs. Crespi and Generali (1995) highlight the significance and value of this process when working with young people.

Personal qualities of the counsellor

We have described the required foundations of a proactive counselling approach for young people as being constructivism grounded in existentialism. We believe that the next requirement for successful counselling of young people is that the counsellor be able to demonstrate particular personal qualities (see Figure 8.1). The personal qualities required include:

1. A sound understanding of adolescent developmental processes.
2. An ability to connect with the counsellor's own inner adolescent.
3. An ability to symbolize and model individuation.
4. Rogerian qualities of congruence and unconditional positive regard.
5. An ability to relate easily and with empathy to young people.

A sound understanding of adolescent developmental processes

When counselling young people it is essential that counsellors have a clear and in-depth understanding of adolescence, including adolescent development, developmental needs and tasks. An overview of adolescence is given in Part 1. However, counsellors who specialize in working with young people may wish to explore the underlying developmental theory of adolescence more fully by referring to the references cited in Part 1.

There is no doubt that counselling young people requires special skills and abilities. We believe that all counsellors working with young people require continuing supervision from suitable professionals who are themselves experienced in counselling young people. Clearly, this is particularly important for new counsellors.

An ability to connect with the counsellor's own inner adolescent

In the transactional analysis model of communication between adults, each individual is seen as having within them a 'parent', 'adult' and 'child' (Berne, 1996). We believe that the standard transactional analysis model omits a significant part of the human personality – the adolescent. We believe that each person has within them a capacity to get in touch with those parts of themselves that are associated with parent, adult, adolescent and child cognitions and behaviours. We carry with us the adolescent part of our personalities and are capable of activating that part whenever we choose (and sometimes without realizing what we are doing). It is likely that most readers will be able to recognize a friend, acquaintance or client who makes considerable use of their inner adolescent by exhibiting adolescent thinking and behaviours. Interestingly, for some people the adolescent part of their personality emerges strongly in mid-life when some of the major responsibilities of adulthood, such as raising and providing for a family, are diminishing.

The adolescent is part of self and is a part of all of us. Adolescence does not just represent an in-between stage linking childhood and adulthood; it is a valid stage of lengthy duration that has its own characteristics as described in Part 1. Just as aspects of the child persist in our personalities, so, in the same way, aspects of the adolescent persist, providing us with an 'inner adolescent'. The inner adolescent is not a part of us which needs to be discarded, but is a part which can be useful. It is the part of our personalities that encourages risk-taking, exploring and experimenting with new behaviours, having fun and thinking creatively. The adolescent part of self is freer and less constrained cognitively than the adult and is therefore more able to think and conceptualize with fewer boundaries.

Counsellors who wish to join with young people so that they are 'on the same wavelength' need to be able to get in touch with their own inner adolescent. We are not suggesting that a counsellor should behave exactly *like* a young person. To do that would be phoney and confusing for the client. We are suggesting that counsellors need to be able to get in touch with, and make use of, their own inner adolescent so that they can be freer to accept the client's constructs without being overly impeded by adult thinking, can be more readily able to perceive the world as the young person perceives it and can be better prepared to meet the client on their own ground.

All parts of self need to be valued

Clearly, counsellors also need to be able to utilize the adult part of themselves much of the time during the counselling process. Figure 8.2 illustrates various communication patterns (a to f) that might occur between a young person and counsellor; the arrows indicate the communication paths.

It is obvious that some communication patterns are preferable to others. In Figure 8.2, (a) and (b) show common communication paths between young people and counsellors. In Figure 8.2 (c) the counsellor uses their inner adult to communicate with the young person's inner adult, but the young person responds from their inner child. Figure 8.2 (d) shows an even worse communication pattern, where the client perceives the counsellor as a parent and responds either from their inner child or inner adolescent to the counsellor's inner parent. Such communication is clearly very unhelpful in counselling, having some similarities to the transference relationship described by psychoanalysts. In this situation there is a danger that the counsellor will assume the counter-transference position and respond from their inner parent, creating the communication pattern shown in Figure 8.2 (e). We believe that Figure 8.2 (a) demonstrates the most useful way for an young person client and counsellor to relate. However, Figure 8.2 (b) can also be useful, as both (a) and (b) allow for the mentor–student relationship described previously.

Sometimes it is both appropriate and necessary for the counsellor to communicate by using their own inner adolescent as shown in Figure 8.2 (f). At times, this is highly desirable to enable joining to occur. As stated previously, this does not mean that the counsellor behaves exactly like a young person, but it does suggest that the counsellor makes use of the inner adolescent part of their personality to think and communicate, at times, in a way that has some matching with the style of communication of the young person. Thus, the counsellor will not remain locked into using only their inner adult, but will also be able to make use of their inner adolescent. If the counsellor is able to

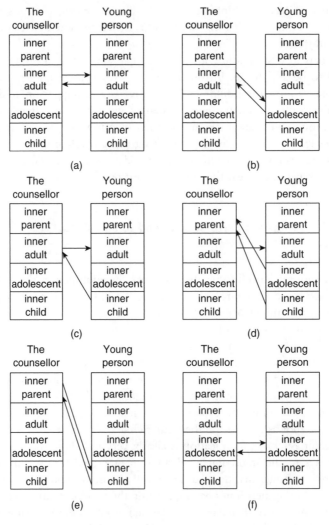

FIGURE 8.2   *Possible communication paths (arrows) in the relationship between the young person and counsellor*

switch from using their inner adult to their inner adolescent and vice versa with ease, a spontaneous and dynamic counselling interaction is possible. Young people are themselves very adept at changing their own styles of communication. As they are moving away from making use of their inner child, they naturally experiment with using both adolescent and adult ways of relating. If the counsellor is able authentically to match such behaviour, joining may be enhanced. However, the counsellor needs to be able to do this naturally and with ease, or it will not fit and will be seen to be phoney.

Interestingly, if a counsellor is able to use their inner adolescent to communicate with the young person's own inner adolescent, then the young person is likely to start to model on the counsellor and to follow when they move into an adult communication mode. Switching in this way allows counselling sessions to be creative, lively and spontaneous.

An ability to symbolize and model individuation

Counsellors working with young people require the ability to communicate their own individuation symbolically by demonstrating their personal individuality and in the process joining with the client. When counselling young people, the counsellor needs to join their own 'self' with the young person in a dynamic process (Fitzgerald, 1995). We believe that the counsellor needs to be proactive in this process if the process is to be dynamic. The way the counsellor dresses, sits and speaks can indicate to the young person that individuality is encouraged and respected. If the counsellor is able to project qualities prized by young people, such as risk-taking, resilience, flexibility, vulnerability and creativity, combined with appropriate humour and gravity, the young person will be likely to have an experience of acceptance and one that values and honours uniqueness.

Joining is clearly critical when counselling young people. Joining at a more personal level than is appropriate when counselling adults can be useful provided that ethical boundaries are respected. The young person is, as has been discussed, inquisitive, and may seek to connect with the counsellor and to get to know who the counsellor is at a personal level rather than as someone hidden behind a professional façade. Young people are more likely to do this if they have some interests in common with the counsellor, and/or if they recognize some similarities between the counsellor's behaviours and ways of relating and their own. Clearly though, as stated, professional ethical boundaries must be maintained. These should not be difficult for the young person to respect if they are framed in terms of the counsellor's own individuation needs.

Rogerian qualities of congruence and unconditional positive regard

Two of the qualities identified by Rogers (1955, 1965) as desirable in counsellors are *congruence* and the ability to demonstrate *unconditional positive regard* towards the client. Many authors since then have accepted that these qualities are useful. We believe that they are not only useful but are necessary for successful counselling of young people.

- *Congruence*: When counsellors fail to be congruent, young people are quick to recognize this. They will easily identify counsellor behaviours that are inconsistent and not genuine. Young people are inquisitive about other people because they are seeking models of adulthood, so they are likely to be critical in assessing the attributes and behaviour of the adults they meet.
- *Unconditional positive regard*: This involves unconditional, non-judgemental and positive acceptance of the client regardless of their behaviour. It is difficult, and at times may be impossible, to achieve unconditional positive regard, but without this quality the counsellor will have difficulty in creating a useful working relationship with the young person.

Young people easily feel judged

The behaviours of young people are not always consistent with the standards of adult behaviour. Not surprisingly, young people frequently feel judged and criticized by adults and also sometimes by peers. They tend to be very quick to recognize disapproval. Consequently, they are unlikely to talk freely with counsellors if they believe that negative judgements are being made about them. Moreover, making negative judgements does not fit with the constructivist approach which demands that the counsellor work from the client's frame of reference to explore the client's own constructs concerning their behaviour. Counsellors need to be able to accept the young person's story and constructs and it can be helpful in doing this if counsellors stay in touch with their own inner adolescent. To do this they may need to deal actively with their own personal feelings, at times, in order to stay within the constructivist paradigm. If a counsellor fails to do this, the young person is unlikely to feel able to talk freely about personal experiences and beliefs.

Being non-judgemental and offering unconditional positive regard to a young person whose behaviour is, by the counsellor's own standards, unacceptable, may not be easy. As stated, being non-judgemental will at times be impossible. However, being non-judgemental and treating clients with unconditional positive regard are goals which counsellors should strive to achieve if they are to work successfully with young people. Where this is difficult, the counsellor needs to explore in supervision any personal issues that may be interfering with their ability to be more accepting.

An ability to relate easily and with empathy to young people

Some counsellors have personalities that allow them to relate easily with young people so that the young people they meet feel comfortable when in their presence and are able to talk to them freely. These counsellors have a natural advantage which, when combined with counselling skills and strategies, can enable them to achieve success in their work with young people. Other counsellors may find working with young people more difficult but can still achieve success if they have a good understanding of the processes required for successful outcomes.

Rogers (1955, 1965) also identified *empathy* as important in counselling. Empathy is the ability to understand fully and share the client's feelings. In being empathic, the counsellor joins effectively with the client, understands their constructs, and is able, at some level, to share the feelings of the client in a way which the young person can recognize. Although we strongly believe that counsellors must be able to demonstrate appropriate levels of empathy when working with young people, we also believe that they need to be able to disengage from the young person's feelings at times. This disengagement is required so that they can protect themselves from being overwhelmed by the client's feelings, and so that they can observe the client and the counselling process and make decisions about that process.

It is essential for the counsellor to be able to convey warmth and caring. Although young people expect their counsellors to be warm and caring, they also tend to be tentative when building relationships and want to preserve their individuation. In order to enable satisfactory joining to occur, the counsellor needs to parallel the young person's cautious behaviour and to demonstrate warmth and caring in ways which are appropriate and not overwhelming, or the young person's individuation will be compromised and the counsellor may be perceived as shallow and lacking congruence.

Particular qualities of the relationship between the young person and counsellor

The qualities of the counselling relationship will clearly depend on the philosophical base for counselling (existential and constructivist), and on the personal qualities of the counsellor (see Figure 8.1). It is widely accepted that the outcome of any counselling intervention is determined by the quality of the relationship between the counsellor and client. This is certainly true for young people where the quality of the relationship is critical in influencing outcomes and client satisfaction (Eltz et al., 1995; Kendall and Southam-Gerow, 1996). For successful outcomes, it is desirable that the counselling relationship should have the following qualities:

1. An authentic person-to-person relationship.
2. The relationship be accepting and understanding.
3. The relationship has appropriate levels of warmth and empathy.
4. The relationship has an element of balance.
5. The relationship takes account of cultural issues.

These relationship qualities are ones that counsellors of young people should strive to achieve. However, sometimes there are specific environmental and/or internal stimuli, including the counsellor's own prejudices and unresolved issues, which make it difficult for the desired relationship qualities to be achieved. It is here that counsellor supervision can be invaluable in helping a counsellor to identify reasons why particular client–counsellor relationships are impaired, and to enable the counsellor to resolve their own personal issues regarding the relationship.

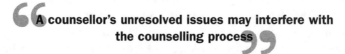

> **A counsellor's unresolved issues may interfere with the counselling process**

An authentic person-to-person relationship

The world, as experienced by young people, is an uncertain one in which all aspects of relationships are tested. The young person's relationships with adults will be different from what they were during childhood. Consequently, the young person needs to try out new ways of relating with adults and may be unsure of the adult expectations. In order to help a young person who seeks counselling to feel relaxed and have a sense of trust, the counsellor will need, above all else, to be congruent (as explained above), open and honest, sincere and respectful. By demonstrating these characteristics, an authentic person-to-person relationship can be created.

The relationship be accepting and understanding

Young people are striving for acceptance in the world outside their families. Generally, young people believe, and come to counselling believing, that no one has understood them, and doubting whether anyone will be able to understand them. In relationships with them it is therefore of major importance that counsellors are able to convey the message that they have heard and do understand. Additionally, as discussed above, the relationship needs to be one where the client feels accepted and valued regardless of their behaviour.

The relationship has appropriate levels of warmth and empathy

Warmth and empathy are essential, but they need to be appropriately demonstrated. The young person is striving for individuation and is unlikely to want to be enveloped in an overwhelming blanket of caring. The young person may also be wary of new relationships, particularly with adults, and may see high levels of warmth emanating from a stranger as incongruent and lacking in genuineness. While recognizing the need for a warm, caring, empathic relationship, counsellors need to allow an appropriate relationship to develop at a pace and intensity comfortable for the client.

The relationship has an element of balance

The relationship between a young person and counsellor does not need to be a predominantly heavy one. It should be balanced, so that although serious and distressing matters may be discussed, there can additionally be some pleasant times involving friendly conversation and/or the use of humour. It is interesting to note that humour has been found to be a useful treatment technique when working with young people (Mann, 1991; Bernet, 1993; Chapman and Chapman-Santana, 1995).

The relationship takes account of cultural issues

While most helping professionals work with limited information concerning their clients' environmental backgrounds, this may present difficulties where the young person and counsellor are from different ethnic and cultural groups (Ivey et al., 2012). Tharp (1991) found that clients prefer counsellors from their own ethnic group and concludes that, whenever possible, counselling for all young people should be in the context of their family's and community's belief systems, relationships and language. We will discuss in more depth cultural considerations when counselling young people in Chapters 9 and 19.

KEY POINTS

- the proactive approach is based on an existentialist philosophy, constructivist thinking, personal qualities of the counsellor, and particular qualities of the counselling relationship
- the existentialist view is that we make sense of our existence through personal experience
- young people are continually forming constructs about the world in which they live: these constructs are not fixed but change as new experiences are encountered
- counsellors of young people need an understanding of adolescent developmental processes, and the ability to connect with their own inner adolescent, to symbolize and model individuation, to be congruent, to have unconditional positive regard, and to relate with ease with young people
- the counselling relationship should be authentic, accepting, understanding, appropriately empathic, and take into account cultural issues

FURTHER RESOURCES

For readers interested in further developing their counselling skills, 'Counselling MindEd' is an e-learning portal developed by the British Association for Counselling and Psychotherapy (BACP) that provides online training for counsellors working with children and adolescents. It can be access via a link from the 'MindEd' website introduced in Chapter 6.

- www.minded.org.uk

9

The Proactive Process for Counselling Young People

In Part 1 we discussed the nature of adolescence, and in Chapters 7 and 8 we have explored the counselling needs of young people and the foundations of the proactive approach. The process used when counselling young people using the proactive approach needs to be understood in the context of all the information discussed previously.

When young people are progressing satisfactorily along their developmental path from childhood to adulthood, they feel good and usually do not need counselling help. When problems arise in their lives, these interfere with, and block, the natural developmental process. Generally, young people will then successfully draw on strategies and resources within themselves to overcome challenges. Alternatively, they may be able to deal adaptively with these problems with the aid of peers, parents or significant others, as shown diagrammatically in Figure 9.1. Sometimes problems may be more serious, severe, accumulative or extremely private, and young people may be unable to manage them without counselling support. If a young person is unable to resolve or negotiate a block in the path of normal development, and is unable to receive the necessary counselling help, there are likely to be resulting maladaptive behaviours in response to stress. Typically, these behaviours might include withdrawal, aggression, truancy, substance abuse, self-harm and/or suicide.

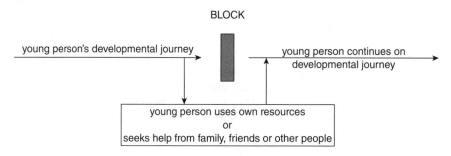

FIGURE 9.1 *Young person's problem-solving behaviour*

We will explain the proactive counselling process by describing:

1. Proactive counsellor behaviours.
2. Flexibility of the counselling process.
3. The primary counselling functions.
4. The use of single or multiple sessions.

Proactive counsellor behaviours

Proactive counsellor behaviours are supported by the foundations described in Chapter 8. Thus they are based on existentialism, constructivism, the personal qualities of the counsellor and particular qualities of the counselling relationship.

We believe that there are five essential characteristics of appropriate counsellor behaviour when working with young people. These are:

- being responsive to the young person's developmental needs
- believing the young person
- joining an adolescent style of communication
- being proactive
- respecting the young person's disclosure processes.

Most counsellors of young people are adults, although there are some young people who have been specially trained to counsel their peers. Many adult counsellors either have, or have parented, adolescent children of their own. Some counsellors from this group may find it hard to accept some of the suggestions in the following paragraphs. This is almost inevitable because it can be difficult for counsellors who are parents to avoid using the *parent* part of themselves. This can make it hard for them to join with young clients as counsellors by using the *inner adolescent* and *inner adult* parts of themselves, which is what is needed (see Chapter 8). However, we know that this can happen because although we are parents ourselves, we are able to enjoy the satisfaction of joining with and helping young people.

Many counsellors make strong statements about the need to meet adult clients with empathy and to join in their perceptions of their world. However, surprisingly, there is often resistance to the idea that counsellors of young people should, at times, use the adolescent part of their personality. Yet using this part of the personality enables close matching and joining with a young person.

Joining with the young person is essential for successful outcomes

As stated in Chapter 8, using the inner adolescent does not mean behaving like a young person or pretending to be a young person. It does involve recognizing and getting in touch with the young person within ourselves so that we are able to think, conceptualize, perceive the world, examine constructs about the world and communicate in a way similar to that of our young clients. If we are not able to do this we will not join with them as counsellors but may be seen as parental. They may perceive us as telling them what we think they should do and how they should behave. This is certain to disempower and alienate the young people we are trying to help.

In exercising unconditional positive regard, we also need to uncritically accept typical adolescent behaviours such as changeability and unreliability. These are developmentally normal. At times, young people will present counsellors with challenging behaviours (Mabey and Sorensen, 1995) because some young people regard adults with suspicion and may act out their feelings within a counselling session. They may become withdrawn, unwilling to trust or may be openly hostile or surly. In response, the counsellor needs to be accepting, flexible and adaptable.

Being responsive to the young person's developmental needs

It is essential that counsellors working with young people understand the adolescent developmental processes, as described in Part 1, so that they are able to make informed use of the counselling process described in this chapter. They also need to be actively responsive to the young people's developmental needs during each counselling session. In attending to developmental needs, fundamental adolescent issues of power and autonomy need to be addressed.

Young people are generally moving from a situation where their lives are heavily controlled by others to a situation where they have more autonomy and responsibility. Counsellors therefore need to allow young people to express their autonomy and individuality within the counselling experience. This may, at times, be uncomfortable for the counsellor. If so, the underlying counsellor issues need to be addressed by the counsellor in supervision.

The young person needs to have choice about how to use each counselling session within mutually agreed limits regarding what is relevant and appropriate. They also need to have the right to decide whether to come to appointments or not. Where counselling is mandated, the young person still needs to feel able to choose to come or not, taking into account the consequences of that decision. Contracts need to be mutually negotiated and agreed so that the young person feels equally responsible for determining these. With regard to ongoing appointments, the young person needs to know that they have control of the decision to come back or not. As young people are seeking control in their lives they will be less likely to return if they believe that the counsellor is trying to make a decision for them.

Believing the young person

First, we need to define what we mean when we refer to 'believing the young person'. When, in the proactive counselling of young people, we say that we believe the client, we mean that we will listen to their story and will accept it at face value as the young person's truth even if the story stretches our credulity. We will be totally accepting of the story and will not challenge its veracity. However, if there are inconsistencies in the story we will draw attention to them and explore them, provided that the client is happy to engage in such exploration with us.

Young people will often tell counsellors stories that are difficult to believe. However, such stories fit with the constructs which the young person is currently using. If counsellors are to help young people to move ahead to the point of reviewing and challenging existing constructs, then it is essential that they first accept without question what the client is saying. However, where inconsistencies arise in the client's stories these can be discussed so that existing constructs can be revised where necessary (see Chapter 12).

> **Believing the young person helps them to review their constructs**

It is well known that young people often feel that they are misunderstood and not believed by adults. If counsellors are seen to behave in a way which matches young people's stereotypical perceptions of adults by not believing their stories, then the possibility of building helpful counselling relationships where the client trusts the counsellor is diminished. Additionally, young people often have stories to tell which the young person may legitimately feel are difficult to believe. They may be true, but difficult to believe. It is therefore essential that we believe what we are being told. If we do not believe what we are told, then we will not be trusted and we are unlikely to be able to help the young person to move forward into telling stories which more accurately reflect adult perceptions.

We know that some counsellors will disagree with the suggestion that we should always believe the client. However, in our experience, by doing this, trust develops and the client is empowered to review and evaluate constructs, discarding those which do not fit with reality and replacing them by more adaptive constructs. In the process, more objective truth is revealed. However, the counsellor does need to be alert to the possibility of the symptoms of mental disorder, as described in Chapter 6, and to refer to appropriate helpers when necessary. Believing the client is an essential component of proactive counselling.

Joining an adolescent style of communication

As will be discussed more fully in Chapter 10, the conversational style of young people is generally not the same as that of most adults. Many young people are likely to move in and out of the conversational process, flit from one idea to another and desire to be in control of the conversation at all times. As counsellors, if we are to be able to join effectively with young people we need to deliberately parallel their conversational style rather than trying to contain it. Thus, digressions may be actively and deliberately encouraged. At times the counsellor can make use of such digressions to help in the joining process, and then later return to discussion of the young person's problems.

Parents often feel that their adolescent children are intrusive in wanting to talk at inappropriate times. They also often find that their adolescent children will not talk about personal issues when invited but want to talk at length at times which are inconvenient. This is developmentally normal adolescent behaviour. Counsellors need to respect and take advantage of this.

Young people who have difficulty in talking about the things that trouble them most will want to do this in their own time. They therefore need to be allowed to digress and move towards and away from discussing matters of importance. Thus, rather than running away from important issues in the counselling conversation, the young person may well be diverting temporarily, waiting for a time when it is more comfortable to continue. The counsellor need not be dismayed by this process but merely needs to follow the young person and add energy to the conversation. This may involve being patient and actively deciding to enjoy listening to a conversation that, at times, may not seem to be directly relevant.

As noted above, counselling conversations do not need to be continually heavy and serious. It is more helpful in putting a young person at ease if friendly conversation and humour are encouraged, to balance the impact of the discussion of serious issues.

Being proactive

When working with young people the interactional style required differs markedly from the style of interaction that commonly occurs when counselling adults. Adults seem to cope well with structured counselling sessions where the counsellor stays within the boundaries of a well-defined counselling contract. They are generally clearer than young people about why they are engaging in counselling and are generally more confident within the counselling process.

In contrast with adults, young people are often restless and uncertain when engaged in counselling. It is usually not sufficient for the counsellor to be a quiet listener. Young people are generally restless beings who need to be actively engaged. They quickly become impatient and bored, so the counselling relationship needs to be dynamic. This requires spontaneous behaviours combined with creativity, and the use of a more active counselling process than that used with adults.

The proactive counselling approach enables counsellors to meet a young person's needs, as described in Part 1, by proactively selecting counselling skills and strategies from commonly used, well-established and tested counselling theories and methods. The selection of counselling skills and strategies is carried out in response to the young person's immediate needs, as they are identified at any point in time, during the counselling session. Decisions regarding the timing of the introduction of particular skills and/or strategies are critical to the proactive process. Thus, sessions are dynamic, with the counsellor deliberately choosing particular skills and introducing specific strategies as these are required. This does not mean that counselling sessions are chaotic. They are not, but the process will continually shift and change in response to the young person's conversation, behaviour, mood, issues and needs.

> ❝ **The proactive counsellor is dynamic in responding to immediate needs** ❞

It is essential to proactive counselling that the counsellor should be active, lively, spontaneous and creative. Most importantly, the counsellor needs to be quick, flexible and *opportunistic*. This means responding quickly and actively through the selection and use of appropriate skills and strategies, so that opportunities are not lost. Thus, the counselling process becomes energized. The use of the proactive counselling approach will be illustrated in Chapter 20 by case studies.

Respecting the young person's disclosure processes

Perhaps the most important factor in counselling success with young people is to enable them to self-disclose. By self-disclosing, they have an opportunity to express themselves openly, they receive validation about the content of their disclosure, gain a sense of control over issues discussed and, most importantly, are enabled to review and revise personal constructs. All of this assists in the adolescent development process (Rotenberg, 1995).

Self-disclosure in young people serves as a catharsis for both positive and negative emotions. It allows young people to experience strong emotions connected with their stories and to identify issues and constructs related to these emotions. If counsellors are able to join with young clients by expressing similar emotional responses to them when listening to their stories, the clients' experiences will be validated and they may be able to release their emotions more fully with cathartic effect. Having done this they can move on to reviewing and revising constructs which will determine future behaviours.

As discussed in Chapter 7, in their everyday lives young people initiate, build and maintain relationships with their peers, in part through the use of mutual self-disclosure. In particular, young people are attracted to others through the disclosure of similar experiences. This mutual sharing creates a sense of safety and intimacy. Just as self-disclosure promotes closeness and intimacy in peer relationships, a level of mutual story-telling during counselling can be useful in establishing trust because it parallels the young person's experience with peers.

Many counsellors, particularly those who are used to working with adults, have concerns regarding counsellor self-disclosure. Counsellor self-disclosure should not be used to satisfy the counsellor's needs. It must be limited to preserve boundaries which are appropriate for the counsellor's own personal individuation and most importantly to respect professional and ethical boundaries. However, when counselling young people, a limited level of counsellor self-disclosure is required in initiating, building and developing the counselling relationship. The use of counsellor self-disclosure will be discussed more fully in the next chapter.

Young people are continually exploring new constructs and comparing them with their own. Often they will make strong statements about their own beliefs while at the same time being open to, and interested in, other people's ideas. They may either directly or indirectly invite peers, parents, teachers and counsellors to share their ideas with them so that they can test their own constructs against those of others. It is important for counsellors to recognize this typical behaviour of young people and to make use of it in the counselling process.

The issue of *confidentiality* is crucial to the willingness of young people to disclose. They expect confidentiality and loyalty in the counselling relationship in the same way that they expect it from peer friendships (although they do not always get these things from their peers).

Unfortunately, the issue of confidentiality is complicated because of the rights of others to have information. Many young people are living at home and may be brought for counselling by their parents. Those who are in care may similarly be brought for counselling by carers. Parents and legal guardians have a right to receive information concerning young people in their care. However, many parents and carers will respect the young person's right to have confidential counselling, provided that they know that they will be told if there are matters of major concern.

Initially, when young people are brought for counselling by parents or other carers, it can be useful to discuss the issue of confidentiality in the presence of the young person and the adults concerned so that agreement can be reached regarding confidentiality and its limits. Where a young person has taken the initiative to set up a counselling interview for themselves, it may be possible for the counsellor to respect confidentiality fully. However, this will be subject to legal, ethical and professional obligations. Where there is disclosure of abuse, or of suicide plans, or of plans to harm others, counsellors have a duty of care to the client and others, and need to take appropriate action. At times like this, it is important to talk with the young person about the necessity of informing others. Whenever possible, after taking account of legal, ethical and professional requirements, the client should be given the right to decide *how* and *when* disclosure will take place. This enables them to have some control of the disclosure process and, it is hoped, a sense of some control over the consequences of disclosure. To do otherwise disempowers the client, and is likely to result in disillusionment with the counselling process. If this occurs, the client may never seek counselling again.

Being open about confidentiality and its limits helps build trust

When young people are brought to counselling by parents or carers, once confidentiality issues have been negotiated and agreed, it is usually best to talk with the young person first in order to be able to obtain their trust. Young people who are under pressure to attend are usually reluctant to engage in the counselling process. If their parents or other adults are consulted first, they may conclude that unfavourable reports about them have been made before they have a chance to state their own points of view.

A good way to respect the rights of the parents and retain the confidence of the young person is to meet with parents or carers only at times when the young person is present, or to meet with the whole family with the young person present. By doing this, the young person can hear what parents (or other family members) are saying, and what the counsellor is saying, and is free to offer alternative points of view or versions of reality (Barker, 1990). When a third party is involved in setting up a counselling contract for a young person, it is vital that the issues of confidentiality, and of further communication between the counsellor and the referral source, are clarified before counselling starts.

Confidentiality is a way of providing the young person with privacy in which to discuss issues that are too difficult to disclose to others. However, as discussed above, there are limits to the extent to which the confidentiality can be offered, and counsellors have a responsibility to be open with young people about these limits. Different countries, and states within countries, have varying policies on the rights of young people, and concerning the responsibilities of counsellors and other professionals. It is essential that counsellors are familiar with the ethical, professional and legal issues relating to confidentiality when working with young people.

Flexibility of the counselling process

When compared with counselling children or adults, counselling young people needs to be more flexible and freer in structure. The counselling process will generally not be as well defined and predictable. Young people are less likely to stay engaged in a counselling process that follows sequentially through stages of therapy over time. They are often unable to see the big picture of the world in which they live because they are struggling with changing constructs. They may also have difficulty in articulating their difficulties and may only be able to focus on, and describe, fairly discrete parts of their world which tend to be disconnected from the broader picture. Their discovery process is one that involves trying to connect and make sense of differing parts of their picture. The counselling process therefore needs to take account of this, with counsellors using strategies which will enable young people to draw their ideas and beliefs together to form constructs which will help them to make sense of their world.

The counselling process needs to allow young people to explore in ways which are similar to those which they use generally. Thus, they may jump from subject to subject and wish to explore seemingly disconnected parts of their world and experiences. The proactive approach allows for this as it requires the counsellor to be spontaneous, creative, flexible and opportunistic, while attending to the primary functions of the counselling process.

The primary counselling functions

Figure 9.2 illustrates diagrammatically the process for counselling young people using the proactive approach. The counselling process depends on a central core of *primary counselling functions*. The three primary counselling functions are:

- relationship building
- assessing the problem
- addressing the problem.

Details of these primary functions will be discussed below. The three functions do not necessarily occur in sequence, but may overlap or be performed concurrently. Each function may happen continuously or be repeated several times during a counselling session. At all times, during a counselling session, the proactive counsellor is involved in attending to one or more of the primary functions. To do this, whenever necessary, the counsellor draws on counselling micro-skills, as illustrated by the arrows in Figure 9.2 (micro-skills are discussed in Chapter 11), or may allow diversions by paralleling the

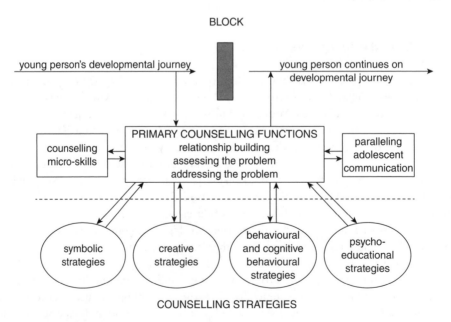

FIGURE 9.2 *The proactive counselling process*

young person's conversational style, as indicated in Figure 9.2. These diversions should not be viewed as lost counselling time because they serve a useful purpose by contributing to the primary counselling functions. Engaging in the young person's general conversation can be useful for relationship building and also in helping the counsellor to learn about and understand the young person's constructs about their world.

Counselling strategies used to operationalize the primary counselling functions

The ellipses in Figure 9.2 describe four different groups of counselling strategies that can be useful when counselling young people. It is the proactive counsellor's task to select from these groups of strategies and to use those strategies which are appropriate at particular points within the counselling session. During one counselling session, one or more strategies may be utilized. The strategies are an available resource. The counsellor needs to be opportunistic and skilled in selecting and using relevant strategies at particular times. *The proactive counsellor takes full responsibility for orchestrating the counselling process to fulfil the primary functions, while allowing the young person freedom within the process to explore and resolve issues.* This is central to proactive counselling of young people. Counselling strategies are selected in response to the young person's cognitive, emotional, somatic, verbal and non-verbal behaviours and the issues being discussed. The strategies selected are the ones which the counsellor believes will promote the most successful outcomes.

A proactive counsellor is quickly responsive to the client's needs

The timing of the introduction of strategies selected is particularly important because this will influence the young person's level of interest and engagement in the counselling process. If the timing is inappropriate, the young person will not be engaged in the use of the strategy. In addition, if the strategy selected does not fit the immediate needs, personality and mood of the young person, then it is likely to fail. The strategies within each group are discussed in Chapters 14 to 17, together with information about the selection and suitability of each strategy.

Each session is complete in itself

In the proactive counselling approach each of the three primary counselling functions is used in every counselling session. Thus, if a young person comes to several counselling sessions, all three functions will be involved in all sessions. However, the balance between the use of the three functions may change as required. Thus each session is complete in itself so that if the client does not return for further counselling useful work has been achieved.

Making each counselling session complete in itself is particularly important for young people. This is because many young people will come to see a counsellor at a time of crisis but will stop coming as soon as the crisis is over. They may then come back later when a new crisis occurs. It is clearly advantageous if counsellors can not only help young people to deal with current crises but also enable them to make changes, so that when new crises occur they have the skills to deal with the new crises themselves without the need for counselling.

When we are counselling young people it is useful to remember that because of their developmental stage in life they may be unreliable with regard to keeping appointments. Consequently, it can be useful for us to assume that each appointment with a young person may be the final appointment. We can then endeavour to achieve a level of completion in the counselling work undertaken in the session.

Relationship building

This primary counselling function involves:

- joining with the young person
- developing a relationship with the young person
- contracting with the young person.

Joining with the young person

Joining with young people is the most critical part of counselling them. It can sometimes be difficult, but without joining effective counselling cannot take place. Young people have a natural tendency to want to move away from the influence and control of parents and other adults, so they are likely to regard adult counsellors with suspicion and mistrust. They may ask questions such as 'How is this person different from my parents or teachers?' and 'Why should I expect them to treat me as a person or individual of value rather than as a child who needs to be told what to do?' Proactive counsellors join by understanding and paralleling some commonly used behaviours of young people. They make use of important components inherent in adolescent friendship formation and particular communication and disclosure processes of young people, which are described in the next chapter. Thus, proactive counsellors model some of their own behaviours on commonly used behaviours which young people use at a personal level when connecting and talking with their peers. This does not mean that proactive counsellors behave like young people, but it does mean that they make sensible use of some communication processes which young people commonly use themselves in their relationships with peers. Additionally, the joining process is enhanced by selectively making use of particular counselling micro-skills, as discussed in Chapter 11.

Clearly, joining is most critical at the start of, and during, the first session of counselling. However, joining does not just happen at the start of a session, but is a continuing process. Young people tend to be changeable and sometimes fickle in their evaluation of friends. They are quick to take offence or to disengage through restlessness or lack of interest. Consequently, the counsellor should continually attend to the need to maintain and develop a positive connection with the client.

Developing a relationship with the young person

The development of a relationship with the young person involves a deeper level of joining than the initial connection that occurs on first meeting. Initial joining needs to occur at the beginning of each counselling session, not just the first session. Such joining engages the young person in the counselling process, and enables the development of a more complete and trusting relationship so that work which may be intensely personal can occur. The development of such a relationship needs to be ongoing and to occur throughout the counselling process. Counsellors need to be constantly attending to relationship development and maintenance because young people continually re-evaluate their relationships. They are most likely to be vigilant in re-examining their relationships with counsellors because counsellors are generally adults, and young people are particularly sensitive to relationship issues with adults.

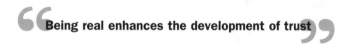

Being real enhances the development of trust

As rapport develops between a counsellor and young person, a relationship which involves the qualities described in Chapter 8 can develop, enabling the client to feel safe in talking about troubling personal issues. The counselling relationship creates a climate in which useful counselling work can take place. Additionally, it is helpful in itself because it may provide a useful setting in which the young person can examine and revise constructs about relationships, can experiment with the relationship itself and can discover new relationship skills. There is safety in doing this in an environment where there can be some level of confidence that judgement and/or disapproval are unlikely to occur. Thus, the counselling relationship can provide an opportunity for the development of social competence and can be used as a model for future relationships.

Contracting with the young person

During the initial joining process, the counsellor needs to make an agreement, even if loose, with regard to the purpose and possible duration of counselling. This agreement may need to be updated and amended from time to time.

Young people who are not used to the counselling process need to be familiarized with the opportunities and limitations of counselling. They will need to know:

- that it is OK to take time to talk things through
- that the counsellor will not provide solutions but will try to help them to find their own solutions

- that what they say will be in confidence but that there may be limits to that confidentiality
- that coming to counselling is their choice (although for some there may be consequences if they decide not to attend)
- that they will have choice about what they do, and do not do, within the counselling process
- that one session may be all they need or want, but that if they wish to continue coming for further sessions that can be discussed so that mutual agreement can be reached.

Assessing the problem

This primary counselling function involves the following:

- listening to the young person's story and believing it
- identifying themes, issues and problems
- evaluating the young person's emotional state.

It needs to be remembered that this function does not occur at a particular point in the overall counselling process. It may happen continuously and/or at various times during a counselling session.

Listening to the young person's story and believing it

As discussed in Chapter 8, listening to the client's story without judgement and believing it are essential to the constructivist basis of the proactive approach. By believing the client's story, we mean that we accept it totally as the young person's truth so that their experience is one of being believed. As the young person tells us their story, being empathic, we match emotional responses, and we verbally affirm the client's experience. Thus the client feels validated. At times, the young person may experience a sense of relief at being believed by an adult. This is particularly so if the story stretches credulity.

By believing the story, the counsellor is entering the young person's world and has a sense of what it is like to be in that world. Where there are inconsistencies, the counsellor may be puzzled, and may share this with the young person. Thus, the counsellor will be seen to be congruent and, most importantly, to be keenly interested in trying to fully understand the young person's world and its inconsistencies.

Identifying themes, issues and problems

As the young person tells their story, the counsellor will progressively piece together a picture relating to that story. Further, as the story is expounded, the counsellor can identify themes, issues and problems, and may feed these back to the client, seeking clarification if necessary. The counsellor may select particular strategies and/or techniques to make it easier for the client to clearly identify and clarify themes, issues and problems. Suitable strategies and techniques are described in Part 3.

Evaluating the young person's emotional state

Evaluation of the client's emotional and mental state, including mood, feelings, thoughts and perceptions, is necessary to provide a complete picture for the counsellor of how the young person is coping. This is needed so that the counsellor can make decisions regarding strategies to be used during counselling, and also to enable the counsellor to determine whether mental health problems that need specialist treatment are in evidence or are developing.

In making an assessment, counsellors need to draw on their knowledge of adolescent development, and understand the impact that past and current experiences have had on the young person's life (see Part 1). This evaluation needs to be seen as an ongoing process throughout the course of a counselling session or series of sessions.

Assessment is an ongoing process

Specific counselling skills to evaluate the young person's emotional and mental state will be discussed in Chapter 11. Young people generally tend to like assessment techniques which they believe might help them discover and understand who they are, or what they might be feeling. This explains why many of them show an interest in philosophies such as astrology or numerology. Consequently, some young people find it interesting to do self-report inventories. Recognizing this, some counsellors find it helpful to use formal assessment tools such as depression inventories or self-esteem assessments. These may be particularly useful in identifying mental health problems. However, many experienced counsellors who work with young people are able to make assessments using clinical judgement alone. This is satisfactory for the purpose of counselling those who are not experiencing mental health problems, and fits with our own practice.

Addressing the problem

This primary counselling function involves the following:

- working through the problem
- exploring solutions
- planning to experiment.

Working through the problem

Young people generally come to counselling seeking solutions to problems, so during the counselling process there is likely to be commitment to the resolution of specific issues. The counsellor therefore needs to select and use strategies which will be appropriate for the task.

Some young people may only wish to explore their issues in counselling and come to a clearer understanding of their problems without seeking solutions. These clients may wish to seek solutions later without counselling help. This fits with a young person's need for individuation. Such clients should be encouraged to do as they wish and be complimented because they are accepting responsibility for finding their own solutions. They can be commended for their confidence in their own ability. Additionally, they can be invited to seek counselling in the future if they think that it might be useful.

Exploring solutions

Working through the problem will often lead naturally to the discovery of possible solutions that will need to be evaluated. The evaluation should take into account positive and negative consequences associated with solutions and the extent to which the young person seems comfortable with each possible solution. Some solutions may not fit with the client's fundamental beliefs or constructs. When this occurs, there is an opportunity for re-examination of beliefs with possible revision of constructs. Solutions which are more inviting need to be considered in terms of the young person's ability and commitment to using them. The only solutions that will work are ones that appeal to the young person, fit with their personal constructs, or revised constructs, and are ones that the young person has the will and capacity to put into practice.

Planning to experiment

Young people are inexperienced and sometimes devise solutions that seem to be attractive but which may be impractical or have undesired consequences. As counsellors, we need to remember that most human beings learn best through personal experience. Having found a possible solution to a problem does not necessarily mean that the problem is solved. The solution needs to be tested.

Young people are vulnerable and may feel a deep sense of failure when solutions do not work out in practice. Counsellors should therefore discuss the need to test solutions by putting them into practice. This can be framed in terms of doing an experiment to test a solution. Where an experiment demonstrates problems with a particular solution, the experiment can be seen not as a failure but as having been useful in providing new information. That new information can be used to revise constructs and formulate other solutions.

The use of single or multiple sessions

Many young people will benefit from a single session of counselling, finding resolution of their problems and thus resuming their developmental journey with relative ease. However, for others this will not be the case and they may require further counselling help. Unfortunately, making appointments and maintaining a commitment to counselling is difficult for many young people. In particular, open-ended counselling contracts may be daunting for some. Even when contracts are made for ongoing counselling, many young people will not turn up regularly but will be inconsistent in their attendance.

Several research studies have compared the effectiveness of short-term or brief counselling with longer-term counselling of young people (for example, Slavin, 1996; Warner, 1996), and other studies have examined the issue of young people attending counselling where they have been sent by others and not self-referred (DiGiuseppe et al., 1996). These studies do not make definitive recommendations regarding the most desirable and effective duration of the counselling relationship. However, it is clear that, generally, young people can benefit from single-session or short-term brief interventions (Fitzgerald, 1995; Mabey and Sorensen, 1995; Mortlock, 1995). Short interventions are more in keeping with the way in which young people run their lives.

> **Each counselling session should be complete in itself**

Proactive counsellors encourage young people to be in control of the decision about whether to return for further counselling. This is achieved by encouraging them to examine their needs and readiness for either short- or longer-term counselling without introducing options prematurely, so that their own decision-making processes are not unduly contaminated by the counsellor. However, it is appropriate for a counsellor to provide feedback and information regarding their own perceptions of the young person's suitability for brief or long-term counselling. Where clients have high ego strength, single-session counselling is likely to be effective, but this is unlikely to be so for clients with low ego strength, who may require a longer and more supportive process (Alexander, 1965).

When a young person decides that further counselling sessions would be helpful and expresses a wish to have these, a contract regarding continuing counselling needs to be negotiated collaboratively by the counsellor and young person. This may result in a specific contract for counselling sessions with firm dates and times. However, some young people prefer an open-door arrangement that will allow them to come to counselling when they feel that they need it. If this is suitable for the counsellor, an open-door policy can be used. Where an agreement is reached and further appointments are made, it is desirable that the young person be invited to cancel appointments if they become unnecessary or are no longer desired. This is to encourage them to be in control of the process.

Clients who drop out

Young people drop out of counselling for a number of reasons:

- They may find the joining and engaging process too threatening.
- The counselling experience may have been unsatisfactory for them and may have failed to meet their expectations.

- They may have hoped for magical solutions and be disappointed when they realize that, ultimately, they themselves are responsible for finding solutions and putting them into practice.
- They may believe that the counsellor does not see their problems as sufficiently important.

Young people who have been sent to counselling by parents or other referral sources are most likely to want to withdraw when painful issues are confronted or awareness of issues is heightened.

It is often assumed that the main reason why clients drop out of counselling is because they are dissatisfied with the treatment received or because facing their problems is too overwhelming. However, research on people who drop out of all forms of therapy reveals that most clients who drop out do so because they have accomplished what they intended.

Many clients who drop out of counselling report as much improvement as those who stay on for the longer term (Talmon, 1990; Budman and Gurman, 1992; Rosenbaum, 1994; Kaffman, 1995). Counsellors of young people are well advised to recognize this, because coming to counselling regularly does not fit very comfortably with the lifestyle of many young people. Additionally, young people tend to be impatient and want quick results. Often, a single counselling session may be enough to help them to overcome their block and continue on their developmental journey. It is therefore wise for counsellors who work with young people to realize that the first session may also be the last, although it may also have been a useful and complete counselling experience which will predispose the young person to seek counselling again in the future, if the need arises.

Counsellors need to take account of the young person's developmental needs for power and autonomy. It is essential that they are given free choice about whether to continue with counselling or not. If this choice is not offered, then the client may become extremely resistant to the counselling process and avoid offers of counselling in the future. Paradoxically, if the client is offered a free and open choice about whether to continue, resistance and hostility are likely to be minimized. It is important for counsellors to be clear with their clients that they are committed to providing continuing counselling, if it is required. They need to let their young clients know of their willingness to work with them for as long as is needed, provided that useful goals are recognized.

Cultural considerations

Before bringing this chapter to a close, we would like to highlight the importance of cultural considerations when counselling young people. Indeed, being aware of and sensitive to both your own and your clients' cultural values is an essential task when working with young people from cultural backgrounds different from your own (Leebert, 2006). Understanding another culture is a complex undertaking, particularly as culture is an ever-changing construct that can mean different things to different people (Chantler, 2005). You may like to take a moment to reflect on the way culture has impacted your own values, beliefs and identity. Has this changed over the course of your life? How might your cultural values impact on the client–counsellor relationship? We touch more on cultural considerations in Chapter 19, although interested readers may like to refer to Ivey et al. (2012), which provides a comprehensive overview of cultural considerations throughout the counselling process.

KEY POINTS

- throughout the counselling process attention needs to be given to the primary counselling functions of relationship building, assessing the problem and addressing the problem
- being proactive involves energetically responding to the young person's immediate needs through:
    - o the use of selected counselling micro-skills
    - o the use of communication processes familiar to young people including digression and appropriate self-disclosure
    - o the introduction of symbolic, creative, behavioural, cognitive behavioural and psycho-educational strategies
- the proactive counsellor is responsive to the young person's developmental needs for autonomy and individuation
- the proactive counsellor has the ability to bring the inner adolescent part of their personality into the counselling process
- believing the young person's story is respectful and assists in building trust
- it is sensible to inform the young person about the extent of confidentiality which can be provided
- the session needs to be complete in itself so that useful work has been achieved even if the young person does not return for further counselling
- testing solutions by putting them into practice can be framed as doing an experiment so that if the solution doesn't work the outcome is not experienced as failure

FURTHER RESOURCES

For a review of the various approaches to therapy please refer to the 'Counselling Directory' website. What approaches fit well with the proactive approach we have described in this chapter?

- www.counselling-directory.org.uk/counselling.html

10

Making Use of Adolescent Communication Processes

We have noticed that many counsellors find it difficult to join with young people and engage them in a way that enables them to talk freely. This can be a serious problem because it is impossible for a helpful counselling process to develop unless the counsellor is able to gain the trust of the young person so that they feel comfortable enough to talk about intimate personal issues. In our opinion this is the biggest problem that counsellors face when trying to help young people. When we think about this problem we shouldn't be surprised by the difficulty counsellors have in trying to engage young people in a counselling process because there is abundant evidence in the literature to support the notion that young people are generally reluctant to talk to adults about sensitive issues (Boldero and Fallon, 1995).

As we have explained previously, young people are in a process of individuation. They need to become individuals in their own right with a level of separation from their parents and other adults so that they can make decisions for themselves. It is appropriate for them to make friends with their peers. As noted by Readdick (1997) and Santrock (1993), they tend to associate more frequently with their peers than with adults.

We know that parents commonly complain that their adolescent children won't talk to them openly. This is not surprising, as avoiding talking about particular topics is the way that individuals create boundaries in their relationships, as a number of authors including Guerrero and Afifi (1995) and Ryder and Bartle (1991) point out. Thus by avoiding talking about sensitive personal issues with parents and other adults, young people establish their boundaries so that they can satisfactorily perform their task of individuation.

We also need to recognize that young people are going to be reluctant to talk to adults about sensitive or personal issues, as doing so might be embarrassing or lead to them becoming emotionally overwhelmed. If they refrain from sharing such information they retain their privacy and avoid the possibility of becoming closer to an adult at a time when they are trying to individuate. In particular, by withholding disclosure from their parents about their daily activities, young people create arenas of privacy and protect themselves from parental interference and unwanted supervision (Buhrmester and Prager, 1995).

" Young people are generally reluctant to confide in adults "

If we take account of the reasons why young people tend to avoid confiding in adults, we shouldn't be surprised by the fact that many young people are reluctant to talk to counsellors. However, if we are to be effective in helping young people, we need to discover useful ways to engage them in conversation and this is made easier by understanding the ways in which they themselves communicate comfortably. As described in the literature, and from observation, it is clear that commonly used adolescent communication processes are in some ways different from commonly used adult communication processes.

If we want to have a fuller understanding of normal adolescent communication processes, it can be useful to observe young people as they talk to each other. Because they may object to being observed and may behave differently when they are being observed, such observations can often best be done in public places. For example, if you are travelling on a train or bus or are sitting in a restaurant with young people nearby, you may find it easy to listen into their conversation without being intrusive. If you notice the processes that they use, you will probably discover that many young people use several distinct processes when talking with peers.

When young people meet with and join with peers at a personal level they usually engage in some of the following behaviours (Rotenberg, 1995; Seiffge-Krenke, 1995):

- They positively connote aspects of the other person's presentation, including appearance, behaviours and adornments or possessions.
- They use direct closed questions to get information.
- They disclose information about themselves and assume that the other person will similarly self-disclose.
- They validate the other person's views, if possible.
- They use praise when relevant.
- They are very direct about what they like and do not like.
- They match and exaggerate the other person's emotional expressions in response to story-telling.

Additionally, we have noticed that many young people tend to:

- frequently digress, move away from a topic of interest, and then return to it
- take the lead in a conversation and feel as though they are in control of it
- give and receive advice.

If, as counsellors, we are to engage young people in conversation, then we can learn from their communication processes so that we ourselves can make use of these processes when appropriate. We believe that it can be helpful if counsellors working with young people are able to proactively engage in behaviours such as those listed above.

However, as counsellors, we do need to behave naturally so that what we do fits with our own personalities and is not fake. Thus, counsellors helping young people need to be able to get in touch with, and use, their own inner adolescent, while remaining true to themselves as adults.

Because of the importance of paralleling at some level normal adolescent communication processes, we will discuss those processes in more detail and consider their relevance when counselling.

The use of direct closed questions to get information

When young people make use of direct closed questions in their typical peer conversations they demonstrate the way in which they tend to be more direct and inquisitive in their conversations than older people. Consequently, in the counselling situation, many young people like to have a direct approach from the counsellor, whereas older people probably prefer counsellors to be more circumspect in the questions they ask. As counsellors, we don't think that it is useful to be limited to direct closed questions. Moreover, we doubt whether it is useful to use many direct closed questions at all. However, we can learn from the way in which young people like to have direct and open communication. Such communication can be achieved by using a wide range of questions that come from a variety of therapeutic approaches. These useful questions will be described in the next chapter.

Mutual self-disclosure

It is interesting for us to note that many parents are troubled because their adolescent children are not prepared to talk with them about sensitive personal issues. However, we have also noticed that not many parents are willing to talk openly with their adolescent children about their own personal issues. Consequently, in many families there is little or no mutual self-disclosure between young people and their parents. Although it is easy to understand why most parents are unwilling to disclose personal information of a sensitive nature to their adolescent children, their reluctance to do this increases the likelihood that their adolescent children will similarly be reluctant to disclose to them. Many young people would be uncomfortable with an unequal and unidirectional self-disclosure process in which they self-disclosed to their parents but their parents did not self-disclose to them. The self-disclosure situation between peers is usually quite different. Good peer relationships are equal relationships where mutual self-disclosure is appropriate. Moreover, there is considerable evidence to support the notion that self-disclosure is important when developing friendships and establishing intimacy (Monsour, 1992; Derlega et al., 1993; Berndt and Hanna, 1995; Parks and Floyd, 1996).

The value of self-disclosure to young people is described by Buhrmester and Prager (1995). They point out that by self-disclosing, young people are able to evaluate for themselves the appropriateness and correctness of their opinions, attitudes, beliefs, values and standards as they share their thoughts with someone else. This is clearly very important in adolescence, as during this stage in life the young person has to re-evaluate for themselves the beliefs, values and standards which they have inevitably learnt from their parents and others. By doing this re-evaluation they are able to reject what doesn't fit for them and accept what does, so that they can develop their own personal moral belief systems. By mutual sharing with a peer they are able to compare their own ideas with those of another person who is in the same life stage as themselves.

Mutual self-disclosure can provide an opportunity for a young person to share pent-up feelings, express them, and also to release them. Additionally, while self-disclosing, the young person implicitly invites the listener to offer emotional support and advice (Cutrona et al., 1990). Self-disclosure is therefore a useful way for young people to deal with stressful issues that are troubling them.

Mutual self-disclosure when counselling young people

Most counsellors who work with adults believe that counsellor self-disclosure should either be strictly limited or not occur at all. However, there are exceptions to this view. For example, feminist counselling theory suggests that self-disclosure in counselling by both the client and counsellor is essential in order to be respectful, achieve equality and minimize the power imbalance occurring between the client and counsellor. We ourselves generally limit the amount of self-disclosure we use when counselling adults because we believe that it is more important for us to value the client by focusing on them and their lives rather than introducing material of our own. However, we believe that the situation is quite different when working with young people, and that there are good reasons for deliberately making use of appropriate counsellor self-disclosure.

When working with young people we like to parallel normal adolescent communication processes. We believe that appropriate counsellor self-disclosure enables young people to feel more comfortable when self-disclosing to us. When a counsellor shares personal information with a young person, the young person is implicitly invited to relate to the counsellor as an equal. They are likely to see the counsellor as a real person who has feelings and experiences which may have some similarity with their own. However, there do need to be some clear limits to counsellor self-disclosure. It is not appropriate or ethical for the counselling process to lead to undesirable closeness with the client and over-involvement by the counsellor.

Appropriate counsellor self-disclosure can assist in developing trust

Generally, counsellor self-disclosure should not involve talking about the counsellor's own past or present problems, unless these are both minor and resolved, and are useful for joining or are directly related to demonstrating a depth of understanding of the young person's situation. For example, if a young person is discussing their response to a recent parental separation and the pain involved in that experience, and if the counsellor has suffered a similar experience, then disclosure might be appropriate. Through such self-disclosure by the counsellor the grief experience can be normalized and the young person may be encouraged to disclose more information. Such disclosure should only occur if the counsellor's own issues relating to the relevant events have been fully resolved by the counsellor, in counselling for themselves or in supervision. Otherwise, the counselling session might be inappropriately used to enable the counsellor to work through their own problems. The focus must always be on the client's problems.

Self-disclosure by a counsellor may help a young person to gain a sense of confidence, believing that it should be possible for them to come to terms with, work through and continue on their developmental journey to achieve success, just as the counsellor has done. Generally, when self-disclosing, counsellors should not describe the complete process of their experience around any significant event. It is helpful to provide only a summary which is sufficient to enable the client to recognize some similarities. Additionally, counsellors need to let their young clients know that there will inevitably be differences between the client's experiences and responses and their own. If the differences are not acknowledged, then the young person may believe that the counsellor is merely pretending to understand fully, whereas full understanding is impossible because two people's experiences will never be identical. This needs to be acknowledged. In addition, young people may be tempted to match their own responses inappropriately to those of the counsellor in an attempt to normalize their experience.

Validating the young person's views

Generally, but not always, young people will validate each other's points of view. By doing this their conversations become collaborative explorations rather than one-sided and argumentative. Together, they will share their beliefs, attitudes and constructs, examine these together, and quite possibly revise them. Even if we do not agree with a young person's point of view, if we can validate what they are telling us by letting them know that we understand their beliefs, attitudes and constructs, and accept them for who they are, then collaboratively we have the opportunity to help them explore, review and revise their constructs. By letting them know that we understand their point of view, even though we may also let them know that we have a different point of view, we show them that they are valued as a person. Thus we join with them and create a genuine, open and honest relationship, where they can feel safe in exploring their own ideas with us.

Use praise when relevant

Because of their developmental stage most young people are continually questioning themselves and their achievements. They generally use praise in a natural way when communicating with each other. Similarly, counsellors can usefully give praise and other positive feedback when appropriate. Clearly, when we do this we need to be careful to ensure that we are seen to be genuine and not patronizing.

Being direct about what we like and do not like

Most young people are very direct about what they like and what they don't like. If we are to build a useful counselling relationship with them, they need to see us as real people who are open in our communication with them about who we are. Whereas when working with adults, most counsellors are cautious about disclosing information about their likes and dislikes, when working with young people it can be very useful to be direct in this regard. In doing this, we need to be respectful of the young person by letting them know that we accept them fully with their own likes and dislikes, even though they may be different from us.

Matching and exaggerating the other person's emotional expressions in response to story-telling

As discussed previously, young people typically match and exaggerate each other's emotional expressions when they are talking to each other about things that have happened to them or to other people. As counsellors, we can learn from the lively and dynamic ways in which young people communicate. Young people generally put a great deal of energy into their conversations with their peers. We can learn from this, and be energized ourselves when we communicate with them, rather than being measured in our speech and flat in our tone of conversation.

Digression

A very common feature of adolescent conversation is that young people tend to frequently digress from a topic of interest, talk about something else, and then return to the topic. Of course, some adults do the same. However, we believe that, especially for young people, this tendency to digress and then return to the topic of conversation serves some useful purposes. Because young people are continually revising their constructs, they are often trying to grapple with many differing thoughts and ideas at the same time. While a friend is talking to them, a new idea will come into their consciousness and they will want to move away from what they were listening to, or talking about, and discuss something else. Realizing that they have moved away from something which might have been of interest or importance, they may later return to that topic. By digressing they are able to deal with new thoughts without putting them on hold. A more mature person might stay on track and talk about new ideas later. However, for young people, there is an impatience to be heard and often an impulsive need to talk about their latest thought without waiting.

Digression also has a very useful function in allowing a young person to move away from something that is very troubling for them. By changing the topic they can stop talking about issues which are emotionally disturbing and instead talk about less troubling things. They may then return to talking about the emotionally troubling issues after having a period of time during which the conversation has been less intense. If they were not allowed to digress, then it is likely that they would shut down the conversation altogether to avoid talking about issues that were distressing for them.

We have noticed that when young people are talking with peers, digression is often a mutually employed process. It is usually accepted as normal behaviour rather than as inappropriate.

Using digression when counselling young people

Young people are often troubled by extremely powerful emotions as they confront new and challenging experiences. As a consequence, in a counselling situation they may at times worry about getting in touch with strong emotions, or feel overwhelmed by their emotions. At these times they can find it very helpful to be allowed to move away from talking about their troubling issues by digressing. If they know that they have the opportunity to digress when they want, they are more likely to feel safe in the counselling environment rather than finding it threatening or worrying. Additionally, they will experience something more like a peer conversation than a conversation between an adult and a young person. Clearly, this is likely to be more comfortable for them.

When talking about a serious issue, sometimes a young person will become distracted and temporarily withdraw from the counselling process. They may play with their shoes or jewellery, or look out the window at something that is happening outside. This distraction may serve the same purpose as a digression. It may allow the young person to escape from continuing to talk about an important but very troubling issue. However, we also need to recognize that they may have just lost the energy and desire to continue talking and consequently have become distracted.

When a young person becomes distracted, the counsellor has an opportunity to introduce a digression and by doing so to join more closely with the young person. For example, if the young person starts to play with their shoes, the counsellor might comment on their shoes and ask about them, saying something such as 'They're colourful; where did you get them?', or 'I had some shoes rather like those, but mine weren't very comfortable. What are yours like?' Notice that if the counsellor digresses in this way, the conversation will no longer involve addressing issues, but instead a low-key conversation will develop which will be likely to help the young person relax. Also, the young person is likely to experience a closer connection with the counsellor through this mutual sharing and self-disclosure about something of common interest. Consequently, the climate in the counselling room will change. A friendly and relaxing conversation will take place which will enable the young person to re-gain energy, and join more effectively with the counsellor. After having such a conversation, it is easy for the counsellor to help the young person return to addressing an important issue. This can be done by using a transitional question, as described in Chapter 11.

> **Actively promoting digression can have positive outcomes**

As discussed, we believe that it can be useful for a counsellor to join with a young person when they digress and also useful for the counsellor to deliberately introduce digressions at appropriate times. Digressing and self-disclosing about everyday matters can considerably enhance the relationship between the counsellor and a young person. Don't be worried if at times a counselling session becomes an enjoyable chat about irrelevancies. When working with young people, this is the key to establishing a good relationship.

Controlling the conversation

Many children grow up in families where they have to do as they are told much of the time. As young children they are usually not allowed to control their conversations with adults. As they grow older and enter adolescence, they want to be more in control of their world. They don't want to be told when they can speak and when they can be quiet. When they talk with their friends, they expect that there will be a mutual sharing, with control of the conversation moving from one person to the other and back again. In particular, they do not like being told what to talk about or when to talk about it.

Adults, particularly when talking with a professional such as a medical practitioner, often have an expectation that the professional will have a considerable amount of control over the process of the conversation. It is usually quite different when young people talk among themselves. They expect to be in control of the conversation rather than to be influenced either directly or indirectly into talking about specific issues.

Control of the conversation when counselling young people

When counselling adults, some counsellors, particularly person-centred counsellors, try to give the client control of the direction of the conversation. Even though they do this, they do adhere to a particular process in giving their responses, and in our view this process has a big influence in controlling the quality and direction of the conversation. Other counsellors, while respecting the client needs as much as they can, deliberately direct and control the counselling conversation.

We believe that when we are working with young people we do need to be proactive. As described in later chapters, this means that we have to take responsibility for responding to the young person's current emotional state by proactively introducing new direction and strategies into the counselling process as described in Chapter 9. However, while doing this we need to try to ensure that the young person is empowered to control the conversation when and as they wish.

Just as with peer conversations between young people, an effective and comfortable counselling conversation with a young person involves handing control of the conversation backwards and forwards between the two participants. However, at all times, it is essential to try to ensure that the young person understands that they have *choice* about what they say and do, so that they do not feel inappropriately controlled during those times when the counsellor takes the initiative by deliberately influencing the process.

Seeking advice

Typically, when young people are uncertain about what to do, or what decision to make, they will talk to a peer or a number of peers, and will ask for advice. This is something that they would be less likely to do with a parent, because they want to make their own decisions without parental direction. When they ask for advice from a friend of their own age, it is unlikely that either they, or their friend, will expect that they will necessarily take the advice. This is different from parent or adult advice-giving. When adults are asked for advice and give it, they usually have an expectation the advice will be taken and may feel aggrieved if it is not. In contrast, when peers seek advice they are usually just trying to get another point of view, and to draw on another person's experience. Advice-giving, then, for young people, involves the sharing of ideas about possible solutions rather than an injunction that these solutions should be adopted. This is consistent with the notion that young people strive to explore constructs, discard those that don't fit and discover those that do.

Giving advice when counselling young people

Most counsellors who work with adults try to avoid giving advice and instead try to empower their clients to find their own solutions. It is obvious that this is also a good policy with young people, as they don't want to be told what they should do. However, it is well documented that young people generally have expectations that counsellors will give advice (Gibson-Cline, 1996). Additionally, they have expectations that counsellors have experience and knowledge which they do not have themselves.

Counsellors working with young people have an obligation to share information with them that has been gained through either education or life experience. When a young person asks for advice, we believe that, rather than declining to give it, it is better to join with the young person and offer them an invitation to explore their situation with us, so that together we might come up with a possible solution. By doing this, the young person is invited to join in a collaborative process in which there is a mutual sharing of ideas and information, as discussed in Chapter 13. Solutions can be explored, together with their consequences.

> ❝ Young people expect counsellors to have expertise
> through life experience ❞

Where possible it can be useful for a counsellor to confirm that they believe that the young person's choice of a particular option seems to be a sensible one. Of course, the counsellor can only do this if they believe that the solution chosen *is* a sensible one. Additionally, the counsellor needs to be careful to make it clear that they think that it is possible that the young person might change their mind and do something different; that it is up to them to do what they believe feels right for them at the time rather than stick to a predetermined option. Giving this message is very important, as young people are continually changing their points of view. If they do not follow through on a decision made in a counselling session, they need to believe that they will not invoke the counsellor's disapproval.

Paralleling adolescent communication processes

As has been discussed in this chapter, it can be very useful for counsellors to parallel typical adolescent communication processes as by doing this they may be able to establish a comfortable and effective counselling conversation with a young person. For example, through the use of appropriate counsellor self-disclosure a level of equality in the counselling relationship can be demonstrated and in some situations such self-disclosure can be normalizing for the young person. Also, the active use of digression, rather than trying to maintain a particular direction in the counselling conversation, can enhance the counselling relationship, may enable the young person to avoid being overwhelmed by emotions, and has the potential to contribute to enhancing the counselling relationship.

KEY POINTS

- young people usually prefer to confide in peers rather than adults because they are in a process of individuation
- typical communication processes used by young people in their conversation with peers differ from typical adult communication processes
- it can be advantageous for a counsellor to make use of typical adolescent communication processes as this can help in building and maintaining the counselling relationship
- appropriate counsellor self-disclosure may encourage a young person to self-disclose, help in promoting a level of equality in the relationship, and assist with normalizing
- actively promoting or joining in digression can encourage the development of a comfortable and effective counselling relationship

FURTHER RESOURCES

The 'Department of Communication Studies at the University of Texas' has produced a number of publications that focus on relational communication. For a list of their publications about adolescent communication please refer to their website.

- commstudies.utexas.edu/research/relational-communication

11

Useful Counselling Micro-Skills

In the previous chapter we discussed the way counsellors can make use of typical adolescent communication processes such as mutual self-disclosure and digression. We also discussed issues of control and advice-giving. In this chapter, we will discuss a variety of counselling micro-skills which, when counselling young people, can be used to promote change. We strongly believe that these micro-skills need to be used in a context which at some level parallels the normal adolescent communication processes as described in the previous chapter.

Counselling micro-skills commonly used with adults are also useful when counselling young people, but there are some important differences in the way in which they are selected and used when working with young people.

Many counsellors who work with adults typically make extensive use of those particular counselling micro-skills which fit with their primary theoretical frame of reference. This is sensible, even for counsellors who claim to be eclectic, because it enables them to bring some consistency and structure into the counselling process. A detailed description of the most commonly used counselling micro-skills coming from a variety of therapeutic models is provided in our books *Practical Counselling Skills* (Geldard and Geldard, 2005, available in the UK and Europe) and *Basic Personal Counselling* (Geldard and Geldard, 2012a, available in Australia and New Zealand).

Counselling young people involves different demands from those encountered when counselling adults. By making use of a very wide range of counselling micro-skills, the counsellor can create a changing and dynamic process to engage the curiosity and interest of the young person. The skills can be used in a process that parallels the relatively low level of structure which is common in adolescent developmental processes. Counsellors who work with young people will therefore have an advantage if they have the knowledge and ability to enable them to use the widest possible range of counselling micro-skills. These need to be proactively selected at appropriate points in time to take advantage of presented opportunities in the counselling process, so that the young client becomes engaged and energized in seeking to discuss and resolve problems.

In this chapter we will describe a wide range of counselling micro-skills and, wherever relevant, will indicate how these can be of particular use when working with young people. The counselling micro-skills we will describe need to be used within the overall counselling process, as shown in Figure 9.2. It needs to be recognized that the micro-skills are used in the context of the primary counselling functions of relationship building, assessing the problem and addressing the problem.

Counselling micro-skills can be used either in direct response to the needs of the counselling process or in conjunction with any of the counselling strategies described in Chapters 14 to 17. Counselling micro-skills can be broadly grouped under the following headings, although there will be some overlap:

- observation
- active listening
- giving feedback
- use of questions
- challenging
- instructions
- the use of humour.

Observation

Observation can be extremely useful in contributing to the overall assessment of a young person's presentation. It needs to occur continually, as an ongoing activity, during each counselling session. However, when counselling young people, we have to be careful how we interpret our observations because they may sometimes be misleading. What a counsellor observes, when counselling a young person, is an external presentation which may disguise what is happening internally. This is because young people are uncertain about themselves and are uncertain about how open they can be if they are to continue receiving acceptance. Because they are in a state of change, their cognitive processes are complex, and they tend to make use of their defences more quickly than most adults.

While recognizing that our observations of a young person may be observations of a façade hiding the real person, we need to respond to that façade as though it were the real person. By accepting and responding to the façade we demonstrate to the young person that we are accepting of what they are presenting to us. In effect, we are doing as described in Chapter 9: we are believing the young person. By accepting the façade we can create trust, and through that trust the young person is more likely to feel safe in showing us what is behind the façade. In addition, by accepting the façade, we validate the individual presentation that the young person wishes to show to us.

If we wanted to join with someone who only spoke a foreign language, we would need to learn that language in order to communicate effectively with them and join with them. Similarly, when counselling a young person, we need to learn from the young person's behavioural and verbal language. We can do this by observing their behavioural, speech and language patterns. We can then, at an appropriate level, parallel their communication processes so that, in effect, we speak the same language. By doing this we can gain the young person's trust, join with them and enter their world. When paralleling a young person's communication processes we need to be careful not to behave as though we ourselves were young people, but to use similar processes to theirs while remaining congruent and true to ourselves.

It helps to speak the young person's language

Observation can provide information about the young person with regard to mood, culture, self-esteem, creativity and social influences. Important attributes of the young person which need to be observed include:

- general appearance
- behaviour
- mood and affect
- speech and language.

General appearance

A young person's general appearance is a reflection of the way in which they wish to be seen and gives an indication of how they would like to be. It is an outward expression of the internal attempt to form a personal identity. Counsellors need to be careful about the way in which they interpret a young person's general appearance. Unfortunately, as counsellors, we all have our own personal prejudices and personal stereotypes. Consequently, a young person's appearance can seriously influence the way we feel towards and relate with them. We need to be careful that we do not over-interpret and we need to take time to get to know them so that we understand who they are and discover what is happening internally for them.

Imagine a young person who has tattoos and body piercing. Such a person might be aggressive and anti-social, or might be a person who is gentle, caring and vulnerable but wishes to appear to be tough and individualistic. We can't know which is true just by observing appearance.

A young person's appearance can tell us the extent to which they feel free to express themselves, and the extent to which they are constricted and constrained and unable to express themselves freely. Where a young person has put a lot of effort into presenting themselves in a particular way, they may be wanting to give the message 'Hey, take notice of me'. If this is the case, it may be extremely helpful in joining, for the counsellor to respond to the implied request, 'Take notice of me', by letting the young person know that they have noticed. This can be done by commenting on, and positively connoting, aspects of the young person's appearance.

Behaviour

A young person's behaviour can give a counsellor useful information about ways in which to match and join. For example, consider the case of a young client who is really talkative and has poor boundaries. In this case, it would be inappropriate for a counsellor to respond by being quiet and withdrawn; instead, the counsellor would need to match the conversational style of the young person and in this way allow joining to occur with ease. If the counsellor were to do otherwise, the young person might receive an implied message which said 'The way you are behaving is not OK'. Similarly, consider the case of an young person who has poorly defined boundaries: it might be tempting for a counsellor to respond by modelling and displaying well-defined boundaries to try to get the young person to modify their behaviour. Unfortunately, this would be likely to undermine the joining process and alienate the client. To join, the counsellor needs to match the young person's behaviour while being congruent and appropriate. By doing so the behaviour is validated and the young person receives a message that this behaviour is acceptable for the counsellor. To do otherwise gives the young person the message that they are being judged and are not OK and are not accepted by the counsellor. Consequently, the chance of joining will be diminished.

When young people behave in ways which seem to be socially inappropriate it needs to be recognized that they may not have the skills to enable them to behave more acceptably. Although, at times during the counselling relationship, counsellors may be able to model desirable behaviours, the processes of joining and engaging demand that counsellors should to some extent modify their own behaviour, within the limits of their own personal identity, to match and satisfy the needs of the young people they seek to help. If they are unable to do this, their young clients are unlikely to be able to relate comfortably with them because they may not know how to relate differently.

Young people are in a process of learning how to relate in new ways as they move from childhood into adulthood. Thus it is not surprising that often their ability to use socially mature behaviour is limited. Modelling is certainly useful in helping young people to learn new behaviours but can only be effective within the context of an effective relationship.

Adolescent behaviours such as restlessness, agitation and lethargy can give a counsellor an indication of a young person's current emotional state. However, as will be discussed, some caution needs to be exercised in assessing mood from the observation of behaviour because many young people are skilled at hiding their true feelings.

Mood and affect

When observing young people we need to be clear about the difference between mood and affect. *Mood* is the internal feeling or emotion which often influences behaviour and the individual's perception of the world. *Affect* is the external emotional response (World Health Organization, 1997). The underlying mood of a young person may be disguised by the presenting affect. For example, it is not uncommon for young people who are suffering from an underlying emotional state of depression to present not as depressed, but as anxious and agitated.

"Mood may be hidden behind affect"

Consider the case of an adolescent boy whose parent has died. He may be inwardly experiencing a high level of depression and sadness, but may outwardly demonstrate hostility and anger. In such a situation, the counsellor needs to be able to go beneath the presenting affect so that the young person is able to identify, own and experience the underlying mood. In order to do this, the counsellor needs to observe the presenting affect and deal with that fully so that, as a consequence, the client can move into a deeper level of experiencing with recognition, acceptance and ownership of the underlying mood of depression and sadness.

Often, the presenting affect will be appropriate for the young person's situation. It is, for example, understandable that a young person whose parent has died might respond angrily, even though the underlying mood is depression and sadness. By recognizing the presenting affect, the counsellor can reflect it back and also normalize it as being appropriate and normal at that stage in the young person's grieving process. Observation of the *absence* of affect is particularly important, especially where young people have suffered traumatic or stressful experiences. In these cases, an absence of affect might indicate that a young person is dissociating or is out of touch with reality and may be developing serious mental health problems.

Clearly, a major goal in counselling is to help the client to feel better. This means that in the long term both affect and mood need to be influenced by the counselling process. The first step in achieving this is for accurate observation to occur.

Speech and language

When observing the speech and language of young people, counsellors need to attend to:

- what is said
- how it is said
- the language used.

What is said

The content of what the young person says tells the counsellor what they are thinking and gives an indication of their beliefs, ideas and general constructs about their world. While listening to the client, the counsellor can gain information about the young person's intellectual functioning and thought processes. This will include information about their ability to remember things accurately, to think logically, to use abstract thinking and to concentrate. This information is required to enable the counsellor to select suitable counselling strategies. For example, it is clearly not going to be helpful for a counsellor to use a counselling strategy that requires a high level of intellectual ability with a client who does not have that level of functioning.

How it is said

How the young person talks is also important. We need to remember that many young people typically flit from subject to subject as a normal part of their communication. However, the counsellor needs to note whether the conversation has some logical sequence or is totally disjointed, with the continual introduction of unrelated ideas.

Sometimes a young person's conversation may be disjointed as a consequence of them being overwhelmed by current circumstances. In this case, the counsellor may need to help them to structure the conversation so that information is presented more clearly. Where young people are flitting from subject to subject between clauses, in other words where derailment is occurring with no meaningful relationship between the ideas being expressed, then the presence of severe mental health problems may be indicated.

The language used

The language used by the client gives an indication of the client's ability to be articulate and to be able to express ideas clearly. This information can be helpful in enabling the counsellor to select counselling strategies to match the client's intellectual ability. Some young people will use 'street language' when talking with a counsellor. This language involves the use of a vocabulary of jargon words which are commonly used by the young person's peer group. The use of these words may be meaningless or confusing for many adults, particularly as such vocabularies are subject to change with the inclusion of new words and new meanings from time to time. Counsellors working with young people need to learn the meaning of these jargon words, so that they can understand and join with the language of the client. Where a counsellor is unsure of the meaning of a particular word it is best to be honest about this and to ask the young person directly: 'What does that word mean – it's new to me?' It might also be useful to seek clarification of words which can have a variety of meanings in contemporary situations.

Active listening

As when counselling adults, active listening is designed to help the client to recognize that the counsellor is attending carefully to what is being said, to help the counsellor join empathically with the client and to encourage the client to continue talking. Active listening includes:

- non-verbal responses
- encouragers
- accenting and amplifying
- reflection of content and feelings
- matching the young person's language
- summarizing
- noticing what is missing.

Non-verbal responses

The counsellor's non-verbal responses are likely to give a young person an indication that the counsellor is listening, an indication of the counsellor's level of interest in what is being said, and information about the counsellor's attitude to them. Non-verbal responses include making appropriate eye contact, acknowledging what has been said by nodding or by using appropriate facial expressions, and matching the young person's body posture and movements.

Encouragers

To signify that the counsellor is listening and to encourage the client to continue talking, counsellors can use a range of minimal responses or encouragers such as 'ah-hm', 'mm-hm', 'yes', 'right', 'really' and 'OK'. It needs to be recognized that these responses not only indicate that the counsellor is listening attentively, but also carry meaning. They may convey indications of a counsellor's attitudes, including approval and disapproval. There are also a number of short responses such as 'Tell me more', 'I see', 'I understand', 'Is that so?', 'I hear', and 'Go on', which can be used non-intrusively and similarly to the single-word minimal encouragers. When responding to the client, the counsellor's tone of voice and speed and volume of talking need to match the client's style and energy.

Inappropriately delivered encouragers may be perceived as judgemental

Generally, counsellors working with adults need to be careful to ensure that minimal encouragers convey a non-judgemental attitude. Many counsellors who work with adults will listen quietly and with a level of seriousness during the initial stages of counselling, and will demonstrate a fairly low level of emotional affect because they do not want to intrude on the adult's thought processes and conversation. Although, generally, counsellors working with young people also need to convey a non-judgemental attitude, joining with young people requires an emotional responsiveness which parallels the young person's communication processes. Young people tend to be more direct and open with each other about their feelings and attitudes. Counsellors therefore need to deliver minimal encouragers proactively so that the emotional energy and tone of the young person are appropriately matched. Additionally, counsellors working with young people may give an indication of their own attitudes, when responding minimally, where this is appropriate and is not likely to make the client feel judged or criticized.

Accenting and amplifying

Accenting and amplifying involve a combination of verbal and non-verbal messages to feed back and emphasize what the client has said. The counsellor can do this verbally and also by using gesture, facial expression and voice intensity so that what the client has said is intensified and made newsworthy. By doing this the counsellor demonstrates positive support for what the young person is saying and encourages them to continue.

Accenting and amplifying are particularly important skills to use when counselling young people and should be used more than when counselling adults. This is because these skills enable the counsellor to validate what the young person is saying and also to join proactively with enthusiasm in the conversation, paralleling typical adolescent communication.

Reflection of content and feelings

Reflection of content and feelings were skills identified by Rogers (1955, 1965) as being important in counselling. Reflection of content involves reflecting back the content of what the client has just said. For example, if a young person has been talking about the way in which they have been in conflict with their brother recently, a reflection of content might be 'Your brother and you have been fighting recently' or 'You've told me that your brother and you have been fighting recently' or 'So, your brother and you have been fighting a lot recently'. When reflecting content, counsellors do not repeat what the client has said, but pick up the most important content information and, using their own words, feed this back to the client.

Reflection of feelings involves reflection of the perceived emotional affect of the client. The reflection may be as a result of things that the client has directly told the counsellor or may be the result of non-verbal behaviour by the client. For example, the counsellor may have noticed tears or a change in tone of voice. Examples of reflection of feeling are 'You're feeling sad' or 'You feel sad' or 'You're sad'. Sometimes, reflection of content and feelings are combined, as in the statement: 'You're sad because you've lost your best friend.'

When we are counselling young people we generally need to be careful not to overuse reflection. Instead, we need to use reflection in a limited way just to help the young person know that they are being heard and understood. The reason that we caution against the over-use of reflection when working with young people is that they do not, as a general rule, use reflection in their peer conversations. If as counsellors we want to join effectively with young people, we need to use a conversational style that is comfortable for them. Young people who are very verbal may be comfortable with a higher level of reflection than others. Unfortunately, many young people respond to reflection by sitting silently and not continuing to talk. If we are to encourage them to continue talking we need to use more proactive micro-skills. As we will discuss later, there is a wide range of different types of questions which are extremely useful in raising the energy of a conversation with a young person and encouraging them to talk.

Matching the young person's language

Three ways in which counsellors need to match the use of language by young people involve:

- the use of vocabulary
- representational style
- metaphor.

Use of the young person's vocabulary

Some young people make use of words from culture-specific adolescent vocabularies. They may also attribute meanings to words which are different from commonly accepted meanings. Use of such vocabularies commonly occurs with young people who belong to peer groups or gangs associated with particular activities. If counsellors wish to join effectively with these young people and to communicate effectively with them, they need to understand, and perhaps use, language which is familiar, natural and comfortable for them. Counsellors may therefore need to learn from their clients so that they are able to understand and communicate with them using words which have meaning for them, rather than being restricted to using words which are in general use in adult conversation.

We can learn from our young clients

Matching representational style

Counsellors need to match the representational style which each individual adolescent client uses to think and communicate. As described in neuro-linguistic programming, people typically think by using one of three different representation modes (Grinder and Bandler, 1976). Some people tend to think visually and conceptualize pictorially, others think verbally and frame their thoughts in terms of things which they hear, and a third group think mainly in a sensory, kinaesthetic or feeling mode. Someone who thinks in a visual mode might say 'I have difficulty seeing myself apologizing to Fred', whereas a person who thinks in an auditory mode might say 'I really can't hear myself saying sorry to Fred'. Another person might use a kinaesthetic or feeling mode, and might say 'I'd feel uncomfortable apologizing to Fred'. It is helpful if counsellors can join with their young clients by using the modes of expression which they use.

Use of metaphor

Young people will often talk metaphorically. For example, a young person might say 'A black cloud seems to be over my head wherever I go'. In this case the metaphor of a black cloud might be being used to describe feelings of despair and depression. Where the client uses a metaphor, it is useful if the counsellor continues to use the client's metaphor. In the example quoted, the counsellor might explore the young person's feelings towards the cloud or might explore what the client believes would need to happen for them to be able to move from under the cloud into the sun. The counsellor might also refer back to the cloud at a later stage of the counselling process, thereby continuing the use of the metaphor (see Chapter 14 for a fuller discussion of the use of metaphor).

Summarizing

As with reflection of content and feelings, summarizing was identified as useful by Rogers (1955, 1965). Summarizing is very similar to reflection. When summarizing, counsellors feed back, in their own words, a brief and concise summary of what the client has said. This summary does not cover all the details of those things the client has discussed, but picks out only the most salient features. Summarizing lets the client know that the counsellor has heard and understood, and also enables the client to clarify thoughts, identifying what is most important.

Noticing what is missing

It is not sufficient just to notice what the client has said; it is also important to notice what is missing. The counsellor needs to look for gaps and unfilled spaces in the client's story, and for evidence of conflicting information and hidden meanings. By sensitively, and without intrusion, inviting the client to explore these gaps or unfilled spaces, useful information may emerge. Through this process the young person may find alternatives and opportunities that are being missed. Noticing what is being missed is a concept which comes from narrative therapy (White, 2007).

We have discussed a range of skills which come under the heading 'active listening'. If the counsellor proactively introduces these skills wherever appropriate, the counselling conversation will be enhanced and the possibility that the young person will be effectively engaged may be enhanced.

Giving feedback

As discussed, we can make use of reflection to feed back information which a young person has provided. This is one form of feedback. There are a number of other ways in which feedback can be given to young people:

- giving compliments
- giving affirmations
- cheer-leading
- normalizing
- reframing
- use of statements.

Giving compliments

Young people often find themselves in situations where they are told that they have done things which they should not have done. This is inevitable, considering their lack of adult experience and their developmental need to experiment with new behaviours. Consequently, many young people expect that adults will be critical of them.

The counselling situation can provide an opportunity to give young people positive feedback to help them to feel OK about themselves. It is appropriate for counsellors to compliment young people on their behaviour during the counselling process where such feedback is likely to be useful. They can also be complimented for decisions which they have made or actions they have taken which demonstrate their personal growth.

Compliments need to be used sensibly otherwise they may be seen as patronizing. Appropriately given compliments enable the young person to feel OK and to continue developing with confidence. Compliments given as feedback may also indicate that the counsellor has heard and understood the young person's story. For example, a young person may have been unduly provoked but may have responded with uncharacteristic control. After hearing the story, a counsellor might say 'Well done, that must have been very difficult to do'. Thus the behaviour is positively connoted and the young person is able to feel good about what they did.

Giving affirmations

Affirmations acknowledge and reinforce a personal truth that has been discovered by the client and shared with the counsellor. For example, a young person may have, in conversation, recognized that they are managing to achieve good results in a situation which is difficult for them. The counsellor might offer the affirmation 'You are obviously coping extremely well under difficult circumstances'. Notice that in this affirmation the counsellor did not say 'You believe that you are coping very well in difficult circumstances', but said 'You are coping very well'. This is the difference between affirmation and reflection. If the counsellor had used reflection, he would have said something like 'You believe that you are coping very well', which would have been a true reflection of what the young person had said. However, this is not very affirming and does not convey the message that the counsellor believes the client has done well.

Reflection and affirmation are not the same

Cheer-leading

Cheer-leading is a skill which comes from solution-focused therapy (O'Connell, 2012). Counsellors engage in cheer-leading when they show enthusiastic reactions of emotional support when clients relate that they have used new behaviours which are positive and different from behaviours which they have used before. Cheer-leading is based on the assumption that the young person has taken control and is responsible for the changes that have occurred.

Cheer-leading uses both questions and statements to encourage the young person to continue to describe the changing process. For example, the counsellor might ask, or say, with enthusiastic interest:

'How did you do that?'
'How did you manage to make that decision?'
'Well done. That must have been really difficult to do. How did you do it?'
'That sounds good!'
'That's amazing!'

Such counsellor responses help the young person to take responsibility for, and feel proud of, their success in achieving some change. Additionally, the client is encouraged to continue exploring the change and the process of change. This reinforces the idea that they can take responsibility for, and control, their behaviour. Such positive reinforcement is likely to help the young person to continue to take responsibility and control in their life, thus promoting the possibility of further change and a move towards adulthood.

Normalizing

Young people are in a changing world. As a consequence, they frequently become troubled by their emotions, responses and behaviours. Often these troubling emotions, responses and behaviours will be normal for the situation. Even so, at times, young people may believe that they are starting to 'go crazy' because they are experiencing high levels of emotional feelings which they have not previously experienced. In situations such as these it can be helpful for counsellors to tell young people that what they are experiencing is normal for the situation, providing that is genuinely the case.

Sometimes young people may react in ways which are disappointing for them, and they may have expectations of themselves that are unrealistic. Once again, it can be useful to normalize such responses and behaviours. Clearly, normalizing needs to be done in cases where unacceptable responses and behaviours are not already minimized.

We know that when young people are disclosing personal information with peers, a major goal for them is to validate their own experiences by checking out whether their peers have had similar experiences (Rotenberg, 1995). Young people are very concerned with what they appear to be in the eyes of others, as compared with what they feel they are (Erikson, 1987). Normalizing is therefore one of the most important counselling skills when working with young people.

Reframing

Reframing is an idea which is particularly useful when working with young people. It was developed as part of neuro-linguistic programming (Bandler and Grinder, 1979). Young people often have a very compartmentalized view of their world and are unable to see the broader picture. This can lead to unrealistically negative perceptions at times. Reframing encourages the young person to consider not just the part of the picture that they have been considering, but to see their part of the picture as part of a larger picture. It is as though the young person had a frame around a small part of the whole picture and was looking at what was within the frame. By choosing a larger frame, what was in the original frame is seen in a wider context.

To illustrate reframing, consider the example of an adolescent girl who is complaining that she frequently has to look after her younger nephew, whereas her twin sister never has to do this. In exploring the wider picture, it might emerge that she is allowed much more freedom than her twin sister and that she gets satisfaction out of being able to parent her nephew more competently than his mother (an older sister). A suitable reframe might be: 'My impression is that you may be more mature than both your sisters. Even though it must be tiresome for you looking after your nephew, you seem to be proud of your ability to parent him more capably than his mother, and your parents seem to trust you by giving you more responsibility and freedom than your twin sister'. This reframe might then enable the counsellor to help her explore her attitude and feelings related to wider issues of freedom and responsibility inherent in moving towards adulthood.

It is essential that reframes do not discount or deny the part of the picture which was initially in focus, but incorporate this part into the wider picture. Failure to do this would invalidate the perceptions of the client. The reframe must embrace the young person's perception, but build on that and enlarge it. They may then be able to recognize that what they have said has been believed and may be able to accept the reframe.

Reframing needs to be done tentatively so that the young person has the opportunity to reject the reframe if it does not fit for them. Reframing can enable clients to accept negative, destructive or oppressive situations or processes by viewing them within a wider, more positive context.

" A reframe needs to fit with the young person's perceptions "

Use of statements

Counsellor statements are extremely useful when counselling young people and can be used in a number of ways:

- Statements can be used to provide feedback when the young person is carrying out an activity associated with a counselling strategy (as described in Chapters 14 to 17). For example, if a young person is having difficulty in carrying out a particular task, the counsellor might make a statement like 'You seem to be finding it difficult to choose a symbol'.

- Statements can be used to enable the counsellor to feed back to the young person observations of the counselling process. For example, a counsellor might say 'I've noticed that we seem to be going round in circles without finding a solution'.
- Statements can be used to feed back to the young person things that they are doing. For example, the counsellor might give feedback to the young person by saying: 'I notice that your hands are clasped together really tightly'. This type of feedback statement comes from Gestalt therapy.
- Statements can be used paradoxically and with humour to feed back and exaggerate what the young person has said so that they will then challenge the exaggeration and recognize personal strengths. For example, the counsellor might say 'So, you are absolutely hopeless and nothing you do ever succeeds. You are a total failure'. This paradoxical approach should only be used with those young people who have the ego strength to deal with the implied challenge, and needs to involve humour or it could be damaging.

Statements are also useful for purposes which are not related to feedback, such as:

- Statements can be used to help the counsellor clarify what might be happening to the young person at a particular moment. For example, a counsellor might suspect that a young person is really pleased with themselves as a result of something that they have done and might say 'If I were you, I would feel really pleased with myself'.
- 'I' statements can be used to model taking responsibility for feelings, thoughts and behaviours. For example, the counsellor might, instead of saying 'People don't bother about that these days', say 'I don't worry about that nowadays'.
- The counsellor can also use statements to structure the counselling process. For example, statements can be made about the levels of confidentiality which are available.

You may have noticed that, as with active listening, there are a number of different skills that can be used when giving feedback. If these skills are proactively selected, the counselling conversation can be enlivened so that the young person's interest is maintained.

Use of questions

When we are working as counsellors with adults we are careful not to over-use questions. To do so might make the counselling conversation more like an interrogation. Similarly, when working with young children we are careful not to use too many questions. This is because when young children are asked questions by adults they will more often than not respond by saying what they think the adults want to hear. We believe that counselling young people is very different from counselling adults or children. In a counselling setting young people need to be engaged so that their interest is maintained. A good way of promoting such engagement is to make use of suitable questions at appropriate times. There are many types of question taken from a number of counselling approaches that are particularly useful in helping to engage the interest of young people. We will describe each of these, but before we do we need to consider two important types of question.

Questions can be divided into two types: closed questions and open questions. Closed questions demand a specific response which may be very limited. An example of a closed question is 'Do you use drugs?'; this question is likely to lead to the answer 'yes' or 'no' and little else. When dealing with a young person before joining has occurred, the answer to this question is most likely to be 'no', regardless of whether the young person uses drugs or not.

An open question is one that elicits a wide range of descriptive answers. For example, instead of asking the closed question 'Do you take drugs?', the counsellor might ask the question 'What do you think about taking drugs?'. This invites the young person being questioned to think about possible answers and to describe an attitude or belief. It is more likely to result in an open discussion than a single-word answer.

Both types of question are useful, although generally the open question is more helpful in counselling because it encourages a conversational response and makes self-disclosure more likely.

At times, closed questions can be useful, particularly when specific information is required. For example, when enquiring about a young person's possible intention to commit suicide, answers to closed questions might enable a counsellor to make decisions about the ongoing safety and protection of the young person. We don't see a problem in asking young people closed questions at times. Indeed, we need to remember that young people are often very direct in seeking information from other young people. It can therefore be helpful for us to model their behaviour in this regard when appropriate. However, it can be risky to ask too many closed questions at a time because, if we do, the counselling session will be almost certain to degenerate into a question-and-answer session.

Overuse of questions results in an interrogation, not counselling

There are several different types of open question that are especially useful when counselling young people and these will now be described.

General information-seeking questions

We commonly use general information-seeking questions in everyday conversation in order to get information. Young people do the same with their peers. Often, when these questions are prefaced with words that indicate the counsellor's genuine curiosity and interest, the young person is likely to feel important as a source of information. For example, the counsellor might say 'I'm curious about your interest in collecting comics. What kind do you enjoy the most?' or 'I don't know much about the skateboard scene. Can you fill me in?'

Questions to heighten the client's awareness

These questions are commonly used in Gestalt therapy (Clarkson, 2013). The aim of these questions is to help the client to become more fully aware of what is happening within them, either somatically or emotionally, so that they can intensify those bodily or emotional feelings, deal with them, and move on to discussing associated thoughts. Typical questions in this category are:

'What are you feeling emotionally right now?'
'Where in your body do you experience that emotional feeling?'
'Can you tell me what's happening inside you right now?'
'What's happening inside you right now?'

If a young person is starting to cry, the counsellor might ask 'Can you put words to your tears?' This may enable the young person to verbalize thoughts related to the internal experience. By doing this, these thoughts can be processed, the counsellor is aware of them, and can achieve empathic joining and help the client move ahead. Similarly, if a young person seems to be stuck and unable to speak, the counsellor might ask 'Can you tell me what is happening inside you right now? What are you experiencing internally?'

Circular questions

Circular questions come from the Milan Systemic Model of Family Therapy (Palazzoli et al., 1980). A circular question is a non-threatening way of getting information from a young person. Instead of asking the young person directly about how they feel or what that they think, or what their attitude is, the counsellor asks the young person how someone else feels or thinks, or asks what the other person's attitude might be. For example, a counsellor might ask 'I wonder what your brother thinks when your mother starts yelling and screaming at you?' By asking circular questions such as these, the counsellor effectively invites the young person to talk about someone else's feelings, thoughts, attitudes or beliefs. This is less threatening than asking the young person to talk about themselves. Often, having answered a circular question, the client will continue by talking about their own feelings, thoughts, attitudes or beliefs to make it clear whether they agree or disagree with the person who was mentioned in the circular question.

Transitional questions

Transitional questions are particularly useful when counselling young people because such questions typically occur in the everyday conversations young people have with their peers. Examples of transitional questions are:

'Previously you talked a great deal about how your mother feels and how your stepfather feels. I'm wondering where your sister fits in?'

'Earlier you talked about the option of leaving school. I'm wondering about how you're feeling about that option now?'

'Earlier you mentioned that you had had a troubling experience. I'm wondering whether you would like to tell me more about that?'

Transitional questions can be used for the following purposes:

1. To encourage the young person to return to discussion of an important topic or issue, particularly after the introduction of a digression (see Chapter 10).
2. To encourage the young person to move from talking about one aspect or topic to another.
3. To make it clear that the counsellor is an active participant in the conversation.
4. To enliven the conversation.

When using transitional questions the counsellor is proactive, having made a clear decision to be an active participant in the conversation, to introduce change and/or to enliven the interaction. It needs to be remembered that the emphasis, when working with young people, is different from that commonly used by counsellors who work with adults. With adults, greater emphasis is often placed on the need to stay with the adult's processes rather than for the counsellor to be proactively engaged as a participant. By comparison, with young people we need to parallel their conversation, and transitional questions are extremely useful for this purpose.

> Following a digression, a transitional question can reintroduce an important issue

Transitional questions do need to be used with some caution. They should only be introduced at points where the young person is not likely to be deflected away from discussion of important and/or painful material.

Choice questions

Choice questions have their origin in Reality therapy (Glasser, 2001). These questions imply that the client has choice about the way they think and behave. Examples of choice questions are:

'What would have been a better choice for you to have made at that time?'

'What would you like to do now? Would you like to continue talking about this issue or would you like to leave it there for now?'

'What alternative ways could you respond to that?'
'If the same situation arises during the coming weeks, what do you think you will do? (Will you do this, or will you do that?)'

Such questions about the past, present or future enable the young person to look at the likely consequences of different behaviours. By exploring choices and consequences, they are likely to be better prepared for future situations.

The guru question

Guru questions have their origin in Gestalt therapy (Clarkson, 2013). When using this type of question, counsellors first invite the client is to stand aside and look at themselves from a distance, and to give themselves some advice. For example, the counsellor might say 'Imagine for a minute that you were a very wise guru and that you could give advice to someone just like you. What advice would you give them?' Guru questions are particularly useful with young people because they commonly give advice to their friends. When they are invited to take up the guru position, they can often give themselves useful advice. Having heard the 'guru's' advice they can then evaluate whether or not they want to follow that advice.

Many young people enjoy giving advice

Career questions

Career questions are questions that exaggerate and extrapolate beyond the young person's present behaviour. They help the young person to recognize that they have choice about the direction in which they are heading and that this choice might lead to extremes of lifestyle. An example of a career question is: 'What would it be like for you to make a career out of being an extremely high achiever who set an example for everybody else by giving up everything except study?' This question raises the client's awareness of a path or journey along which they can progress, if they wish. It enhances their ability to make choices to bring about change, at the current point in time, which might have long-term consequences.

Career questions have a level of paradoxical intent in that, it is hoped, ensuing discussion will result in satisfying behaviours which are not extreme. We need to be careful to use these questions with discretion or they may become self-fulfilling prophecies. Consider the question: 'Would you like to continue your shop-lifting behaviour, take more risks, and move on to becoming a career criminal?' This question would be useful for some young people, but for others might encourage them to follow the 'suggested' career.

Externalizing questions

These questions have their origins in Narrative therapy (White, 2007). Externalizing questions separate the problem, or central issue, from the person. By doing this, the client is able to feel that they can control their problem, or central issue, if they wish, because it is something external to them which can be controlled, rather than something inherent in them which cannot be controlled.

A good example of the use of an externalizing question relates to anger control where a counsellor might externalize the anger of a young person by saying: 'My impression is that your anger has control of you rather than you having control of it. How does your anger manage to trick you into letting it control you?'

Externalizing questions often lead to discussion about issues of control. Control issues are important for young people who are struggling with the desire to have more control of their lives but may be reluctant to accept responsibility for controlling their own behaviour. Externalizing questions are often followed up with exception-oriented questions to help promote change.

Exception-oriented questions

A number of useful types of question have their origin in Brief Solution-focused Therapy. These include exception-oriented questions, questions which exaggerate consequences, miracle questions, goal-oriented questions, scaling questions and questions which presuppose change (O'Connell, 2012).

Exception-oriented questions aim to promote change by drawing attention to times or situations where an undesirable behaviour does not occur. Examples of exception-oriented questions are:

'When do you not get angry?'
'When do you not get into arguments with your father?'
'In what situations do you have control of your impatience?'

Exception-oriented questions aim to help the young person discover that there are times and/or situations where they behave differently, and to recognize what it is that enables them to behave differently. Gaining understanding in this way allows them to recognize that they can take more control of their behaviour and/or their environment. By recognizing this, they may be able to make choices to bring about positive change.

Discovering exceptions can lead to possibilities for change

Questions which exaggerate consequences

Examples of this kind of question are:

- 'How come things aren't worse?'
- 'What stopped total disaster from occurring?'
- 'How did you avoid falling apart?'

These questions can be used to help a young person recognize that they have coped extremely well under adverse situations. These questions are aimed at encouraging the client to view their behaviour in a positive light and discover unrecognized strengths. Such questions can be extremely useful for young people who are unsure about how well they are coping with life.

Miracle questions

Miracle questions are used to help the client begin to find hypothetical solutions to the problems they are experiencing. Typical miracle questions are:

'If a miracle happened and the problem was solved, what would you be doing differently?'
'If things changed miraculously, what would life be like?'

This sort of question appeals to some young people because it lets them use their imagination to explore what would be different if their situation changed for the better.

As a result of thinking about ways in which things might change, they are likely to explore new ideas that might be useful in helping them to make changes.

Goal-oriented questions

Goal-oriented questions are direct questions and are similar in some ways to exception-oriented questions because they invite exploration of ways in which things could be different. They help young people to identify broad changes that they might like to make. In exploring how things could be different, goal-oriented questions invite the client to look ahead to the future. Examples of goal-oriented questions are:

'What do you think your life would be like if you didn't get angry?'
'How would you know that you had resolved this problem?'
'Can you tell me what your life would be like, and what sort of thing you would be doing, if you were no longer feeling miserable?'
'If you had a particular goal that you wanted to achieve with regard to . . ., what would it be?'
'How would you like things to be?'
'When you think about . . ., can you identify any particular goals?'

Other goal-oriented questions identify perceived restraints, which in the young person's mind interfere with their ability to achieve particular goals. They help the client to identify ways to overcome these restraints. Examples are:

'What stops you from achieving your goal?'
'What would you need to do to achieve your goal?'

Scaling questions

Scaling questions have their origin in Brief Solution-focused Therapy. Scaling questions often lead into goal-oriented questions as they are related to goals. They help the young person to be specific when identifying and discussing goals. Examples of scaling questions are:

'On a scale of 1–10, 1 being hopelessly incompetent and 10 being really competent, where do you think you fit right now?'
'On the scale of 1–10, 1 being very depressed and 10 being ecstatically happy, where would you like to be in the future?'
'If 1 corresponded to being an honest and upright citizen and 10 corresponded to being a hardened criminal, where would you like to be?'

Scaling questions lead into goal-oriented questions. For example, the counsellor might ask: 'What will you need to do to reach this point on the scale?'

Questions which presuppose change

An example of a question which presupposes change is: 'What has been different or better since you last saw me?' This question presupposes that some change has occurred and may help a young person to identify things that have improved, so that they can feel good. Quite often, positive change goes unnoticed. For example, although there may have been fewer arguments during the week, the young person might not have recognized this. By using a question which presupposes change, the counsellor can bring the change which has occurred into focus and make small changes newsworthy, so that there is a recognition that improvement has begun. Once improvement has been identified, there is an incentive to make further improvement so that significant change can occur.

Challenging

There are a number of situations where counsellors need to challenge adolescent clients. Challenging needs to be done in a way that does not offend them but invites them to question what they have said, what they believe or what they are doing. In their peer relationships, young people are usually direct in challenging each other. Similarly, counsellors need to be direct, but in a way which is not threatening to the young person's ego. Situations in which challenging might need to occur are:

- Where the young person has been talking about things in a way that is confusing because what they are saying is inconsistent or contradictory.
- Where the young person is engaging in behaviour which is inevitably self-destructive, but they are not recognizing this.
- When the young person is avoiding a basic issue which appears to be troubling them.
- Where a young person is excessively and inappropriately locked into talking about the past or the future and is unable to focus on the present.
- When a young person is going around in circles by repeating the same story over and over again.
- When the young person's non-verbal behaviour does not match their verbal behaviour.
- Where undesirable processes are occurring in the relationship between the client and counsellor; for example, where dependency or transference is occurring or where a client withdraws or shows hostility, anger or some other emotion towards the counsellor.
- Where the young person is failing to recognize possible serious consequences of their behaviour.
- When the client is out of touch with reality with regard to a specific situation, but is not exhibiting a mental health problem.

In situations such as these, counsellors may challenge their clients by sharing what they feel or are observing. A good way to challenge is to use the following process:

1. Reflect or give a brief summary of what the client has said so that the client feels heard and understood.
2. Possibly include a statement of the counsellor's own feelings at the time.
3. Make a concrete statement of what the counsellor has noticed or observed. This needs to be given without interpretation.

Sensitivity is required when challenging

Examples of challenging responses are:

'You have just told me that . . . but I'm puzzled because I've noticed that several times you have briefly talked about your relationship with your sister and then have started to talk about something quite different.'
'You have talked about your relationship with your mother. However I'm confused; you've told me that you care very much about your mother, but you have also said that you are deliberately planning to try to hurt her.'

Instructions

When counselling young people, there are a number of types of instruction which can be useful. When instructions are given, they need to be given in a way that is neither patronizing nor parentified or the young person is likely to be alienated. During a pro-active counselling process counsellors select counselling strategies, as explained in Chapter 9, to facilitate the exploration of the young person's issues. When using these strategies, counsellors need to give instructions to implement the selected strategies and help structure the process. This means that at times they need to be directive.

Being directive

Before starting to give direct instructions related to the use of a particular strategy, the counsellor needs to give the young person a choice about whether or not to engage in the strategy concerned. In addition, the young person needs to be told that they have a choice about whether or not to do as directed. If these conditions are not met, the young client will be disempowered and, if the session continues, the client–counsellor relationship will be likely to deteriorate into a parental type of relationship. Negotiation about involvement in a particular process is essential to enable the young person to join co-operatively with the counsellor in accepting, or choosing not to accept, particular directions.

In being directive, the counsellor needs to give clear, concise instructions such as:

'Tell me how you feel now.'
'Tell me more.'
'Tell your football coach how you really feel.' [*in role play*]
'I would like you to stand over here and imagine that you are your teacher.' [*in role play*]
'Change places and be your grandmother.' [*in two-chair work*]
'Choose a symbol to represent your disappointment.' [*when choosing symbols*]

It is important for counsellors to monitor the outcomes of their directions. If a strategy is not working, the instructions and directions being used need to be modified. This might mean that a counsellor may need to abandon a strategy at a particular point.

The use of humour

Humour can be particularly useful when working with some young people as it can help to lighten the conversation. It is important for counsellors to be able to get in touch with their own inner adolescent and to use humour which is appropriate for the situation. Humour can be used directly to influence change as well as to create an easier climate.

In using humour to promote change, we can make use of paradoxical interventions. Paradoxical interventions have their origins in Strategic Family Therapy (Madanes, 1981, 1984). Frankl (1973) described paradoxical intervention as a technique to enable the client to develop a sense of detachment from their neurosis by laughing at it. By making a ridiculous suggestion the counsellor may encourage a young person to think creatively about new or alternative solutions to problems. For example, if a young person has been expressing anxiety about needing to achieve a very high standard in assignments, the counsellor might say in a deliberately humorous way: 'Well, maybe you should read your assignments through twenty times to make sure they are OK and then show them to half a dozen friends to get them to check and make suggestions, and then revise them before you hand them in'. Clearly, this approach should only be used with students where the counsellor has confidence that a positive outcome will be achieved.

Humour in counselling should never be hostile or derogatory. Young people themselves use humour by teasing, mimicking or acting out. These are clearly not suitable counsellor behaviours. The successful use of humour in counselling depends on sensible choice of content, and timing, with the counsellor being sensitive to the vulnerability of the young client. What may be amusing for one individual may not be for another.

KEY POINTS

- a wide variety of micro-counselling skills can be used to engage and join with the young person and to enable them to resolve issues and feel better
- observation can be used as an assessment tool in providing information about the young person with regard to mood, intellectual functioning, self-esteem, attitudes, beliefs, creativity and social influences
- it can be useful to match the young person's conversational style through the use of digression, self-disclosure, their vocabulary, representational style and the use of their metaphors
- a wide variety of questions and feedback statements can be used to energize the counselling interaction, engage the young person, and promote joining
- humour is particularly useful in helping to provide balance in the counselling conversation

FURTHER RESOURCES

'Quizlet' is an online study tool that provides, among other topics, resources to study counselling micro-skills. After checking out the micro-skills resources, perhaps you might like to explore other topics covered by 'Quizlet'?

- quizlet.com/9996625/counseling-micro-skills-flash-cards/

12

Promoting Change in Young People

In previous chapters we have discussed the proactive counselling approach when counselling young people. We have described the way that this approach makes use of adolescent communication processes together with counselling skills and deliberately attempts to make the counselling process relevant for young people. We have described the foundations of the proactive approach and the process used to address the primary counselling functions.

Because facilitating change in a person is central to any counselling process, we think that it is important for a counsellor to understand the various mechanisms for change that may come into play when using the proactive approach with young people.

Research has shown that positive change in counselling can occur regardless of the model of counselling used (Prochaska, 1999). Further, it has been shown that the relationship between a client and counsellor is a more important factor in facilitating change than the model of counselling used. Even so, we believe that change is likely to occur more quickly and effectively if the counselling process used is one that fits for the client. In our view, the advantage of the proactive approach is that it does generally suit adolescent clients because it is compatible with their developmental stage.

What kinds of change are useful?

Human beings are often troubled by unhelpful or intrusive thoughts, by uncomfortable emotions, and by behaviours that have negative consequences for them. Central goals in counselling young people are to help them to feel better and function more adaptively so that they can lead more satisfying lives. Thus, when counselling young people the aim is to facilitate change in the way they think, feel and behave.

It is obvious that there is a definite connection between a person's thoughts, emotions and behaviours. For many years counsellors, psychologists and others have had various opinions about the precise nature of the relationship between thoughts, emotions and behaviours.

"Thoughts, emotions and behaviours are interconnected"

Some people believe that change in cognitions (thoughts) is sufficient to produce emotional and behavioural change. Others think that changing emotional feelings will inevitably produce changes in thinking and behaving. Not surprisingly there are other people who believe that changing behaviours will produce changes in a person's thoughts and emotional feelings. Trying to determine which comes first in promoting change is rather like asking the question 'Which comes first, the chicken or the egg?' We don't think that we need to find a definitive answer to the question 'Should we target emotions, or thoughts or behaviours in order to produce positive change?' It seems to us that emotions, thoughts and behaviours are interdependent, so if we are able to facilitate change in any one of these attributes, the others may also change.

Consider an example

Imagine a teenage girl who starts to find her schoolwork too challenging for her. As a consequence, she feels overwhelmed and starts to misbehave in class in a subconscious effort to draw her attention away from worrying about her inability to focus on her set work. Her self-esteem is affected by her lack of achievement and the negative feedback she receives about her behaviour. As a result, she starts to think negatively about herself, saying to herself 'I am not good at anything'.

Changing her emotions

Imagine that a counsellor was able to help her change her emotional feelings so that she did not feel overwhelmed, but instead felt as though she could cope. If this happened, what do you think the effect would be on her thoughts and behaviour? Although we can't be sure, it is possible that if she was not feeling overwhelmed she would be able to focus on her schoolwork so that her performance improved. If she could do this, her behaviour might also change as she would no longer want to misbehave in class. Additionally, because she was able to attend to her schoolwork and not get into trouble in class, she might start to think more positively about herself.

Changing her thoughts

Imagine that a counsellor was able to help the young girl to change her thoughts so that instead of saying 'I am not good at anything', she could say to herself 'I can do reasonably well at most things if I put some effort in'. Once again, we can't be sure of the outcome, but it is possible that she might also feel better and behave differently. For example, once she realized that she was capable of doing reasonably well if she tried, she might begin to put more effort into her work. Thus her behaviour would have changed. Additionally, the positive message she would now be giving herself together with the changed behaviour might help her to feel better emotionally.

Changing her behaviour

Imagine that a counsellor was able to help the teenager change her behaviour so that she stopped misbehaving in class. This might have an effect on both her emotions and thoughts. Because her behaviour had changed she might start to feel better about herself and think about herself more positively.

Can you see from this example how it is sometimes possible to bring about change in emotions, thoughts and behaviours just by targeting one of these? Sometimes it may be possible to simultaneously target all three attributes, although often counsellors will begin by addressing either thoughts, or emotions, or behaviours, with the goal of eventually promoting change in all three.

Facilitating emotional change

As we know, most young people come for counselling help when they are experiencing a level of emotional distress. For some, their emotions are clearly expressed, either verbally or non-verbally. For others, although they may exhibit levels of anxiety or confusion, their emotional expression is more contained. Many young people are unable to identify with clarity the emotions they are experiencing. Sometimes their emotions are so repressed that in the early stages of counselling it may be impossible for them to get in touch with them at all.

Have you noticed that when you release your emotions you tend to feel better and enter into a calmer state? Let us consider an example. Have you ever felt very sad, maybe after someone you cared about died, or as a result of a broken relationship? If you have, did you cry? If you did cry, did you feel less distraught after crying? Our experience is that when we let our emotions out we usually feel better. Thus, when we are sad, crying helps. Although we may not feel happy after crying, we are likely to feel more comfortable and be less emotionally disturbed. Similarly, if we are very angry, we may need to release our anger in some way. This may be by shouting, punching a pillow or engaging in a symbolic ritual. It is the same for young people. They are likely to feel better if they have some way of releasing their emotions. Thus, one way in which a counsellor may help a young person feel better is to help them achieve catharsis through emotional release.

A good way to help young people get in touch with their emotions is to use Rogerian reflective skills and feedback of non-verbal behaviour (see Chapter 11). If you watch a young person's non-verbal behaviour, including facial expression and tone of voice, you may be able to identify the way they are feeling emotionally and reflect that back to them. As a consequence, they may get in touch with strong emotions. It can be helpful to allow the young person to fully experience any emotions which emerge (subject to safety when dealing with clients who are very angry).

Generally, if a young person starts to cry, it is useful to allow the crying to continue until it stops naturally. Consequently, emotions are released and catharsis occurs. With regard to other emotions, such as frustration, anger and despair, encourage the young person, through reflection of content and feelings, to get in touch with and talk about their emotions rather than avoid dealing with them.

Some counsellors worry when a young person cries because they are afraid that they won't stop. Generally, this is not the case. Typically, human beings self-regulate and after a while will stop crying naturally. After many years working with young people, we, the authors, have never been confronted by a situation where a young person has not stopped crying after they have adequately expressed their emotions. Clearly, if this were to happen, a psychiatric assessment would be needed.

You might ask 'Is emotional release sufficient in itself?' Pierce, Nichols and Du Brin (1983) in their book, *Emotional Expression in Psychotherapy*, are clear in their belief that when feelings are fully expressed they lead to new ways for clients to view themselves and their world. In other words, their perception of their situation changes and they think about things differently. The authors go on to say that the new ways of thinking and viewing the world then lead to more satisfying behaviours. However, they recognize that this process does not necessarily happen automatically.

Limitations of emotional release

We ourselves believe that emotional release is an important component of the healing process, but we do not believe that it is sufficient in itself. In our experience many young people who release emotions in counselling are unable to make significant changes to their thinking and behaviour without also being invited to deal directly with their thoughts and behaviours. Unfortunately, young people who are unable to make changes in their thinking and behaviours are quite likely to experience problems in the future. This may be because they continue to use self-destructive thought patterns or continue to engage in unhelpful behaviours. Additionally, when new troubling situations arise, they may not have learnt how to respond cognitively and behaviourally in adaptive ways.

Emotional release alone may not be sufficient

Another problem with relying on emotional release to help young people feel better is that a significant proportion of young people have trouble getting in touch with strong emotions in a counselling setting. As a consequence, they may not be able to use the emotional release process effectively.

Counsellors need to be careful when working with young people who have a tendency to become violent. First, if they are invited to let their anger out in a counselling session they may well act out in a way which is damaging to themselves, the counsellor, or the counselling room. Second, and more importantly, encouraging them to let their anger out may be unhelpful to them as they may learn to do this inappropriately in the wider social system. It is often better to help such young people learn how to manage their anger so that they can express it in adaptive rather than maladaptive ways. Hence, for them, facilitating change in thinking and/or behaviour may be more appropriate than emotional release.

Facilitating changes in thinking

If we want to help a young person change the way they think we have several options. For example, we could use:

- a psycho-educational strategy (see Chapter 17)
- a symbolic or creative strategy (see Chapters 14 and 15)
- a cognitive behavioural strategy (see Chapter 16).

We will discuss the use of each of these in promoting changes in thinking, but first we need to understand the normal processes young people generally use to change their constructs or perceptions of the world in which they live. These processes have been described by Young et al. (1999).

Normal adolescent peer conversations are generally egalitarian and reciprocal. This is appropriate in adolescence as such relationships are consistent with young people seeking to develop their own individual selves as they strive to become autonomous. In such egalitarian relationships young people have the opportunity to review their constructs, beliefs, attitudes and opinions in a climate where they are accepted and respected. As they talk with each other they define their individual positions and, in the process of conversation, re-examine and refine their constructs, adjusting them as they share information with each other. Together with one another they can co-operatively and collaboratively challenge their own and others' constructs, review them, accept those that fit and replace those that do not. It is not surprising, then, that young people report that they rely on friends and peers as their primary referents (Boldero and Fallon, 1995). It is through interaction with each other, in the safety of mutually respectful relationships where they can discuss and explore their constructs, that young people are often able to change the way they view the world.

As counsellors who want to be effective in helping young people to change, we need to recognize the way that young people challenge and review each others' constructs. Then we can use a similar interactional style when trying to help them change. As explained earlier, we need to establish a respectful and as far as possible egalitarian relationship. We are then in the best helping environment to facilitate change by co-operatively and collabora-tively working with the young person in the process of challenging, reviewing and revising constructs. By doing this we facilitate change.

Using a psycho-educational strategy to change thinking

In Chapter 17 we discuss a number of psycho-educational strategies which can be use-ful in helping young people to change the way they think.

As explained previously, young people are in a stage in life where they are exploring new ideas, beliefs and constructs. Although they may resent being told what to do by adults, they do have an expectation that counsellors will be able to provide them with information and ideas which they don't have themselves. When they come to see a counsellor they legitimately expect that the counsellor will have some expertise and will be willing to share it with them. Even though generally they don't like being told what to do, they are often receptive to new information and enjoy receiving it, provided it doesn't come from parents or significant others whom they perceive as being in a power situation relative to themselves. Consequently, young people are often receptive to new ideas when they are suggested by counsellors, and these ideas may promote change.

Using a symbolic or creative strategy to change thinking

Another way to produce change in a young person's thinking is to raise their awareness sufficiently for them to gain additional insight into their situation. It is interesting to note that psychoanalytic therapists believe that raising insight produces change, and similarly Gestalt therapists believe that raising awareness produces change. There is a clear parallel between the two styles of therapy (this is not surprising because Gestalt therapy grew out of psychoanalysis). We have found that the best way to help young people raise their awareness and gain insight is often by making use either of a symbolic strategy (see Chapter 14) or of a creative strategy (see Chapter 15).

Symbolic strategies can be particularly useful in cases where the issues troubling a young person are so distressing or personal that they are unable to talk about them directly. By using symbols the young person may be able to share their thoughts about issues which are difficult for them to discuss without talking about the issues directly. As they share their thoughts in this way, changes to their thinking may occur.

Many authors draw attention to the usefulness of creative strategies in bringing about changes in thinking and perceptions. For example, Clarkson (2013) identifies the way creative processes can bring dormant insights into awareness and provide the opportu-nity for this awareness to be shared so that change occurs.

Using symbolic or creative strategies is often more effective than just encouraging a young person to talk about their thoughts. This is especially true for those young peo-ple who do not have a high level of verbal skills. Creative and symbolic strategies enable them to make discoveries about themselves and others, and help raise their awareness and gain insight without a heavy reliance on language. Equally, these strategies can be very useful for those young people who have a high level of verbal competence. This is because such strategies tend to move the young person away from talking 'about' things in a way which is personally detached, and instead help them to get more fully in touch with their inner experiences and thought processes.

Symbolic and creative strategies are not reliant on verbal ability

Using a cognitive behavioural strategy to change thinking

As discussed previously, young people are continually revising their constructs and beliefs. Because of this, they often have beliefs that are at best unhelpful and at worst self-destructive. Often self-destructive beliefs will relate to unrealistic expectations of themselves or of others. A young person who has self-destructive beliefs can be helped if these beliefs are challenged. They can then be encouraged to find alternative beliefs that are more helpful (see Chapter 16). Usually, replacing self-destructive beliefs by more constructive beliefs will result in the person feeling better and behaving differently.

Facilitating changes in behaviour

Up to now, we have discussed ways of bringing about change by using methods which involve emotional release and changes in thinking. For some young people releasing emotions and/or changing ways of thinking is sufficient to produce behavioural change, but for others the counselling process needs to be more strongly directed towards behaviours.

When directly targeting behaviours, counsellors can make use of choice questions which were described in the previous chapter. If the young person is encouraged to look at their choices with regard to different behaviours, and the consequences of these behaviours, they will often recognize that it is in their own interests to change their behaviour so that they get better outcomes for themselves.

Sometimes young people will be clear in expressing a desire to change their behaviour but will be experiencing difficulty in putting the desired change into practice. In such cases it may be useful to try to check out what is driving the behaviour and what rewards, either practical or psychological, are associated with the behaviour.

Consider an example. A young person might be genuinely concerned about their continuing use of illegal drugs and be clear in their own mind that they want to stop. When exploring the situation more fully, the counsellor might discover that the young person's best friends are drug-users and are active in trying to undermine the young person's resolve. Consequently, there is a clear reward for them when they continue to use drugs. By using drugs, they join more fully with their close friends. However, if they stop using drugs their friendships are likely to be compromised, so there is a cost involved in changing their behaviour. Once the problem is seen in its context, it is obvious that it may not be an easy matter for the young person to make the desired change. If they are to give up their drug habit they will first have to think through the process of how to do this, and decide whether they are prepared to put this process into action or not. In order to stop using drugs they may have to confront their friends directly, or relinquish some friendships. To do this they may have to make significant changes to their social life. In such a case the client and counsellor need to work collaboratively in drawing up a plan of action. Then role-plays may be needed to help the young person learn suitable communication skills which may be necessary if the plan is to succeed.

As an action plan is being put into practice there needs to be an opportunity for the client, in collaboration with the counsellor, to review whether or not the plan is working. When doing this, the counsellor must continue to be non-judgemental and supportive, particularly if setbacks occur. Setbacks need to be explored to determine how the plan needs to be modified to suit the needs and desires of the young person if the goal is to be achieved. When engaged in the review process it can be helpful for the counsellor to remember that the young person is doing the best they can, and may feel uncomfortable when admitting to failure.

When a young person succeeds in achieving progress they can be encouraged to give themselves a reward so that they feel good, not only as a result of achieving progress but also because they can enjoy the reward.

Using motivational interviewing to support change in behaviour

Motivational interviewing is a collaborative client-centred approach used to promote change in an individual's behaviour. It has a growing research base for use with adolescents, particularly with respect to substance use. Indeed, with a focus on promoting autonomy, motivational interviewing is well suited to the adolescent developmental period (Naar-King, 2011). There are many elements that comprise motivational interviewing, including the underlying client-centred principles, foundational skills (in particular, the micro-skills that we covered in Chapter 11), encouragement and reinforcement of 'change talk' and the spirit or philosophy guiding the approach (Rosengren, 2009). Due to its complex nature, readers who are interested in motivational interviewing are encouraged to seek training and supervision to develop their skills in this area.

The role of the young person's family in promoting change

We touched on the possibility of combining individual and family therapy when supporting young people in Chapter 7. Here, we consider how the family may support or hinder change for a young person. Systems theory, as we discuss in our book *Relationship*

Counselling for Children, Young People and Families (Geldard and Geldard, 2009), views the family as individuals who interact within a system (Dattilio, 1998). The family system is made up of smaller subsystems, such as the parental subsystem, and sits within a number of larger systems, for example, the school system. We will focus on the impact of the family system itself in this chapter. However, for an overview of the various systems that may impact on an adolescent please refer to Chapter 5.

An important concept of family systems theory is that of homoeostasis: a family system will act to maintain a state of dynamic balance. If change happens in one part of the system, such as in a young person participating in counselling, the family may respond by resisting this change in order to maintain homoeostasis. As such, family therapy may play a complementary role within the counselling process by developing a supportive family context in which the adolescent can be empowered to make, and maintain, change. As we noted in Chapter 1, a key developmental task of adolescence is for a young person to gain independence from their family. Therefore, as counsellors, we believe it is important to respect our clients' choice in whether or not they would like their family to be involved within the counselling process.

KEY POINTS

- thoughts, emotions and behaviours are interconnected so changing one of these may change the others, although this will not necessarily happen
- for change to be most effective, thoughts, emotions and behaviours all need to change
- emotional release can be cathartic but may not result in changes to thoughts and behaviours
- psycho-educational, symbolic, creative and cognitive behavioural strategies can be used to promote changes in thinking
- action plans are useful when targeting behaviour change

FURTHER RESOURCES

In this chapter we touched briefly on motivational interviewing to support behaviour change in young people. For readers who are interested, 'Headspace' has produced a summary of the evidence for using motivational interviewing when working with young people. Readers may also like to explore the other resources available on the 'Headspace' website.

- www.headspace.org.au/what-works/resources/-evidence-summaries

13

Maintaining a Collaborative Relationship

As has been discussed in earlier chapters, a counsellor needs to be proactive in order to be able to continually engage a young person's interest in the counselling process. We explained, in Chapter 9, how it can be useful for the counsellor to engage in particular proactive behaviours and to make use of adolescent communication processes in order to join with the young person in a way which will be therapeutically helpful. However, even when using the most effective strategies for working with a young person it is inevitable that at times their energy and interest in the counselling process will diminish. If the counselling process is to have a satisfactory outcome a counsellor will need to be attentive, recognizing changes in the young person and their behaviour, and responding appropriately.

In recent years a considerable amount of literature has been written with regard to the effectiveness of counselling. Research studies have identified the influence of particular 'common factors' and what has been called 'the therapeutic alliance'. Important contributors in the field have been Frank and Frank (1991), Horvath (2001) and Wampold (2001).

Common factors

Common factors have been identified as helpful for counselling to be effective. These have been described in different ways by different authors and generally include:

- the counsellor's personal qualities
- the client–counsellor relationship
- the client trusting the counsellor as being able to be of help
- client factors
- the influence of hope and optimism.

The counsellor's personal qualities, the client–counsellor relationship, and the need for the client to trust the counsellor as being able to be of help, have been discussed in some detail earlier in this book with particular emphasis on their relevance when working with young people. When considering the importance of maintaining a collaborative relationship with the client, it can be useful to take into account both client factors and the influence of hope and optimism.

Client factors

You might like to consider the question 'Is it the counsellor who is effective in promoting change in the client, or is it the client who generates change in themselves?' It seems to us that many young people have within them the resilience and ability to heal themselves, and this fits with Carl Rogers' beliefs with regard to the client having the ability to find their own solutions. So what is it that the counsellor does? The counsellor acts as a facilitator, working collaboratively with the client to promote, amplify and extend the possibility of change (Bohart and Tallman, 1996). The proactive approach described in this book is an approach that depends on a collaborative working together between the young person and the counsellor. Although this makes good sense and is easy to describe, it is not always easy for a counsellor to be able to maintain an effective relationship so that the young person is engaged in working collaboratively with them.

Some clients are highly motivated, whereas others are not

As counsellors, we need to recognize that each young person who comes to see us for counselling is a unique individual, and that their individual motivation to consider alternatives for change is likely to influence the counselling relationship. Some young people will be highly motivated to join with the counsellor in exploring their issues and in making decisions which will enable them to function more adaptively. Others will be less ready to undertake what might be the painful work involved in exploring their issues, taking personal responsibility for what is theirs, and considering alternative ways of thinking and behaving. Clearly, if the counsellor doesn't recognize this and respond appropriately by respecting the young person's current understanding of their personal situation, and respecting their constructs and beliefs that support this understanding, the chance of working collaboratively with the young person will be compromised.

The influence of hope and optimism

When His Holiness The Dalai Lama was in conversation with psychiatrist Howard Cutler (Dalai Lama and Cutler, 2000), they agreed that for a person to change in attitude the person must first realize that this is possible, must wish to do so, and then implement the changes. If we accept that this is correct, then as counsellors, it is clearly useful for us to help the young people who come to see us to have hope and the expectation that change is possible.

Hope and optimism are processes used in varying degrees by most people to cope with daily life. In particular, many young people are able to spontaneously get in touch with hope and optimism at times. Unfortunately, we know that because of the stresses of adolescence, and other factors associated with this developmental stage, most young people are subject to mood swings. However, it can be helpful if, during counselling, we are able to help young clients to tap into their potential for hope and optimism. We have to admit that, as with other people, we ourselves will sometimes sink into thinking negatively and become pessimistic. Are you the same? We have discovered that being in a negative frame of mind is uncomfortable for us, so when we recognize our negativity we are motivated to change our attitude so that we are more positive and hopeful. By sharing this information about ourselves with young people they may discover that they can do the same.

A useful question is 'How can we use counselling to engender hope in our clients?' Frank and Frank (1991) suggest that a counsellor who is hopeful can contribute to a client's sense of hope and optimism. They also suggest that the explanation the counsellor gives about why the client is experiencing the presenting problem can also lead to the client's sense of hope for the future. Taking note of their ideas we also suggest that being hopeful is in some way contagious, and that if, as counsellors, we are hopeful about outcomes for a young person who comes to see us, they are more likely to start to feel hopeful themselves.

Hope and optimism can be contagious

The therapeutic alliance

The concept of the therapeutic alliance has been discussed by many authors, over many years, including Bordin (1994) and Safran and Muran (2000). Included as attributes of the therapeutic alliance are:

- the bond between the client and counsellor
- the counsellor's empathic understanding
- a level of agreement between the client and counsellor with regard to the goals and tasks of treatment.

Research involving adult clients has shown that the quality of the alliance fluctuates over time, even within a particular session (Safran et al. 2011). Counsellors who work with young people can confirm that this is especially so for the adolescent age group.

It is important to recognize, however, that the therapeutic alliance is one of the best predictors of psychotherapeutic change (Horvath and Symonds, 1991). It is therefore essential that when we are working with young people we pay attention to the quality of the therapeutic alliance throughout a counselling session.

The value of being collaborative

In our view, an effective therapeutic alliance extends the relationship between the client and counsellor to enable them to work together *collaboratively* throughout the whole process of counselling. If this is done successfully, the reason why the person seeking help has come for counselling will be discovered and the purpose and goals of the counselling process will become clear as the counsellor collaborates with the client. Further, through collaboration solutions will be found.

Collaboration enhances the possibility of solutions being discovered

Creating a therapeutic alliance ensures that the person seeking help is valued as a person, as explained in Chapter 2. They are respected as being capable of working towards the discovery of solutions. However, rather than being a bystander, the counsellor collaborates with the client in a working relationship. This enables the counsellor to enter into a respectful partnership with the client in exploring new ways of addressing problems and of finding solutions. In this working relationship the client brings their innate skills, competencies, resources and natural ability to self-heal into the relationship while the counsellor collaborates by offering their counselling expertise and skills, and sharing their ideas as an equal, rather than as an expert, with the young person. This collaboration is effected with the client's full knowledge and understanding so that they are aware of their own and the counsellor's roles.

Being collaborative while showing respect for the client's competence

We are convinced that, using the proactive model, it is advantageous with regard to achieving successful outcomes for the counsellor to be able to establish and maintain a collaborative working relationship with the young person. It is interesting to note that some counselling models place a much stronger emphasis on client–counsellor collaboration than other models where this is seen to be less important.

In Client-centred Counselling there is a strong emphasis on the ability of the client to find solutions from their own resources. The counsellor is a facilitator who facilitates a process which enables the client to use their own inner processes in order to resolve issues and find solutions. Other approaches, such as Narrative Therapy and Solution-focused

Counselling, emphasize the need for the counsellor and client to work together as equal partners in finding solutions, while still respecting the client's competence. In these latter approaches the counsellor is active in using questions to propose and explore possible alternative solutions with the client. Clearly, there are differences in emphasis with regard to the extent of client–counsellor collaboration when comparing various models of counselling. Some counsellors believe that primarily we need to facilitate a process which relies on the client's ability to discover their own solutions, while others believe that while respecting the client's abilities it is also beneficial to focus on engaging in a collaborative process to discover solutions. Clearly, you will want to decide for yourself what fits best for you.

If a useful counselling relationship is to occur, the counsellor must respect and value the young person as capable, as explained in the early chapters. It is extremely important for a counsellor to respect the client's competence and to hold the belief that the client has the inner resources needed to deal with troubling issues, find solutions to problems, make decisions to change behaviour, and put desired changes into action. It is inevitable that some young people will come to counselling believing that they do not have the inner resources and capability to do such things. Their expectation is that the counsellor will help them by finding solutions for them. They may, at the time when they come for counselling, be unable to get in touch with their inner sense of personal power and self-confidence which they need if they are to be self-reliant. However, if the counsellor maintains the belief that the young person does have the required inner strength and competence required for self-reliance, then they will be in a position to enable the young person to get in touch with their own strengths and resources, to become self-reliant, to make decisions which suit them, and consequently to gain in self-esteem. In facilitating this process the proactive counsellor may, as a collaborative partner, introduce new ideas that can be explored with the young person. If this is done with sensitivity and respect, the client can continue to be encouraged to explore their issues, make their own decisions, and find solutions which fit for them. Also, the counselling conversation can be enriched by the introduction of additional ideas by the counsellor. In this situation the young person is likely to believe that the counsellor cares enough to be involved as an equal partner in the exploration of problems and the search for solutions, thereby enhancing the client–counsellor relationship. Thus, the counsellor is actively helpful and involved in a process which is purposeful while working collaboratively with the client as an equal partner by contributing their own skills and attributes to the counselling conversation. During this collaborative process the counsellor shows respect for the young person's competence and ability as they explore troubling issues, and make personal decisions which fit for them.

Recognizing when the therapeutic alliance is weakening

Research has demonstrated that the quality of the working alliance is significantly associated with positive change in young people (Hintikka et al., 2006). Unfortunately, while research has been carried out on ways to deal with breakdowns in the therapeutic alliance with adult clients, to date similar research relating to young people continues to be limited, even though this lack of research was identified several years ago by DiGiuseppe et al. (1996). As has been discussed earlier in this book, many counsellors consider that establishing and maintaining an effective therapeutic alliance with young people can be a challenging task. However, in our experience as counsellors we have found that working proactively as described in Chapter 9 together with the use of adolescent communication processes as described in Chapter 10 can minimize the risk that the therapeutic alliance will be seriously compromised. Even so, whenever working collaboratively with a young person it is very important for us to be able to recognize when our connection with them is starting to weaken.

We would like to invite you to think for a moment about how, during a counselling session with a young person, you would start to recognize that the strength of your relationship with the young person was weakening.

In our experience, the first step in recognizing that the therapeutic alliance may be about to be compromised is to use our own awareness of our own emotional feelings to gain a sense of the level of contact that we have with the young person. If we start to feel as though we are not joined with the young person, then we can be fairly sure that the young person is unlikely to be joined with us. In addition to our own feelings we might use information gained from our observation of the client. We might notice any of the following about them:

- they seem disinterested and continually deflect away from dealing with their issues
- they are quiet without actively participating in the conversation
- they no longer make eye contact
- they are sceptical or negative in attitude
- they seem keen to end the session.

Once we recognize that the therapeutic alliance is weakening we believe that it is preferable to be proactive in directly addressing the situation rather than trying to manipulate the situation. In our view it is more important to be transparent in our relationship with the young person rather than to try to use surreptitious methods to re-energize the relationship.

> **Being proactive can help strengthen a weakening therapeutic alliance**

In being proactive we need to:

- relate to the young person openly and honestly
- feed back what we are experiencing or have noticed
- check out what is happening for the young person
- offer the young person alternatives.

It will be difficult to re-establish a collaborative working relationship unless we are upfront with the young person. If the relationship is less than satisfactory for therapeutic gains, then we need to be open in recognizing this and sharing our feelings with the client. In this way we are being respectful of them and can offer them choices with regard to continuing the counselling session or ending it.

We might use statements such as:

> 'I'm concerned because I sense that I'm failing to join with you in a way that feels comfortable for you. I am wondering whether you're experiencing the same?'
> 'I am getting the impression that I am not meeting your needs right now, and wonder whether I can do things differently so that you will feel more comfortable in talking to me about your situation?'
> 'What would be most helpful for you at this point?'
> 'Would you like to continue exploring your situation in the way that we have been, or would it be better if we tried a new and different approach?'
> 'Would you like to continue talking with me about the things that trouble you or would you prefer to go away, think about things, and maybe come back later?'

By using statements like these we can be open with a young person, rather than pretending that the relationship is fine and that they are getting their needs met in a way which is comfortable for them. Notice that by using statements such as those above, the young person is given choice. When inviting a young person to make a choice about what to do in the current situation, it is important to identify alternatives rather than offering just one option. For example, if a counsellor were to say 'Would you like to continue talking to me about your worries?', it might be difficult for some young people to say 'No I don't want to do that'. Alternatively, if the counsellor was to say 'Would you like to continue talking to me about your worries or would you prefer to go away and possibly come back another time?', they would be giving the young person an invitation to either continue talking or to feel OK about deciding not to continue in the counselling session.

Provide a young person with alternatives when offering them a choice

Giving positive messages

Whatever decision the young person makes in response to the counsellor's enquiries related to the weakening of the therapeutic alliance, it can be useful for the counsellor to take the opportunity to give the young person some positive feedback. For example, feedback might include the ability of the young person to be open about what they want to do, or might be related to the way in which the young person has been able to explore the issues in the counselling setting. If the young person decides that they would like to end the counselling session, it is sensible and appropriate to assure them that they would be welcome to come back at another time.

Potential barriers to maintaining a collaborative relationship

A number of potential barriers to maintaining a collaborative therapeutic relationship may arise throughout the counselling process. Potential challenges may stem from the counsellor, the young person, the nature of the therapeutic relationship itself or from external influences (Manassis, 2012). As counsellors, we approach the therapeutic relationship with a number of values and attitudes. These attitudes may relate directly to the therapeutic process, for example, ideas about what counselling 'should' be and our counselling framework and philosophy. Other values are broader and guide our thinking, decisions and actions. Both our attitudes towards counselling and our broader values can impact on the client–counsellor relationship. We would like to invite you to take a moment to reflect on your attitudes and values. What attitudes and values do you hold that may impact on a collaborative counselling relationship? Another aspect that we, as counsellors, need to be aware of is our professional competence. Practising within our limits of competence is an ethical duty (British Association for Counselling and Psychotherapy, 2010) that also impacts on our ability to maintain a collaborative relationship: practising outside our competence could potentially lead to clients deciding to discontinue counselling (Block and Greeno, 2011). What areas of practice are you comfortable with? Which areas do you feel need to be developed? We find that being proactive and self-reflective can help to limit the influence of attitudes, values and professional competence on the development of the client–counsellor relationship. This process of self-reflection can be supported by seeking supervision, particularly when a client presents with an issue outside our professional competence.

Just as the counsellor brings attitudes and values to the therapeutic relationship, so does the client. While some young people may be motivated and engaged, other adolescents may be wary of the counselling process. This may be particularly true of clients who have been referred, for example, by a parent or teacher. Adolescents who have not self-referred are likely to have less motivation to engage with you, the counsellor, and are more likely to stop accessing counselling support (Block and Greeno, 2011). Finally, the developmental stage of adolescence may be a barrier to forming a collaborative relationship in itself. Seeking counselling help suggests dependence in a time of growing independence and autonomy. There are also elements of the therapeutic relationship itself that may be barriers to forming a collaborative relationship with a young person. For example, both the power imbalance and formal nature of the therapeutic relationship can be deterrents for adolescents who prefer a more equal and informal client–counsellor relationship (Block and Greeno, 2011). Proactively using the strategies and skills outlined in earlier chapters will go a long way in addressing the challenges that clients and the nature of the therapeutic relationship may bring. These strategies and skills focus on creating an environment in which the young person can feel empowered to make choices about the counselling process, thereby addressing many of the barriers highlighted above.

There are a number of external influences that can impact on a collaborative therapeutic relationship. Here we will touch on the young person's family and social environment. For more information on external factors that may impact on the counselling process please refer to Chapter 5. An adolescent's family, as touched on in the previous chapter, may influence the counselling process, including the young person's ability to form a collaborative relationship. In particular, parental attitudes towards counselling, such as the perception of barriers, have been found to be correlated with poorer counselling outcomes (Block and Greeno, 2011). Family therapy could be considered as a response to challenges from the family system as long as the young person is happy for their family to be involved in the counselling process. Family therapy may help to create a supportive environment in which the adolescent is empowered to participate in the counselling process. For interested readers, we touched on family therapy in Chapter 7, and our book, *Relationship Counselling for Children, Young People and Families* (Geldard and Geldard, 2009), explores in much more detail how family therapy can be used in conjunction with individual therapy. Finally, an adolescent's peer group can impact on the development of a collaborative therapeutic relationship. A young person may resist a therapeutic alliance if not supported by peers or if their peer group holds negative views about seeking counselling support (Block and Greeno, 2011). Here, it is again important to focus on the proactive strategies and skills described in previous chapters in order to build a therapeutic relationship that provides the young person with the independence and autonomy sought during this developmental period.

In conclusion

As counsellors, we can maximize our opportunity to create and maintain a collaborative working relationship with a young person if we use the strategies described in earlier chapters. In particular, we believe that it is important to use a proactive process which makes use of typical adolescent communication processes.

When we recognize that a young person's interest or energy is diminishing it can be advantageous to proactively, in collaboration with the client, introduce a strategy that will interest and re-energize the young person.

As counsellors, we do need to be vigilant with regard to recognizing when the therapeutic alliance is starting to weaken. We can do this by trusting our own feelings and taking into account what we observe. Having recognized that our working relationship with a young person is starting to be compromised, we need to be open in sharing our experience with them and in giving them options to continue or terminate the session.

KEY POINTS

- counselling effectiveness has been shown to be related to common factors, including the therapeutic alliance
- being collaborative enables the counsellor to enter into a respectful partnership with the young person in addressing problems and finding solutions
- a counsellor needs to be proactive when recognizing that the therapeutic alliance is weakening
- counselling may need to address a young person's motivation and to emphasize their choice with regard to participating in the counselling process
- helping a young person to get in touch with hope and optimism can be useful in promoting change
- there are a number of potential barriers to maintaining a collaborative relationship; responding proactively to these barriers can help to limit the impact on the therapeutic alliance

FURTHER RESOURCES

The 'American Psychological Association (APA)' has interviewed Dr Wampold about what makes therapy effective. To see Dr Wampold's interview and explore other resources available, readers may like to visit the 'APA' website.

- www.apa.org/news/press/releases/2009/12/wampold.aspx

Part 3

Counselling Strategies

14

Symbolic Strategies

In this chapter we will consider five symbolic strategies, using:

- metaphor
- ritual
- symbols
- sand tray
- miniature animals.

Although these strategies are all symbolic, they are not interchangeable and need to be selected having regard to the relevant primary counselling function required at the time. (Readers may wish to refer back to Figure 9.2 regarding primary counselling functions.)

The use of metaphor

A metaphor is a figure of speech containing an implied comparison: it expresses one thing in terms of something else (Meier and Davis, 2011). Rather than making a direct description of some specific aspects, situations or processes within the client's life, the metaphor provides an alternative description. It uses an alternative picture and its contents to represent the real-life picture symbolically. If a young person says 'I'm trapped in a maze. Every time I turn a new corner it leads to a dead end' to describe feelings of frustration and inability to find resolution of problems, the maze is a metaphor for the real-life situation. In using metaphor, there is an underlying assumption that if some aspects of the metaphor agree with reality, that other aspects will also agree. This assumption can be useful in enabling a counsellor to make use of the client's metaphor to explore the client's perceptions of their actual situation more fully.

The value of using metaphor

Many authors have discussed the usefulness of metaphor in counselling and have suggested that it can be used to achieve the following:

1. Metaphor can be used to *heighten the client's interest* and thus improve co-operation with the counselling process (Sommers-Flanagan and Sommers-Flanagan, 1996). Because young people are searching, exploring and looking for new ideas, many of them enjoy the use of metaphor, and become interested and excited by the creation, discussion and expansion of particular metaphors. By becoming interested in a particular metaphor they are likely to become more fully engaged in the counselling process and become joined with the counsellor in the exploration of that metaphor. Joining can be enhanced if the counsellor matches and uses the young person's own metaphors and language.

2. Metaphor can be used to *stimulate insight* and present new constructs and paradigms for adaptive behaviour (Divinyi, 1995). By exploring a metaphor, a young person may more fully explore their life situation and its associated issues, beliefs and feelings, and discover aspects of their situation that had previously not been brought into awareness. Sometimes this will happen when a young person is surprised to discover unexpected similarities between the metaphor and their own situation. Thus, the use of metaphor may enhance insight and enable the young person to discover parts of themselves and issues which were hidden in the subconscious.

3. Metaphor may be useful in *providing solutions* to problems. Often, young people are unable to identify solutions to their problems because their problems overwhelm them. Metaphor can be used to create an externalizing frame so that the person is separated from the problem and can exercise control over it (Peterson, 1994). By using an externalizing frame, young people are able to put some distance between their own selves and the painfulness and/or vulnerability associated with reality. Sometimes a solution is then discovered within the metaphor, and this may trigger off ideas about how to provide a real-life solution.

4. Metaphor can be useful in *promoting behavioural change* because, as discussed, solutions may be self-generated through exploration of the metaphor (Brown et al., 1996).

5. Metaphor can be used to *promote significant life changes* involving not only behaviour but also roles. Consider the example of a young person who describes herself as rowing a boatload of friends down a river, while at the same time taking responsibility for steering the boat so that it does not crash into rocks. That person may discover other options, such as becoming a passenger in the boat, or taking a risk by leaving the boat and swimming to safety. As a consequence, she may see herself in a new role, as a person responsible for herself, rather than as someone who is responsible for the safety of others.

6. Sometimes, when using metaphor, the client will *gain therapeutically* by staying with the metaphor, without the need to make the transition consciously to discussion of real life. At other times, it will be useful if the counsellor helps the young person to relate the metaphor back to real life. For example, a counsellor might say 'I notice that you have talked about the possibility of jumping out of the boat on to dry land. What is it, in your life, that stops you from doing that?'

7. Metaphor can be used to help in the *exploration of conflicts* and increase empathy (Leavitt and Pill, 1995), to help in the exploration of feelings (Holland and Kipnis, 1994) and to give permission for the expression and acting out of thoughts, feelings and behaviours (Madonna and Caswell, 1991).

8. Metaphor can be used to *set the scene* for safe, non-threatening conversation and self-disclosure (Kingsbury, 1994). Because of this, metaphor is particularly suitable for use with young people. It provides a very non-threatening way of enabling them to talk about troubling situations and issues. Through the use of metaphor, the client is able to talk freely because, if they wish, they can disown those similarities between their own life and the metaphor which may be too troubling. This makes it safer for them to commence disclosure of those things that are difficult to discuss with someone else.

9. Metaphor can enable a person to *tell their life story* (Mazurova and Rozin, 1991). This is particularly relevant for adolescents. Sometimes it may be too hard initially for a young person to share their life story with a counsellor. However, they may be able to do this indirectly through the use of metaphor.

10. Metaphor can be used to help in the *avoidance of resistance* (Briggs, 1992). As describing life situations metaphorically is less threatening than direct disclosure, resistance is less likely to be encountered.

11. Metaphor may provide a *link to other elements* of the client situation (Angus, 1990). Sometimes the use of metaphor will enable the young person to recognize other aspects of their situation that initially did not seem to be important or relevant.

Ways to use metaphor

Counsellors working with young people can make use of metaphor in the following ways:

1. By exploring the young person's own metaphor.
2. By extending the young person's own metaphor.
3. By inventing a metaphor to describe a particular event or situation.
4. By using metaphor to tell a story.

Metaphor may also be used in conjunction with expressive arts, such as drawing, story-telling and guided imagery.

Exploring the young person's own metaphor

Young people often spontaneously use metaphors in their conversation. For example, a young person might say 'I've got a rocky road ahead'. Having introduced the metaphor of a rocky road to represent their expectations of future events, the counsellor now has an opportunity to take up that metaphor and use it. The counsellor can use the young person's own metaphor to invite them to describe the metaphor itself or parts of the metaphor in more detail. For example, the counsellor might ask 'Can you tell me more about that rocky road?', 'What is it like?' or 'Describe it to me'. Alternatively, the counsellor might invite the young person to talk about how it would feel to be travelling down the metaphorical road.

This might enable them to get in touch with feelings which are similar to those that will be confronted in the real-life situation, which the metaphor parallels.

Extending the young person's own metaphor

Using the example in the previous paragraph, a counsellor might use the metaphor by asking 'Do you think you will be able to ride your bike over this road or will you have to walk?' By asking this question, the young person's own metaphor can be explored further. There could be a number of outcomes from this. It may be that the young person will start to talk about different ways to reach their destination, and this may lead to the discovery of new ways to reach real-life goals.

> ❝Building on the young person's metaphor can enhance the relationship❞

Inventing a metaphor to describe a particular event or situation

Sometimes it can be useful for a counsellor to invent a metaphor to describe a particular event or situation. For example, a counsellor might say 'It sounds to me as though you are walking along the edge of a cliff and are a bit worried about falling off'. The young person may then accept or reject the counsellor's metaphor. If the metaphor is rejected, the young person might replace the counsellor's metaphor by an alternative one, by saying, for example, 'Oh no, it's not like being on the edge of a cliff, it's more like trying to cross a rickety bridge over a pond'. In this case, the counsellor can explore the differences between the two metaphors, and then focus on the client's metaphor.

Alternatively, the young person may agree with the counsellor's metaphor. In this case they might develop that metaphor and, for example, say 'What's worse, my best friend looks as though she is going to push me over the edge of the cliff'. In this instance, the metaphor immediately connects with the young person's real life. Of course, they might respond by saying 'I'm pretty good at walking around the edges of cliffs'. This would give the counsellor an opportunity to help them to explore their strengths and the ability to cope with difficult situations.

Using a metaphor to tell a story

This particular technique is used by narrative therapists (Hoffman, 1993). Sometimes young people will recount stories of their lives which suggest that they have behaviours or roles which have become pervasive. For example, a young person might incorporate all of the following in a description of self:

- I am the member of the family who stops my mother and father from fighting when they are intoxicated.

- I have been, and continue to be, responsible for preventing my young nephew from being abused by his mother.
- I act as peacemaker in situations when my friends and peers are in conflict.

This information suggests that the young person's self-perception is of a person who rescues others from unpleasant situations. The counsellor can describe the young person metaphorically as 'a rescuer', and can then encourage them to explore the possibility of using alternative metaphors (for example, 'observer', 'ostrich' or 'adviser') so that outcomes will be different.

Some narrative therapists encourage their clients to change their story or their metaphor by externalizing their problem (White, 2007). This approach encourages clients to see their problem as a separate entity, external to themselves. By externalizing the problem, clients often find it easier to loosen the restraints that stop them from changing.

The use of ritual

Rituals form a part of the lives of everyone. They are used to mark occasions, events and transitions. For example, many people help celebrate their friends' and relatives' birthdays by using rituals such as buying a birthday cake, singing a song and blowing out candles, or giving a present.

> " Use of rituals is a natural part of human behaviour "

Rituals have been used in ancient and contemporary cultures to mark transitions from one state to another, such as from childhood to adulthood. Examples of culture-specific rituals are the bar mitzvah in Jewish culture and initiation ceremonies in Aboriginal culture. Rites of passage involving initiation are often characterized by external 'ordeals', such as body piercing, tattooing and recitation of passages from holy books. The externally observable ritual associated with rites of passage is paralleled by inner changes within the person which, it is hoped, enable them to get in touch with inner resources in response to the external ordeals. In such situations, young people draw on their ideas about their new roles, and get in touch with those parts of themselves that they will need when preparing for these roles. The transition involves a movement from being *what is* to becoming *something different*, and this is symbolized in the ritual.

Rituals are especially important for young people because they are continually in a state of transition. They mark their transitions by using rituals to demonstrate to themselves and to others that changes are taking place. For example, a young person who has had their hair shaved off may be saying to peers and adults 'I now have the choice to present myself as I wish. I am moving from being a child controlled by my parents into becoming an adult who can control their own life'. The head-shaving is therefore a ritual which demonstrates the rite of passage from childhood to adulthood.

Young people need to engage in rituals or they may feel constrained and unable to develop. In ancient cultures, initiates were able to get in touch with many different roles, parts of self and images, which came from their society's beliefs and cultural myths.

Initiates were able to draw on these to enable the shift from one state of being to another. Unfortunately, contemporary Western society is somewhat impoverished in this regard as a consequence of the move from a multi-dimensional culture to an emphasis on individuality and separateness. It can therefore be useful to help young people get in touch with the various parts of their inner selves and to create and enact rituals to mark significant points in their journey to adulthood.

The use of ritual in counselling

Counsellors, in conjunction with their young clients, can proactively and imaginatively devise rituals for specific purposes. Such rituals can be devised to achieve catharsis and enable young people to move along their developmental path. For example, if a young client has been victimized and abused, they might be invited to draw a sketch of their oppressor and then burn it. The burning would enable them to act out their anger towards the person who abused them. This would allow for cathartic release and completion, and could be followed by cognitive resolution of issues.

Letter-writing can be used as a ritual. The process of putting down on paper thoughts and feelings that have not been openly expressed can often be cathartic and bring completion to troubling events. The letter does not have to be sent. Often, the ritual will be completed just in the writing of the letter.

Rituals can often be used in conjunction with symbols (see below). For example, where a young person needs to let go of an idea, thought, feeling or relationship, the young person might be encouraged to choose a symbol to represent the thing to be discarded. The symbol can then be ritualistically buried, disposed of in another way, or destroyed. During the ritual, the counsellor can help the young person explore their feelings and thoughts as they let go of their connection with whatever it is that the symbol represents. The main purpose of ritual is so that the young person can move on into a future that is less troubled by thoughts and feelings related to past events.

The use of symbols

Symbols for use in counselling young people are specific physical objects that can be used to represent feelings, thoughts, beliefs, people, relationships and a range of other things. It is useful for counsellors to have a collection of symbols available on a shelf or in a particular place in their room. Sometimes, counselling work with young people occurs in their own environment, and in this case anything that happens to be available can be used as a symbol.

A counsellor's own set of symbols should preferably include items that might be of interest to young people. These might include a rock, a piece of wood, a feather, an ornament, a toy, a miniature animal, a crystal ball, a pencil, a ball, a cushion, a candle, figurines, a box with lid, other containers and many other small articles.

The importance of symbols

Jung (1968) believed that symbols can be helpful in uncovering unconscious material. Accessing unconscious material can be particularly useful when working with young people because the process of adolescent individuation involves an interaction between the unconscious and conscious self. By using symbols, a counsellor may enable a young person to bring unconscious material into conscious thinking, with the consequence that they gain in self-knowledge. With increased self-knowledge, they are likely to have more choice and control about how to behave and change.

Symbolic work can access material from the unconscious

Using symbols

When counselling young people, symbols can be used for the following purposes:

1. To help the young person access and disclose information consciously.
2. To enable the young person to get in touch with, and explore, feelings, beliefs and thoughts.
3. To represent particular alternatives so that these alternatives can be anchored for comparison.
4. To represent polarities within self so that these can be explored.
5. To represent particular people so that role-played dialogue between these people can be created.
6. To represent something of positive or negative value that may need to be discarded or dealt with in some way.

For each of the above purposes, the young person is first invited to select a symbol or symbols to represent whatever is relevant. Sometimes they will choose a symbol and be sure that it is the symbol they want for a particular purpose. At other times, they may find it hard to choose a symbol and may spend a considerable amount of time picking up and putting down symbols, or looking at them and thinking about them. In this case, the counsellor may choose to give feedback about the process that is occurring. For example, the counsellor might say 'You seem to be having trouble picking a symbol'.

It is then likely that discussion will follow concerning the young person's difficulty in choosing a symbol, and this may yield useful information. It may be that they will say that no single symbol can satisfactorily represent the item in question. In this case, the counsellor might invite them to select more than one symbol to represent whatever it is that they are wanting to symbolize.

Once a symbol has been selected, the young person can be invited to describe the symbol and its qualities. The counsellor might say 'Tell me about this symbol', or ask 'What can you tell me about this symbol?' or 'What is this symbol like?' Notice that the questions do not ask the young person to interpret the symbol, but encourage them to describe the symbol itself. By inviting them to describe the symbol, it is possible that qualities of the symbol may be identified that relate to whatever the symbol represents, but which surprise the young person because they had not previously been recognized. These qualities and related ideas may have been previously suppressed in the subconscious. Thus, previously inaccessible subconscious ideas may be drawn out through discussion of the symbol and made accessible.

As well as discussing the symbol as described, the counsellor can focus on the 'here-and-now' experience involved in choosing and describing the symbol. For example, the counsellor might ask 'What are you feeling emotionally as you pick up that symbol?', 'What thoughts do you have as you experience that emotion?' and 'Can you tell me what's happening inside you (or what you are experiencing emotionally) as you describe the symbol?' Thus, the experience of choosing a symbol and describing the symbol provides an opportunity for the young person to examine and explore their current feelings and responses related to the tasks of choosing and describing the symbol. This Gestalt 'here-and-now' approach may enable the young person to get in touch with important unconscious and conscious feelings and thoughts. In addition, the counsellor might provide feedback statements about the young person's behaviour. For example, the counsellor might say 'I notice that as you are talking about your symbol, you are becoming more excited'. Throughout the process, the symbol remains important because of what it represents and the increased awareness that it engenders. When a symbol is an externalized part of a young person it needs to be treated sensitively and with respect for the young person's vulnerability.

Using symbols to access and disclose information

When a counsellor notices that a young person is having difficulty talking about a situation, event or experience, then it may be appropriate for the counsellor to invite them to choose a symbol to represent whatever is under discussion. For example, imagine a client who is having difficulty talking about what it is like at meal times at home. A counsellor might say 'Choose a symbol to represent what it is like in your house at meal times'. When the young person begins to describe features and characteristics of the symbol it is possible that they will also be able to get in touch with, and disclose, information that had been blocked from consciousness.

Using symbols to get in touch with and explore feelings, beliefs and thoughts

Sometimes it can be useful to ask a young person to choose a symbol to represent a particular feeling, belief or thought. The counsellor can then invite them to describe the symbol fully. In this discussion it is likely that additional information will emerge about the young person's internal responses to whatever it is that the symbol represents. The young person can also be invited to talk to the symbol, and to tell the symbol anything they might wish to say.

Imagine, as an example, that a young person picks a symbol to represent resentment which they have towards a particular person. That resentment might be annoying the young person by troubling them continuously. After representing the resentment by a symbol, the young person might be able to express anger towards the resentment and to tell it to go away. The young person could then be invited to reply as the resentment. The counsellor might say 'I want you to imagine that you are the resentment represented by that symbol and to reply to what has just been said to it'. Thus a dialogue is created between the young person and their resentment which might enable them to deal with the troubling feeling. Externalizing a feeling in this way can empower a young person to take control of a feeling and its troubling intrusions.

Using symbols to anchor alternatives for comparison

Often a young person will be confused about various alternatives or choices available to them. In such a case, the young person can be invited to choose symbols to represent each of the available choices. The selected symbols can be processed by inviting the young person to describe each symbol. Then the counsellor can give the instruction: 'Arrange the symbols you have chosen in this space here [counsellor indicates a space] to indicate the way in which they relate to each other'. By inviting the young person to do this, it may be that two alternatives which are similar are placed together and a third option that is quite different is placed a long way away. Discussion of the arrangement of symbols can then be useful in raising the young person's awareness with regard to available choices.

Use of symbols can assist in decision making

The young person can next be invited to touch one of the symbols and to continue touching it while talking about it and describing the advantages and disadvantages associated with the alternative that it represents. By touching the symbol while talking about it, the young person anchors ideas related to that symbol on to the symbol. By moving from touching one symbol and talking about it to doing the same with another, the young person is able to get in touch with the positives and negatives associated with each alternative.

Sometimes it can be useful for the young person to create a dialogue between alternatives. To do this the young person needs to be instructed to touch one symbol while arguing for the option it represents. The young person can then touch another symbol, representing a different option, and argue for that. As this process continues, the young person may decide to move the symbols so that their relative positions change as levels of preference emerge. The visual image the young person gets from observing the placement of symbols is helpful as it externalizes the conscious and unconscious ideas that they have by representing them symbolically in concrete form. The method described above, using symbols, should be compared with the selection of choices by using cushions, as described in Chapter 15.

Using symbols to represent polarities within self

Symbols can also be used to represent polarities within the self. While young people strive for personal identity and individuation, it can be liberating for them to realize that within themselves there exist opposites. For example, young people, like adults, have the potential to be kind or cruel, to love and to hate, to be generous and mean. We all have these characteristics within us. To accept that these polarities exist can be a relief to a young person and may allow them greater freedom to choose, and take control of, how they behave.

Where a client is troubled by uncertainty about such polarities, it can be useful for a counsellor to invite the client to select symbols to represent each of the polarities in question, and then engage in a similar process to that used when exploring alternatives. Through this exploration the young person may be able to integrate the two polarities and recognize that it is possible to move along the continuum joining them, and to take up a specific position on that continuum at any particular point in time. For example, on the generous–mean continuum, a young person may decide to be fairly, but not overly, generous in a specific situation, and to be mean in another situation. Thus, the young person is empowered and able to decisively take control of their behaviour, rather than being constrained by rigid thinking introjected from external sources. As with using symbols to select alternatives, this technique, and the technique described below, need to be compared with the psychodramatic technique where dialogue is created between cushions (see Chapter 15).

Using symbols to represent people so that role-played dialogue can be created

Symbols can similarly be used to create dialogue between a symbol representing a young client and symbols representing other people. When doing this, it is important for the young person to anchor what is being said in the dialogue by touching the relevant symbol while talking on behalf of the person it represents. This technique is particularly useful when a young person is troubled by relationship problems with others. In this situation it may provide insight into the young person's own issues as well as some understanding of other people's responses to them.

Using symbols to represent something which may need to be discarded

This has been discussed in the section on the use of ritual.

The use of a sand tray

Sand-tray work has traditionally been used with children, but can be extremely useful when working with young people (and also when working with some adults). When using the sand tray, we need to remember that young people are moving out of childhood, so it is important to reassure them that sand-tray work is not childish but is a technique that is used by some counsellors with adults. With some young people it may be useful to describe briefly the history of sand-tray work. Sand-tray work was initially developed by Margaret Lowenfeld (1967). She worked with children by using symbols in a sand tray to encourage non-verbal expression which was less influenced by rational thinking. She collected small objects, coloured sticks and shapes of paper, metal and clay and kept them in what her child clients called her 'Wonder box' (Ryce-Menuhin, 1992). This approach grew out of Lowenfeld's desire to find a way to help children to talk without the use of language.

Dora Kalff moved on from Lowenfeld's work to create a framework within which to work with young people and adults. She discovered that more could be gained through the use of symbolic representation in the sand tray than through talking directly. Kalff believes that sand-tray work gives the counsellor and client a non-verbal image that can represent meanings which are not yet known or fully grasped by either the client or the counsellor (Kalff, 2004). When counselling a young person, these non-verbal images can be explored as they place symbols in the sand tray. They can be invited to discuss the arrangement of the symbols and their relationship to each other. The counsellor uses the sand tray to help them to think by visually observing concrete symbolic representations of their ideas in the tray, so that these can be put into language.

Equipment and materials

You will need a sand tray, which is an open box. A large tray is preferable so that there is space for different environments within the tray. The tray must be rectangular so that there are corners to symbolize places of safety or entrapment. A square tray with sides measuring about 75 cm by 75 cm and about 15 cm high would be suitable. The depth of sand in the tray should be about 7 or 8 cm, giving a space between the surface of the sand and the top edge of the tray when the sand is spread evenly.

Symbols to be used in the sand tray consist of a variety of small objects that are chosen because they have properties which enable them easily to assume symbolic meaning. Items such as the following are useful:

- rocks, shells, stones and pieces of wood
- small boxes and containers with lids
- ornaments
- beads
- padlocks and keys
- toy fences, vehicles, animals, trees
- small figurines.

There are really no restrictions on the types of article that can be used as symbols. Some symbols may be better for representing abstract ideas; for example, symbols such as feathers or crystal balls.

Reasons for using the sand tray

When counselling young people, we need to remember the importance of keeping them interested and engaged in the counselling process. Most young people enjoy trying out new ways of expressing themselves. Using the sand tray provides a novel way for them to do this.

When using the sand tray some young people enjoy getting back in touch with their childhood experiences and happily regress into childlike behaviours. However, for most young people, the use of the sand tray involves very different behaviour from this as it presents an interesting challenge for them. They will work in a very mature and early adult way in setting up and processing the contents of the tray. Generally, with young people, the sand tray can be used to help the young person to:

- tell their story
- explore feelings, thoughts, situations and issues relating to their story
- explore past, present and future situations and events
- gain a cognitive understanding of the elements or events occurring in their life.

Using the sand tray

A good way to start is by inviting the young person to choose and use any symbols they wish to make a scene or picture in the sand to represent the life events or story they wish to describe. Sometimes a young person will start to tell the story without initially selecting any symbols. In this case the counsellor can interrupt and say 'OK, you've just told me that you were riding your bike over to your mate's place. Would you like to put a symbol in the sand to represent your bike and another one to represent your mate's place?' In this way the young person is encouraged to symbolize the story as it is told.

Some young people will spontaneously describe the story they are telling, as it develops in the sand tray. Other young people may start to build a picture, by placing symbols in the sand, without speaking. The counsellor then has a choice and can either just observe until the picture is complete, or can ask the young person to describe the story as it is created. The counsellor might say 'Would you like to talk about what you are doing as you build your picture?' However, while the picture is being constructed, it is important to observe the process carefully and to allow it to develop without unnecessary interpretation or intrusion. Some young people may prefer to complete their work in silence before discussing their picture. With other young people, counselling skills may be used to help process information, feelings and issues related to the picture, as the picture develops. Once the picture is complete, it needs to be fully processed by using counselling skills.

In processing a sand-tray picture it is important not to go beyond the meaning that is understood and used by the young person in connection with either the symbols or the picture. Feedback of observations about the placement of symbols in relation to each other is particularly useful when processing sand-tray work. For example, a counsellor might say 'I notice that your story has developed in this corner of the sand tray. Can you tell me what happens in the rest of the space?' In this way the counsellor can explore absences or omissions in the young person's picture as these may have significant relevance to the young person's story. Additionally, reflective skills are of value when responding to the thoughts and feelings expressed.

The purpose of sand-tray work is to encourage disclosure of material that will help young clients gain a greater understanding of themselves and of their current life situations. With this disclosure, and with heightened awareness of their situation, comes growth and the opportunity to feel empowered, make choices and have control over the direction of their lives.

The use of miniature animals

This technique has a high level of appeal to most young people. If it is introduced casually, but with enthusiasm, it can be very useful for initial ice-breaking and joining. When young people are invited to use this technique, they become engaged in a task that may be treated lightheartedly or with seriousness. Often, when they start using a lighthearted approach, important information of a serious nature will emerge, with the young person becoming actively engaged in the counselling process. The technique involves the use of miniature animals which are used as symbols to represent people in the client's family or social system. It is a projective technique that focuses specifically on exploring the interpersonal relationships of the young person.

❝Miniature animals can help in the exploration of relationship issues❞

The advantages of using a projective technique

There are considerable advantages in using projective techniques with young people:

1. Clark (1995) points out that projective techniques enhance the client–counsellor relationship, help in the understanding of the client and can be useful in clarifying goals and determining the course of counselling.
2. Reyes (1994) talks about the usefulness of symbols in shifting the perspective of a counselling conversation from an outside-in to an inside-out perspective. Using an outside-in perspective, the client and counsellor try to look from the outside at what is happening within the client, whereas by using an inside-out perspective, the client reveals through projection what is happening inside, so that it can be outwardly observed.
3. Waiswol (1995) points out that not only do projective methods facilitate communication, but they also allow for the overcoming of inhibitions, in effect bypassing resistance.
4. Projective techniques are less threatening for a young person because of the indirect way in which they access personal information.

The use of miniature animals allows sensitive material to be discussed in relation to the symbols used, rather than in direct relation to the young person's real-life situation. The young person is, during this process, able to compare information related to the symbols with real life, selecting what fits and rejecting what does not fit and what is too painful or risky to own. By using this technique, we believe that we often identify important things that need to be addressed in a young person's life which may not be disclosed using other strategies.

In this technique the young person projects ideas from their family, peer group or other social system on to the miniature animals that are used as symbols, but has the freedom to exaggerate or modify these projections. They may access ideas and beliefs that have been suppressed into the unconscious because of fears about the consequences of recognizing and/or owning those ideas and beliefs. Additionally, the method allows the young person to attribute characteristics and behaviours to the symbols that they might initially be unable to own with regard to the real-life situation. In so doing, the young person is likely to make important discoveries about relationships within their social environment and to take advantage of the opportunity to talk about them.

❝The use of miniature animals involves a projective process❞

Materials

A variety of small toy animals and other creatures, such as the following, are used in this technique:

- domestic animals
- farm animals
- jungle animals
- zoo animals
- dinosaurs
- reptiles
- insects
- sea creatures.

The animals and other creatures should preferably be made of plastic, and be as representational as possible of those animals. The appearance and nature of the animals will suggest particular behavioural and personality characteristics for them, enabling the young person to choose particular animals to represent particular people. This can occur more easily if the miniature animals look realistic, rather than being caricatures of animals.

Method

The method involves four well-defined stages:

1. Choosing animals.
2. Arranging the animals in a picture.
3. Exploring various configurations.
4. Rearranging the animals so that they are comfortable.

By using this structured process, the work moves from initial engagement through to active exploration of relationships, and then to satisfying closure involving processing of the projective work so that use can be made of the information disclosed.

Choosing animals

The counsellor begins by inviting the young person to choose an animal to represent themself. The counsellor will do this by saying 'Choose the animal that is most like you'. The wording of this instruction is critical. The aim is to encourage the young person to choose an animal that is most truly representative of themself, rather than the animal that they would most like to be.

Once the animal is chosen, the counsellor encourages the young person to describe the characteristics of the animal they have chosen as most like them. The counsellor might say 'What is this animal like?' or 'What can you tell me about this lion [or whatever animal the young person has chosen]?' It is often useful for the counsellor to follow up the young person's response to such questions by asking them to elaborate on their description. The counsellor might say 'Tell me more'. Finally, the counsellor might elicit more detailed information by asking the question

'Is there anything else you can tell me about this animal?' These supplementary questions often bring out significantly more useful information as these questions
encourage the young person to think more deeply about the animal's characteristics.
Often, when they do this, they will discover characteristics of themselves that have
not been previously recognized.

Once the young person has chosen an animal to represent themself, they are invited
to choose animals to represent other people in their social system. The counsellor
might say 'Choose an animal that is most like your mother/father/brother [and so on]'.
As each animal is chosen, the counsellor will invite discussion of that animal, using the
same questions as were used when the animal chosen to represent the young person
was discussed.

Arranging the animals in a picture

The counsellor then invites the young person to arrange all the animals in a picture.
This is not unlike the process used in family sculpting in family therapy. Once the
young person has arranged the animals in the picture, the counsellor can use statements
to feed back to them what they notice about the arrangement. The counsellor might
say 'I notice that the giraffe is a long way away from the lion' or 'All the animals are in
a circle'. These feedback statements are likely to encourage the young person to explain
the reasons why the animals have been positioned as they have.

Exploring various configurations

In this stage, the counsellor instructs the young person to move the animals into
different positions. For example, the counsellor might say 'Move the lion so that it is
facing the zebra' or 'Put the monkey next to the elephant'. Each time the young
person moves an animal, the counsellor can make use of circular questions to invite
the client to explore the emotional responses of the animals to the changes in position. For example, the counsellor might ask 'How does the rabbit feel with the
dinosaur standing close to it?' or 'How does the elephant feel when he sees the rabbit and the dinosaur together?' Throughout the process, the counsellor continues to
give the young person feedback by making statements of observations of the
arrangement of the animals. Through this process, the counsellor can explore various
configurations of closeness and distance between animals, and can help the client to
think about and discuss alliances, alignments, absences and hierarchical structures
within the animal group.

During this process, and throughout the use of the miniature animals, it is important for the counsellor to maintain the projective nature of the technique. The
counsellor does this by referring to 'that animal' or using its name (for example, 'the
lion'). The counsellor does not call an animal by the name of the person it represents

and does not imply that the animal is that person. Referring to the animal as 'that animal', or by its animal name, allows the young person to distance themself from the chosen animal, so that although it represents the young person or a member of their family in some way, it is not the same as they are. The young person can then project qualities, characteristics and behaviours on to the animal with safety. The animal, and not the person represented, becomes the owner of negative, positive, acceptable and unacceptable attributes. This enables the young person to feel freer in attributing negative and undesirable behaviours they may recognize in themselves and others but may not be ready to own.

To enable the young person to stay connected with the projective process, it is also advisable for the counsellor never to touch or move the animals. Instead, the counsellor instructs the young person to move the animals during the process, and observes how they touch and move the animals. By using this approach, valuable information may be observed which can then be fed back to the young person. For example, the counsellor might say 'I noticed that when you moved the rabbit near the dinosaur, you hesitated and eventually moved the rabbit a little further away'. The feedback of this observation might help the young person recognize suppressed information about the relevant relationships.

Rearranging the animals so that they are comfortable

Finally, the counsellor will terminate the projective process by inviting the young person to arrange the animals in a new picture so that they all feel comfortable. This allows the young person to close the process in a way which, it is hoped, leaves them feeling comfortable. There are usually differences between the termination picture and the initial picture. Sometimes it can be useful to explore the differences between these pictures. This may help bring into focus internal processes that may have taken place, during the work with the animals, in the young person's perceptions of the interpersonal relationships involved.

In summary

Symbolic techniques are particularly suitable for young people, as many are restless and like to do things that maintain their interest and concentration. Symbolic techniques particularly appeal to them because they involve choice of visual objects as symbols and also activity in the use of those symbols. Consequently, it is easy to keep a young person engaged, interested and enthusiastic with regard to the counselling process.

Using symbols also challenges the young person's new-found cognitive skills of abstraction and the use of imagery. It helps them to disclose material that may otherwise be inaccessible or difficult to talk about. Working with symbols, however, will not suit all young people. The counsellor therefore needs to be proactive in deliberately and actively selecting the appropriate strategy for each young client.

KEY POINTS

- symbolic strategies include the use of metaphor, ritual, symbols, the sand tray and miniature animals
- metaphor can engage a young person, stimulate interest, help in discovering solutions, and enable the young person to talk about difficult issues in a safe and indirect way
- rituals can be useful in enabling a young person to achieve catharsis so that they are able to continue along their developmental path
- symbols are useful in enabling a young person to access information that may be suppressed in the unconscious, and to talk about information that would be difficult to disclose in a counselling process which relied only on verbal conversation
- symbols can be useful in enabling a young person to explore alternatives, to explore polarities within themselves, and to engage in role-play dialogue
- sand-tray work can be useful in enabling a young person to tell their story, particularly if they have limited verbal skills
- miniature animals are especially useful for helping young people to explore relationship issues, particularly those within their own families

CASE STUDY

Imagine you work in a government-supported counselling centre specializing in working with individuals who have experienced trauma. You have been working with 17-year-old Jake for a few sessions now. Jake is finding it too overwhelming to discuss his early home experiences, often saying that he can't remember what happened when his father drank too much. He has shared that his mother has told him that his father got quite violent and Jake would make sure his siblings were safely hidden away. Jake has also talked about the way he tends to be the 'peacemaker' among his peers. What type of symbol work discussed in this chapter might help Jake to explore his early home experiences? What strategies might be helpful in exploring Jake's role as a 'peacemaker'? How might you go about introducing symbol work in your sessions?

FURTHER RESOURCES

There are a number of resources available that can support symbol work with young people. We particularly like those produced by 'Lighthouse Resources', 'St Luke's Innovative Resources' and 'Sandtopia' in Australia. Sand trays can be purchased from sandtrays.co.uk and symbols from 'Stepping Stones' in the UK.

- www.lighthouseresources.com.au
- www.innovativeresources.org
- www.sandtopia.com.au
- www.sandtrays.co.uk
- www.steppingstonestherapy.co.uk

15

Creative Strategies

Young people are in a phase of their lives where they are experimenting with new and complex cognitions. They are able to think more abstractly than before and consequently are generally able to understand and use symbols, metaphors and other forms of creative representation. Many young people use artistic methods to express themselves and convey meaning about their lives to others. For example, young people are often seen sketching and/or using graffiti to express themselves, release emotions and convey messages to other people. In this chapter we will discuss a number of creative strategies under the following headings:

- art
- role play
- journals
- relaxation
- imagination
- dream work.

These creative strategies are particularly appealing to young people because they involve activities that are interesting and dynamic.

Counsellors need to be sensitive to a young person's personal preference when selecting creative strategies. Some young people will readily engage in art or drawing activities, whereas others will feel threatened. Similarly, some young people will feel relaxed and comfortable when writing or using journals, whereas others will not. Role play and drama may be threatening for some young people, who may fear embarrassment and exposure, whereas others will enjoy the dynamic and energized processes involved.

Art

Visual arts are non-threatening for most young people and provide a way for them to express innermost thoughts, feelings and ideas. Drawing a picture can enable them to externalize thoughts or feelings, by placing them in a picture, so that they can be

observed as separate from themselves. Doing this is generally less threatening than owning painful thoughts and feelings directly. There is safety in the use of a picture, provided
that interpretation of the picture is done by the young person themself so that they have
control over what they choose to disclose.

Art can be used in counselling to:

- understand current issues and problems
- explore feelings
- develop insight.

There are many different ways of achieving these purposes by using visual art. We have
selected, and will describe, a few methods that we have found to be useful.

We recognize that some art therapists hold strong beliefs about their ability to be interpretative when using art in counselling. However, we prefer to leave interpretation to our
young clients. We believe that it is true that the presence of some commonly identifiable
features in works of visual art may be an indication of particular issues or psychological
problems. However, we believe that, generally, it is unwise for counsellors to attempt to
be interpretative. It is better for them to invite their clients to interpret their own work
and to disclose whatever meanings are relevant for them and safe for them to disclose. If
we become interpreters of our clients' work, we run the risk of contaminating their work
through projection on to their work of our own ideas, beliefs, feelings and issues.

Use of art to understand current issues and problems

Three ways to use art to help a young person to understand their current issues and
problems are:

1. The use of free drawing.
2. The use of a family picture.
3. The use of shapes, lines and colours.

The use of free drawing

In the course of getting to know a young person, a counsellor might discover that they
have an interest in drawing and/or art. Their artwork may be a valuable source of
information concerning their current issues and problems. Therefore it can be useful
for a counsellor to invite a young client to bring artwork, such as drawings and paint-
ings, to a counselling session. They can then be invited to talk about their art and to
share the feelings, thoughts, ideas and beliefs associated with it and the responses which
it evokes. The counsellor may then be able to give the young person positive feedback
with regard to their talents and skills and affirm their ability to use art as a means of
personal expression.

> **"It is advantageous to make use of a young person's creative interests"**

Art allows a young person to make strong statements that may be either socially acceptable or unacceptable. Currently, in Western society, there is considerable emphasis in the media, which targets the adolescent population, on violence, surrealism, sadistic and cruel themes, domination and Satanic and other undesirable rituals and practices. The covers of CDs, DVDs and magazines that target young people, often reflect negative and socially unacceptable practices. The same is true of some advertisements. Young people are likely to reflect this current cultural bias in their own artwork. As counsellors, we need to recognize the cultural influences at work in our society so that we do not incorrectly impose sinister or dysfunctional interpretations on our young clients' work. Instead, we need to invite them to explain the meaning of their work.

A useful way for a counsellor to begin to process a drawing or painting is to ask 'Can you tell me about your drawing?' This might be followed up by the question 'Can you tell me more?' The second question may seem unnecessary, but is often extremely useful because it encourages the young person to think more deeply. As a consequence, important information may emerge. It can be useful for counsellors to give concrete feedback, without interpretation, about attributes or features that they notice in a drawing or painting. For example, a counsellor might say 'I notice that this section of your picture is brightly coloured' or 'There is a lot of detail in this shape'. Such non-interpretative feedback will often result in a young client getting more fully in touch with feelings, meanings and ideas that are being expressed through their art.

If a drawing (or painting) contains pictures of figures or people, it can be useful for the counsellor to invite the young person to imagine that they are a person or figure represented in the picture. The counsellor might say 'Imagine that you are this monster. What are you like? Describe yourself to me'. A Gestalt therapy technique can then be used to invite the young person to continue imagining that they are the monster and, as the monster, to say something to another creature or part of the picture. For example, a counsellor might say 'As the monster, what would you like to say to the baby [or the clock] in the picture?' This might be followed up by asking 'As the baby [or the clock], what would you like to say in reply?' Thus, a dialogue can be created between various parts of the picture, enabling the young client to enter, in their imagination, into the underlying story. By doing this, they are likely to discover feelings and issues related to the story. Sometimes, when a picture is processed in this way, information may emerge which the young person spontaneously relates to their own life and issues. When this does not occur, the counsellor might ask questions such as 'Does this fit with anything that is happening in your life at the moment?' or 'Do you ever feel that way?' By asking these questions, information about the current issues relevant for the young person may emerge.

The use of a family picture

Inviting a young person to draw a family picture helps them to explore current family relationship issues and talk about them. There are two different ways of drawing a family picture: either a traditional representational picture of the family can be drawn, or the family can be depicted in an abstract picture, where shapes, colour and symbols are used to represent family members. Having provided coloured felt pens and paper, a counsellor might say 'Draw a picture of your family'. In response, some young people will ask questions about the type of picture required, in which case the counsellor might say 'When you think of your family what comes to mind?' and 'Just draw your family as you picture it'.

Sometimes a counsellor might ask a young person to use symbols, lines, shapes and colours to draw a picture of their family. The counsellor might say 'Draw a picture of your family using just lines, shapes and colours but nothing real' or 'Draw a picture of your family and use symbols to represent each member of your family'. Some young people may have difficulty understanding a request to use symbols in their drawing, and for them it can be useful to give examples of the use of symbols. For example, a member of the family could be drawn as a soft, cuddly cushion if that fitted their personality and behaviour, or a member of the family could be drawn as a worm if they were sneaky.

Processing a young person's drawing is critical in understanding their perception of relationships within the family. As noted above, the most essential part of processing a picture is to give specific, non-interpretative feedback about things the counsellor observes or notices. It can be useful to feed back information regarding the arrangement of family members in the picture. The closeness or distance between family members and the alignment of some with others are relevant. In giving feedback, a counsellor might say, for example, 'I notice that the blue shape which is your mother and the pink shape which is your father are on opposite sides of the page'. The counsellor might also find it useful to comment on absences and additions within a family picture. For example, 'I notice that there is a big space in this part of your picture' or 'I notice that your younger brother is missing from this picture'.

> ❝ **Interpretation needs to be made by the young person themselves** ❞

Significant information about a young person's family and about how the young person perceives relationships within the family can be gained through discussion which evolves in response to non-interpretative feedback. Most importantly, using this approach gives the young person an opportunity to talk about their family, without feeling vulnerable as a consequence of premature discussion of sensitive material. They have control over what is disclosed, so that they do not feel threatened but perceive the counselling environment as safe.

The use of shapes, lines and colours

The use of shapes, lines and colours combines many of the features of the previous methods of using art. The young person is asked to create a picture that represents their world just by drawing lines, shapes and colours, but nothing real. During the drawing they are invited to put themself in the picture. The counsellor might say 'Where will you put yourself in this picture?' Once the drawing is completed, the counsellor may invite the young person to imagine that they are the shape that has been drawn to represent self and to talk to other shapes in the picture. The counsellor might say 'I'd like you to talk to the shapes around you. Tell them who you are and what you would like to say to them'. In response a young person might reply by saying 'I'm a solid, strong shape and none of you can get the better of me'. The counsellor can then encourage the young person to imagine being another shape in the picture, and to reply to what was previously said. Thus, a dialogue can be created between parts of the picture. Finally, the young person can be invited to explore whether the dialogue between shapes in the picture relates in any way to their current life.

Use of art to explore feelings

Research confirms that drawing can be used to help a young person to get in touch with emotional feelings and explore them. Jolley and Thomas (1994) explored sensitivity of young people to metaphorical expression of mood in abstract art. Their results confirm that young people can associate formal properties of painting with the correct labelling and comprehension of mood. Additionally, Morra et al. (1994) found that young people could successfully draw symbols to represent emotions. Two ways of using art to explore feelings are:

- Drawing a picture of how you feel now.
- Drawing parts of self.

Drawing a picture of how you feel now

At times, during a counselling session, a young person is likely to experience strong feelings. At these times, a counsellor can invite them to draw a picture of how they feel at that moment. The counsellor can begin by reflecting back to the young person observations about their behaviour. The counsellor might say 'You sound angry. Draw a picture of how you feel emotionally now'. When the drawing is complete the counsellor can invite the young person to talk about the drawing. Drawing the emotional feeling currently being experienced can help a young client to talk about that feeling and the things that contribute to it. By expressing feelings, they are likely to feel better, with more positive feelings emerging.

Drawing parts of self

Young people often experience conflicting feelings that relate to different parts of self. For example, a young person might feel both ashamed and proud of a particular behaviour as described in the following example:

- Being ashamed might be because the behaviour contravenes socially acceptable norms. Knowing this might bring the young person in touch with the part of self that wants to be seen as responsible and mature.
- Being proud might be because part of the young person wants to confront and challenge society's norms.

Conflicting feelings such as these can be confusing and troubling to a young person who is attempting to make sense of their world. In such a situation, encouraging them to draw the two conflicting parts of the self can be useful. There are three ways in which this can be done:

1. Lines, shapes and colours might be used to represent the conflicting parts of self.
2. Symbols might be used to represent conflicting parts of self (for example, a hammer and a sea shell might be drawn).
3. Two self-portraits showing differing expressions might be used.

Usually, we give a general instruction which allows the young person to choose freely about how to depict the parts of the self. Drawing conflicting parts of the self allows the young person to visualize, explore and discuss them. If appropriate, a dialogue can be created between the two parts of the self as described in Chapter 14 in the discussion of the use of symbols to anchor alternatives for comparison. As a consequence, the conflicting parts of the self will, it is hoped, be understood and accepted, so that they can coexist comfortably.

Use of art to develop insight

The following strategies can be useful in enabling a young person to gain personal insight:

- Drawing a fruit tree to represent self.
- Drawing a self-portrait.

Drawing a fruit tree to represent self

As discussed in Chapter 14, the use of metaphor is a safe and easy way to enable a young person to get in touch with, and talk about, personal information. A fruit tree can be used as a metaphor for "self" to enable a young person to gain personal insight and disclose personal constructs, beliefs, feelings and issues (Geldard et al., 2009).

When using this technique, the counsellor might begin by inviting the young person to imagine themself as a fruit tree and prompting them with regard to features of the tree which might be included. For example, the counsellor might say, 'How big are you?', 'What shape are you?', 'What colour are you?', 'Do you have fruit?', 'Do you have leaves?' and 'Where are your roots?' Processing the young person's drawing of themself as a fruit tree requires the skills used when processing other metaphors (see Chapter 14). It is important for the counsellor to continue focusing on the metaphor, rather than what it might represent, until it has been fully explored. Doing this enables the young person to feel safe and, if they feel safe, they are more likely to be able to disclose information.

While processing the drawing, the counsellor might ask the young person to continue imagining that they are the tree by saying 'You are that fruit tree'. Then the counsellor might ask questions such as 'Where are you?', 'Do you have fruit all the time?', 'What happens to your fruit?', 'What happens to the fruit that falls from the tree?' or 'When the wind blows strongly how does the fruit tree feel?'

Encourage the young person to stay in role as the fruit tree

During processing of the drawing of the fruit tree it can be useful for the counsellor to observe the verbal and non-verbal behaviour of the young person, and give feedback about this. For example, a young person might appear to be very sad when saying that flocks of birds had eaten all their fruit. Feeding back what had been observed, the counsellor might say 'Fruit tree, you seem to be sad when you say that birds have eaten your fruit'. After hearing the response to this statement, the counsellor might continue by asking if there was anything the tree would like to say to the birds. This might be followed by encouraging dialogue between the tree and the birds.

To finish processing the drawing of the fruit tree, the counsellor might ask the young person whether anything that was said about the fruit tree fits with their own life. It is likely that this will be the case because the young person will have inevitably projected ideas from their own life on to the tree. If they have attributed feelings to the fruit tree, the counsellor might ask 'Do you ever feel that way?'

Drawing a self-portrait

Sometimes inviting young people to draw pictures of themselves can be useful in helping them to gain insight and to explore personal attributes, including strengths and weaknesses. As with art generally, interpretation is best done by the young client rather than by the counsellor. Interpretation can be encouraged by the counsellor feeding back specific aspects of the picture, such as 'You have drawn yourself as a very small person on a very large page' or 'Your hands are coloured green'.

Role play

Role play can incorporate the use of specific techniques from a variety of therapeutic models, including psychodrama, Gestalt therapy and rational emotive behaviour therapy. Role play is an excellent way of keeping the energy flowing. When role playing, many young people become actively involved in a very dynamic process. They can play out parts of their lives in a highly charged and physical way, which for many young people is easier and more comfortable than just sitting down and talking through issues.

Engaging in role playing does not suit all young people. Some are too self-conscious to allow themselves to play a role creatively. It is therefore essential for counsellors to check out whether a client is willing or not to use role play. Sometimes young people will be willing to try out role playing if it is made clear to them that they may withdraw if they find that role play is not comfortable or useful for them. It is often helpful, in setting up a role play, for the counsellor to model role-playing behaviour and then encourage the young person to join in. When using role play it is essential for the young person to feel in control of the process and also to feel supported in what they do. Thus, the counsellor needs to provide a balance between allowing the young person to take risks in the role play, and giving support.

Role play can be used for the following purposes:

- To gain an understanding of roles and relationships.
- To get in touch with feelings.
- To explore parts of the self.
- To make choices.
- To externalize beliefs or feelings.
- To practise and experiment with new behaviours.

Sometimes these purposes will overlap. It is part of the proactive counsellor's job to set up role plays opportunistically, at points in the counselling process where they are likely to achieve useful purposes and/or positive outcomes.

When a young person is involved in role play it is important for the counsellor to continually observe their verbal and non-verbal behaviour in order to detect underlying emotional feelings. When a counsellor notices behaviours that suggest underlying emotions, which are not being openly acknowledged, it can be useful to feed back the observed information to the young person. For example, the counsellor might say 'I noticed that, as you spoke, you clenched your fists very tightly, clenched your mouth and closed your eyes' or 'As you said that your voice sounded sad'. Such observational feedback is extremely important because it enables the young person to get in touch with emotional feelings which otherwise might not be recognized and might be being avoided because they are painful. Unfortunately, issues related to such painful emotions cannot be resolved unless the emotions are first accepted and released.

Use of role play to gain an understanding of roles and relationships

Role play can be useful in helping young people explore their relationships with others and gain a better understanding of the issues involved in these relationships, both from their own point of view and from the perspectives of others. During role play a young person can act out, both verbally and non-verbally, ways in which they behave in their relationships with others. By changing roles – that is, by taking the role of another person within a role-play situation – they may be better able to observe their own behaviours more objectively, and understand the behaviours of other people.

Exchanging roles can increase insight

Role play can be used to help young people recognize the difference between roles which they believe are functional and productive and roles which are dysfunctional and unproductive. They then have the opportunity to expand their repertoires of roles by learning to play new roles which have not been used previously.

The Gestalt two-chair approach

In helping to explore issues connected with relationships, role-play methods from Gestalt therapy, using two or more chairs, can be valuable. In the two-chair approach, if a young person has relationship issues with another person, that other person is imagined to be in an empty chair facing the young person's chair. The young person is then encouraged to talk to the imagined person in the empty chair, and to say to them whatever they wish. Some young people will initially be reluctant to talk to an empty chair. In order to support and encourage the client in this process, the counsellor can stand beside them and model the appropriate behaviour by making a statement on behalf of the young person to the imagined person in the empty chair. In doing this, the counsellor needs to use the first person and, speaking on behalf of the client, say, for example, 'Mary, I'm furious with you because . . .' (where Mary is the imagined person in the empty chair). The young person can then be invited to add to that statement, or to change it.

Once a young person has spoken to the imagined person in the empty chair, they can be invited to experiment, by changing roles, sitting in the other chair, and imagining that they are the other person. They can then be invited to reply, as though they were the other person, to the message that they initially gave when in their own chair. Thus, a dialogue can then be created with the counsellor directing the role play by indicating to the young person when to move from one chair to the other. This movement from chair to chair is necessary so that the young person anchors both themself and the other person in the correct chairs and speaks on behalf of the person they are representing at any particular time. At all times during this process, the young person must be encouraged to use 'I' statements. For example, when in the other person's chair, the young person may be tempted to say 'Well, Mary would say . . .' If that happens, the counsellor needs to give a clear instruction that this is a role play, and say 'I would like you to imagine that you are Mary and to talk on her behalf'. The counsellor might then model an 'I' statement which could be made by Mary, such as 'I disagree with what you have said . . .'

From the role-play experience, it is likely that the young person will gain an understanding of their own issues, feelings and thoughts, and will also gain some level of understanding of the other person's perspective. It is often not necessary to do any processing of the role play while using the two-chair approach, although it is likely to be useful to feed back non-verbal indications of emotional feelings and to explore them. During role play the young person will experience something of what it is like to be the other person, and that experience may be sufficient in itself.

After the role play is completed, the young person may be encouraged, through the use of counselling micro-skills, to deal with current feelings and thoughts. In this stage of the process it is likely to be counterproductive to ask the client questions about how the other person in the role play might have felt or thought. To do that would take them away from their own experience and invite them to try to do something which might be both difficult and threatening. They have already role played that other person and have some sense of what that person's perspective might be, and that is sufficient. Pushing the young client to talk about the other person's perspective might lead to resistance and possible unwillingness to return for further counselling.

The psychodrama approach using cushions

An alternative to using the two-chair Gestalt therapy approach is to use a technique derived from *psychodrama*. Psychodrama originated in the work of Moreno in the 1940s (Vondracek and Corneal, 1995). In this approach, the young person is initially invited to choose from a pile of assorted cushions of various colours and styles. Some cushions may have patterns on them, while others are plain, some may have fringes, some may be soft and fluffy and others thin and hard, some may be small and some large. The young person is asked initially 'Choose a cushion to represent you'. Having chosen the cushion, the young person is then asked to describe the cushion. The cushion is effectively a symbol for the young person so, by describing the cushion, the young person may well discover information about themselves which they have not previously recognized. Clearly, this is a projective technique.

The young person is next invited to put the cushion somewhere on the floor and to choose another cushion for the other person with whom there is a problem. It may be that there is more than one other person involved. If this is the case, the young person can be invited to choose cushions for each of the people concerned. Having chosen each cushion, the young person can be invited, if the counsellor wishes, to describe each of the cushions and, in doing so, the attributes of the person represented by that cushion may be discovered. Once the cushions are selected, the young person can be invited to place them in an arrangement on the floor to demonstrate their relationships. Thus, a relationships sculpture is formed. This sometimes involves one cushion being on top of another.

> **“ A cushion sculpture can raise awareness of relationship issues ”**

The young person is then coached in the use of the cushions, each of which represents a person. Initially, the young person is invited to stand behind their own cushion and to face another cushion representing the person who will be the target of whatever the young person wishes to say. As in two-chair work, the counsellor may stand beside the client and act as their alter ego, adding to what the client says and repeating what is said with more energy and emotional feeling. The young person can then be invited to stand in a new position behind the cushion of the person who was addressed, to role play that person, and to respond verbally to what was said. The process can continue with the counsellor directing a drama by moving the young person into playing the roles of different people represented by the cushions. When playing a particular role, the young person is encouraged to stand behind the relevant cushion.

This process is very similar to two-chair work but has the following advantages:

- It is more flexible because it allows for easy movement of cushions as relationships change in the young person's perceptions.
- Using cushions instead of chairs enables the drama to unfold more quickly, because rather than having to stand up and sit down each time a role change occurs, the young person can quickly move across from one cushion to another.
- Experiments can easily be done with regard to changes in relationships. For example, the counsellor may move a cushion nearer to another and check out the young person's response.

In this process the counsellor needs to direct the drama proactively. Thus, the young person is moved from cushion to cushion so that energy is maintained and a useful dialogue is created among the imagined participants. At some point in the process, the counsellor may observe that resolution of issues has occurred. The young person can then be invited to leave the cushions, sit down and talk about their current emotional feelings. When resolution does not occur, the counsellor can summarize the process so that the young person's awareness of feelings and issues is raised. By doing this, the possibility of future change is promoted.

It is important to note that it is generally not useful to talk about the drama itself because that would involve an attempt to re-run what has already been experienced. What is required is for current 'here-and-now' feelings to be explored after the drama has been completed. Dramas created using cushions provide an opportunity for a counsellor to proactively introduce paradoxical counselling skills and to make use of humour in the counselling process. Properly directed dramas may be energized, lively and, at times, amusing, capturing the young person's interest and imagination. Equally, it is possible for dramas to be intense and/or charged with emotion, with the young person displaying strong emotions by shouting or crying.

Readers who are interested in learning more about useful ways to help young people explore relationships both within and external to their family may wish to read our book *Relationship Counselling for Children, Young People and Families* (Geldard and Geldard, 2009).

The use of role play to get in touch with feelings

Role play as described above, using either Gestalt two-chair work or the psychodramatic method with cushions, can be used effectively to help young people explore and express emotional feelings. A technique which can be used when encouraging expression of feelings during role plays is the psychodramatic technique of *doubling*. In doubling, the counsellor stands beside the young person and acts as the young person's alter ego (as described in the examples above). If the young person is extremely angry with a friend called Martin, for example, it may be that the young person, standing beside their own cushion, will say 'I am very angry with you, Martin', using a low, flat and quiet tone of voice. If this were to occur, the counsellor could stand beside the young person and shout in a loud, energy-charged voice 'I am furious with you, Martin!' The counsellor might also add words, including expletives, from the young person's own declared vocabulary. Through this, the young client may be able to model on the counsellor and express feelings with energy and congruence. Thus, a dynamic role play can be created. This can be very cathartic for the young person because it can help in the release of strong feelings that may have been bottled up.

Some counsellors worry about using the techniques described with young people. They argue that modelling such behaviour in drama might encourage young people to behave disrespectfully or abusively in real life. Clearly, this is not the intention, so counsellors need to make sensible decisions about the suitability of this method for particular clients. Generally, when young people are allowed to express their feelings powerfully in a safe therapeutic environment, catharsis occurs with the consequence that they re-enter the outside world feeling more relaxed and thus more able to respond appropriately.

The use of powerful role plays needs to be seen in context. After completion of such role plays, a satisfactory counselling process will continue by encouraging the young person to explore adaptive options for dealing with the relationship problems in the future. These options will not be abusive or provocative, but will include the use of assertive behaviour and conflict-resolution skills. Strategies to enable young people to learn such behaviours and skills are described in Chapter 16.

The use of role play to explore parts of self

Young people often become troubled and confused because they are striving to establish an individual and unique identity which is consistent and congruent, but while doing this they are almost certain to experience different parts of themselves which are in conflict and appear to be inconsistent with each other. Young people are naturally complex, and have to deal with opposing desires and with conflicting beliefs and emotional feelings, which are certain to trouble them.

These different parts of self, although appearing to be in conflict, comprise the individual uniqueness of the young person. Young people who are able to discover and accept that their personalities are not homogeneous, but are made up of various differing parts, may experience a sense of relief which will enable them to integrate the differences within themselves. To help in the processes of discovery and integration, counsellors can use strategies similar to those described in Chapter 14, where the use of symbols to represent polarities within the self was described.

In order to explore conflicting parts of self, or polarities within self, cushions can be selected to represent these conflicting parts or polarities. For example, a young person may recognize their ability to be both vindictive and forgiving, and may be confused about how to integrate these two conflicting parts of self. In this case it could be useful to ask the young person to choose a cushion to represent the vindictive part of self and a cushion to represent the forgiving part of self. The cushions can then be placed on the floor on opposite sides of the room. Role play, as described in the previous section, can be encouraged to enable the young person to role play each of the parts of self. Thus, the young person can be supported in creating a dialogue between the two parts of self, standing behind one cushion and arguing for that part of self, and then moving to the other.

As the role-played argument continues, the counsellor might suggest that the young person experiment with taking up various positions on the line joining the two cushions. The young person can then be asked to describe what it is like to be in a particular position on that line and can be encouraged to move along the line to experience what it is like to move along a continuum between opposites. This process can help them to integrate the opposites by accepting them both as being available for use. The young person may then recognize that they do not need to be locked into either extreme, but can exercise personal control in making use of parts of self. Thus, they can move to a position on the continuum that suits them best at a particular time in a particular situation.

Recognition of the ability to move between extremes can be empowering

The use of role play to make choices

This strategy is similar to the strategy described in Chapter 14 on using symbols to anchor alternatives for comparison. However, in place of symbols, cushions are used to represent the various options. The young person is then encouraged to move from cushion to cushion. While standing behind a cushion, the young person argues for that option, as well as talking about both its advantages and disadvantages. Also during the role play the counsellor may help the young person challenge irrational beliefs, as described in Chapter 16.

The use of role play to externalize beliefs or feelings

Often messages from the past influence how young people believe they should behave in the present. These messages may be connected to cultural and spiritual beliefs, and may be very strong. For example, a young person may have incorporated a belief that they need to be nice to everybody regardless of the treatment they receive from others, but may be experiencing inner conflict because that belief is causing them to allow other people to be abusive towards them. Beliefs (or feelings) such as this can be externalized by encouraging the young person to choose a cushion to represent themself and a cushion to represent the belief or feeling. A dialogue is then created between the young person and the externalized belief.

The counsellor may take part in this dialogue and use paradoxical statements, in conjunction with humour, in order to challenge the young person into reviewing particular beliefs. For example, in the case described, the counsellor might take up a position behind the 'belief' cushion which represents 'being nice to everyone at all times'. The counsellor might then say to the young person who is behind their own cushion 'Look, mate, if someone pours red paint all over you, you should smile, shake their hand and say thank you'. The young person is almost certain to challenge this provocative and humorous statement. The young person then has choice about the degree to which they hold on to the belief, give up the belief or integrate part of the belief into a revised construct.

The use of role play to practise and experiment with new behaviours

Role play can help young people to gain better control over their lives by learning new behaviours (Gladding, 2012). During role plays the counsellor can use a technique from psychodrama called *mirroring*. Mirroring requires the counsellor to replace the young person during the role play. The role play is then continued, so that the young person can watch the drama unfold and gain a more objective awareness of themself with regard to interactions with others.

It can also be useful to record role plays on DVD or a digital device. This enables the young person to get feedback about their behaviour through observation of the recordings. Consequently, they may become more involved in changing their behaviours (Furman, 1990). Young people can be encouraged to repeat role plays using new and different behaviours which have been learnt through previous role-play experiences. This provides them with the opportunity to rehearse and practise new behaviours.

Additionally, videotaped role plays have been found to increase significantly the ability of young people to maintain an internal locus of control (Dequine and Pearson-Davis, 1983).

Journals

Many young people like writing. They enjoy writing diaries, lyrics and poetry, so that keeping journals is a task that is interesting, familiar and satisfying for them. This can be very useful in conjunction with counselling because it has been found that diaries written by young people provide an opportunity for them to disclose personal and intimate information (Rotenberg, 1995). They can record reflections about, and emotional responses to, present and past personal experiences. Journals can be written in a variety of ways, as described by Weinhold (1987). Daily logs and dream logs are especially useful.

The daily log

The daily log closely resembles a diary and serves as a running record of the young person's subjective experience of daily life. It is important for the daily log to be reviewed regularly so that the young person can reflect, gain insight and explore opportunities for positive change.

We find it useful to follow guidelines for writing daily logs adapted from those suggested by Nelson (1992). The young person is invited to record the events of each day using particular headings as follows:

- *What I did*: Under this heading the young person simply records the content of the day's events. For example, 'I got up', 'I had a shower', 'I had breakfast', 'I went to school' and so on.
- *How I viewed the day*: Under this heading the young person is encouraged to pretend that they are looking through a window at the day and to make comments such as 'Today was a disgusting day' or 'Today I got lots done'.
- *How I felt emotionally*: Under this heading the young person is encouraged to write down the positive, negative or mixed emotional feelings that were experienced during the day. For example, 'Felt great when I was eating my cereal, but felt depressed when I thought about going to school, but was happy when I arrived there'.
- *Relationships or lack of relationships*: Under this heading the young person is encouraged to record information about relationships with others, including both contact and lack of contact with others, and also the influences of others during the day. For example, 'I didn't see my father all day and wasn't allowed to go and visit my friends, but had an argument with Paula which made things worse'.
- *Things I learnt from today*: Under this heading the young person is encouraged to record anything they learnt from the day's events. For example, 'Today I learnt that not having any social contact with my friends is just as bad as not having any contact with my father'.

By looking at places in the journal where different choices could have been made, the young person may be able to identify possibilities regarding the use of different behaviours and/or the achievement of different outcomes. If used over a period of time, the young person may identify patterns of behaviour that have been either useful or unhelpful, and may identify goals for the future. Through discussion with the counsellor, they may also be enabled to explore underlying motivations for particular unsatisfactory behaviours, allowing change to occur.

> " **Diaries can be useful in identifying repetitive behaviour patterns** "

The dream log

Young people often show great interest in their dreams. Sometimes they are troubled by them, particularly if they are continually recurring. Dreams can be a very useful way of helping a young person to access important personal information. In order to be able to use the information from a dream, it is helpful if as much detail about the dream as possible can be remembered.

In cases where it is likely that a young person will return for further counselling, and it is clear that they would like to explore a dream, it can be useful to invite them to keep a log of the dream. To keep a log of the dream, they need to keep a pad of paper and a pen beside the bed. On waking, whenever they remember a dream or part of a dream, they need to write details in the log immediately. The log should preferably be written in three parts as follows:

- *Part 1*: The content of the dream, including a full description of what happened in the dream.
- *Part 2*: The emotional feelings experienced during the dream.
- *Part 3*: Thoughts about the dream.

The log can then be used as described later in this Chapter under the heading 'Dream work'.

Relaxation

Some young people find it helpful to learn relaxation techniques. However, it needs to be recognized that not all young people find this useful. For some, relaxation performed in a structured way is not helpful because they are unable to enter happily and comfortably into the experience. Relaxation training can be useful for the following:

- To help young people who are troubled by anxiety and/or tension.
- To teach young people how to cope actively with anxiety and a variety of other problems that result from stressful situations (Forman, 1993).
- As a prerequisite to the use of guided imagery.

How to help a young person learn to relax

First, it is important to determine the young person's attitude to taking part in a relaxation exercise. Many young people will have already been exposed to some form of relaxation exercise. Some of them will have found this useful, and others will not. There may be little point in trying to help a young person learn relaxation techniques if they have previously had unsatisfactory experiences with them.

When undergoing any relaxation technique, it is important for young people to feel that they are in control rather than the adult who is helping them to learn the relaxation process. Failure to observe this requirement disempowers the young person and might lead them to believe that they need to be dependent on the help of an adult in order to achieve their goals.

Before starting the relaxation procedure, the young person needs to be informed that they have a choice about whether to observe the instructions given by the counsellor or not. They also need to be told that they have a choice about whether to continue with the exercise or not. It is important to rehearse the way in which the young person would stop the relaxation exercise, if that was what they wanted to do. It is insufficient for a counsellor just to say 'If you want to discontinue this exercise, discontinue it'. It is important to ask how they will stop the exercise. Will they raise a hand, will they open their eyes and say 'Stop' or will they just get up and say 'I don't want to do this any more'? Failure to go through this process of checking out how the young person will discontinue, if they want to, may make it difficult for some young people to feel that they are in control.

Relaxation cannot easily occur in a brightly lit, noisy environment. For relaxation training to be most effective, the environment needs to be one in which there are no intrusive noises and where the lighting is subdued. Young people undergoing relaxation training need to be seated in a comfortable position. We prefer to ask them to make themselves as comfortable as possible on a bean bag. Asking them to lie on the floor would not be appropriate because for some young people, particularly those who have been abused, lying on the floor may make them feel vulnerable and unsafe. With a bean bag, they have more control; they can shape the bean bag so that they are reclining, if they wish, or sitting in a more upright position, if that is what they prefer.

Giving the relaxation instructions

In giving relaxation instructions, it is important for the counsellor to talk in a fairly monotonous, flat tone of voice. There needs to be a pause between all statements to allow time for the young person to respond to instructions and continue relaxing. The relaxation process can be started in the following way:

Make yourself comfortable on the bean bag by shuffling yourself around. When you are ready, close your eyes. Notice the way you are sitting and recognize any part of you that is not comfortable. If any part of your body is not comfortable, move it.

Check your feet and your legs. Are they comfortable? If not, shuffle them into a better position.

Check your body. Is it comfortable? If not, move it.

Check your arms, your neck and your head. Make them comfortable.

If necessary, move completely to get more comfortable.

Once the young person is comfortable, the relaxation process continues as the counsellor says words such as:

During this exercise breathe naturally, and silently say to yourself the word 'relax' every time you breathe out.

Whenever there is silence, you might want to focus on your breathing, and say 'relax' silently to yourself, each time you breathe out.

If intruding thoughts come into your head, don't worry about them, but focus again on your natural breathing.

The counsellor can then observe the young person for a short while and, whenever they breathe out, say quietly 'relax'. The young person is then helped to relax their body progressively from their feet to the top of their head as the following instructions are given:

Wiggle your toes and your feet and allow them to feel relaxed.

Notice your breathing. [The counsellor now says 'relax' each time the person breathes out for a few breaths.]

Now notice your feet. Wiggle your toes, and as you breathe out allow them to relax. Notice your legs. Tighten the muscles in them gently. As you breathe out say 'relax' to yourself, allowing your legs to relax. Let the relaxed feeling flow from your legs down through your feet into the floor.

Notice your lower back and your stomach. Gently tighten the muscles in them, and as you breathe out, silently say 'relax' as you let the muscles relax.

Allow a relaxed feeling to flow from your stomach, through your lower back, your legs and your feet into the floor.

Relax, relax, relax [said quietly in time with breathing].

Notice your chest and your arms, tighten the muscles in them gently and let them relax as you breathe out.

Allow the relaxed feeling to flow from your arms, down your chest into your legs and your feet and into the floor.

Notice your hands, tighten the muscles gently, let them relax and allow the
relaxed feeling to flow from your hands through your arms, your body, your legs to
the floor.

Allow yourself to sink deeper into the bean bag, and focus on your breathing, silently
saying 'relax' every time you breathe out.

Tighten the muscles in your head and neck slightly, and allow yourself to relax as you
breathe out, notice the relaxed feeling flowing from your head down through your
body to your feet and out into the floor.

You can continue relaxing by saying 'relax' to yourself each time you breathe out.

The counsellor can now allow some time for the young person to experience being
relaxed and can say:

I won't say anything for the next two or three minutes. I'll just let you practise focusing
on your breathing and on saying 'relax' to yourself. If intruding thoughts come into
your head, don't worry about them, just focus on your breathing.

After a while the counsellor can say:

It is time for you to start to move towards finishing this relaxation exercise. I'd like you
to start preparing yourself for becoming alert and active again.

Then, with a pause between statements, the counsellor can continue by saying:

Instead of noticing your breathing and saying 'relax', notice that you are sitting on
the bean bag.

Shuffle around a bit on the bean bag to become aware of it.

Move your head and neck, and open your eyes.

Look around and notice things that are in the room with us.

When you are ready, get up carefully, remembering that you have been relaxed, so it
might not be a good idea to stand up suddenly.

After teaching relaxation, it is sensible to tell the young person that they may be feeling
more relaxed than usual, and that it may therefore be inadvisable to engage in any activity which demands a high level of alertness. For example, if the young person has
become very relaxed, it would not be sensible to send them off to ride a bike through
traffic, along a busy street, because they may not be alert enough to cope properly. This
could result in an accident.

Once a young person has learnt to relax, it can be useful to help them to general-
ize this relaxed behaviour to situations that are anxiety-provoking or stressful. This can
be done by inviting them to stand upright, and then suggesting that they take a few
deep breaths (do not allow hyperventilation to occur). While taking these breaths, tell

them to allow their body to relax as they silently say 'relax' to themself. Thus, in a standing position, they learn to relax the muscles in their hands, arms, neck, shoulders, body and legs so that, although they are standing, they become relaxed by taking a few deep breaths. This ability to relax when standing may be useful when confronting stressful situations.

Imagination

Four important ways to use imagination are:

1. To change self-perceptions.
2. To establish new emotional and behavioural patterns.
3. To reconstruct negative memories.
4. To go on an imaginary journey.

In achieving the above goals, imagination enables the young person to replace old memories with new memories that are more helpful and adaptive.

Use of imagination to change self-perceptions

The self-perceptions of a young person originate from childhood but will change and develop during adolescence. Unfortunately, past self-perceptions tend to continue to influence the way young people think about themselves and to affect their relationships with other people.

Traumatic and/or abusive experiences in childhood and adolescence often lead to dysfunctional and unhelpful self-perceptions. For example, young people who have been abused might believe that they are undesirable, unworthy of affection, helpless, untrustworthy and unreliable. Such negative self-perceptions may mean that they continue to behave in ways that are consistent with, and support, these beliefs. Imagination can be used to help young people change such perceptions and beliefs.

The first step in using imagination to change self-perceptions is to bring the influence of unhelpful beliefs into full awareness. This is done by discussing current behaviours and the way in which they are influenced by entrenched thinking. The counsellor also needs to raise the young person's awareness of behaviours that are used to avoid painful thoughts about themselves. For example, they might present a façade of being tough and robust, but this façade might be a way of hiding feelings of helplessness and vulnerability.

Once negative self-perceptions and their origins have been identified, guided imagery can be used to bring about change. The young person is encouraged to remember the negative past experiences (where, for example, they may have felt victimized or helpless). Then, in a guided imagery exercise, they are encouraged to re-live those experiences but to change the way they behaved so that they can feel good about themself.

The process used is as follows. First, the counsellor uses a relaxation exercise and then, when relaxed, the young person is invited to remember a negative experience from the past. Then, while continuing to stay relaxed with their eyes closed, they are invited to describe the scene and events which they are imagining from the past. Next, the counsellor asks the young person to suggest ways in which they might change that picture, or the events, so that their feelings and the outcomes would be different. The young person is then invited to return to the beginning of the imagined scenario and to rerun the script, so that events occur differently with positive outcomes and so that they experience good feelings about themself.

In such an exercise, a young person might imagine events from the past where they were bullied in the playground as a young child by several older and bigger children. During the re-experiencing of these memories, they might be encouraged by the counsellor to replace the aggressive and violent behaviours of the bullies with behaviours which would indicate that the young person was accepted and valued by peers in the playground. This would allow them to get in touch with their positive attributes such as friendliness, helpfulness, sense of humour and loyalty. The counsellor might then highlight these attributes, make them newsworthy and help the young person to construct a new, different and positive perception of themself. This new perception might, in the future, enable the young person to engage in positive social relationships.

Use of imagination to establish new emotional and behavioural patterns

This is a rational emotive behaviour therapy approach (Dryden et al., 2010). Sometimes young people are troubled by failures from their past. These may be either recent past experiences or experiences which occurred some time ago. For example, a young person might remember an episode in the playground at school, involving three or four other students, which resulted in an abusive exchange. As a consequence, they may have been called to the principal's office, along with the students involved and a teacher who witnessed the event. During the discussion in the principal's office the young person may not have found an opportunity to explain their perceptions of the event. They may have been prevented, through interruption, directions by the more powerful members in the meeting and their own ignorance of the procedures of the meeting, from putting their point of view forward. This encounter may have left them feeling powerless, disrespected and inadequate.

In order to change the young person's feelings about the event, the counsellor might first use a relaxation exercise. While relaxed, the young person might be invited to imagine the events as they actually occurred and to talk about them as they are imagined. The counsellor might then invite them to re-run the story in their imagination and to describe it so that events occurred differently and in a way that was satisfying for them. By re-running the revised story several times, it is hoped that the young person will become less troubled by the past memories. They may also begin to feel more comfortable and confident that in the future they will have the skills to deal with similar situations in an appropriate and empowering way.

Use of imagination to reconstruct negative memories

Often young people who have been traumatized have difficulty putting their story together in a sequence which makes sense to them. This may be because some pieces of information are missing from their memories. The fragmentation of their stories prevents them from feeling a sense of completion of their experiences, resulting in anxiety. In addition, as their stories are fragmented, they may experience a sense of not having been able to control events, because the events are not remembered as following a logical and understandable sequence. They may also be troubled by flashbacks which result from triggers that are difficult to identify. If traumatic events can be reconstructed so that they follow a complete sequence that is fully understood, then a sense of control may be achieved, and triggers may be identified and reduced in power. Additionally, ways to manage responses to triggers may be explored.

A good way to help such young people to reconstruct their story, so that it makes sense for them, is to help them to imagine the story when relaxed, and to talk about it as they imagined it, so that the story flows from beginning to end. In this way they can make sense of what happened. It does need to be remembered, however, that the story as recounted may not in fact be completely accurate, but may include material that has been invented.

The first step in the process is for the counsellor to invite the young person to relax and, while relaxed, to recall their memory of the traumatic experience. During their recollection the counsellor might promote exploration of the event by asking questions such as, 'When you remember what happened, do you see any pictures in your mind?', 'What are you wearing?', 'Are you aware of any sounds, smells or activity around you?' The purpose of asking such questions is to help the young client to get in touch with the more sensory components of their experience because triggers associated with traumatic events are often related to sensory experiences. Once such triggers are recognized, the young person is likely to be better able to deal with them. After this exercise, the young person is encouraged to identify any new or enlightening information which may have changed their original perceptions of the event. These new insights may help them make sense of the original trauma.

Use of imagination to go on an imaginary journey

Imaginary journeys can be used either to take young people into a pleasant place which they might like to visit in their imagination in the future, or to help them get in touch with past troubling experiences.

To get in touch with a pleasant place

In helping a young person to get in touch with a pleasant place, continue a relaxation exercise by inviting them to move, in their imagination, to a place that they find pleasant and enjoyable. Consequently, they have the opportunity to choose a place, which for them will be comfortable and pleasant. While they are imagining the pleasant place with their eyes closed, the counsellor might invite them to talk about their imagined experience.

To get in touch with past troubling experiences

When the imaginary journey is used to enable a young person to get in touch with past experiences which may have been troubling, the counsellor takes them on an imaginary journey which leads them back to a time and place where the events occurred. The young person may then be invited to imagine, as a sequence, that:

1. They are looking at the troubling scene from the past.
2. They are part of the scene.
3. They are able to say anything they like to anyone in the scene, to hear responses from those people and to do anything that they would have liked to have done at the time of the actual event.
4. They can complete their imaginary journey by doing or saying anything that they wish to do or say before leaving the journey.
5. Finally, they are invited to leave the imaginary journey and be fully aware of their actual situation in the counselling room.

After the journey has been completed and they have been invited to open their eyes and leave the journey, they may be invited to draw or sketch, using coloured felt pens, anything that comes into their mind with regard to the journey. After completing the drawing, they may be invited to talk about it. The counsellor may comment on the picture, with statements such as 'I notice that there is a large red blotch over here' or 'I notice that there is a space in this part of the picture'. Thus, by making non-interpretative statements of fact about the picture, the young client is invited to disclose information about their picture, if they wish, without being troubled by intrusive questions.

> **"Processing an imaginative journey by drawing a picture is non-threatening"**

An alternative is to use a more open and less structured imaginary journey, so that the young person has freedom to choose where they go in their imagination. For example, a counsellor might suggest that they imagine they are standing in front of a door, and that when they open the door they will see a scene which they remember. This sets a very open agenda, but often the scene remembered will be a very significant one. The numbered sequence described above can be used so that the young person is invited to look at the scene, move into the scene, talk to people in the scene and do anything they wish to do before leaving the scene. It is important that they are invited to leave the scene, in their imagination, in the same way as they entered. Thus, they should be invited to come back through the door, close the door and leave. By doing this, in their imagination, they have completed their journey and are able to resume life within the counselling situation rather than being invited to stay in the imaginary situation.

The journey can be processed by drawing a picture, as described above. It is likely that, when a counsellor processes the experience of going on an imaginary journey of this type, the young person will disclose information about real-life situations. This provides an easy opportunity for the sharing of personal information.

Dream work

Most young people are very interested in their dreams. They tend to be intrigued by them and often attach particular significance and importance to them. Sometimes they will believe that their dreams are almost prophetic in nature and consequently will wish to have them interpreted. We believe that the only person competent and able to interpret a young person's dreams is the young person themself. It is their own interpretation that matters.

As discussed previously, young people who wish to work with their dreams may be encouraged to keep a dream record, made immediately on waking. Sometimes, however, young people will come to a session without a journal, but remembering a dream quite clearly and wishing to discuss it.

Two different ways of processing dreams will be discussed: one is through the use of art, and the other is a psychodramatic or Gestalt therapy approach (there is considerable overlap between psychodrama and Gestalt therapy).

Use of art to process dreams

When using art, the young person is invited to draw or sketch a picture of their dream, using coloured felt pens. This picture may be a representational picture or it may be abstract with just shapes and colours. Sometimes, while the picture is being drawn, the young person will talk spontaneously about the dream. At other times, they will draw silently and, after the picture is complete, the counsellor might say 'Tell me about your picture'. This question can be followed up by the useful statement 'Tell me more', which encourages the young client to think more deeply and disclose important information which comes into their awareness. Further processing can occur by the counsellor inviting them to imagine that they are an object or person within the picture. As that object or person, they can be invited to describe how they feel and what they are thinking. They may also be asked if they would like to say anything as the object or person. While imagining that they are the object or person, the young person might be asked to say something to another object, person or animal in the picture. They can then be invited to imagine that they are the object, other person or animal, and respond to what was said. Thus a dialogue can be created between two parts of the picture. This dialogue will often raise new and unexpected information for the young person that can contribute insight into a troubling issue or event.

Psychodramatic processing of a dream

In the psychodramatic approach to processing dreams, the young person is first invited to describe the dream. Next they are invited to choose cushions to represent significant items or people in the dream. The story is then re-told with the cushions being placed on the floor in an arrangement that creates a picture of the dream. The young person is then invited to take up positions by standing behind relevant cushions. When at a cushion, the young person is asked to experience what it would be like to be that item, object or person within the dream, and talk on behalf of the item, object or person. By moving from cushion to cushion, dialogue is created between various parts of the dream. During the psychodramatic process, the counsellor needs to observe and give feedback about both verbal and non-verbal behaviour. Thus, the young person's awareness of emotions and associated thoughts is raised and these can be processed.

In summary

We have described a number of creative strategies that can be used in helping young people to explore issues, deal with their feelings and make changes. All of these creative strategies require activity on the part of the young person, and must therefore be chosen to suit the abilities and needs of the young person. We strongly believe that it is essential to give young people choice about participation in activities during counselling. With all the strategies discussed, the technique itself is of limited value unless the work done is properly processed by exploring the thoughts, emotional feelings, attitudes and beliefs that emerge during the process.

KEY POINTS

- creative strategies include the use of art, role play, journals, relaxation, imagination and dream work
- artwork can be used to help a young person understand current issues and problems, explore feelings and develop insight
- it is preferable for interpretation of artwork to be made by the young person themself

- role play engages a young person in an active and dynamic way and can be used to help them get in touch with feelings, explore relationships, explore parts of self, make choices and practise and experiment with new behaviours
- daily logs and dream logs can be useful in raising a young person's awareness of emotional and relationship issues and of unhelpful repetitive behaviours
- relaxation exercises can be helpful in enabling young people to reduce tension, particularly in stressful situations
- the use of imagination can be helpful in enabling a young person to change their self-perceptions, to establish new emotional and behavioural patterns, to reconstruct negative memories, to get in touch with troubling experiences and to move into a comfortable space

CASE STUDY

Mid Term 3, an art teacher at the school in which you work as a Guidance Counsellor referred one of her students saying she is quite concerned about the violent content of 14-year-old Emily's artwork. The teacher also noted in her referral that while Emily was shy in Term 1 she was still clearly engaged and doing quite well at school. Things changed in Term 2, with Emily becoming more withdrawn and her grades dropping. How might you engage Emily in a counselling process to which she did not self-refer? Would you encourage Emily to process her existing artwork? How? What other creative strategies in this chapter could you use to support Emily?

FURTHER RESOURCES

The 'Expressive Therapies Institute of Australia', founded by Mark Pearson and Helen Wilson, provides training in expressive therapies, including symbol work and creative strategies, throughout Australia and South East Asia. They also provide a description of the various expressive modalities and useful links for practitioners on their website, including a list of publications the Institute has produced. For workshop and training options in the United Kingdom, please see the 'Integrative Therapies' website.

- www.expressivetherapies.com.au
- www.integrativetherapies.co.uk

16

Behavioural and Cognitive Behavioural Strategies

In Chapters 14 and 15 we looked at symbolic and creative strategies. These can help young people to understand and gain insight into themselves and change their behaviours by becoming more fully aware of troubling emotions and underlying issues. Symbolic and creative strategies are also useful in helping young people to define, understand and change beliefs and values, as a consequence of which changes in behaviours will often occur. In this chapter we will discuss behavioural and cognitive behavioural strategies. These methods rely on structured, goal-oriented approaches, collaboration between an active counsellor and an active young person and emphasis on current issues (Kutcher and Marton, 1990). Behavioural and cognitive behavioural strategies specifically target behaviours, whereas symbolic and creative strategies influence behaviour indirectly. In targeting behaviours directly, there is an assumption that when behaviours change, emotional feelings will also be positively influenced.

Behavioural and cognitive behavioural strategies have been successful, to varying degrees, when working with young people who are anxious, depressed, aggressive, oppositional and unmotivated, and with young people who have difficulty with interpersonal and social skills (Valliant and Antonowicz, 1991; Finch et al., 1993; Wilkes et al., 1994; Biswas et al., 1995; Reinecke et al., 2006).

Behavioural and cognitive behavioural strategies will be discussed under the following headings:

- self-control
- challenging self-destructive beliefs
- anger management
- assertiveness training
- setting lifestyle goals
- making decisions.

Self-control

There are four stages involved in learning behavioural self-control:

1. Identification of problem behaviour.
2. Observation of behaviour.
3. Evaluation of behaviour.
4. Setting consequences for behaviour.

When self-control issues need to be addressed it can be useful for a counsellor to describe these stages to the young person so that, together, they can plan a programme for behavioural change.

Identification of problem behaviour

In counselling, a young person may be able to identify one or more behaviours that have been causing problems. For example, they may be fighting with a younger sibling and getting into trouble as a result. A young person with this sort of problem might initially complain about a younger brother's behaviour and blame him for what is happening. It is the proactive counsellor's responsibility to help the client recognize that they cannot change other people's behaviours. To help them acknowledge this, a counsellor might ask questions such as 'Do you think your brother is likely to change?' and/ or 'Do you think that you can change your brother's behaviour?' As a consequence of these questions, which challenge the young person's beliefs, they will hopefully recognize that the only behaviours they can change are their own.

Observation of behaviour

If young people wish to change their behaviours, the first thing they need to do is observe their current behaviours so that they can fully understand them and their consequences. Often, simply observing when an unwanted behaviour occurs, and when it does not occur, will result in change in that behaviour. For example, if a young person notices each time conflict arises with a younger sibling, then the very act of observing this may decrease the conflict. This is because, as soon as the targeted behaviour starts to occur, the young person's awareness of it will be raised, so that action can be taken immediately to change what is happening.

The use of a diary

The use of a diary may be helpful to those young people who would like to observe their unwanted behaviour. They can record situations and/or events where the unwanted behaviour occurs, and record both antecedent behaviours and the consequences of the unwanted behaviour. A good way to keep a diary for this purpose is to use a notepad where the pages are divided into three columns headed:

1. The behaviour of others and self prior to the situation/event (and my feelings).
2. Description of the situation/event (and my feelings).
3. The outcome for self (and my feelings).

Thus, under each heading, the young person is invited to describe their feelings at the time.

It can also be helpful for the young person to divide each day in the diary into parts so that changes in the frequency of the targeted behaviour can be determined. Suitable parts might be:

- before school
- during the morning
- during the afternoon
- after school.

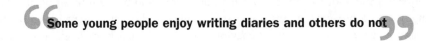

Some young people enjoy writing diaries and others do not

The number of times the unwanted behaviour happens in each of these parts of the day may give useful information about times and situations where problems in management of the unwanted behaviour occur. Keeping a diary in this way can be 'homework' for the young person between counselling sessions. However, it needs to be remembered that young people will only do homework of this kind if they find the task interesting and useful.

Evaluation of behaviour

In this stage the young person is invited to evaluate their own behaviour against criteria which they set for themselves. For example, a young person may make a decision to try to reduce the number of times they fight with their younger brother by 50 per cent. Setting a level of 50 per cent is more realistic than trying to extinguish the behaviour completely, which might set them up for failure.

Young people often become discouraged if they believe that they are not making good progress in achieving change. To avoid this and to provide motivation and incentive for continuing change, a young person can be encouraged to monitor quantitatively the success actually being achieved in meeting predetermined goals. To make the exercise more interesting, they can be helped to chart or graph the targeted behaviour so that comparison can be made with a baseline established during an observation stage.

Setting consequences for behaviour

If a young person is to be motivated to achieve self-control, there will need to be rewards for the achievement of goals. Often, rewards occur naturally because, as undesirable behaviours change, negative consequences diminish and positive consequences are experienced. However, in the early stages of change, such naturally occurring consequences may not be noticeable. It is therefore sensible to put in place formally a system of positive rewards. These rewards can take a variety of forms. They may be specific rewards, such as a new possession or participation in a desired activity for achieving target criteria, or they might be in the form of tokens that can be cashed in later for a specific reward.

As an important goal is to encourage self-control in young people, it is preferable for the young person themself to be in control of determining what kinds of reinforcement or reward they should receive. In some cases, parents or significant others can be involved in the process of reward-giving. For example, a young person might negotiate a deal with their father by saying, 'Dad, if I'm able to cut down my fighting with Bill so that I only fight with him three times a week, will you drive me to soccer on Saturday?' Thus, the young person has an external incentive, which they were personally responsible for establishing, thereby demonstrating their own ability to take responsibility for change.

Challenging self-destructive beliefs

Young people commonly hold a range of beliefs which lead them to behave, or think, in ways which are destructive for them. Albert Ellis, the originator of rational emotive therapy, which is now more commonly known as rational emotive behaviour therapy (REBT), drew attention to the need for counsellors to challenge what he described as clients' 'irrational beliefs'. Readers who would like to make significant use of rational emotive behaviour therapy may wish to read Dryden et al. (2010). Ellis's ideas, and the way in which they have been developed, are extremely useful when working with young people.

Irrational beliefs (which we prefer to call 'self-destructive beliefs' when counselling young people)

In rational emotive behaviour therapy, beliefs are considered to be 'irrational' if they prevent people from achieving their basic goals and purposes, are illogical (especially, dogmatic) and are empirically inconsistent with reality. Labelling beliefs this way appeals to many adults, but young people tend to be less convinced. Many young people are simplistically logical and like to argue. If we use Ellis's term 'irrational beliefs', they may argue that some so-called 'irrational beliefs' are not irrational, but do have a logical rational base. Thus, calling these beliefs 'irrational' invites unnecessary argument.

However, if we call these beliefs 'self-destructive beliefs' there is unlikely to be any argument and most young people will understand the concept and agree with the definition. We believe that counsellors are therefore on safer ground, when working with young people, if they use the term 'self-destructive beliefs'.

The REBT theory of change

Rational emotive behaviour therapy (REBT) theory regarding change is very useful when working with young people. This is sometimes described as the ABC framework where:

> *A* is the *Activating* event.
> *B* is the *Belief* which conditions the response to the event.
> *C* is the *Consequence* of the response.

When an *activating event* occurs, the young person responds automatically by using current beliefs. These beliefs condition the person's response and there are consequences related to this response. Thus, when a young person has self-destructive beliefs, these will condition their responses to external events and are likely to result in negative consequences for them, so that they will feel bad.

Behavioural change can promote emotional change

If the young person changes a self-destructive belief and replaces it with a more useful constructive belief (or, in REBT language, a 'rational belief'), then they will respond differently to an activating event as a result of the new belief. Having behaved differently, there will be a positive emotional consequence for the young person, who will be more likely to feel good than to feel bad, in the way they did when they responded in accordance with the self-destructive belief.

Types of self-destructive belief

Table 16.1 shows a list of self-destructive beliefs compared with a list of useful constructive beliefs. Self-destructive beliefs fit into the following categories:

- should, must, ought-to and have-to beliefs
- catastrophizing beliefs
- always and never beliefs
- intolerance-of-others beliefs
- blaming beliefs
- negative self-perception beliefs.

TABLE 16.1 *Self-destructive beliefs and constructive beliefs*

Self-destructive beliefs	Constructive beliefs
Should, must, ought-to and have-to beliefs	
My friends *should* be loyal to me.	Sometimes my friends won't be loyal to me; that's the way it is. It doesn't mean there's something wrong with me.
Other people *should* live up to my expectations.	Other people won't live up to my expectations.
I *must* conform to my peers.	I can be an individual and do my own thing.
I *must* win.	According to the law of averages most people only win 50 per cent of the time. I don't need to win to feel OK.
I *ought to* please my brother rather than do what I want.	I need to attend to my own needs so that I feel OK. Then if I feel OK, I can care about other people too.
I *have to* visit my dying uncle everyday.	I have a choice. I can choose whether or not to visit my dying uncle every day.
Catastrophizing beliefs	
I can never go back to school again.	I am me, I am OK. Everybody makes mistakes at times.
It would be too embarrassing. I wouldn't be able to face the other students.	I'm normal and proud to be me.
I might as well stop work on the project altogether because it is a total failure.	I've done really well to take on such a hard project. It's not a *total* failure. I can still get some positives out of it.
It's all too much. I just can't cope anymore.	I can cope. I always have in the past, and I will now.
Nobody will ever respect me again.	I don't need other people's respect to feel good about myself I am OK.
Always and never beliefs	
I'm not going to ask my mother because she *always* says 'no'.	I am going to ask my mother because she might say 'yes'.
I *never* succeed in anything.	Sometimes I succeed and sometimes I fail. I'm human and I'm OK.
Everybody *always* criticizes me.	People sometimes criticize me, but that's OK because it's impossible to please everybody all the time.

(Continued)

TABLE 16.1   *(Continued)*

Self-destructive beliefs	Constructive beliefs
I should *never* make mistakes.	Everybody makes mistakes. The only way to avoid making mistakes is to do nothing, and that's not me.

Intolerance-of-others beliefs

She makes me mad because she borrows my library books and then returns them late. She deliberately gets me into trouble.	She's just careless. I know that and I have a choice about whether to lend her my library books or not.
He didn't turn up to meet me after class as we arranged. He deliberately stood me up to make me look foolish.	He probably forgot – that's the way he is, and there is nothing I can do about that. He's the one who's made the mistake. I can feel OK about me.
My little brother makes me mad because he never does his share of the work.	My brother is lazy. I can't change him so I'll ignore his behaviour and be proud of being a hard worker myself.

Blaming beliefs

I can't do my homework because my sister keeps asking me to play with her.	I don't have to play with my sister when I have important things to do for me.
If he didn't keep annoying me I wouldn't hit him. It's his fault that I get into trouble.	I can choose other ways to deal with his annoying behaviour so that I don't get into trouble.
I am always late for class because they are so slow at the tuckshop.	I can only blame myself if I'm late because I don't get to the tuckshop earlier. I am in control of what happens.

Negative self-perception beliefs

I'm a victim.	I'm powerful.
I'm a loser.	I'm a winner.
I'm no good.	I'm OK.
I'm worthless.	I'm worthwhile.
I'm helpless.	I'm resourceful.
I'm a bad person.	I'm a good person.
I'm incapable.	I'm capable.
I'm stupid.	I'm smart.
I'm unlovable.	I'm lovable.

A printable version of this table is available to download from https://study.sagepub.com/geldardadolescents

Should, must, ought-to and have-to beliefs

These beliefs are demonstrated by the use of statements such as:

Other people *should* always be responsible.
I *must* conform to my peers.
I *ought to* please my brother rather than do what I want.
I *have to* visit my dying uncle every day.

At times, these beliefs may be self-destructive for young people. The beliefs set them up to have expectations that may not be met and/or to do things which other people want done rather than to attend to their own needs.

Catastrophizing beliefs

Catastrophizing beliefs lead the young person to believe that they have few options left, and that a disaster of enormous proportions has occurred, or will occur. For example, a young person may believe that:

I can never go back to school again. It would be too embarrassing. I wouldn't be able to face the other students.
I might as well stop work on the project altogether because it is a total failure.
It's all too much, I just can't cope any more.
Nobody will ever respect me again.

These statements are clearly very destructive because they leave no options for the future and inevitably lead the young person to feel hopeless and depressed.

Always and never beliefs

'Always' and 'never' beliefs are an exaggeration of the truth and leave the young person feeling bad because times when positive things do occur are ignored or denied. Typical 'always' and 'never' statements are:

I'm not going to ask my mother because she *always* says 'no'.
I *never* succeed in anything.
Everybody *always* criticizes me.
I should *never* make mistakes. [*This is a combination of a 'should' and a 'never' belief.*]
I must *always* complete my assignments on time. [*This is combination of a 'must' and an 'always' belief.*]
I *never* get any free time. I *always* have to work.

Intolerance-of-others beliefs

Intolerance-of-others beliefs are beliefs which suggest that other people are intrinsically hopeless, bad or malevolent, don't do as they should and generally don't live up to the young person's expectations. For example:

She makes me mad because she borrows my library books and then returns them late. She deliberately gets me into trouble.

He didn't turn up to meet me after class as we arranged. He deliberately stood me up to make me look foolish.

My little brother makes me mad because he never does his share of the work.

These beliefs lead to negative feelings and damage relationships.

Blaming beliefs

With these beliefs young people blame other people for their situation. By blaming, they excuse themselves from the need to change, and instead want someone else to change. This is clearly self-destructive because no one can make another person change, so the unsatisfactory situation is certain to continue. Typical examples of blaming beliefs are:

I can't do my homework because my sister keeps asking me to play with her.

I am always late for class because they are so slow at the tuckshop.

If he didn't keep annoying me I wouldn't hit him. It's his fault that I get into trouble.

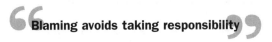
Blaming avoids taking responsibility

Negative self-perception beliefs

Negative self-perception beliefs are where people describe themselves in negative ways. Examples are:

I'm a victim.
I'm a loser.
I'm no good.
I'm worthless.
I'm helpless.
I'm a bad person.
I'm incapable.
I'm stupid.
I'm unlovable.

Constructive beliefs

Constructive beliefs to replace all of the examples of self-destructive beliefs described in this section are given in Table 16.1.

The origins of self-destructive beliefs in young people

When counselling young people it is important to understand the origins of their self-destructive beliefs because it is the origins of these beliefs which give them validity in their minds. Most young people's self-destructive beliefs are accumulated during child-hood as a consequence of messages given directly and indirectly by adults in the child's environment. Some of these messages are appropriate during childhood and provide a framework for social and moral development, but in adolescence and later in life can become self-destructive and most unhelpful.

Most children are continually told that they *should, must, ought to* and *have to* do things that adults require them to do. They are often told that things *always* or *never* happen, and they are frequently led to believe that if they do not do the right thing a *catastrophe* will happen. Additionally, they are often treated with intolerance if they do not behave in ways that are acceptable for adults. Consequently, they learn to be *intolerant* of others themselves. Children are often blamed for things that go wrong when they make mistakes. This is inevitable. However, it leads them to start engaging in beliefs that rely on *blaming* other people for their behaviours. Children model on the behaviours they observe in adults, and for most children the modelling behaviour of adults suggests that some beliefs which will later be unhelpful for them are the ones that they should have.

How to challenge self-destructive beliefs when counselling young people

When using REBT techniques with young people, we need to modify the challenging processes that are normally used with adults by taking account of the young person's developmental process. As counsellors, we need to recognize that young people are different from adults. They are in a process of moving out of childhood where they have naturally and inevitably absorbed beliefs that now need to be changed.

If a counsellor working with a young person uses the usual REBT technique of directly and actively disputing self-destructive beliefs, there is a risk that the young person will be alienated. This is because beliefs that the young person has rightly held for years will be treated disrespectfully and will not be validated.

When counselling young people, challenging self-destructive beliefs needs to involve two stages:

1. The young person needs to be complimented for existing beliefs. These need to be validated as having been useful in the past, during childhood.
2. Existing beliefs need to be challenged as now being self-destructive and needing to change as a consequence of the young person's movement from childhood into adulthood. The young person no longer needs to be constrained by these beliefs but is free to reject them if they choose.

The challenging needs to be done by debating the issues in a way that parallels the way in which young people debate issues. This debate, in paralleling adolescent communication, may involve a level of self-disclosure. It is appropriate for a counsellor to disclose and share with a young person their views and beliefs in a way that allows the young person to integrate these beliefs into their own belief system. For example, a counsellor might say 'I have some difficulty when people tell me that I *should* do things. I prefer to do things that I *choose* to do rather than necessarily doing things that other people believe I should do'. By making a statement such as this, the counsellor is disclosing their own need for individuation, and their desire to take responsibility for their own decisions without being excessively influenced by other people's expectations.

Having made a statement such as that described, the counsellor has a responsibility to help the young person to fit in with the demands of the real world where we cannot do exactly as we like, but have to make choices about when and where to conform to other people's expectations. The counsellor might continue by saying 'Sometimes, I choose to do what other people want. For example, because I choose to work at a school I have to comply with the rules here'. Thus the message is given that as a general rule it can be self-destructive to use *should* beliefs, but that there are times when we might choose to comply with other people's expectations because we want to avoid the consequences of not doing so.

> **The consequences of choices need to be considered**

Modelling a process for dealing with self-destructive beliefs may also be helpful for a young person. The counsellor might talk about having held a certain set of beliefs in the past, and having changed them because they were unhelpful. A counsellor might usefully ask 'Where does that belief come from? Who told you that you always had to perform to the highest standards?' By doing this, the counsellor is inviting the young person to recognize that the beliefs they hold may have been appropriate for them as a child. As a child, their parents had the right to tell them what to do, and to teach them particular values and standards. However, these beliefs, values and standards may need to be amended because their parents are no longer running their life as they once did.

In challenging self-destructive beliefs with young people, we prefer to use a conversational style where the beliefs of both client and counsellor are respected. Also, existing beliefs and values are validated as having been useful, but then questioned in terms of their current usefulness. By discussing beliefs and their origins, the young person is given permission to become more flexible in their thinking. The counsellor's goal is not to replace the young person's beliefs immediately with a new set of beliefs. Rather, it is to leave the young person feeling freer to think about alternative beliefs and with an openness and readiness to explore and change those beliefs that are self-destructive. Thus, the proactive counsellor does not try to impose new ways of thinking on a young person, but sets up a challenge and leaves them to deal with it in their own way.

To help in the development of new beliefs, a white-board may be used to list constructive beliefs that could replace particular self-destructive beliefs. Additionally, if the young person is willing to participate, role play and the use of imagination, as described in Chapter 15, can help the young person explore the outcomes of adopting new beliefs, holding on to current beliefs or rejecting part of an old belief while maintaining some part of that belief.

Anger management

A number of authors have contributed to our knowledge of the management of anger in young people, including Feindler and Ecton (1986), Fodor (1992) and Forman (1993). There is a general consensus that young people who have a problem with anger control need to externalize the problem and understand their own personal triggers and beliefs which may result in inappropriate angry behaviour. There are five clearly identifiable stages in anger management for young people:

1. Identifying the angry response pattern.
2. Externalizing the anger.
3. Identifying personal triggers and catalysts.
4. Focusing on personal power.
5. Choosing control options.

Identifying the angry response pattern

Each young person is unique, so the pattern of behaviour which results in an angry response will be different for each individual. Before the undesired behaviour pattern can be changed, a young person needs to recognize and understand it. To help them do this, a counsellor might invite them to describe the following:

1. *The antecedents to an angry outburst*, including triggers, their own behaviour and feelings, and the behaviour of others before the outburst occurs.
2. *Behaviours displayed during the angry outburst.* For example, being verbally or physically abusive. When describing these behaviours, the young person can be encouraged to talk about their reactions and also their physiological and emotional feelings.
3. *Consequences that arise from the angry episode.* Here, the young person can be encouraged to examine whether the consequences make them feel good, bad or otherwise, in both the short term and the long term.

By discussing all of the above, the young person may recognize influences that are reinforcing the undesired behaviour and/or making it harder for change to occur.

Externalizing the anger

To help the young person understand their behaviour patterns, the counsellor may wish to use a white-board and felt pens to draw the model shown in Figure 16.1. This model externalizes the young person's anger, describing the 'anger' and the young person as separate identities, as though 'anger' has an existence and personality of its own.

> **Externalizing the emotion challenges the young person to control it**

Triggers, which have been setting off the anger, do not act directly on the anger. They act on the young person. The young person has control of whether or not these triggers are allowed to activate the anger and cause a damaging explosion. Between the young person and the externalized anger is a space filled with catalysts (see Figure 16.1). These catalysts are things that cleverly trick the young person into passing the trigger on so that it activates the anger. Additionally, the catalysts give extra power to the triggers.

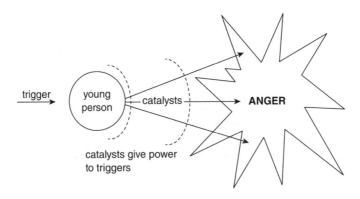

FIGURE 16.1 *Externalizing anger*

The anger model shown in Figure 16.1 presents the young person with a dilemma. They can either choose to be powerful and take control of the triggers, the catalysts and the anger, or they can give their power away so that the triggers, catalysts and anger take control. If the young person chooses to be powerful, triggers will be deflected, catalysts will be neutralized and the expression of anger will be appropriate, non-abusive and less damaging, as shown in Figure 16.2.

In reviewing the personal dilemma of the anger model, the young person needs to recognize that they can, if they choose, be the most powerful component in this model. The counsellor might ask questions such as 'Do you want to be controlled by "anger" or do you want to control "anger"?', 'Who is the stronger, you or "anger"?' and 'Are you going to let the triggers and catalysts trick you into letting "anger" take control, or are you going to be ready to deflect the triggers and neutralize the catalysts?' The young person is likely to recognize that, if they take control, consequences that are

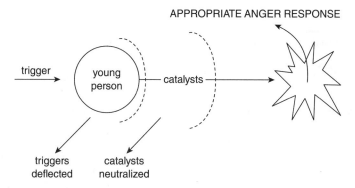

FIGURE 16.2   *Triggers and catalysts deflected*

better for them can be achieved, whereas if the triggers and catalysts are allowed to give power to 'anger', and 'anger' is allowed to take control, negative consequences will inevitably result.

Identifying personal triggers and catalysts

Triggers are external events and precede the angry aggressive outburst. Examples of triggers are given in Table 16.2. Initially, a counsellor might invite a young client to make a personal list of triggers that are commonly associated with their angry outbursts. It can then be useful for the counsellor to explore with the young person whether or not they believe that triggers are inevitably going to occur from time to time in their life. Recognition that triggers are inevitable is an essential part of anger control. Young people need to understand that triggers cannot be stopped, but are a natural part of life. What is important is the young person's response, which they can control if they choose.

TABLE 16.2   *Triggers, catalysts and alternative beliefs*

Triggers (the activating event)	Catalysts (the self-destructive belief)	Alternative belief (to neutralize the catalyst)
Being teased.	Other people should always respect me.	Sometimes people are disrespectful; I can cope with that because I know that I'm OK.
Someone tries to get me to do something that I don't want to do.	They are trying to take advantage of me.	I am me and I can make my own decisions about what to do.
Being pushed.	Other people don't respect me.	I respect myself and I will be assertive when other people try to push me around.

(Continued)

TABLE 16.2   *(Continued)*

Triggers (the activating event)	Catalysts (the self-destructive belief)	Alternative belief (to neutralize the catalyst)
Being shamed.	Other people are better than me.	I am me, and I am OK.
Making a mistake.	Making mistakes is a disaster.	Everybody makes mistakes; that's normal, so I am normal.
Waiting in a queue.	I should be served first.	It would be nice if I were served first but everybody has to queue up, not just me.
Not being able to do something competently.	I'm useless.	There are some things I'm really good at doing and other things I need more practice at; nobody's perfect.
When something is lost.	Someone has taken it.	It's just mislaid; I can find it if I stay calm and take time to look.
Accidental intrusion by others.	They don't respect my rights.	They are careless; I am capable of telling them what I need.
Someone else doesn't do what I want them to do.	Other people should live up to my expectations.	Other people don't need to live up to my expectations.
Being unfairly treated.	I should always be treated fairly.	Life is not always fair and just.
Losing in a game.	I must always win.	If I win 50 per cent of the time I'm doing well.
Being told what to do by someone in authority.	People in authority do not have the right to tell me what to do.	I can accept that in some situations I will be told what to do and that is appropriate.

A printable version of this table is available to download from https://study.sagepub.com/geldardadolescents

Triggers are given power by catalysts. Catalysts are self-destructive beliefs, and examples of these are given in Table 16.2. Consider, for example, the trigger of 'someone trying to get you to do something you don't want to do'. A catalyst that would be likely to give this trigger more power might be the belief that they were trying to take advantage of you. This belief needs to be challenged because it is self-destructive (see discussion above on challenging self-destructive beliefs). Counsellors need to help young people to identify both triggers and catalysts. Catalysts can then be reviewed, challenged and replaced by more helpful beliefs that will not give power to triggers.

Focusing on personal power

Young people are at a stage of life where they want to have control over their lives, so issues of power and control are important to them. The anger control model shown in Figure 16.2 is therefore likely to appeal to young people because generally they will recognize that they do, if they wish, have the ability to exercise power and control over the influence of triggers and that they can neutralize catalysts by replacing self-destructive beliefs with more helpful ones. Additionally, young people generally don't like being controlled, so they may be motivated to control their anger rather than be controlled by it.

Some young people are reluctant to let go of abusive ways of expressing anger because being abusive gives them a feeling of power. It can therefore be helpful for a young person to identify what the pay-offs are from being powerful. By identifying these pay-offs, they may find other ways of obtaining them without being abusive. For example, a pay-off, as a consequence of being aggressive, might be that a young person gains a sense of being respected by others. If they are to give up aggressive behaviour, they will need to explore other ways of achieving respect. Through discussion in counselling, they may realize that as a result of being powerful in a different way, by taking control of their anger, they might gain in respect from others as a consequence of the following:

- increased self-respect
- increased confidence
- being seen as mature
- being seen as tough and in control
- being able to stand up for values and beliefs.

By contrast, when a young person engages in unacceptable ways of expressing anger, there are certain to be negative consequences. The young person may get into a great deal of conflict and trouble with both peers and adults, and particularly with adults who are in authority positions. In such cases, it may be useful for a counsellor to say 'It seems to me that "anger" gets you into a lot of trouble when it gets control. When you're able to control "anger", you seem to be able to avoid trouble'. Clearly, the issue of power and control in anger management needs to be presented in terms of who has the control: does the anger have control of the young person, or does the young person have control of the anger?

Choosing control options

There are a number of strategies that a young person can use in order to deal with triggers and/or catalysts so that they don't fire off unacceptable levels of angry behaviour. These strategies are:

- avoiding triggers
- recognizing symptoms of arousal
- using thought-stopping
- using relaxation

- challenging self-destructive beliefs
- dealing with internalized anger
- using appropriate expression of anger
- finding constructive ways to get needs met.

Avoiding triggers

Once a young person has been able to identify triggers that result in angry or aggressive behaviour, they may be able to identify where triggers might occur more often in some situations than in other situations. During the process of learning improved anger-management strategies, it may be useful for a young person to plan to deliberately avoid situations where triggers are likely to occur. For example, going to a particular spot on the school sports field might be likely to bring them into contact with others who have in the past succeeded in triggering unacceptably angry behaviour. In other situations, a young person might find it useful to leave a scene where their anger has been triggered in order to prevent an aggressive outburst occurring. Although avoiding triggers is a useful strategy, it may lead to the young person internalizing anger, which will need to be dealt with later (see below).

It may be helpful to avoid provocative situations

Recognizing symptoms of arousal

It can be helpful for a young person to learn to recognize the physiological symptoms of arousal that occur in situations that are likely to provoke an angry response. A young person who is starting to get angry may exhibit some, or all, of the following physiological symptoms: sweating, increase in heart rate, clenching of jaw or fists, tensing of muscles, hair standing on end, knots in the stomach, face going red or white, increasingly rapid breathing, or difficulty in getting breath. Once the physiological symptoms of arousal have been recognized, they can be used as a signal to enable the young person to use strategies to prevent the triggers from setting off an angry outburst.

Using thought-stopping

Thought-stopping can be useful in helping a young person to intercept a trigger quickly to prevent it having effect or to reduce its effect. To do this, the young person can be taught to use thought-stopping as soon as physiological symptoms of arousal are recognized. If someone slams a book down on a desk and simultaneously shouts 'Stop!', anyone near will have their thoughts interrupted by the 'Stop' message. In the same way, young people can be taught to interrupt their thoughts suddenly, as soon as they recognize the physiological cues of anger arousal.

It can be useful to pair thought-stopping with one specific physical behaviour. For example, some people, when learning to thought-stop, will wear a loose elastic band around their wrist. When they notice that the physiological cues of arousal are starting to occur, they stretch the elastic band with their other hand so that it flicks back on to their wrist as they silently say to themselves 'Stop!' This provides an interruption to thoughts associated with the anger-arousal process. A relaxation strategy can then be used. Additionally, self-destructive beliefs that might be catalysts for triggering anger can be challenged.

Using relaxation

The use of relaxation can reduce the level of emotional arousal, making it easier for a young person to deflect a trigger, neutralize the power of a catalyst and take control of anger. Relaxation can be used immediately after thought-stopping, which will have occurred following the recognition of the physiological symptoms of arousal.

A relaxation exercise, as described in Chapter 15, can be used to teach a young person to relax. Having learnt how to relax in this way, they can then be taught how to do brief relaxation exercises in a standing or sitting position. To model brief relaxation, first show the young person how to take a deep breath and encourage them to try the technique themselves. You might say, for example, 'Place your hand on your stomach, breathe in slowly through your nose, feel your lungs fill completely with air, and, as you breathe in, your hand should move outward. Once your lungs are completely filled with air, breathe out completely through your mouth'. While doing the breathing exercise two or three times, the young person can be encouraged to allow their muscles to relax each time they breathe out, while silently saying calming words such as 'relax', 'calm down', 'slow down' or 'keep cool'. The deep breathing, muscle relaxation and calming words help to reduce tension and shift the young person's attention away from whatever is triggering their anger and on to their own self-control (Feindler and Ecton, 1986). Clearly, when doing this exercise, excessive breathing that might create hyperventilation must be avoided.

Challenging self-destructive beliefs

As discussed, catalysts are generally the result of self-destructive beliefs and need to be challenged and replaced with more helpful beliefs.

Dealing with internalized anger

It is not sensible to teach a young person to control anger merely by suppressing it, because this is likely to result in a high level of internalized anger. Internalized anger can have psychological and behavioural consequences. It may lead to depression and/or the anger may be expressed in subtle ways that will cause undesirable consequences. It is therefore important that young people have ways of dealing directly with their anger, rather than just suppressing it, so that they can feel better.

One way of dealing with internalized anger is by talking through the issues related to the angry feelings with a counsellor or friend. By doing this, catharsis might occur naturally. Alternatively, a cathartic process might be deliberately planned to enable the young person to release the anger. In counselling, this might be through the use of

Gestalt two-chair work as described in previous chapter, or in the wider environment the young person might act their feelings out in a cathartic and safe way without the involvement of other people. For example, this might be done by going into an open space and yelling out things that need to be said and released. Another way to deal with internalized angry feelings is through the expression of physical energy. For example, a young person might go on a long run or engage energetically in sport. By doing this, they will release natural endorphins which will have a soothing effect. Finally, internalized anger can be released by directly expressing it to the person concerned as described in the following section.

Using appropriate expression of anger

There are times when it is appropriate for young people to express their anger directly. Role playing can be used, as described in Chapter 15, to help a young person to learn non-abusive ways of expressing anger. These will generally involve the young person learning to make statements beginning 'I feel angry because . . .', followed by non-interpretative statements of fact such as '. . . you have accused me of something that I didn't do'. Sometimes, feelings other than anger will be involved. For example, a young person might say 'I feel angry and humiliated because in front of my friends you have accused me of something I didn't do'.

In teaching young people to make appropriate expressions of anger it is important to help them to recognize:

1. That having made a clear statement of their feelings, as described, they need to listen to and validate any response from the other person, rather than becoming involved in counterproductive argument. Being able to let the other person have the last word is a sign of maturity.
2. That there may be undesirable consequences for them if they directly express their anger to the person they feel angry towards. Hence they have to weigh up the likely consequences when deciding whether or not to express their anger directly in this way.

Finding constructive ways to get needs met

In teaching young people to control their anger it is essential to help them find socially acceptable ways to get their needs met. If they are not able to do this, they will inevitably build up angry and resentful feelings and their efforts at anger control may be undermined. They therefore need to learn assertiveness skills that will enable them to communicate with others so that they can express their needs clearly.

Assertiveness training

Assertiveness is a non-defensive way of presenting a point of view, and being heard, without offending others. Being assertive involves the following steps:

1. Listening to the other person.
2. Validating what the other person has said.
3. Believing in your right to present a point of view.
4. Expressing a point of view.
5. Being prepared to negotiate a compromise.
6. Being prepared to accept that differences do exist.

We believe that, for young people, 5 and 6 in the above list are particularly important. If these are not respected, conflict may occur. In seeking individuation for themselves, young people sometimes lose sight of the need for others to be individuals. However, when this is drawn to their attention they are usually quick to accept and respect the rights of others to have different opinions, because this fits with the adolescent frame of reference regarding individuation.

Teaching assertiveness to young people is best done through the use of a combination of didactic teaching on a white-board and role-playing rehearsal as described in Chapter 15.

Listening to the other person

Listening to another person involves (a) attending to the content of the message that is being verbally communicated, and (b) observing and taking account of any non-verbal messages which accompany the verbal communication. It is particularly important for young people to learn to pay attention to incongruence between verbal and non-verbal messages, and to check out whether information being received is correctly understood or not. Often, misunderstandings between young people occur because they do not get the true message being communicated. As counsellors, we need to remember that young people are not experienced in adult communication methods.

Young people need to learn to check out that they have correctly heard and understood the other person's message. For example, a young person might practise asking questions such as 'Are you saying that . . . ?' Similarly, they need to learn to check out incongruence between verbal and non-verbal messages. For example, they might practise making statements like 'I'm confused because you are telling me to go ahead but you sound disappointed. I am not sure what you would really like'. Rehearsing statements of this type, which begin with an 'I' statement of personal feelings, can be very useful.

Validating what the other person has said

It is important for a young person to learn to validate what the other person has said by letting them know that they have been heard and understood. Role play can be used to practise making statements which reflect back the content of what has been heard. Typical validating statements are:

I've heard you say that . . .
You would like it if . . .
You think that it is important . . .
You think that I . . .
You are saying that . . .

Validating involves being sensitive to the other person's needs and/or point of view while continuing to stay in touch with your own needs and/or point of view.

Believing in your right to present a point of view

Young people need to feel confident that they have a right to present an alternative point of view, while at the same time recognizing that other people have the right to have different points of view. This inevitably means that they have to accept the possibility that their own point of view may not necessarily be accepted. Young people often find this difficult because of the adolescent tendency to be egocentric. However, because young people have a strong belief in their right to be respected as individuals, they can usually understand and accept that other people may also want to be respected as individuals with their own points of view. In this regard, it can be useful for counsellors to positively promote the right to be different.

Expressing a point of view

When expressing a particular point of view it is helpful for the young person to state things from their point of view by making 'I' statements. Coaching in the use of 'I' statements, particularly those that express feelings, can be useful. For example, a counsellor might coach a young person to make statements such as 'I feel embarrassed about asking for money, but I want to get to the job interview and I need money so that I can catch the bus'. Young people need to learn that when expressing a point of view, it is important to stay focused and not be distracted by side issues. Additionally, there is a need to be specific, and to avoid making assumptions about the other person's feelings or motives without checking these out.

Being prepared to negotiate a compromise

Some counsellors, who teach assertiveness training with adults, will suggest that assertive behaviour requires the person to continue making their request without deviating, and that this may involve behaving like a cracked record, by repeatedly restating the request. For young people, this approach to assertiveness training can be destructive as it may set them up for failure. Other people are likely to become angered by constant repetitions of a request, particularly when coming from a young person. It is better to teach young people to try to make sure that their message has been heard correctly, and then to negotiate so that compromise can be achieved, if this is possible, in situations where their requests are not going to be granted in full.

Compromise may lead to a satisfactory outcome

Being prepared to accept that differences do exist

There will be times when young people will not get their requests met in any way. Such situations may present strong triggers for anger. Young people therefore need to be prepared for such situations and to rehearse behaviours for dealing with triggers when these occur. Where there are unresolvable differences, the young person needs to learn to be able to back off by saying something such as 'You and I don't think the same, so we may as well stop discussing it'. In saying this, they are implicitly recognizing that expecting that they will always get their needs met is unrealistic and constitutes a self-destructive belief.

Success in assertive skills training depends on good modelling, coaching in specific skills, rehearsal through role play and reinforcement when positive outcomes occur.

Setting lifestyle goals

Young people are at a stage in their lives when they are confronted by new experiences and situations. In addition, they have an unknown future which threatens to present them with unexpected challenges. Because they are moving through unknown territory in their lives, they often have problems in finding an overall direction that makes sense for them. If they lack an overall sense of direction, and do not have clear lifestyle goals, they may become excessively troubled by the uncertainty of their lives.

Lifestyle goals provide a general sense of direction within which other, less global, decisions can be made. They also help to provide motivation. This is important because if young people are to be successful in achieving satisfaction for themselves, they need to be motivated.

Types of lifestyle goals

Goals can be divided into categories as follows (Ford, 1992):

- *Affective*: where goals are described in terms of feelings.
- *Cognitive*: where goals are described in terms of creativity or knowledge.
- *Subjective*: where goals are described as fulfilling spiritual needs.
- *Relationship*: where goals are described in terms of relationships with one's self and others.
- *Task-oriented*: where goals are described as meeting material or mastery needs.

When young people are exploring their goals, it can be useful for counsellors to identify the categories into which possible goals fall.

Selecting goals

It can be useful for young people to list their goals and then develop a hierarchy that prioritizes the goals that are most important for them. Sometimes, when they do this, they will be surprised to find that their priorities are not what they would have expected.

The simultaneous pursuit of more than one type of goal will be the most motivating. For example, combining the affective goal of feeling happy with a relationship goal of being with friends might lead a young person to choose activities, experiences or an occupation which involves working and interacting with others. Thus, it can be helpful for a young person to explore lifestyle possibilities in which more than one type of goal might be achieved simultaneously.

As a young person begins to isolate particular goals, a counsellor might encourage them to consider sub-goals, or targets, which will help in achieving these goals. This is useful, because self-motivation is sustained by the achievement of obtainable sub-goals which lead to larger goals. Success in achieving sub-goals provides reinforcement and incentive to proceed further. It is the proactive counsellor's task to help the young person try to design a lifestyle that offers opportunities for achieving a number of types of goal. Unfortunately, environmental and personal constraints sometimes preclude the possibility of meeting multiple goals.

Once sub-goals have been achieved, it is useful to provide the young person with feedback to help them continue. Feedback includes information that enables them to evaluate their progress, identify hurdles and reinforce the young person's beliefs with regard to achieving desired outcomes. Feedback also provides the young person with information about whether or not they have the skills required to achieve targeted goals.

Suicide and goals

Baumeister (1990) believes that helping to identify goals is essential for young people who attempt or threaten suicide. He has formulated the 'escape theory', which suggests that young people who attempt suicide intentionally fail to attend to the broader goals and values that normally provide meaning to a person's thoughts, feelings and actions. Changes in goals, emotions and personal beliefs are often precursors to suicide. Helping young people to identify both short- and long-term goals can therefore be helpful in suicide prevention.

Due to the serious nature of suicide, we would like to take a moment to share with you, the reader, other approaches, strategies and resources for supporting clients who may be at risk of suicide. At the outset, however, we would like to strongly encourage you to access further training and support, including supervision, if working in this area. Working with adolescents who are at risk of suicide and/or self-harm (as we discuss next) is intense, emotionally draining work with very serious consequences for the young person. It is important for you to be competent, both professionally, in terms of knowledge and skills, and personally, in terms of your own self-care, in order to provide the best support possible. In saying this, it is also important to recognize that, sadly, some young people will continue to self-harm or attempt suicide despite competent and caring support. In light of this high risk of harm, limits to confidentiality are present in the counselling relationship and relevant information will need to be shared with the appropriate people. We discuss the process of disclosure of information in Chapter 19.

James and Gilliland (2013) suggest seven steps when providing crisis intervention support. A primary task that is ongoing throughout the crisis intervention is that of *ensuring the safety* of the young person. One way to determine safety is by performing a risk assessment that identifies the risk and protective factors present in the adolescent's life and putting immediate strategies in place if required, for example, restricting access to means of suicide (Hawton et al., 2012). James and Gilliland's (2013) seven steps are as follows:

1. *Engaging with the client* so as to establish a therapeutic relationship and discuss expectations about what they can expect from you, the counsellor.
2. *Exploring the problem and defining the crisis* by listening with empathy, and without judgement, to the young person's story (the counselling micro-skills we discussed in Chapter 11 are essential here!).
3. *Providing support* through relationship-building and ensuring the young person of your concern for and willingness to offer care without judgement.
4. *Examining alternatives* that are available to the young person by identifying the choices the adolescent has with respect to supports and coping strategies.
5. *Making plans* with the young person by outlining the supports, resources and coping strategies they have access to and steps that the client can own and accomplish.
6. *Obtaining a commitment* from the young person to follow the plan they have made.
7. *Following up* regularly in the next few hours or days (depending on the risk of harm) to ensure the young person of your ongoing care and concern and to check in with how the plan they developed is going.

Guidelines for supporting individuals at risk of suicide are available from the American Psychological Association (APA) at psychiatryonline.org/guidelines.aspx and from the Australian National Health and Medical Research Council (NHMRC) at www.clinicalguidelines.gov.au. A risk assessment tool developed by the Australian Institute for Suicide Research and Prevention (AISRAP) is available to download from www.griffith.edu.au/__data/assets/pdf_file/0004/625846/Handout-2-AISRAP-Suicide-Assess-Tool-2014.pdf.

One group of young people at a higher risk of suicide are those who self-harm (Shiner, 2008). Consequently, in order to address your client's safety, the same seven steps outlined above can be followed. We outline more suggestions for supporting young people who self-harm below.

As discussed in Chapter 6, self-harm can be used as a coping strategy. Therefore, it can be helpful to support young people in identifying the need being met by the self-harming behaviour so that other coping strategies can be explored (Shiner, 2008). One way of doing this is to perform a chain analysis. A chain analysis allows the young person to work through the events leading up to the moment of self-harm and to record the accompanying thoughts, feelings, behaviours, vulnerabilities, protective factors and consequences. Processing this information can help the young person to identify the emotional needs being met by self-harm (Brent et al., 2011). Additionally, many of the creative and symbolic strategies we discussed in Chapters 14 and 15 can be useful in helping the young person to explore their self-harming behaviours.

After exploring the self-harming behaviours with your client, it is important to consider both short- and long-term coping strategies so that young people can act immediately while further developing their emotional management skills. With respect to short-term strategies, distraction techniques can be a good starting point as they buy time during which the intense emotions and urge to self-harm may pass. You may like to engage the young person in brainstorming ideas they could use to distract themselves. Distraction techniques can be activities unrelated to self-harm, such as exercise, music or a creative outlet, or activities simulating self-harm, for example, drawing at the usual site of self-harm using a red felt pen or using ice or flicking an elastic band instead of burning or cutting (Shiner, 2008).

Supporting longer-term emotional management strategies involves developing both external and internal resources. External resources include social support networks (family, peers and significant others), professional supports (GPs, the local hospital, counsellors, mental health workers and so on), online support forums such as Self-Injury Guidance and Network Support (www.lifesigns.org.uk) and crisis support lines such as ChildLine in the UK (www.childline.org.uk) and Kids Help Line in Australia (www.kidshelp.com.au). Supporting internal resources can take many forms, including the use of cognitive behavioural therapy (CBT) and problem-solving therapy. For a review of research on supporting young people who self-harm please refer to Ougrin et al. (2012).

While supporting the young person to develop their emotional management skills, it is expected that they will continue to use self-harm to cope with intense emotions. Therefore, it is also important to discuss harm reduction or minimization strategies with young people. For example, adolescents who cut can be encouraged to use sterile cutting instruments and to not share these cutting instruments with others to decrease the risk of infection. Young people can also be encouraged to learn basic first aid and to identify when they need to access medical treatment for self-harm injuries (Shiner, 2008).

For those readers involved in suicide and self-harm prevention, the National Institute for Clinical Excellence (NICE) website (www.nice.org.uk) and the Living Is For Everyone (LIFE) website (livingisforeveryone.com.au) have information and resources available. As we highlighted at the start of this section, we strongly encourage readers to seek extra training and supervision in this area.

Making decisions

As young people are moving from a stage of being dependent on their parents and family to being independent, they are required to make many decisions for themselves. For many adults, making decisions can be difficult, and for most young people even more difficult. This is because they do not have a body of experience from past decisions on which to base their current judgements. Additionally, they often do not have information about the options available to them or the likely consequences of these options. Sometimes, even though they will understand cognitively what the consequences of particular actions are likely to be, because they have not personally experienced such consequences they may underestimate their importance or severity. Alternatively, they may exaggerate their importance and be afraid to choose alternatives because they believe that the associated consequences will be too severe for them.

Adolescent decision-making processes are often influenced by pressure from peer groups to conform; they may also be influenced by beliefs about other people's motives, abilities and characteristics, where these people's co-operation might be required to facilitate or implement decisions. Young people can often be over-optimistic in their estimates of the outcomes and consequences of their decisions. Because a young person feels optimistic, they may have an illusion of being in control in situations where this is unrealistic.

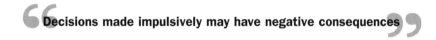
Decisions made impulsively may have negative consequences

Young people frequently make decisions impulsively and/or defensively in response to situational demands without carefully following a properly thought-out decision-making process. Counsellors can help them use their own resources for arriving at decisions but, in the process, provide them with information they do not have because of lack of experience. They need to be encouraged to make the best possible choices, taking account of their personal values and the objectives they wish to achieve (Janis and Mann, 1982).

In helping young people to make decisions it can be useful for a counsellor to identify, for them, the following stages of decision making:

1. Identifying unhelpful decision-making response patterns.
2. Exploring risks associated with change or with not changing.
3. Exploring lifestyle goals.

4. Identifying losses involved in choosing.
5. Examining alternatives.
6. Informing others of a decision.
7. Maintaining a commitment to a decision.

For most important decisions, all of these stages will be required. If any of them are missed out, then it may be that decisions will be reached that cannot be maintained.

Identifying unhelpful decision-making response patterns

It is helpful for young people to be able to identify ways in which they behave when they need to make decisions. Stress is almost always associated with decision making because of anxiety related to the losses involved. Some common ways in which young people respond to the stress of making decisions are as follows:

- They may continue doing what they are already doing.
- They may adopt a new course of action without any prior thought or planning.
- They may hastily adopt a solution that provides immediate relief without looking at the consequences.
- They may procrastinate and try to shift the responsibility of the decision making on to somebody else.
- They may search for information, assimilate the information in an unbiased way and appraise the alternatives to arrive at a decision.

Clearly, the last response is the most useful. Counsellors can help young people identify their responses to the stress associated with decision making. This can be useful in enabling them to recognize unsatisfactory responses in the future.

Exploring risks associated with change or with not changing

When young people are trying to make decisions regarding change, counsellors may need to help them to explore their expectations about the risks involved in changing, or not changing.

Risks in changing

There are often problems for young people when they do decide to change their behaviour, even if the changes are for the better. First, they have to cope with their own emotional feelings with regard to change. Whenever change occurs there are likely to be some losses, and there may be feelings of apprehension and uncertainty about the change.

Not only do young people have to cope with their own feelings, but they also have to cope with other people's responses to any change. Unfortunately, sometimes when young people make decisions which will lead to positive outcomes for themselves (or even for others), parents, other adults and peers will be troubled by the change and will resist it.

When changing, there is usually uncertainty because young people may not have previously experienced using the behaviours that have been chosen. Consequently, they cannot be sure whether the outcomes of these behaviours will be positive or not.

Risks in not changing

Young people often make decisions because their current behaviours are causing problems for them. They are, therefore, usually very aware of the risks associated with not changing. However, it can be useful for a counsellor to ask about these risks so that they are brought into focus in the young person's mind, thus encouraging a decision that will result in positive change.

Exploring the young person's optimism

Risk-taking is very much a part of young person behaviour, so young people will often look forward to new and exciting changes, even though they may be stressful. Thus, many young people will view change with enthusiasm and optimism. However, some young people will feel excessively anxious when making decisions. For them, exploring the risks associated with making a decision to change is an important step in the process of decision making.

Exploring lifestyle goals

As explained above, counsellors can help young people to explore lifestyle goals which are important for them. Once goals are identified, these will influence current decisions.

Identifying losses involved in choosing

In making decisions, young people need to be able to recognize losses that are associated with the alternatives available to them. Almost all decisions involve losses. For example, consider a situation where a young person makes a decision to leave home. As a consequence, the young person will experience the loss of guidance and support from parents, as well as material comfort and security. Typical losses associated with decisions may include the loss of such things as:

- a relationship
- closeness in a relationship
- intensity of a relationship
- support
- security
- freedom
- personal control

- leadership
- power
- material possessions
- personal faith
- previously held values and/or beliefs.

Many decisions involve letting go of something desirable

Sometimes young people may be able to compensate for personal losses such as loss of freedom, loss of control, loss of leadership and loss of power by making decisions that provide other rewards in these areas. At other times, they will need to accept losses without being able to compensate for them. This is particularly so with regard to losses which involve the emotions, such as relationship losses.

Once losses are identified, it may be possible to find ways to minimize them. For example, a young person who is wanting to leave home may recognize the loss of material comforts and security, and as a consequence consider ways to earn money to make up for the loss.

Examining alternatives

Alternatives may be explored using symbolic strategies as described in Chapter 14 or the creative strategy of role play as described in Chapter 15. However, some young people do not enjoy the use of symbolic or creative strategies and may wish to work in a more cognitive way. Sometimes it is possible to combine creative and/or symbolic strategies with cognitive strategies.

It can be helpful for a young person to write up on a white-board alternatives that need to be considered when making a particular decision. While this list is being drawn up, the counsellor might encourage the young person to think of as many options as possible. The options can then be explored by allowing the young person to talk about them in a general way. After this the counsellor may wish to summarize the alternatives clearly and encourage the young person to explore each option individually. When doing this, it can be useful to explore the positive and negative aspects of each option so that the alternatives can be narrowed down to a shorter list. There may be some advantage in encouraging the young person to deal with the most unlikely or least preferred options first. This helps in shortening the list of alternatives, making it easier for a decision to be reached.

When examining alternatives, it is helpful to encourage the young person not only to look carefully at the consequences, both negative and positive, of each alternative, but also to take account of their emotional or gut feelings connected with each alternative.

There are some risks for young people when examining alternatives. These are:

1. The young person needs to understand the difference between decisions that are based on fact and also sit comfortably emotionally, and those which are only based on emotional preference and have little factual basis. Often, because of lack of experience, young people will be carried away by strong emotional preferences and make decisions that may have doubtful or negative outcomes.
2. The young person might get distracted by irrelevant aspects of the alternatives which lead to an unrealistic prediction of outcomes. To guard against this, the counsellor needs to help them to focus on the most significant aspects of each option.
3. The young person's level of stress, self-perception, confidence and self-esteem will often influence their ability to look at alternatives clearly.
4. A young person may be pulled in one direction by thinking that depends on past values and beliefs. In this case, it is important to check out whether these beliefs and values are still important for them. Where a decision fits with their current values and beliefs, it is more likely that there will be commitment to the decision.

After proper consideration of alternatives, the final choice must be the young person's, rather than a choice that is influenced by the counsellor. It is to be hoped that, with careful consideration of the advantages, disadvantages and consequences of choosing each alternative, the young person will be able to make a decision that is best for them. However, this decision may not be the one that the counsellor believes to be the most desirable, sensible or appropriate.

Informing others of a decision

Once a decision has been made it needs to be acted on. However, this may not be immediate. The timing needs to be suitable for the young person and it is sensible to discuss this in counselling.

With many decisions, other people will need to be informed. Often a young person will deliberate about implementing a decision because they are uncertain about how to manage the responses of other people. To deal with this uncertainty, a counsellor might help them to anticipate the possible reactions of others and to decide on possible responses to these reactions. When doing this, it might be helpful for the counsellor to encourage the young person to rehearse the way in which they intend to tell others of their decision. This rehearsal can be done through the use of role play as described in Chapter 15, if desired. Additionally, role play can be used to allow the young person to experience what it would be like to be the recipient of the intended message. To help them in informing others of their decision, the counsellor might also coach them in the use of 'I' statements and assertiveness skills.

Maintaining a commitment to a decision

Adhering to a decision is often difficult for a young person, who may be constantly confronted with challenges and pressures that are contrary to the decision and the chosen direction. In particular, they may receive negative feedback from others regarding the decision.

Following an initial honeymoon period, where the young person is excited about a new decision, there will often be a period of renewed stress in response to the decision. However, young people can often cope with stress at this time more easily than when the decision was initially made. They are often more resilient, having dealt with the earlier stress, so they may be able to continue with their commitment to the decision.

The stability of the young person's decision will be significantly affected by the intensity of feedback, both positive and negative, which they receive from others regarding the decision. In the face of strong and consistent negative feedback, they may abandon a decision and seek an alternative. When this happens, it is important for a counsellor to give the young person positive feedback in connection with having tried out the original decision. They can be told that, in effect, an experiment has been done, with information from the experiment showing that the decision needs to be altered. By framing feedback in terms of a useful experiment, the young person may feel good rather than feel that they are poor at making decisions.

In summary

In this chapter we have discussed cognitive strategies that can be used with young people. These strategies can often be employed in conjunction with the psycho-educational strategies discussed in the next chapter.

KEY POINTS

- young people experiencing anxiety, depression, or aggressive, oppositional and unmotivated behaviour have been helped by behavioural and cognitive behavioural strategies
- writing a diary can help in identifying repetitive unhelpful behaviours
- challenging self-destructive beliefs can be useful in bringing about behavioural and emotional change
- self-destructive beliefs can be challenged by using a conversational approach which is similar to the way in which young people discuss issues with each other
- externalizing emotions such as anger can help give a young person a sense of control of the emotion
- assertiveness training can be useful in enabling a young person to express their needs but should not lead to the expectation that these needs will necessarily be fulfilled

- respecting another person's point of view and the ability to compromise can be useful in reaching satisfactory solutions
- changing behaviour involves risk and making choices often involves loss

CASE STUDY

While 16-year-old Brent was referred by his mother to your private practice, he agrees that he needs to talk with someone about his relationship with his father. For the last year or so there has been increasing conflict, both in number and intensity, between Brent and his Dad. Brent feels that his father is pressuring him to 'follow in his footsteps' and often makes fun of his interests, in particular being in a band with a few friends. What strategies discussed in this chapter would be useful in working with Brent? How would you introduce and use the strategies you have chosen? What if Brent doesn't engage with the strategies you have chosen?

FURTHER RESOURCES

The 'Centre for Clinical Interventions' is a website providing information and resources on mental health for both clients and practitioners. It includes multiple printable resources that can support counsellors when using a cognitive-behavioural approach.

- www.cci.health.wa.gov.au

17

Psycho-educational Strategies

In this chapter we will discuss a range of educational strategies that teach young people about life and may also help them to gain more control over their behaviours. Young people are on a journey of self-discovery and are mostly hungry to learn about themselves and their relationships with others. Gaining such knowledge helps them to develop an identity and make sense of the world around them. The psycho-educational strategies that will be discussed encourage young people to participate actively in ways of learning new information. The processes used are largely ones of self-discovery.

Most young people see counsellors as people who have knowledge and skills in the area of intrapersonal and interpersonal relationships (Gibson-Cline, 1996). Consequently, while learning mainly through self-discovery by using psycho-educational strategies, young people are also likely to gain if they can make use of the personal knowledge and experience of the counsellor about human relationships. Thus, it is useful for counsellors to share relevant knowledge and experience so that their young clients can integrate information that fits into their own body of knowledge.

When using psycho-educational strategies, a counsellor needs to constantly observe the young person's non-verbal behaviour and verbal responses. Through this observation, new material may be discovered about the young person's emotional feelings, beliefs, issues and attitudes. Quite often, a counsellor will need to interrupt the use of a psycho-educational strategy in order to explore issues which are spontaneously emerging for the young person. In this respect, it needs to be remembered that a strategy is only a tool that is used to enhance the counselling process. It is more important for a counsellor to continually watch for, and deal with, underlying issues as they emerge, than to stay with a particular strategy.

There is a risk when using psycho-educational models, that the young person may uncritically accept a complete psycho-educational model and try to fit themself into that model. It is more important that the young person should be encouraged to critically examine and modify the model so that it suits them.

Psycho-educational strategies will be described under four headings:

- strategies to get information
- strategies to explain relationships

- strategies to explain behaviour
- strategies to help change behaviour.

Strategies to get information

Two simple psycho-educational strategies, which can enable young people to find out and share information about themselves, involve the use of rating scales and inventories.

Rating scales

When using rating scales, a white-board or poster paper is needed so that information is visually presented. Rating scales are linear models which depict a range of items from one extreme to another. As indicators they can use either qualitative ratings, such as 'very much' and 'not at all', or numerical ratings, such as 1 to 7. Rating scales can be used to rate and monitor intensity, severity or frequency of behaviours.

Qualitative rating scales

Imagine that a young person is complaining about the restrictive behaviour of parents. A counsellor might draw a rating scale on a white-board as shown in Figure 17.1. The young person could then be asked to put marks on that rating scale to indicate exactly where their mother fits and exactly where their father fits on the scale. Discussion can then follow to help the young person recognize variations in parental behaviour. For example, the young person might have put the marks at the extreme left-hand end, 'never allow me to do anything', but it might emerge in discussion that, at times, this is not correct. The young person could also be asked to mark where they would like their parents to be on the scale. As a consequence, discussion of issues relating to control and responsibility might emerge.

FIGURE 17.1   *Qualitative scale to rate parental permission*

Numerical rating scales

Sometimes it can be useful to draw rating scales using numerical values, ranging from 1 to 10, for example. Rating scales using numerical values are particularly useful for rating behaviour in terms of severity or intensity. For example, it might be useful for a young person to rate their level of anger on a scale of 1–10 as shown in Figure 17.2. Numerical scales can also be useful in rating the frequency of occurrence of behaviours;

for example, the number of times each week a young person intervenes in a dispute between their parents. Such rating scales can be used to provide baseline measures and then to monitor change. Thus, they may be useful in promoting change and in providing information required for setting goals.

FIGURE 17.2　*Numerical scale to rate behaviour in terms of severity*

The use of rating scales to monitor feeling

Rating scales can be used to monitor feelings, at a point in time or over a period of time, using a scale such as that shown in Figure 17.3.

unhappy all the time	unhappy most of the time	unhappy some of the time	sometimes happy, sometimes unhappy	happy some of the time	happy most of the time	happy all the time

FIGURE 17.3　*Scale to rate feelings*

The use of rating scales to give feedback

Rating scales can help a young person to stop and think about their behaviours. Often young people tend to think of their own and other people's behaviours in terms of extremes. When processing the responses of a young person on a rating scale, a counsellor may be able to help them to recognize the way in which behaviours often vary along a continuum between two extremes. This can be done by encouraging the young client to identify times when exceptions to the extremes occur.

A position on the continuum between extremes can be useful

Inventories

Inventories, or questionnaires, are used by mental health workers in assessing a range of mental health problems. In addition, when counselling young people, it can be useful to use informal questionnaires such as those found in popular magazines and those which specifically target young people. Such inventories can be used in a serious or a humorous way to help young people identify information that is consistently true about their perceptions of themselves.

A typical questionnaire is shown in Figure 17.4; this 'How friendly are you?' questionnaire explores a young person's perceptions of their ability to be friendly towards others. Processing of the completed questionnaire can facilitate discussion and exploration of self-perceptions and related issues. The scoring key can also be used for discussion. For example, what does a score of 20 actually mean for the individual concerned?

Even though a counsellor may not believe in astrology, numerology or other new age concepts, horoscopes are popular with many young people and may be useful to help them explore their perceptions of themselves. Similarly, more conventional, established methods of categorizing people and their personalities can be used, such as the Myers–Briggs type indicator (Briggs Myers et al., 1998).

Strategies to explain relationships

Three ways of exploring relationship issues, and helping young people understand the nature of relationships, involve the use of:

- genograms
- ideas from transactional analysis
- strategies for understanding boundaries.

Genograms

Figure 17.5 shows a typical genogram where females are drawn as ellipses, males as rectangles, and the lines are used to indicate various relationships as described in the key.

Most young people like to be engaged in activity. Many of them, therefore, will enjoy drawing genograms of their extended families on white-boards or on poster paper using coloured felt pens. Genograms are a useful way of collecting and organizing information about a family. This information might include the extended family, including grandparents, uncles, aunts and so on. A genogram provides a pictorial layout of a family that can help a young person to recognize their position within the family. This is something that is important for a young person because in adolescence they are striving to find a personal identity, and part of their personal identity is likely to be framed in the context of their family.

HOW FRIENDLY ARE YOU?: circle your answer and check your score!	
1 When other people invite you out, you go... (a) Sometimes (b) Always (c) Not usually	5 Your friends indicate they would like to celebrate your recent athletic win. You... (a) Match their lively behaviour and respond cheerfully (b) Ignore their attempts to engage you (c) Wish that you were at home
2 Your remember a friend's birthday so you... (a) Send flowers (b) Call them (c) Call them only if they remembered your last birthday (d) Say 'Happy Birthday' next time you meet	6 When going for your regular walk in your neighbourhood, you usually... (a) Say 'hello' only to people that you recognize (b) Say 'hello' to everyone that you pass (c) Say 'hello' to no one
3 You haven't heard from a friend since your last outing, during which you had a slight disagreement. You... (a) Call and ignore the issue of the disagreement (b) Call, acknowledge the disagreement by owning your part in it and suggest you both meet at the place you like to hang out (c) Wait until your friend calls you	7 You know that a classmate has been involved in a weekend sporting accident. You... (a) Drop in to see how they are and hear about their ordeal (b) Wait for them to recover fully before you ask them how they're feeling (c) Stop by quickly to let them know that if they need anything you're available to help
4 You are sorting through photos and come across one of an old school friend you have lost contact with. You... (a) Remember the good times you had together (b) Try to get back in touch with them (c) Prefer to remember them as someone from your past	8 You are going on a school excursion by bus. You are likely to... (a) Talk with the person who sits in the vacant seat next to you (b) Take advantage of looking at the scenery (c) Find a seat next to someone already on the bus so that you can chat

HOW DID YOU SCORE?

(1) a = 2, b = 5, c = 0; (2) a = 5, b = 2, c = 0, d = 1; (3) a = 2, b = 5, c = 0; (4) a = 2, b = 5, c = 0; (5) a = 5, b = 2, c = 0; (6) a = 2, b = 5, c = 0; (7) a = 2, b = 0, c = 5; (8) a = 2, b = 0, c = 5.

25–40 points: Being friendly is important to you

You consider friendliness high on your list of priorities in relationships. You try to make other people feel valued and liked in relationships and are willing to persevere in relationships. You will do so even if others don't want to!

10–24 points: You see being friendly as a two-way street

Being friendly is important to you: however, you need feedback from others to continue to be friendly. You are conscious of not intruding on others' privacy.

---

9 points or less: Friendliness is not a priority to you

You are one of the world's rare people who is comfortable with his or her own company, while not being unfriendly. There are other things that capture your interest.

FIGURE 17.4   *Example of an inventory*

A printable version of this figure is available to download from https://study.sagepub.com/geldardadolescents

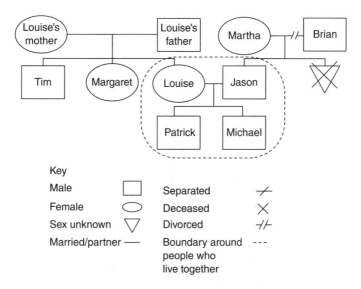

FIGURE 17.5   *Typical genogram: Louise is married to Jason and they have two children, Patrick and Michael. Jason's mother and father, Martha and Brian, are divorced, Jason had a sibling of unknown sex who died. (This genogram is invented and any similarity to a real family is purely coincidental.)*

While a young person is drawing a genogram, discussion is likely to revolve around family characteristics and relationships within the family. Consequently, a genogram may enable a young person to talk about their family in a way which may reveal personal issues. Also a genogram can indicate the closeness and distance of family members in relation to each other. Additional lines may be added to indicate particular relationships. As shown in Figure 17.6, the double line between Louise and Michael indicates a close relationship, whereas the wavy line between Jason and Michael, indicates an unsatisfactory relationship.

Where the wavy line has the small letters 'dv' written beside it, as on the line from Brian to Martha, domestic violence has occurred or is occurring. The dotted lines around clusters of family members indicate those who are living together.

From a genogram, a young person may be able to recognize patterns of behaviour and particular influences which come from generation to generation. For example, the young person may recognize that there has been an inter-generational dependency on alcohol within the family. Once this behaviour has been recognized, the young person may be able to make a decision: either to continue the family tradition and become an alcoholic, or to make a new and different life for themselves by choosing a different path.

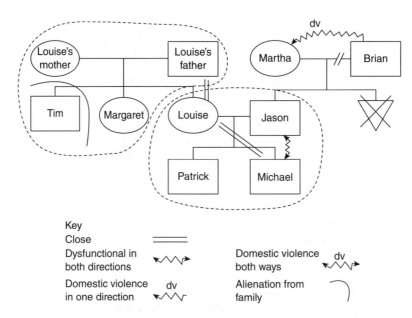

FIGURE 17.6 *Using a genogram to illustrate relationships: Jason's father was violent towards his mother during their marriage. Jason has a dysfunctional relationship with his son Michael. Louise has a close relationship with Michael. Louise is also close to her father. While Louise's parents and sister Margaret live together, her brother Tim is alienated from the rest of the family. (This genogram is invented and any similarity to a real family is purely coincidental.)*

Ideas from transactional analysis

Transactional analysis was originated by Berne (1964) and developed by Harris (1973). Ideas from transactional analysis tend to appeal to young people because they provide easy-to-follow explanations of behaviours within relationships as expressed by people. Transactional analysis models can be represented by pictorial drawings that can be put on to a white-board or poster paper. These drawings provide an anchor for the ideas that are being presented and allow the young person to participate by modifying the drawings to suit their own situation.

In Chapter 8 we described a modified version of the transactional analysis model by showing the inner components of a person as including parent, adult, young person and child. We believe that the modified model given in Chapter 8 is most useful in helping counsellors understand the needs of young people in counselling. However, when the transactional analysis model is used with young people as a psycho-educational tool, we believe that it is better to return to the original model, as proposed by Berne (1964), in which there are only three inner components identified within an individual, as follows:

1. *Inner parent*: The inner parent can be either a critical parent or a nurturing parent. The critical parent is powerful, dominating, rigid and controlling, whereas the nurturing parent is warm, protective and caring. The parent role has a high level of responsibility, including responsibility not only for self, but also for others, when the communication is directed from the inner parent to the other person's child.

2. *Inner adult*: The inner adult:

   - is reality-based and logical
   - is respectful of others rather than seeking to control them
   - seeks information before making decisions, rather than being governed by emotional responses
   - is not submissive but independent and self-sufficient
   - is flexible and able to change in response to new information.

3. *Inner child*: The inner child is childlike and helpless. It may be submissive or rebellious. It is dependent, responds reactively and without thought to emotional feelings, easily takes the victim role, may experience high levels of emotion and is prone to tantrum.

In using this model of personality with a young person, a diagram such as that shown in Figure 17.7 can be used. As this diagram is constructed, the young person can be involved in discussion of the characteristics that apply to a critical parent, a nurturing parent, an adult and an inner child. By doing this, the young person will inevitably become involved in an exploration of parts of themselves.

The young person can next be invited to explore the ways in which relationships are influenced by communications which come from differing parts of the inner self and go to various parts of the inner self of the other person, as shown in Figure 17.8. Figures 17.8(a) and 17.8(b) show examples of communication patterns which are dysfunctional and unsatisfactory because the communication lines cross each other. Many patterns such as these were described by Harris (1973). Parallel communications, as shown in

inner parent	*The critical parent:* powerful, dominating, rigid, controlling, coercive and restrictive. *The nurturing parent:* caring, permissive, protective and with a high level of responsibility for self and others.
inner adult	*The adult:* able to choose responses, self-directed, reality-based and logical. Respectful of others, seeks information before making decisions, independent and self-sufficient. Flexible and able to change in response to new information.
inner child	*The child:* dependent, childlike, helpless, submissive or rebellious. Responds without thought to emotional feelings. Easily takes the victim role, experiences high levels of emotion and is prone to tantrum.

FIGURE 17.7   *The transactional analysis model of personality*

Figures 17.8(c) and 17.8(d) tend to be more satisfactory, although they may still cause problems. For example, if one person is behaving as a child talking to a parent and the other is responding as a parent talking to a child, as shown in Figure 17.8(c), then there is effectively collaboration between the two parties to play particular roles. However, this arrangement may be uncomfortable for both, particularly over a long period of time. The communication pattern between a person who is behaving like an angry critical parent and the other person responding as a dissatisfied child will also be uncomfortable, as in Figure 17.8(d).

Generally, people are more satisfied if the communication lines are parallel and horizontal as shown in Figures 17.8(e) and 17.8(f). Parent–parent and child–child communications can be quite enjoyable and satisfying at times. However, there could sometimes be disastrous consequences from these communications because both parties might collude in undesirable behaviour. The optimum mode of communication is that between adult and adult, as shown in Figure 17.8(e).

Clearly, every person has choice about which inner part they use in communicating with others. This choice is certain to influence the outcome of communication and also to impact on the relationship. Teaching young people the transactional analysis model can help them to understand more about the ways in which they relate to, and communicate with, other people. They may, in addition, become more aware of the likely consequences of their behaviour on relationships. Readers who wish to learn more about transactional analysis might like to read Berne (1996) and Stewart (2007).

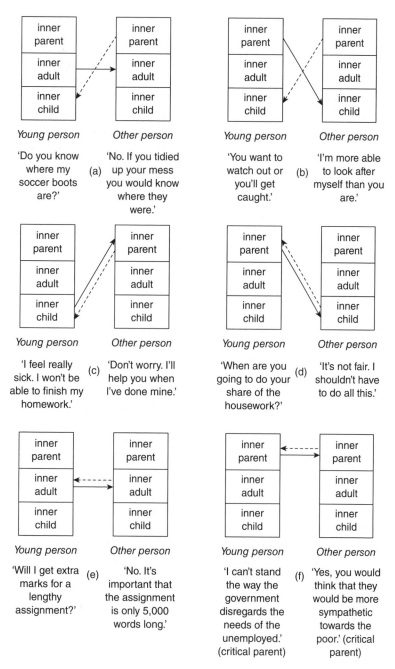

FIGURE 17.8 *Communication interaction patterns (the solid arrows designate the first message and the dotted arrows indicate the response)*

Strategies for understanding boundaries

As described in Chapter 1, young people have a heightened awareness of biological and physical needs. They are changing physically, and becoming aware of the sexual changes in their bodies and of their heightened sexual arousal. For many young people this can be a period of intense discomfort, while at the same time being exciting. They are continually faced with making decisions about personal closeness and intimacy in situations that may be new for them. Consequently, it is often necessary in counselling to help young people explore issues related to closeness and distance in relationships.

During childhood, relationships and friendships are often governed and controlled by parental decisions. This usually changes during adolescence, as the young person starts to have more freedom in choosing, maintaining and relinquishing friendships. Young people also learn that there are different types of relationship. Whereas for a child, another child is either a friend or not a friend, in adolescence there is a growing recognition of the development of a range of relationships. This range varies along a continuum, as follows:

- not a friend
- an acquaintance
- marginally a friend
- one of a number of friends (or part of a group of friends)
- a close friend
- a special friend in an intimate personal relationship.

Managing and maintaining such a range of friendships, and also allowing friendships to change, requires considerable skill, much of which has to be learnt during adolescence.

Dealing with changing friendships can be troubling for young people

Young people often have problems in understanding what they perceive as, and what may actually be, rejection by others. Often rejection by others, or the perception of rejection, is a consequence of others setting boundaries that are important for them. If a young person is able to understand the nature of boundaries, then they will be better able to accept rejection when it occurs, as it inevitably will.

To help young people understand the concept of boundaries, a modified version of the circle concept suggested by Champagne and Walker-Hirsch (1982) can be used. Figure 17.9 shows the circle model, as we will call it, which can be drawn on a large sheet of paper using felt pens.

The circles, in order of size, represent the following:

- *The central circle*: this circle is described as the young person's own personal space, which does not have to be shared with anyone else unless they decide to invite someone to do so. The young person may be invited to write their name in this circle. If another person

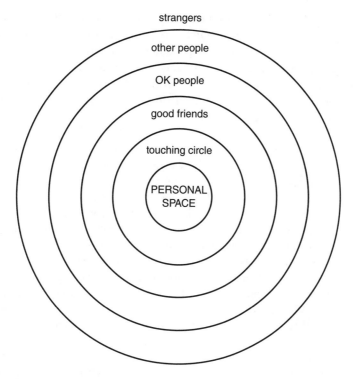

FIGURE 17.9   *The circle model*

is allowed into this circle, intimate behaviour will occur. This might involve the sharing of very private and personal information and/or touching. Sexual behaviour, which might include sexual intercourse, may also occur if that is what is mutually desired.

- *The touching circle*: this circle is one in which the young person might engage in some non-sexual physical contact such as hugging. Relatives and special friends may be invited into this circle.
- *The good friends circle*: this circle is for people with whom there are warm, positive and mutual feelings. Personal and intimate information might be shared with them. However, for many young people, there will be little or no touching or hugging.
- *The OK people circle*: this circle includes people who are in the young person's social system. Relationships with these people are comfortable, but they are not close friends. The young person may not particularly either like or dislike them. These people are part of the group to which the young person belongs. For a person to move from this 'OK people circle' to the 'good friends circle', they would need to spend more time with the young person, share more about themselves and participate more fully in common interests.
- *The other people circle*: this circle includes all those people who the young person might meet but who don't belong within the smaller circles. Thus, familiar faces such as shop-keepers, bus drivers and other people who are recognized but not generally engaged in conversation, are in this circle.
- Outside the outer circle is the space occupied by *strangers*.

When using the circle model, the young person is invited to describe the kinds of people who might be invited into each circle, and to write their descriptions or names within the correct circle. In addition, using a different coloured marker pen, behaviours that are appropriate for each circle are discussed and written in the relevant circle.

The circle model can be used to teach behaviours that are connected with the development of appropriate boundaries and relationships with others. In particular, the young person might learn the following:

1. It is appropriate for young people to have boundaries, which they draw themselves, that set limits to the closeness of relationships with other people. On the circle model, no one has the right to move into a circle closer to the centre without mutual agreement.
2. Other people have their own boundaries, which can similarly be represented by sets of circles, and have the right to decide who may enter a particular circle. Consequently, young people will not be able to control where someone else will place them. Just as they control how close they will allow others to be, so other people will similarly set limits.
3. Relationships are not fixed, but are dynamic. If the young person wishes, they can, on their circle model, allow other people to move from one circle to another. They have the right to be in control of whether or not they allow a person to move from a larger circle to a smaller one. When inviting someone to move into a smaller circle, the young person needs to respect that other person's wishes. It may be that the other person will not wish to move in closer.
4. While young people have control over allowing others to move from one circle to another in their own model, they will not have control over whether they themselves are allowed to move from one circle to a smaller one in somebody else's set of circles.
5. There are different kinds of behaviours that are appropriate for relationships within each of the circles. If the young person wishes someone to move from a larger circle to a smaller circle, then they will need to display behaviours that are inviting and create a climate which encourages the other person to want to move. Equally, if the young person wishes to move from an outer circle to an inner circle, or from an inner circle to an outer circle in somebody else's model, they will need to develop behaviours that are appropriate for achieving this, subject to the other person's co-operation.
6. Behaviours must be developed which will give other people clear messages about where they belong, so that consistent relationships will be developed without unnecessary misunderstanding. These behaviours will involve social skills such as friendship-formation skills, assertiveness skills, negotiation skills and conflict-resolution skills. The ability to have some level of flexibility is also useful, provided that boundaries are not inappropriately transgressed.
7. Boundaries need to be respected and violations addressed. The young person needs to respect other people's rights to set their boundaries. Additionally, it is important for them to learn assertive behaviours to let other people know when their own boundaries are being infringed. For example, if someone who is not in the touching circle touches them, they need to be able to say clearly that this is not OK. In this regard, the counsellor may need to role play situations so that the young person can learn appropriate responses.

> **"Respect for other people's boundaries is essential"**

Strategies to explain behaviour

Under this heading we will deal with three different models:

1. The distracting role assignment model.
2. The goal-oriented role assignment model.
3. The cycle of violence model.

These models deal with repetitive maladaptive behaviour patterns that have been learnt. Often it will be difficult for a young person to recognize these repetitive patterns of behaviour because they are entrenched and habitual. If a young person is not able to recognize the repetitive pattern, they are unlikely to be able to learn to control its use, see that it is only used at appropriate times or change it altogether, if that is what they want to do. The first step, therefore, in dealing with repetitive behaviour patterns, is to help the young person to identify a pattern that fits personally.

The patterns that will be described are patterns that are frequently encountered, but will need to be modified to suit the particular behaviours of each individual young person. The process of using the role assignment model and the cycle of violence model invites the young person to develop a personal model that describes their own behaviour.

The distracting role assignment model

The distracting role assignment model is illustrated in Figure 17.10. There are four stages in the circular process involved in this model:

1. The antecedent event.
2. Distracting behaviour by the young person.
3. The response from others.
4. Relief.

The antecedent event

This event marks the beginning of the cycle. It is usually an event that raises the young person's anxiety level. Examples of antecedent events are:

- a fight between their parents
- a close friend consuming too much alcohol
- a friend doing something dangerous.

Distracting behaviour by the young person

During this stage of the cycle the young person engages in behaviour to distract, with the hope that by doing this the heat will be taken out of the situation. Distracting

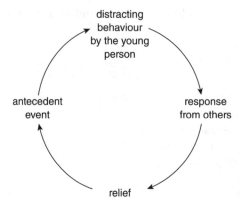

FIGURE 17.10 *The role assignment model*

behaviour is usually behaviour that the young person has used in the past, and which has been successful in reducing tension and anxiety. As a consequence of the distracting behaviour, the young person assumes a particular role. Examples are:

- During a parental fight, a young person might distract their parents by behaving in a way that results in the parents disciplining them for unacceptable behaviour. Thus, the focus has been shifted from the parental fight to the young person, who, as a consequence, has taken on the role of 'scapegoat' in order to reduce their anxiety concerning the parental fight.
- A young person might use humour as a distraction and consequently be assigned the role of 'clown'.
- A young person might become excessively protective of one parent and take on the role of 'rescuer'.
- A young person might become parental and mediate between fighting parents, thus adopting the role of 'parent'.

The response from others
During this stage there will be a response from others to the young person's distracting behaviour. This response usually deflects attention away from the antecedent event and shifts the focus from that event to the distracting behaviour. The young person's anxiety is consequently reduced, leading to the final stage of the cycle.

Relief
As a result of the young person engaging in a repetitive learnt behaviour pattern, the outcome is predictable. Both the young person and the other people involved may recognize the pattern, and respond in a consistent and predictable way to the young person's intervention. Relief from anxiety and tension is experienced by the young

person and the other people involved in the interaction. However, the use of such repetitive behaviour is almost certain to have negative consequences for the young person, as will be explained later.

The goal-oriented role assignment model

In this model the young person becomes locked into an entrenched role in the family or wider environment. By playing this role, they provide safety and stability within the system in order to try to reduce their own anxiety, but are precluded from getting some of their own needs met and may become stressed by the responsibility of the role. Examples are:

- A young person might become locked into the *protector* role because they believe that they need to rescue a young sister from the aggressive bullying tactics of an older brother. In doing this, they may need to be highly vigilant and protective of the younger sister. This vigilant behaviour will inevitably prevent them from pursuing their social needs and may result in them spending most of their social time with their younger sister rather than developing and forming relationships with their own peer group.
- A young person might be locked into a *hero* role. The hero performs well at school, is good at sport and is socially adept. By doing this, the hero may believe that they will make their dysfunctional parents feel better because they will be able to feel proud of having raised a successful child. The problem is that the hero feels driven to perform in order to avoid letting people down, and is constantly stressed by the performance expectations of others.
- A young person might take on, or be assigned, the role of *peacemaker*. The peacemaker does not like people expressing strong emotions, but likes to negotiate solutions for others. Unless the peacemaker fulfils this role they will become anxious because of their fear of strong emotions being expressed, which may result in more intense levels of conflict.

Dealing with role assignment

The problem with the use of repetitive patterns, such as those described that result in role assignment, is that the young person gets locked into a particular role which may be extremely unsatisfactory for them in the long term. In particular, by using this role, they may be unable to get important needs of their own met. Instead of getting in touch with their own needs, and using their inner adult to step back from the situation and make logical decisions so that they can assertively state their own needs, the young person becomes engaged in behaviour that has been learnt, merely to bring about temporary relief from anxiety.

Clearly, the learnt repetitive behaviour helps in the immediate avoidance of tension. However, part of the process of young people growing up is for them to recognize that at times they need to face tension, so that they can make decisions that will enable them to get their own needs met. This may sometimes involve a recognition that others may have to take responsibility for looking after themselves.

❝Sometimes difficult decisions are required❞

When helping young people who have become locked into role assignments, either of the distracting or the goal-oriented type, the counsellor can find ways to help them to recognize the role they have assumed and the reasons why they have assumed that role. Self-destructive beliefs can then be challenged and ways to interrupt the repetitive behaviour can be explored. New skills can then be rehearsed so that more adaptive behaviours can be used.

The cycle of violence model

This model is illustrated in Figure 17.11, which shows the seven stages. Some young people become locked into the cycle of violence. This can have disastrous consequences for them, for their relationships with others and for others with whom they relate. Describing this model to a young person who is caught in the cycle may enable them to identify their repetitive pattern of behaviour and to recognize the early stages of the cycle. By recognizing the early stages, they have a choice about whether to continue around the cycle or to use an alternative behaviour. The cycle of violence model may be used in conjunction with the anger-management strategies described in Chapter 16.

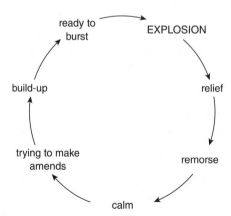

FIGURE 17.11   *The cycle of violence model*

The seven phases of the cycle of violence are:

1. The build-up phase.
2. The ready-to-burst phase.
3. The explosion phase.

4. The relief phase.
5. The remorse phase.
6. The calm phase.
7. The trying-to-make-amends phase.

The build-up phase

During the build-up phase, the young person experiences increasing and rising levels of inner tension. The reasons for this build-up of tension can be usefully explored during counselling. In the build-up phase the young person may experience feelings of intolerance, impatience, frustration and may engage in the use of self-destructive beliefs with unrealistic expectations of others (see Chapter 15). Sometimes the build-up of angry feelings will be in response to the actions of a particular person or to a particular situation or event. However, for some young people it may be generalized, and may be a response to a wide range of situations. This is most likely to occur when a young person is experiencing high levels of anxiety or where there is a mental health problem. Where mental health problems are suspected, referral to a mental health professional for assessment is strongly recommended.

The ready-to-burst phase

Without the appropriate skills to deal adaptively with the tension experienced during the build-up phase, a young person may become overwhelmed by their emotional state and have difficulty in monitoring and controlling their behaviour. During the ready-to-burst phase, the young person will probably give out verbal and non-verbal signals that demonstrate a very high level of angry feelings. Consequently, other people, who relate with them, may feel as though they are treading on eggshells and that they are waiting for an explosion. This is clearly damaging for relationships.

The explosion phase

In the explosion phase, the young person acts out anger in a destructive way, either verbally or physically. However, the consequences for others are certain to be damaging, and there will be repercussions for relationships and the well-being of the young person.

The relief phase

Once the explosion is over, the young person experiences an immediate sense of relief from built-up energy and tension. It is the relief phase that reinforces the young person's cycle of violence behaviour.

The remorse phase

During the remorse phase, the young person recognizes that their behaviour has been unacceptable, and feels guilty and apologetic. They may apologize to people, but will often attempt to minimize their behaviour by blaming others for what they perceive as provocation. They may believe that they do not have another way of dealing with their stress.

The calm phase

The calm phase is a phase in which the young person feels less emotional and is able to re-evaluate. It is in the calm stage that the young person is most likely to be able to recognize the repetitive behaviour pattern and to make decisions to avoid repetitions occurring. It is important for the young person to learn to recognize the physiological symptoms that indicate the build-up of anger (see anger management in Chapter 16).

The trying-to-make-amends phase

During this phase, the young person makes attempts to repair damaged relationships and restore comfortable relationships with others. Many young people do not have the repertoire of skills needed to do this, and experience increasing frustration as their attempts fail. This frustration tends to lock them into repeating the cycle.

Breaking the pattern

Whenever young people are locked into the cycle of violence, counsellors have a responsibility to be proactive in raising their awareness of this, so that they can learn new ways of behaving. By using the cycle of violence model, the young person can be helped to recognize that at any stage around the cycle, before the explosion occurs, they may use different behaviours, thought patterns and beliefs to break their repetitive pattern of violence. It is the counsellor's responsibility to teach the young person the skills of anger management as explained in Chapter 16. Additionally, it is important for the counsellor to be clear in letting the young person know that it is *their responsibility* to change their behaviour so that they don't continue going around the violence circle. As part of the process of breaking the cycle of violence, education can be given regarding the following four important and essential messages:

1. *'Abuse is not OK'*: Abuse includes both verbal and non-verbal behaviour that is damaging or disrespectful of others, and is never acceptable behaviour.
2. *'Provocation is not an excuse for abuse'*: Provocation is best dealt with through the use of non-abusive responses. These will vary with each particular situation. Suitable responses to provocation can be explored and rehearsed in counselling.
3. *'An abusive person is responsible for their abusive behaviour regardless of the behaviour of others'*: Taking responsibility is the key to changing abusive behaviour and it is sometimes hard for young people to recognize and accept this. When they were children, other people would have taken much of the responsibility for controlling their behaviour. They are now in the stage in life where they want more responsibility for controlling their lives but may still be reluctant to accept responsibility for making difficult changes. The issue of responsibility therefore needs to be explored fully, so that it is seen to extend to the control of unacceptable behaviour.
4. *'Provocation is abuse'*: Young people who are violent often like to blame their violence on other people's provocation, but often provoke other people themselves. This is not surprising because being provocative is a way, maladaptive though it is, of expressing frustration and anger. Therefore, it is important for young people to hear two messages

about provocation: first, as discussed, provocation does *not* justify an abusive response; and second, being provocative is not OK, but is abusive.

Clearly, the negative messages about abuse, which the young person learns in combating the cycle of violence, should be accompanied by skills training to enable positive relationships to be built.

Helping young victims of the cycle of violence

Unfortunately, many young people are subjected to, or witness, violence in their homes. These young people need specialist help to deal with their post-traumatic stress and to enable them to make decisions to protect themselves in the future. In our work with both children and young people who have been traumatized in this way, we have found that the cycle of violence model can be useful in helping them to understand the process they are experiencing or have experienced. Once they have recognized the process, it may be easier for them to devise a plan to protect themselves in the future.

Victims, during the build-up phase of the cycle, feel as though they are walking on eggshells. Often victims, unable to stand the emotional strain of the tension of the build-up phase, will precipitate the explosion by doing something provocative. Thus, they get the explosion over and can experience some relief, although they have risked serious injury in the process. As counsellors, we need to remember that children, young people and adults are killed each year through domestic violence. It is therefore important to ensure that all steps possible are taken to ensure our young clients' safety in ways that are acceptable to them.

Strategies to help change behaviour

Many of the strategies described in Chapters 14, 15 and 16 and earlier in this chapter can be used to change behaviour. In this section we will describe three additional strategies that can be useful in this regard:

- problem solving
- the use of timelines
- collapsing time.

Problem solving

In Chapter 16 we discussed the process of decision making with young people. While problem solving follows similar lines, it is more helpful to use the problem solving technique when discussing or exploring ways of dealing with everyday issues that require simple decisions. Figure 17.12 gives six steps that a young person can follow to solve problems.

STEP 1: *Identify the problem*

Discuss the events and highlight the main troubling issue. Write down what you think is the main problem.

STEP 2: *List all the possible solutions*

Write down all the ideas you can think of to solve the problem. Be as creative as you like.

1
2
3
4

STEP 3: *Make a list of the advantages and disadvantages of each solution*

Advantages	Disadvantages
1	
2	
3	
4	

STEP 4: *Choose the best solution* that takes into account your skills, money, time, resources. Write it down.

STEP 5: *List the steps you will take* to reach the desired result. List the things you need at each step to help you carry out your solution.

Steps	Things I need

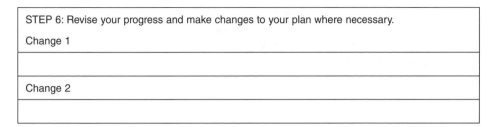

STEP 6: Revise your progress and make changes to your plan where necessary.

Change 1

Change 2

FIGURE 17.12 *Problem-solving steps*

A printable version of this figure is available to download from https://study.sagepub.com/geldardadolescents

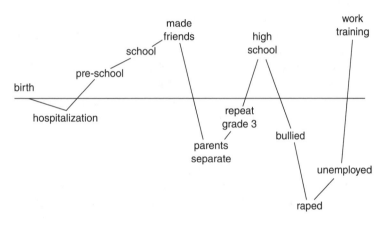

FIGURE 17.13 *Timeline to chart both positive and negative significant events*

The use of timelines

Timelines can help a young person gain a perception of changes that are occurring with time. They can be useful in conjunction with decision making, as they provide a pictorial representation of the path along which the young person is travelling. A typical timeline is shown in Figure 17.13. Timelines can be based on chronological age, beginning from childhood and moving through to adulthood, or may use dates to indicate positions along the line.

Timelines can be used to chart the sequence of important events, and to evaluate the events in the young person's life that have been negatively or positively significant. They can be useful in enabling young people to recognize repetitive behaviours that have occurred over a period of time. By indicating on a timeline that the same behaviour has occurred on various dates over a long period, the young person may recognize repetitive behaviour and be encouraged to make decisions to break the cycle that causes the repetition. Timelines can help young people gain a sense of where they have been and where they are going, and to highlight successes that can then be used to provide incentives for further change.

Collapsing time

Collapsing time can be useful in helping a young person recognize the need to make decisions and take action to change behaviour, rather than just allowing things to continue as they are. In collapsing time, a counsellor might draw a horizontal line on a whiteboard or on a large sheet of poster paper to demonstrate time. The timeline might start, at the left-hand end, from some time in the past (say six months ago) and move to a point in the middle of the line representing the present and then to a point at the right-hand end representing a particular date in the future. Intermediate dates can be added to the line as discussion occurs.

After the timeline is drawn, the young person might be encouraged to talk about ways in which changes to their behaviour have occurred at various times. These changes can then be marked on the timeline. Discussion might then move to the behaviour that currently needs to be addressed. Time can be collapsed by encouraging the young person to think about whether the target behaviour will have changed in six months' time, a year's time, two years' time or five years' time. Thus, the timing of any proposed change is brought into focus.

The use of a timeline helps raise a young person's awareness of the need to make decisions and implement them in order for change to happen. As a consequence, there may be a recognition that it is not sufficient just to talk about wanting to change. If change is to occur, then there needs to be a specific target with regard to the timing of that change. Understanding this is particularly important for young people, many of whom are extremely good at procrastinating and not doing things which they do not feel pressured to do immediately.

In summary

In this chapter we have discussed a number of psycho-educational strategies that can be used with young people. These can often be used in conjunction with one or more of the strategies described in Chapters 14, 15 and 16. When using a psycho-educational strategy it is particularly important to ensure that the young person continues to be interested and engaged in the counselling process. It can be useful to remember that it is more important to attend to the quality of the counselling relationship than to persist in using a strategy that the young person doesn't find very appealing. However, provided that a sound therapeutic alliance is maintained psycho-educational strategies can be very helpful indeed with regard to gaining information, explaining relationships and behaviour, and in helping to change behaviour.

KEY POINTS

- psycho-educational strategies work best if they involve a process of self-discovery
- rating scales can be useful in enabling a young person to work towards, and monitor, behaviour change
- genograms encourage a young person to discuss information relating to their family environment
- transactional analysis strategies can be used to help improve a young person's understanding of their own and other people's communication processes
- the circle concept can help in enabling young people to understand how to manage changing relationships
- the distracting role assignment and goal-oriented role assignment models of behaviour temporarily reduce anxiety in a young person, but lead to negative consequences
- the cycle of violence model can help the perpetrators and victims of abuse in understanding how to bring about change
- other strategies useful in helping change behaviour include problem solving, timelines and collapsing time

CASE STUDY

Kara has always been described as 'quiet' and tends to shy away from conflict, typically by agreeing with others' ideas or suggestions. Her parents have referred her to you after they found out that Kara has been experimenting with alcohol and marijuana with her friends. Her parents are also concerned that Kara may be sexually active, stating that a '16-year-old is too young to be intimately involved with boys'. How would you join with Kara in the counselling process? What strategies introduced in this chapter might be helpful for exploring the choices Kara is making?

FURTHER RESOURCES

There is a wealth of websites designed to provide young people with information about a range of topics that they may be curious about or need support for. Such websites can be a valuable supplement to psycho-educational strategies used during a session. A few websites readers may be interested in include those provided by 'Childline' (in the UK) and 'Kids Helpline' (in Australia).

- www.childline.org.uk
- www.kidshelp.com.au

18

The Use of Technology when Counselling Young People

Technology has become an everyday part of contemporary life. While technology does present challenges for the adolescent (as we outlined in Chapter 5), there is also the potential for technology to make a positive impact. In this chapter we will explore a number of ways that technology can be applied when counselling young people. In particular, we will summarize how the telephone, video conferencing, the Internet, tablets, smart phones and computer games have been used to support the counselling process when working with adolescents. We will then look at some ethical considerations unique to the use of technology in counselling.

Telephone

The telephone has long played a role in counselling. It is commonly used in conjunction with face-to-face support in order to keep in touch between sessions or to follow up with clients once face-to-face sessions have finished. In addition, multiple telephone counselling services are now available, such as, ChildLine in the UK (www.childline.org.uk) and Kids Helpline in Australia (www.kidshelp.com.au). The Helplines Partnership (www.helplines.org.au in the UK and www.helplines.org.au in Australia) lists 120 telephone services which receive over 11 million calls per year from children and adolescents (Christogiorgos et al., 2010). Clearly, adolescents are comfortable accessing support via the telephone. Indeed, in a phase of growing independence, telephone counselling offers privacy (in the form of anonymity, confidentiality and lack of parental involvement) and control (the adolescent decides when to call and when to hang up). Using the telephone to provide counselling is also convenient, easily accessible and widely available, particularly now with mobile phones and 24-hour phone lines on offer (Riemer-Reiss, 2000; Cruz et al., 2001; Tedeschi et al., 2005; Cottrell et al., 2007; Christogiorgos et al., 2010). A number of studies have explored the Kids Helpline service and found evidence for the effectiveness of telephone counselling in decreasing young people's distress (for example, King et al., 2006b).

Video conferencing

With the increasing availability of webcams and video-conferencing software (Skype has over 300 million users according to blogs.skype.com), using video conferencing in counselling is an increasingly cost-effective option to supplement face-to-face counselling or to develop a distance counselling relationship. Video conferencing has similar advantages to telephone counselling with the added benefit of visual cues, which can aid the counselling process (Alessi, 2000; Riemer-Reiss, 2000). Video conferencing allows increased access to support in a cost- and time-efficient way. However, challenges may also present, such as technical difficulties (Riemer-Reiss, 2000; Nelson and Bui, 2010). Another implication to consider is the security of video conferencing. Clearly, both counsellors and clients want to avoid unauthorized access to their video call. This concern is, however, lessening with the advent of secure websites developed specifically for counselling via video conferencing, for example, usctelehealth.com (Reamer, 2013). While many studies have reported acceptance and satisfaction with video counselling, there is currently a lack of research regarding outcomes (Alessi, 2000). However, the current evidence is looking positive (Riemer-Reiss, 2000; Nelson and Bui, 2010).

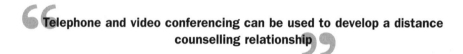

"Telephone and video conferencing can be used to develop a distance counselling relationship"

The Internet

The Internet can be used for information provision or psycho-education, programme delivery, counselling and provision of support groups. Social networking sites can also be used in a variety of ways to support young people within the counselling process. Table 18.1 outlines some of the services available in each of these categories in relation to the type of service delivery, from counsellor-administered to client-administered services, as defined by Carlbring and Andersson (2006). We will explore each of these categories in more detail below before outlining the advantages, disadvantages and research regarding the use of the Internet when supporting young people.

Information provision and psycho-education

There is an overwhelming amount of information available on the Internet. Accessing this wealth of information can be fraught with challenges as there are no limits on who can post information. Therefore, adolescents may access information that is not accurate or helpful in addressing their concerns (Oh et al., 2009). As such, it is important to be aware of websites that do reflect current understandings of the challenges adolescents may face and provide evidence-based suggestions to address these challenges. Some websites are recommended in Table 18.1.

TABLE 18.1 Counselling support for young people available on the Internet

	Psycho-education	Programme delivery	Counselling	Support groups
Counsellor-administered	Online information forum provided by SANE (itsallright.org)		*General online counselling support:* Childline (www.childline.org.uk) Kids Helpline (www.kidshelp.com.au) Kooth (www.kooth.com) E-motion provided by Visyon (www.visyon.org.uk/e-motion/) Youth Beyond Blue (www.youthbeyondblue.com) HeadSpace (www.headspace.org.au) *Drug and alcohol online counselling:* Counselling Online (counsellingonline.org.au)	
Active, but minimal counsellor contact		Cool Teens Program CD ROM-based programme to support anxiety management		Kooth (www.kooth.com) Childline (www.childline.org.uk) ReachOut (reachout.com.au) Youth Beyond Blue (www.youthbeyondblue.com)
Mostly client-administered with counsellor guidance		'Project CATCH-IT' (Competent Adulthood Transition with Cognitive-behavioural, Humanistic and Interpersonal Training) Web-based prevention programme for adolescents at risk of depression		

	Psycho-education	Programme delivery	Counselling	Support groups
Client-administered	British Association of Counselling and Psychotherapy (BACP) (www.itsgoodtotalk.org.au)	*Programmes to support young people with anxiety:*		
	Childline (www.childline.org.uk)	The Brave Program developed by the University of Queensland		
	Kids Help Line (www.kidshelp.com.au)	The Panic Centre (www.paniccenter.net)		
	Kooth (www.kooth.com)	Fear Fighter (www.fearfighter.com)		
	ReachOut (reachout.com.au)	*Programmes to support young people with depression:*		
	SANE (itsallright.org)	MoodGYM (moodgym.anu.edu.au)		
	Blue Pages (bluepages.anu.edu.au)	*Programmes to support young people with anxiety and depression:*		
	Youth Beyond Blue (www.youthbeyondblue.com)	Beating the Blues (www.beatingtheblues.co.uk)		
	Online Counselling	*Programmes to support young people with alcohol concerns:*		
	Information about drug and alcohol concerns (onlinecounselling.org.au)	Drinker's Check Up (www.drinkerscheckup.com)		

Programme delivery

A growing number of programmes are becoming available online. Many of these programmes draw on cognitive behavioural therapy (CBT) and range from entirely self-administered interventions to programmes designed to supplement face-to-face counselling (Edwards-Hart and Chester, 2010). Most programmes available for adolescents address anxiety and depression; however, programmes to support young people with drug and alcohol concerns are also available. Table 18.1 provides some examples of programmes currently available online.

Counselling

Most counselling services provided over the Internet are counsellor-administered. However, adolescents do hold more power in online, compared to face-to-face counselling, in light of the increased control they have, for example, over session length and timing (Edwards-Hart and Chester, 2010). As with telephone counselling, young people can also choose to remain anonymous. Hence, adolescents may feel a higher level of privacy, which may support disclosure. Online counselling can be offered in multiple formats, including email (Riemer-Reiss, 2000), video conferencing (as described in the previous section) and real-time chat. Please refer to Table 18.1 for some examples of online counselling services available for young people.

Support groups

Multiple support groups have been set up on the Internet to provide young people with forums on which they can access information, understanding and support for the challenges they are facing (Greidanus and Everall, 2010). While some of these forums are entirely run by participants, there are forums available that are monitored, guided or led by a range of professionals. Table 18.1 provides some examples of forums available for adolescents.

Social networking

Many adolescents use social networking to connect with offline friends or create new relationships online, as highlighted in Chapter 5. Due to the wide use of social networking sites, such as MySpace and Facebook, it is important to explore ways in which such sites can be used to the support the counselling process. For example, setting up a profile page on a social networking site is an exercise in identity exploration. Therefore, the adolescent can be encouraged to reflect on what their profile says about them or, if willing, to share their profile with the counsellor during a session in order to explore questions of identity (Clemens et al., 2008). The connectivity that social networking sites provide can also be used to support adolescents. For example, there is a function on Facebook that allows users to report suicidal comments. An email is then sent to the individual who posted the suicidal comment encouraging them to access crisis support either by telephone or online (Reamer, 2013). To date, there is a lack of evidence for using social networking sites to support adolescents. However, this is an important area for future research in light of the high use of such websites.

> ❝ The Internet affords many opportunities to support the counselling process ❞

Advantages of using the Internet in counselling

Perhaps the greatest advantage of using the Internet is the amazing access it affords, reaching, for example, into remote areas or into the homes of those unable to leave them (Hoffmann, 2006; Australian Psychological Society, 2011). The Internet also provides a sense of security and privacy due to increased anonymity, thereby encouraging disclosure. Adolescents may also find the sense of control and balance of power in the client–counsellor relationship an advantage. Provision of support over the Internet is time- and cost-efficient, convenient and flexible. In addition, the Internet is a familiar, and therefore safe, setting for young people (Chester and Glass, 2006; Bambling et al., 2008; Glasheen and Campbell, 2009; Oh et al., 2009; Williams et al., 2009; Edwards-Hart and Chester, 2010).

Disadvantages of using the Internet in counselling

With respect to text-based online counselling, one of the major concerns is whether a sufficient client–counsellor relationship can be developed without verbal and visual cues. Misunderstandings, particularly in identifying emotion, can also be more common without these verbal and visual cues. Exchange of information is slower using text-based communication; therefore, time constraints may limit effective counselling processes (King et al., 2006a; Bambling et al., 2008; Fukkink and Hermanns, 2009; Glasheen and Campbell, 2009; Williams et al., 2009). Another disadvantage inherent with technology is technical problems: sometimes technology fails (Hanley, 2012). It is also important to keep in mind that online support is not appropriate for some clients, for example, clients who are suicidal or experiencing psychosis (Chester and Glass, 2006). Text-based interventions may be better suited to those with higher levels of computer literacy and written expression skills. Unique security issues may also present with respect to unauthorized access to client information being transmitted over or stored on the Internet (Edwards-Hart and Chester, 2010).

The evidence base for using the Internet in counselling

While in its early stages, there is a growing body of evidence for support provided over the Internet. This research has mainly focused on the provision of online counselling. However, there is also some research into self-help programmes provided on the Internet (Australian Psychological Society, 2011). Reviews have concluded that there is promising evidence for the efficacy of online counselling and programme delivery, although more studies are needed (Rochlen et al., 2004). There are also indications in the current research that exposure to accurate mental health information, such as provided by Beyond Blue, may support increased awareness of mental health (Oh et al., 2009). The research evidence for the effectiveness of online support groups is mixed: some find a positive impact, others no impact at all (Barak and Dolev-Cohen, 2006).

Tablets and smart phones

Making use of the functionality of tablets and smart phones in counselling is beginning to emerge. Indeed, there has been significant growth in the number of Apps claiming to support individuals with a number of challenges, including mental health. Unfortunately, there is currently no quality control to ensure the Apps that are available are appropriate or effective in supporting young people (Epstein and Bequette, 2013). Additionally, there is little research evidence for the use of tablets and mobile phones in counselling. There are, however, a number of reviews becoming available that are designed to support counsellors and other professionals in choosing appropriate Apps to use in counselling and to recommend to clients. For example, the IMS Institute for Healthcare Informatics (IMS Health, 2013) conducted an evaluation of health care Apps currently available, including Apps to support mental health. In addition, ReachOut provides App suggestions relevant to young people (reachout.com.au).

Some Apps are designed to address specific concerns, such as Recovery Record for individuals with eating disorders (recoveryrecord.com; Epstein and Bequette, 2013). Other Apps have more general applications, for example, there are a number of mood tracking Apps, which is a common component of many counselling approaches. Other Apps can be adapted to the counselling domain. For example, there are a number of mind mapping Apps that can be used to support clients to map their behaviour, thoughts and feelings about a challenging event they are facing (Warren, 2012).

Apart from Apps, there are also other ways that tablets and smart phones can be used to support the counselling process. Text messages, for example, can be used to send young people information between sessions to support the counselling process (Sude, 2013) or as an intervention in its own right (Epstein and Bequette, 2013). In addition, reminder messages have been found to increase attendance (Sude, 2013). Tablets or smart phones can also be used to photograph or record (either audio or video) information during a session or as between-session homework (Epstein and Bequette, 2013).

Advantages of using tablets and smart phones in counselling

The ability to record information on tablets and smart phones means better quality information can be recorded and shared more easily between client and counsellor.

Access to information and activities that support the counselling process is more convenient and young people may be more motivated to engage in phone-based activities compared to their paper counterparts. In addition, using tablets and smart phones is an acceptable social activity, and therefore won't draw attention to young people using their devices to engage in therapeutic activities (Matthews et al., 2008; Epstein and Bequette, 2013; Sude, 2013).

Disadvantages of using tablets and smart phones in counselling

One concern regarding the use of tablets and smart phones within the counselling process is that of confidentiality (Epstein and Bequette, 2013). Information about the client can be accessed by unauthorized users if, for example, the device is lost or stolen. Unencrypted information kept on devices connected to the Internet can also be easily accessed without the client's consent. Therefore, it is important to encourage security measures, such as password protection and data encryption (Epstein and Bequette, 2013). Another disadvantage is the possibility of technology failure, for example, messages not being sent or received without the knowledge of the sender (Sude, 2013).

> There are a number of Apps designed for counsellors to use in session and that can be recommended to clients

Computer games

Computer games are enjoyable and motivating for many adolescents, and therefore have the potential to be an effective means of supporting young people (Knox et al., 2011). There are two categories of computer games that can be used when counselling young people: games specifically designed to be used within the counselling process and commercially available games that can be adapted to support young people. Here we provide some examples from both of these categories.

Computer games designed for counselling

A number of role-playing games have been developed for the specific purpose of supporting young people. For example, Zora is a virtual reality game that allows users to develop their own avatar to inhabit a virtual world of their own creation. In addition to the physical characteristics, users can also assign moral values to their creations. This makes Zora unique among virtual reality games and lends it to supporting young people. Zora is particularly well suited to exploring identity (www.ase.tufts.edu/DevTech/projects/zora.asp; Bers, 2006).

Computer games have also been developed in order to support the introduction and learning of relaxation techniques, such as deep breathing and visualization, through biofeedback. This approach has been found to support the reduction of anxiety and somatic symptoms. The Journey to Wild Divine is one such example (www.wilddivine.com; Knox et al., 2011).

Another approach is adventure computer games with a focus on making decisions and solving puzzles. One such game is Personal Investigator, placing the young person within a detective academy as they uncover solution-focused therapy principles to address a personal challenge. Players make a note of their discoveries in a virtual notebook that they print out to keep once completing the game (www.aplayspace.com/projects/personalinvestigator.html; Reamer, 2013).

Commercially available computer games

There are a number of virtual reality games that can be used to support the counselling process. Second Life, for example, has been used as a platform for online counselling within a virtual therapy room attended by avatars (Reamer, 2013). Virtual reality games also naturally lend themselves to the exploration of identity as they allow adolescents to develop their own avatar, and therefore experiment with their self-image (Villani et al., 2012).

Potential ethical implications

Professional bodies in both the UK and Australia have developed guidelines specifically addressing ethical issues arising from the use of technology in counselling. Here we will highlight some of these ethical implications as identified in the guidelines produced by the Australian Psychological Society (APS, 2011) and the British Association of Counselling and Psychotherapy (BACP) (Anthony and Goss, 2009). Where relevant, we will also refer to the British Psychological Society (BPS, 2013) guidelines for research conducted over the Internet. For those readers interested in including technology in their work with young people, we would encourage you to access these guidelines in full in addition to reviewing other sources of information specific to your practice. Sude (2013), for example, provides guidelines specific to the use of text messaging. Similarly, overviews of the ethical implications in relation to using email in practice are presented by Mehta and Chalhoub (2006) and Bradley et al. (2011). More general e-therapy guidelines are outlined by Prabhakar (2013). There is also a growing number of organizations that have been founded to support counsellors and other practitioners using technology. The International Society for Mental Health Online (ISMHO), for example, provides resources and information for a range of professionals who use technology to support mental health, including standards for online practice (ismho.org). Readers may also like to explore the Association for Counselling and Therapy Online (www. acto-uk.org) or the Online Therapy Institute (onlinetherapyinstitute.com).

Technology presents a number of unique ethical considerations

Counsellor expertise

Both the APS and BACP acknowledge the specialty skills and knowledge needed to successfully incorporate technology into the counselling process. As such, counsellors are encouraged to increase their understanding and skills related to providing services with the aid of technology. As part of this up-skilling, counsellors also need to consider the current research evidence and any relevant legal and registration requirements, particularly when providing services outside their registration area. The BACP encourages counsellors to seek supervision specific to their work with technology to further support their skill development.

Informed consent

When conducting research over the Internet, the BPS stresses the importance of including comprehensive information about the use of technology so that individuals can make an informed decision. This is, of course, equally important when using technology to support the counselling process, as highlighted by the APS and BACP. It is recommended that the information provided to clients includes the advantages and disadvantages of technology use along with evidence for its effectiveness and any potential risks. When conducting distance counselling, it is advised to take steps to establish the identity of the client to ensure, for example, the offered service is appropriate for the client's age and situation, and, in particular, that parental consent is not required. Not knowing the client's identity also limits the responsive action counsellors can take in crisis situations. To address this ethical dilemma, Manhal-Baugus (2001) suggests gathering contact details (a physical address and phone number) in addition to local emergency numbers before offering distance counselling. Holding an initial face-to-face or video conferencing session can confirm a young person's identity before making use of code words in distance counselling sessions to protect against imposters.

Confidentiality

The APS, BACP and BPS all highlight the importance of confidentiality when using technology for either research or counselling support. In particular, counsellors are encouraged to outline specific limits to confidentiality inherent in technology use and the means put in place to protect clients' privacy. Safeguards to consider include secure storage and back up of electronic information and the use of passwords and encryption. Counsellors are also encouraged to discuss with clients the steps they can take to ensure their information is protected, for example, not forwarding personalized information on to others and using password-protected devices.

Boundaries

Maintaining professional boundaries is another important aspect highlighted by the APS and BACP. This is a particularly important consideration in light of the potential for technologies such as mobile phones and email to be seen as personal rather than professional. To help maintain professional boundaries, the APS and BACP recommend outlining expectations with respect to technology use with all clients. This may include expectations around time frames with respect to responding to electronic communications, the number of text messages or emails clients can expect between sessions and when the counsellor will check their phone messages and email accounts. It is also important to maintain the use of professional language when using technology such as text messages or email.

In summary

While research evidence is lacking regarding technology and counselling, this is starting to change and promising evidence is beginning to emerge. Therefore, in light of the large role that technology plays in many adolescents' lives, it is important to consider the ways in which technology may be used to engage and motivate young people within the counselling process. Technologies that may be used to support adolescents include the telephone, video conferencing, the Internet, tablets, smart phones and computer games.

KEY POINTS

- the telephone, video conferencing, the Internet, tablets, smart phones and computer games can all be used to supplement the counselling process. Some technologies (telephone, video conferencing, Internet) are also being applied to develop distance counselling relationships with young people.
- the research base for technology use in counselling is beginning to emerge and, at this stage, is looking positive.
- there are a number of unique ethical considerations when using technology to support the counselling process. Guidelines produced by the APS, BPS and BACP encourage counsellors to consider implications with respect to counsellor expertise, informed consent, confidentiality and professional boundaries.

CASE STUDY

Below are described some clients who have presented to your private practice. You offer both distance and face-to-face counselling. To which clients would you offer distance counselling? What form of distance counselling would you suggest? Which clients would you encourage to engage in face-to-face counselling? Is there any technology that you would consider to supplement face-to-face sessions? What factors influenced your decision-making process?

1. Sarah (13 years old) has been referred by her mother who is concerned about an increase in family conflict. Sarah's parents have recently separated and she has refused to talk with her father since he moved out. She is arguing more frequently with her mother and younger sister (10 years old).
2. Seventeen-year-old Elijah has self-presented. He recently moved to the city from a rural area in order to commence university. In addition to missing home, Elijah has recently broken up with his girlfriend and is failing half of his subjects. He reports feeling 'down' most days and has had fleeting thoughts of 'ending it all'.
3. Saying she needs to talk through some 'relationship stuff', Nina (15 years old) has been feeling pressured to sleep with her boyfriend of the same age.
4. For about a year now, 16-year-old Ruby has been self-harming to manage her intense emotions after being sexually abused. Having recently discovered Ruby self-harming, her parents are very concerned and have referred Ruby for counselling support.
5. Riley (14 years old) reports worrying about 'everything' all of the time. His worry is keeping him up at night and he is beginning to find it difficult to concentrate at school. His father has noticed Riley's increasing attentional difficulties and has suggested he talk with someone about it.

FURTHER RESOURCES

The 'Learning App Guide' is an online database of reviews completed by a Speech Language Pathologist on a wide variety of Apps. You can get a 'sneek peek' of some of the reviews on the 'Learning App Guide' website, although you do need to subscribe to access the full guide. There are a number of other free resources available on the website.

- www.learningappguide.com

Part 4

Proactive Counselling in Practice

19

Professional and Ethical Issues

It is sensible and ethically responsible for all counsellors to be familiar with the codes of professional and ethical conduct relevant for counsellors in the country where they practice. For example, counsellors in the United Kingdom need to be familiar with and observe the requirements of the British Association for Counselling and Psychotherapy (BACP). Additionally, when working with young people we have to take account of their special needs related to their stage in life. In this regard it is important for us to respect each young person who meets with us, to recognize our professional obligations to them, and to do what we can to ensure that we are competent in attending to their needs.

Respect for the young person

This involves attending to:

- the rights of the young person
- confidentiality
- limits of the client–counsellor relationship
- cultural diversity.

Rights of the young person

Perhaps the most important right of the young person who comes to counselling is to be respected by the counsellor as an individual person who has feelings, opinions, beliefs, thoughts and constructs which need to be valued as authentically theirs. They have a right to be believed, as explained in Chapter 9, and to be respected when they disclose sensitive personal information.

" The young person needs to be valued "

Inevitably there are limits to the rights of young people, as at times there may be conflict between what the young person considers are their rights and the rights of parents and other adults who may have authority over them. As a consequence, there may be dilemmas for the counsellor with regard to particular issues such as confidentiality and the need to ensure the safety of the young person. Where these dilemmas arise, ethical considerations usually demand that the counsellor is open with the young person so that they are aware of the counsellor's position. Also, it is appropriate for such dilemmas to be discussed by the counsellor in supervision.

The incidence of such dilemmas is likely to be reduced by a counsellor ensuring that, at all times, the young person is clear about the counselling relationship, confidentiality and any obligations of the counsellor. It is essential that with regard to these issues a young person is invited to give informed consent. As discussed by Corey et al. (2011), the use of informed consent can empower the client and consequently may have therapeutic as well as ethical significance. We believe that this is particularly so when working with young people, as inevitably, due to their stage in life, they will frequently have issues with regard to lack of personal power.

Confidentiality

Counsellors who work with young people are frequently challenged in balancing the young person's need for confidentiality with parents' desires for information (Benitez, 2004). Additionally, in many cases there are other interested parties (for example, school-teachers). In practice, counsellors often have to find a balance between revealing too much and too little information to parents (Corey et al., 2011).

When a young person comes to talk with a counsellor they will often be sharing information that they are unable to talk about with any other adult. Consequently, they are likely to expect that the information they share will be held in confidence and that their privacy will be respected. In some situations there will be limits to the extent of confidentiality that may be accorded, and in these cases it is incumbent on the counsellor to be clear with the young person about the level of confidentiality which can be provided. Clearly, this will depend on the nature of the information that is being disclosed. Where the safety of the young person themselves, or of others, is at risk, the counsellor may have an ethical, and in some cases legal, responsibility to disclose the information to other people. These may include parents, people in authority such as teachers, and statutory bodies (for example, a child protection agency).

" There are limits to confidentiality when working with young people "

Respect for the young person demands that first, the young person should be informed of the limits of confidentiality. Second, they should be invited to give informed consent where disclosure to others is not essential. Third, where it is essential for ethical reasons to disclose information to others, where possible and appropriate, the young person should be consulted with regard to the way in which the information is to be passed on to other people. For example, the young person may wish to pass information on themselves, either alone or with the help of the counsellor, or they may want the counsellor to pass information on in their absence. Additionally, it is desirable that, whenever appropriate, the young person should have control of the timing of any disclosure, otherwise they will be likely to feel disempowered.

Also relevant to confidentiality is the process of recording and storing documentation related to the counselling process. In particular, it is important to ensure the security of any client information and that this information is accessible only to the counsellor. Both storage of paper and electronic data needs to be considered. Lockable filing cabinets and rooms should be commonplace and use of encryption and password protection has also become essential in this digital age as we discussed in Chapter 18.

Limits of the client–counsellor relationship

When working with clients of any age, the client–counsellor relationship cannot be an entirely equal relationship. This is especially true when working with young people, where inevitably, whether the counsellor wishes or not, the counsellor is in a position of power and influence. Young people who come to see counsellors are often in highly emotional states and are consequently very vulnerable. Because the counsellor devotes much of their energy to listening with empathy and understanding the client, a young person may perceive them as unrealistically caring and giving. This perception may make the young person vulnerable to offers of friendship and closeness. As has been described in Chapter 3, young people are particularly vulnerable with regard to relationships as these typically undergo change during adolescence. Also, young people are susceptible to powerful feelings of romantic love and may sometimes develop inappropriate feelings of romantic attachment to a counsellor. Consequently, it is essential for counsellors working with young people to set appropriate boundaries so that their client's individuality and separateness is not compromised by the counselling relationship.

"Clear boundaries between the young person and counsellor are required"

It is inevitable that some young people may experience a period of dependence on counselling or on the counsellor. Such a temporary dependence is not necessarily problematic for the client (Corey et al., 2011), provided that it is recognized by the counsellor and responded to appropriately so that long-term dependence doesn't develop.

Lamb and Catanzaro (1998) identify situations where nonsexual relationships can prove to be ethically questionable. This includes multiple relationships with clients, and physical touching of current or former clients. This issue is particularly relevant when dealing with young people who, as discussed before, are particularly vulnerable. School counsellors are sometimes in a position where they have multiple relationships with young people. They may act as counsellor, part-time teacher and/or sports coach. These multiple relationships intensify the need to set appropriate boundaries at all times.

Cultural diversity

As counsellors, it is important for us to recognize and respond appropriately to cultural issues. This is particularly relevant when working with young people. Many young people from ethnic groups are faced by challenges as a consequence of dilemmas created by differences between the cultural backgrounds of their families and the general cultural background of the society in which they live.

Reddy (2006) suggests that to be competent culturally, a counsellor requires awareness and knowledge of the individual, social and cultural context of the client. Consistent with this, some counsellors believe that it is best for clients to have counsellors from their own ethnic group. Unfortunately, it is unrealistic to expect that a counsellor will necessarily have awareness with regard to a young person's culture. Additionally, counsellors from the same ethnic group as a particular young person may not be available. What is the responsible and ethical answer to this dilemma?

"Abandon the role of cultural expert"

As explained by Tervalon and Murray-Garcia (1998), we need to leave aside the role of cultural expert and instead become the student of our ethnic clients, working with them in collaborative partnerships in the counselling relationship. It is respectful for us to be open about the limits of our knowledge and seek the information we require from the client. By joining with a young person and working collaboratively with them, they will be empowered to inform us and to help us understand the cultural issues that are troubling them so that they may find solutions that fit for them.

Professional obligations

Included among the professional obligations of a counsellor working with young people are issues related to:

- the requirements of the working environment
- working in conjunction with other professionals
- legal obligations.

The requirements of the working environment

Many counsellors who work with young people have responsibilities to an employing authority. For example, counsellors who work in schools are usually directly responsible to the school administration and are required to carry out their work in the context, and under the limitations, imposed by the school system. Similarly, counsellors who work for a child and youth protection agency must observe and respect the policies and procedures of the agency. Sometimes the requirements of the working environment will be a constraint on the counsellor's therapeutic work. Acting responsibly implies recognizing any conflicts between personal and professional values and dealing with them effectively (Corey et al., 2011). When working in a situation where there are constraints that need to be observed as a consequence of the counsellor's professional role in the particular working environment, it is respectful for the counsellor to be clear with their young clients about these. Such constraints often relate to limits with regard to confidentiality and a requirement to share information with others.

Working in conjunction with other professionals

It can, in some situations, be advantageous for counsellors of young people to work cooperatively with professionals such as psychiatrists, medical practitioners, psychologists, social workers, youth workers and other welfare workers. It is sometimes in the interests of a young person for other professionals to be appropriately informed about their situation. Wherever possible, sensible judgements need to be made in collaboration with the young person about what information can be, and is to be, disclosed and what is to be withheld.

If as a counsellor you believe that it is desirable that sensitive material be disclosed, it is usually preferable for the young person's permission to be obtained. However, in some situations there may be unusual and compelling reasons for not doing so. When a counsellor is uncertain about the appropriate ethical course of action, the matter should be discussed with their counselling supervisor.

Legal obligations

Sometimes client confidentiality may be limited by legal intervention as counsellors may be subpoenaed to give evidence in court, and in such cases withholding information may be in contempt of court. Additionally, mandatory reporting is required by counsellors from certain professions in some countries or states with regard to issues such as child abuse.

Familiarize yourself with your legal obligations

It is important for counsellors be aware that there is the distinct possibility that they could be held legally accountable if a young person engages in self-inflicted injury or if they harm another person. Also, counsellors have a duty to protect property when a minor makes a serious threat to damage or destroy it (Corey et al., 2011). Because national and state laws pertaining to confidentiality for young people are not uniform, it is essential for counsellors to be familiar with the laws of the jurisdiction in which they practise (Lawrence and Kurpius, 2000).

The counsellor's competence

When considering the need for competence by counsellors working with young people, we need to take into account:

- training
- supervision
- responsibility of the counsellor
- attitudes and values of the counsellor
- counsellor competence
- referral
- reflective practice
- the counsellor's need for self-care.

Training

In order to qualify as a counsellor, a person needs to complete an accredited course of study and training, have ongoing supervision, and meet the requirements of the relevant professional body in their country of residence; for example, in Britain the British Association for Counselling and Psychotherapy (BACP), and in Australia either the Psychotherapy and Counselling Federation of Australia (PACFA) or the Australian Counselling Association (ACA).

Because young people are a special client population, distinct education, training and supervised practice are required for counsellors who expect to work with them (Lawrence and Kurpius, 2000). Before counselling young people, it is essential that new counsellors receive specific training in working with them, and that they work under the supervision of a counsellor who is experienced in working with young people.

Counsellor training needs to continue during a counsellor's practice through attendance and participation in professional development activities, including training programmes, conferences, workshops and seminars.

> **A counsellor's training is continuous throughout their working life**

Supervision

Supervision is required for several important reasons, including to:

- enable a counsellor to work through their own personal issues
- enable counsellors to upgrade their skills
- provide an external review of the counselling process for particular clients
- address issues concerning dependency and professional boundaries.

It is extremely important that counsellors working with young people address their own personal issues, particularly in relation to issues that may have arisen during their own adolescence, and in relation to issues concerning the counsellor's values and beliefs regarding young people. However, it is essential for counsellors to address important personal issues which they recognize, even though these may not relate directly to young people, because a counsellor's personal issues can interfere with the counselling process if they are triggered during a counselling session.

To find out more about supervision and accessing supervision, readers are encouraged to contact their relevant professional body. The websites of the British Association for Counselling and Psychotherapy (BACP), the Psychotherapy and Counselling Federation of Australia (PACFA) and the Australian Counselling Association (ACA) are available in the Further Resources section at the end of this chapter.

Responsibility of the counsellor

Counsellors have to be aware at all times of their responsibilities to the community at large. This sometimes raises problems with regard to confidentiality. Whenever a member of the community is at risk, or property is likely to be damaged, or illegal actions are likely to occur or have occurred, then a counsellor needs to make a decision regarding what action is needed. Often such decisions do not involve choosing between black and white, but rather between shades of grey, and sometimes counsellors find it difficult to decide what is most appropriate in order to serve the needs of the client and the community in the long term. At these times a sensible approach is for a counsellor to talk through the ethical issues with their supervisor.

Attitudes and values of the counsellor

When discussing potential barriers to developing a collaborative relationship in Chapter 13, one factor we highlighted was our attitudes and values. Indeed, our attitudes and values not only guide our thinking, decisions and actions, but also our practice as counsellors. Therefore, it is important to be aware of our attitudes and values as well as their influence on the counselling relationship. In our own practice, we have found that being proactive and reflective is helpful to ensure our attitudes and values do not impact negatively on the counselling relationship. This may involve regularly checking in with yourself in order to explore how your attitudes and values may be influencing your practice. You may also find supervision helpful in raising your awareness of your underlying attitudes and values.

Counsellor competence

Counsellors have a responsibility to ensure that they give the highest possible standard of service. This can only be achieved through adequate training, through supervision from an experienced counsellor, and through undertaking professional development activities. Counsellors, including experienced counsellors, need to be aware of the limits of their competence. We all have limits professionally and personally, and it is essential that as counsellors we are able to recognize these limits and to be open with our clients about them. The client has a right to know whether they are seeing someone who has, or does not have, the necessary abilities to give them the help they require.

Referral

Counselling a young person requires special skills, and when clients present with particular problems it may sometimes be sensible to refer them to another counsellor or other professional who has the necessary skills. Before making a referral, it is sensible to talk with the young person concerned to check out how they would feel about being referred to another counsellor or professional. In cases where the young person is adamant that they do not wish to be referred elsewhere, it may be appropriate to continue seeing them under intensive supervision, instead of referring. However, this is a matter that needs to be discussed in supervision.

Where a young person is comfortable with the idea of being referred to another counsellor or professional, discussion with the client regarding what information is to be passed on to the new counsellor and what is to be withheld is required so that the young person has a level of control in the handover process. Clearly, there are some situations where information must be passed on to another professional for ethical reasons. Once again, this needs to be discussed with the client so that the client understands why the information is being transmitted, and can have some input with regard to the way in which the information is conveyed to the other professional, otherwise they are likely to feel disempowered.

Reflective practice

You may have noticed that we often encourage you, as counsellors, to proactively reflect on various aspects related to the counselling process. We believe that reflective practice is essential for ethical and competent practice. Indeed, it is difficult to respond to the areas of our counselling practice that require improvement if we are not aware of them! Readers interested in learning more about reflective practice might like to refer to the book *Reflective Practice in Psychotherapy and Counselling*, edited by Stedmon and Dallos (2009). The book provides an overview of the foundations and frameworks for reflective practice before discussing reflective practice in the context of a range of therapeutic approaches.

The counsellor's need for self-care

You may be surprised to be reading that the need for self-care is being discussed in this chapter. However, we believe that self-care is not only a professional issue but also an ethical one. 'Self-care [is] a basic tenet of ethical practice' (Corey et al., 2011: 63). Counselling is a profession which is very demanding emotionally on the counsellor, as the counselling relationship is in some respects an unbalanced relationship where the counsellor works in collaboration with the client to address their issues while putting their own issues aside. In the counselling process the client receives empathic support which the counsellor provides. Particularly when working with young people who have troubling issues, it can at times be emotionally distressing for the counsellor. As a consequence, it is common for counsellors to go through phases of burnout.

All counsellors experience burnout symptoms at times

A counsellor who is experiencing burnout symptoms will have difficulty in working with a young person collaboratively with regard to addressing troubling emotional issues. Consequently, counsellors have an ethical responsibility to look after themselves and to take what action is needed to recharge when they experience the onset of burnout symptoms. A number of warning signs to look for have been identified by Koocher and Keith-Spiegel (2008: 91) including: 'uncharacteristic angry outbursts, apathy, chronic frustration, a sense of depersonalization, depression, emotional and physical exhaustion, hostility, feelings of malice or aversion towards patients, reduced productivity or lowered effectiveness at work'. In our own practice we have found that proactively engaging in self-care strategies can help decrease the risk of burnout. Common self-care strategies include exercise, music, taking a bath, reading or spending time with friends or family. You may also find regular supervision helpful. What self-care strategies do you feel would work for you? For more detailed information about burnout and self-care, we recommend reading the chapter on burnout entitled 'Looking After Yourself' in one of our books, either *Practical Counselling Skills* (2005; available in the UK), *Basic Personal Counselling* (2012a; available in Australia) or *Personal Counseling Skills* (2012b; available in the USA), to learn more about burnout and how to deal with it.

KEY POINTS

- important professional and ethical issues for counsellors of young people relate to respect, professional obligations and the counsellor's competence
- respecting the young person includes their rights, confidentiality, limits to the client–counsellor relationship and attention to cultural diversity
- there are limits to confidentiality for young people due to safety issues and the rights of parents and/or other adults
- clear boundaries between a young person and counsellor are required
- professional obligations include requirements of the working environment, working with other professionals and legal obligations
- counsellors need to be aware of legal obligations regarding reporting
- counsellors need to provide a competent service by engaging in training and supervision and caring for their own needs
- referral to others is required where a counsellor does not have the relevant skills

FURTHER RESOURCES

Readers may be interested in learning more about their relevant professional body by exploring the websites of the 'British Association for Counselling and Psychotherapy (BACP)', the 'Psychotherapy and Counselling Federation of Australia (PACFA)' or the 'Australian Counselling Association (ACA)'. The 'British Psychological Society (BPS)' and 'Australian Psychological Society (APS)' also have helpful ethical, and other, resources on their websites.

- www.bacp.co.uk
- www.pacfa.org.au
- www.theaca.net.au
- www.bps.org.uk
- www.psychology.org.au

20

Case Studies

To illustrate the proactive counselling process we will describe two case studies:

- *Case 1: Max* underwent a single session of counselling.
- *Case 2: Laura* attended a programme involving six counselling sessions.

In the description of these case studies, the right-hand column indicates the skills and strategies used by the counsellor (as shown in Figure 9.2). They help to illustrate the proactive nature of the counseling process. If the right-hand column is examined, it will be apparent that the counsellor does not follow a set pattern in selecting skills and strategies but spontaneously and opportunistically responds to the current state of the client. The proactive counsellor is an eclectic and integrative counsellor, who deliberately seeks to introduce and employ strategies from differing theoretical frameworks, within one or a series of sessions, at specific times when the chosen strategies are likely to be most effective. However, this alone does not sufficiently describe the proactive process. The process needs to fit within the total framework that has been described in this book.

Case study 1: Max

Max, aged 15, is the youngest son and oldest surviving child of his mother, Mary. Mary is in her third marriage. There are no children to this marriage. Max has a younger 12-year-old sister who has the same mother but a different father. Max's 18-year-old brother Trent committed suicide three months ago. Max and Trent were children of the same father. Mary's history is one of neglect and abuse as a child and abuse and violence in adult relationships. Her sons witnessed this violence. Mary has always had a close relationship with her children and sees herself as her children's friend.

Mary approached a counsellor requesting help for Max following his brother's suicide by taking an overdose of pain-killers. Mary believed that Max needed help to deal with his responses to his brother's death. He dropped out of school after his brother's suicide. Mary is also concerned because Max has become increasingly withdrawn from the family. She believes that he may be using alcohol heavily because he frequently comes home appearing to be intoxicated. Mary describes Max's behaviours now as similar to those of his deceased brother, but different from his behaviour before Trent died. Mary says that Max has been wearing Trent's clothes, playing his music, adopting his mannerisms and socializing with Trent's friends more than with his own friends. Mary is worried that Max may also commit suicide. Attempts by Mary to talk with Max have failed. However, she believes that he is troubled and would be prepared to talk to someone else.

The counselling session

The following is a description of the counselling session that took place. This is not a verbatim report, but a summary of what happened in a session of about one hour's duration.

The counselling session	Skills and strategies used by the counsellor (see Figure 9.2)
The counsellor met Max in the waiting room, and by observing his mood and behaviour assessed that he appeared to be unhappy and anxious about being there.	*Observation*
The counsellor introduced herself informally and cheerfully.	*Relationship building*
To help Max feel at ease and join with him, she gave him a positive message about coming.	*Affirmation*
Once in the counselling room, the counsellor demonstrated her willingness to be honest in the relationship by disclosing that Max's mother had contacted her and that consequently she had some information regarding the background of what had happened in his family.	*Relationship building*
The counsellor invited Max to express what it was like for him to be there. The counsellor listened to his response and observed Max's accompanying non-verbal behaviour.	*Open questions, observation and active listening*

The counselling session

Despite his obvious restlessness, Max denied being anxious and believed he was only there because of his mother's request. This was not directly confronted as the emphasis was on building a trusting relationship at this stage. Instead, the counsellor agreed with Max's point of view and acknowledged that parents can sometimes be powerful influences on their children.

The counsellor then talked with Max about confidentiality issues as part of the joining process and reached a mutually acceptable agreement with him.

The counsellor began to explore Max's beliefs about why his mother thought he should come to counselling. In an attempt to identify the major themes and issues for Max, the counsellor asked 'If your mother was here, what do you think she would say about why she thinks you need counselling?'

Max started to talk about how his mother was 'freaking out about him' since his brother's suicide. He stated that he had noticed her distress, and voiced his concerns about her ability to cope since his brother's death. The counsellor used active listening skills to encourage Max to continue.

In a further attempt to build a positive and honest relationship, the counsellor acknowledged that she had also gained the impression that Max's mother was extremely concerned about him. As a

Skills and strategies used by the counsellor (see Figure 9.2)

Paralleled adolescent communication by agreeing with an adolescent point of view and mirroring Max's language

Relationship building

Assessing the problem through the use of active listening and circular questions

Active listening skills

Paralleled adolescent communication by open disclosure and agreement with the young person's point of view

The counselling session	Skills and strategies used by the counsellor (see Figure 9.2)
result of this disclosure, the counsellor was able to share openly with Max's opinion of his mother and agree with his perception of his mother's distraught behaviour.	
The counsellor now moved the focus on to identifying the major issues for Max himself. She gave him feedback about his current emotional state as he talked about his mother, and invited him to talk about the issues related to his feelings. Max animatedly described how his mother behaved when she 'freaked out'.	*Started to address the problem by using a feedback statement to raise awareness of issues*
Max explained that his mother's behaviour was not good for him. While listening to Max's story, the counsellor assessed Max's emotional state and observed how, as he spoke, he became agitated and sounded angry.	*Used minimal responses and reflection*
Max explained that his mother 'stressed out' when he behaved in certain ways. She cried, told him not to wear his brother's clothes and compared his behaviour to that of his dead brother (alcoholic binges and emotional withdrawal). Max said he felt that his mother depended on him too much. The counsellor summarized Max's comments and feelings regarding his mother's behaviours, and agreed that Max's mother was a problem for him.	*Assessed the problem through the use of a summary*
Max said that he did behave in the ways that his mother described, and that sometimes those behaviours of his were also uncomfortable for him, but that more importantly he was tired of his mother's behaviour and did not know what to do about it. Because Max felt as	*Joining with the young person by matching the adolescent style of communication*

The counselling session	Skills and strategies used by the counsellor (see Figure 9.2)
though the counsellor understood his position he was able to disclose his own feelings more openly.	
During the course of conversation Max deflected and digressed. The counsellor followed his digressions.	*Paralleled adolescent communication*
Max made reference to many relatives and step-family members, and gave descriptions of his mother and extended family. He meandered through his story of a family exposed to violence, separations, losses and traumas.	*Used a range of active listening counselling micro-skills*
The counsellor suggested the use of a genogram to assist Max in his description.	*Psycho-educational strategy*
The counsellor observed and listened as Max talked at length about how he became stressed and angry when his mother behaved in the ways that he described in response to his behaviours.	*Used a range of counselling micro-skills*
The counsellor matched Max's emotional affect and said that she would feel the same as Max in the same situation.	*Paralleled adolescent communication*
The counsellor used scaling questions to explore Max's perspective of his mother's belief about his need for counselling. He was invited to indicate, on a scale drawn on a white-board, how he believed his mother saw him. He was asked 'On a scale of 1 to 10, where 1 corresponded to really needing help and 10 to not needing help at all, where do you think your mother thinks you are?' Max believed that his mother would place him at about 2 or 3 on the scale. In order to explore Max's own perceptions of his resilience and coping	*Psycho-educational strategy*

The counselling session	**Skills and strategies used by the counsellor (see Figure 9.2)**
ability, he was asked 'Where do you think you are on the scale of 1 to 10?' He placed himself at about 6.	
The counsellor affirmed and validated Max's perceptions that he was coping better than his mother thought he was.	*Affirmation and validation*
To understand and assess Max's perceptions of his own coping ability more fully, the counsellor pointed out that she was puzzled because although Max said that he believed he was coping better than his mother thought he was, he had not placed his own score near the top of the scale.	*Assessing the problem through the use of a challenging question*
As a consequence of the counsellor's challenge, Max began to relate the process of his own grieving from the time he first heard news of his brother's death. The counsellor actively listened while Max explained that he had completed his grieving and was getting on with his life.	*Active listening*
As he continued, the counsellor observed that Max became restless, less confident and finally became silent. The counsellor suspected that Max was getting in touch with emotions related to the death of his brother. She decided to focus on the immediate problem of Max's current emotional state.	*Observation*
The counsellor helped Max get in touch with his feelings and thoughts by identifying his bodily sensations and connecting these to his emotional feelings and thoughts.	*Used feedback statement to raise awareness*

The counselling session	Skills and strategies used by the counsellor (see Figure 9.2)
Max cried, and talked about his brother and the loss of his brother. He identified his past dependency on his brother as a father figure and his fear about not being able to get support or advice from now on.	*Minimal responses and reflection*
The counsellor addressed the problem of Max's vulnerability and fear by using a psychodramatic technique to increase Max's awareness of his own innate strength, wisdom and ability to solve problems. The counsellor helped Max to externalize his fear, symbolized by a coloured cushion, and encouraged a dialogue between Max and his 'fear'.	*Creative strategy*
To complete the use of the creative strategy, the counsellor helped Max to explore current emotional feelings so that he could verbalize these and feel more in control.	*Used range of counselling micro-skills*
Max continued to talk about his regret at not having told his brother how much he had valued him as a role model and how he had relied on him.	*Active listening*
The counsellor helped Max to address the problem of his lost opportunity to talk with his brother. The counsellor made use of the two-chair technique to enable Max to role play a conversation between himself and his brother. In this conversation, Max expressed previously unexpressed feelings and thoughts.	*Creative strategy*
The use of this strategy enabled Max to access other thoughts. He explained that he believed that he was just like his	*Reflection of content and feelings*

The counselling session	Skills and strategies used by the counsellor (see Figure 9.2)
brother. He also expressed emotional feelings towards his brother, and expressed anger towards him for committing suicide.	
Max suggested several alternative solutions that his brother could have taken, and implied that he himself would have behaved differently given the same circumstances. The counsellor challenged Max about conflicting information he had given as to whether he was the same as, or different from, his brother.	*Used a challenging question*
To explore the differences between Max and his brother, and to address Max's need, as a young man, to search for an individual and unique identity, the counsellor encouraged Max to draw up two lists. One list was of ways he was like his brother, and the other was of ways he was not like his brother. Max did this enthusiastically.	*Used a cognitive strategy to anchor the differences through the use of a visual list*
From this a discussion ensued about Max's predictions concerning his own future behaviours. The counsellor took the opportunity to help Max explore his lifestyle goals. He now seemed more relaxed and appeared to be pleased with himself.	*Cognitive strategy*
After this discussion had been completed, the counsellor took control by using a transitional question to return Max's attention to the earlier issue regarding his mother's perceptions of his need for help. Using the scale of 1 to 10, the counsellor asked Max to imagine how his mother would behave differently if she gave him a score of 10.	*Counsellor took control by using a transitional question to return to an earlier issue*

The counselling session	Skills and strategies used by the counsellor (see Figure 9.2)
Rather than answer this question, Max began to laugh and said that he would have to change into an almost entirely new person for his mother to be able to give him a score of 10.	
The counsellor made use of humour to maintain the positive relationship and energy of the conversation. She exaggerated by suggesting outrageous behaviours Max might need to use if his mother was to stop worrying (for example, stop wearing his brother's clothes but start wearing his sister's, stop playing his brother's music and listen to Mozart and so on).	*Paralleled adolescent communication and made use of humour*
The counsellor mirrored and matched Max's affect to validate and amplify his responses.	*Paralleled adolescent communication*
The counsellor asked 'Can you think of a time when your mother hasn't been stressed out by worrying about you?' Max was able to identify some exceptions to his mother's distressed behaviour. This included occasions when Max had worn his own clothes, and she had commented on how nice he looked. Max was able to recognize that at times when his mother was positive towards him he felt less hostile towards her.	*Used exception-oriented question*
However, wearing his brother's clothes and using his brother's possessions were comforting for him. Max identified a dilemma about how to meet his own needs and at the same time avoid conflict with his mother. He was encouraged to describe how he would like things to be with regard to wearing his brother's clothes, and with regard to his relationship with his mother.	*Addressing the problem using future-oriented questions*

The counselling session	Skills and strategies used by the counsellor (see Figure 9.2)
The counsellor encouraged Max to use a problem-solving exercise to discover his options and choices in connection with his dilemma. Max continued by suggesting some compromises that he could put in place so that everyone might be happier.	*Cognitive strategy*
Max continued to express his uncertainty about the possibility of having 'a totally stress-free zone' when with his mother. He described his desire to become more independent of his mother and his family. The counsellor normalized Max's behaviour by suggesting that his wish to be separate and become an individual was normal for a person of his age.	*Used normalizing*
The counsellor shared with Max that when she was a teenager and wanted to be more separate, her own mother had found this difficult to accept. This information allowed Max to explore how his mother might be feeling at a time when she had recently lost her eldest son. He was able to elaborate on, and make sense of, his mother's behaviours, and consequently felt more comfortable with his situation.	*Counsellor self-disclosure to impart useful information*
Max decided that it would be useful to return for one more counselling session. The counselor agreed and negotiated a suitable time, but pointed out that if Max discovered later that this was unnecessary, then he could decide not to attend.	*Maintaining a relationship*

Follow-up

Although Max had decided that one more appointment would be helpful, he did not return for more counselling. Max's mother, Mary, did contact the counsellor to say that Max had been able to communicate with her more openly about the loss of his brother, and intended to return to school with the goal of becoming an apprentice. Mary also reported that Max was socializing with his own peer group and, while continuing to experiment with the use of alcohol, had been able to discontinue his previous bingeing behaviour. Max had also begun to form a closer relationship with his stepfather, Brian.

While Mary felt that she and Max were not as close as they had previously been, she recognized that he was behaving normally 'for a boy of his age'. She noticed also that Max continued to wear his brother's clothes and use his brother's possessions. However, this behaviour now seemed less alarming to her because of the other positive changes she had noticed.

Comments on case study 1

Because Max's brother had committed suicide it was important for the counsellor to be alert to any indications that might suggest that Max himself could be harbouring suicidal thoughts. In the absence of such indications, the counsellor believed and accepted Max's construct that the problem belonged to his mother and not to him. By doing this, Max was able to revise his constructs regarding his own and his mother's behaviour, and access and address his own issues. While proactively directing the counselling session by maintaining a focus on the primary counselling functions (as described in Figure 9.2), the counsellor empowered Max to find his own solutions. Existential ideas about anxiety being a part of life were accepted and normalized through counsellor self-disclosure. A variety of strategies and counselling skills from differing frameworks were opportunistically selected and combined to meet Max's current needs. At different points in the process, the counsellor selectively used her inner adolescent or inner adult to communicate effectively.

Case study 2: Laura

Laura was referred for counselling by a youth worker employed in a youth accommodation programme. Laura was a 16-year-old female referred because of concerns about her behaviour. Laura was described as having immature behaviour, lying, stealing, exhibiting poor hygiene, multiple somatic symptoms and low self-esteem. Laura was currently homeless. She had no reservations about attending counselling, believing that she probably needed help.

The counselling sessions

The following is a description of the counselling sessions. This is not a verbatim report, but a summary of what happened in sessions of about one hour's duration each.

The counselling sessions

First session

Laura arrived for her appointment early. In the waiting room she was talkative and on meeting the counsellor commented on the counsellor's clothes. The counsellor responded cheerfully, matching Laura's friendliness and tone.

The counsellor observed that Laura continued to interact in a somewhat agitated but familiar way with her and in general seemed unconcerned about her own or other people's personal boundaries. The counsellor took note of Laura's lack of boundaries.

The counsellor invited Laura into the counselling room, and in joining with Laura congratulated her on the apparent ease with which she was entering into a new situation, and stating that for many young people the counselling situation can be overwhelming. Laura appeared to be unimpressed with this feedback, believing that it was an expectation that she should disclose and communicate everything about herself so that the counsellor could help her. She said that she had many problems and needed lots of help. The counsellor noted that this was inconsistent with what Laura had said to others before coming to counselling, and suspected that Laura may be a very dependent teenager.

Skills and strategies used by the counsellor (see Figure 9.2)

Paralleled adolescent communication and used relationship-building skills

Assessing the problem through observation

Affirmed, normalized and paralleled adolescent communication

The counselling sessions	Skills and strategies used by the counsellor (see Figure 9.2)
The counsellor told Laura that she knew that there were many other people who were helping her, and asked what that was like for her. Laura believed that, with other people helping her, she might be able to stop behaving in ways that were getting her into trouble. The counsellor noted that Laura was relying on external controls to manage her behaviour and not taking personal responsibility for this.	*Assessing the problem by using open questions*
The counsellor then talked with Laura about confidentiality issues as part of the joining process, and reached a mutually acceptable agreement with her.	*Relationship building*
The counsellor actively listened while Laura spontaneously began to disclose information about her childhood experiences, and how she continued to have contact with her father and mother who had separated when she was young. This contact was always initiated by Laura.	*Active listening*
During this first session, Laura was talkative, articulate, anxious and confused, with regard to both recent and past memories. The counsellor observed that Laura needed to talk about herself and her experiences, and that she sometimes had difficulty separating past from current experiences.	*Active listening and observation to assess the problem*
During this session the counsellor invited Laura to draw a genogram to describe her complex family system.	*Psycho-educational strategy*

The counselling sessions	Skills and strategies used by the counsellor (see Figure 9.2)
The counsellor used a timeline to help Laura describe her past and current events and circumstances.	*Psycho-educational strategy*
The counsellor then affirmed and congratulated Laura for her ability to describe in detail her personal experiences within her complicated family system.	*Affirmation*
As she shared this information, Laura's rapid speech and physical restlessness were observed. The counsellor provided feedback to Laura about her observation of this.	*Observation and feedback*
Laura was asked to identify her bodily sensations of physical restlessness, and through doing this to get in touch with her feelings and thoughts.	*Used open questions*
Laura described her restlessness as being due to excitement at meeting with a new person and talking about herself and her family. However, she admitted that the process was stressful for her. The counsellor helped Laura to explore her feelings by externalizing her anxiety. Using cushions as symbols, the counsellor helped Laura to create a dialogue between herself and her anxiety.	*Creative strategy*
During this exercise, it was clear to Laura and the counsellor that Laura felt too fragile emotionally to disclose further information. The counsellor gave Laura feedback statements about how apprehension and anxiety in the current situation were normal.	*Normalizing*

The counselling sessions	Skills and strategies used by the counsellor (see Figure 9.2)
The counsellor shared personal experiences that reinforced this feedback statement.	*Self-disclosure paralleling adolescent communication*
Laura's heightened awareness of her anxiety helped her discover that, in order to disclose more personal information, a relationship of trust would need to be established. She said that her past experiences of trust in close relationships were not positive. The counsellor reminded Laura that she had a choice about whether to disclose or not. Discussion ensued regarding Laura's readiness for continuing counselling.	*Various counselling micro-skills were used*
The counsellor helped Laura to explore options and choices regarding further counselling by using a problem-solving technique. Laura contracted for four more sessions. She identified her goal for these sessions as the exploration of her issues with regard to trust in relationships.	*Cognitive strategy*

Second session

Laura arrived for her appointment appearing more reserved and tentative than last time. The counsellor asked her what it was like to come back for counselling. Laura likened the experience to going to the dentist.	*Relationship building and assessing the problem through the use of open questions*
The counsellor continued to use Laura's metaphor by disclosing her own fears of going to the dentist. Laura and the counsellor chatted together, mirrored each other's views and amplified each other's emotional feelings about visiting the dentist.	*Symbolic strategy and paralleling of adolescent communication*

The counselling sessions	Skills and strategies used by the counsellor (see Figure 9.2)
The counsellor disclosed techniques she herself used to make it less stressful when going to the dentist, and invited Laura to think about her own strategies. The counsellor explored with Laura whether she might be able to generalize these strategies to coping with the counselling situation.	*Self-disclosure and use of cognitive strategy*
Laura identified that being in control was important for her and, together, the counsellor and Laura negotiated ways in which this could occur during counselling.	*Addressing the problem*
The counsellor enquired about her mood and if things had been better or different since her last visit.	*Question which presupposes change*
Laura had been able to recognize that in the last session she had made a decision to explore some important issues in her life and that she was now ambivalent about this decision. The counsellor encouraged Laura to explore the risks involved with regard to her decision by helping Laura identify the gains and losses associated with her decision.	*Cognitive strategy*
Laura then felt comfortable enough to proceed with exploring the goal of trust and loyalty in relationships. The counsellor suggested that a start might be to explore her past and current relationships with her family by using miniature animals as symbols to represent her family.	*Symbolic strategy*

The counselling sessions

From this session it emerged that:

1. Laura believed she was responsible for her parents' marriage failure.
2. Laura's experience of her early childhood was chaotic, with multiple parental separations which resulted in her living with each parent at various times.
3. She believed that she had been sexually abused by her mother's partner over a two- to three-year period and had not been believed by her mother when she disclosed this.
4. Laura believed she was unwanted by both parents and that her siblings were preferred by her parents.
5. It emerged that Laura had a strong desire to be close to her father but not her mother. She believed that her mother could not be trusted.

Laura was able to identify the major issues for her as feelings of:

- being uncared for as a child
- being disempowered
- being neglected.

Third session

Laura arrived complaining of feeling sick. The counsellor explored Laura's 'sickness' and shared memories with Laura of being sick herself.

The counsellor explored what it was like for Laura being sick.

Skills and strategies used by the counsellor (see Figure 9.2)

Various counselling micro-skills were used

Summary

Self-disclosure and paralleling of adolescent communication

Use of questions, reflections and summarizing

The counselling sessions

The counsellor encouraged Laura to make a list of the advantages of being sick and the disadvantages of being sick. Laura saw the main advantage of being sick as having an opportunity to be cared for. She believed that the disadvantages of being sick were that being sick resulted in her being disempowered. She likened the experience of being sick to that of being a child.

The counsellor asked whether Laura's experiences as a child might explain her ambivalence about trusting relationships with others. While, on the one hand, relationships might give her an opportunity to be looked after, on the other hand, they might result in her feeling anxious in case they became disempowering.

Laura responded defensively by talking about the 'hundreds' of friends she had. During this conversation it appeared that Laura was unable to understand the difference between close relationships and newly formed relationships.

The counsellor decided to use the circle model to help Laura recognize variations in closeness and distance in relationships and the need for differing boundaries. Laura was able to identify from her current social circle those people with whom she wanted closeness, and those with whom she wanted more distance. She was not confident of her ability to maintain the boundaries she wished to have. She decided to continue to explore related issues in the next counselling session.

Skills and strategies used by the counsellor (see Figure 9.2)

Cognitive strategy

Used various counselling micro-skills including questions

Various counselling micro-skills were used

Psycho-educational strategy

The counselling sessions	Skills and strategies used by the counsellor (see Figure 9.2)
Fourth session	
Laura arrived for her appointment and the counsellor observed that she was more measured and less effusive than at other times.	*Observation*
The counsellor explored Laura's level of comfort in continuing to have counselling and explored her current feelings and thoughts.	*Relationship building*
Laura was keen to continue exploring the issues of trust in relationships and reminded the counsellor of the goal that had been set in the previous week. During this session the counsellor selected a creative strategy using coloured cushions to represent each end of a continuum. This was to help Laura to integrate the polarities of being totally trusting and of not trusting at all. The counsellor encouraged Laura to explore and experience her emotional responses while she physically moved along the continuum between the cushions. Further issues emerged regarding control over closeness with others. Laura began to understand that she had a choice about where she 'stood' on the continuum in relation to closeness.	*Creative strategy*
The counsellor used cognitive behavioural strategies to help Laura explore the risks, and consequences, of being in control over closeness with others in relationships. This process raised further issues regarding Laura's self-esteem and self-worth in relationships with others. Laura identified exploration of her sense of self as a goal for the next counselling session.	*Cognitive strategy*

The counselling sessions	Skills and strategies used by the counsellor (see Figure 9.2)

Fifth session

The counsellor asked questions that presumed change had occurred during the week to discover how the week had been for Laura.

Questions presupposing change

Laura was keen to relate how things had been different for her during the week. She had experimented with making choices about her level of involvement with others, and had found the experience to be very empowering. The counsellor made her success newsworthy and congratulated her.

Cheer-leading and relationship building

Laura admitted that there were times when her confidence had failed, and as a result she had felt unworthy and undeserving of some relationships. This had happened when she had tried to contact her father.

Active listening

The counsellor invited Laura to draw herself as a 'fruit tree' in order to use the metaphor to explore Laura's perceptions of herself. During the processing of the drawing it became clear to Laura that she had many negative perceptions of herself, which were related to helplessness and victimization.

Creative strategy

The counsellor helped Laura externalize her victimization and separate this from herself so that she could view it as a separate entity. The counsellor encouraged Laura to choose a symbol to represent her victimization and to create a dialogue with the symbol.

Symbolic strategy

The counselling sessions	Skills and strategies used by the counsellor (see Figure 9.2)
The counsellor helped Laura focus on the problems caused by her victimization. Together, the counsellor and Laura spent time rediscovering times when she had not felt victimized. At this stage, an alternative story began to emerge about Laura as a person who could be strong and independent.	*Exception-oriented questions*
The counsellor reminded Laura that the four counselling sessions in the contract, made at the end of the first session, were now over, but gave her the option of continuing, if she wished. Laura decided that she would like to come to one more counselling session. It was agreed that this would be a closing session.	*Relationship maintenance*

Sixth session

Laura presented with an elevated mood, increased sense of optimism, and described encounters with others during the previous week in a positive way.	*Relationship maintenance*
Laura had begun to make plans to move out of the youth shelter into shared accommodation. The counsellor reinforced Laura's goals and invited Laura to describe her plans to achieve these goals.	*Cognitive strategy*
At this point Laura decided not to continue with counselling. She described her life as currently too full. The counsellor affirmed her decision to terminate counselling.	*Affirmation*

Follow-up

While it was recognized that Laura might return for counselling at a later date, the counsellor believed that it was important for Laura to experience a period of integration and normal adolescent behaviour without counselling support. This would enable her in the future to continue to recognize her strengths, abilities and times when she was fully in charge of her life.

Comments on case study 2

This case was very different from that of Max in case study 1. In Max's case, a speedy counselling process could be used because entrenched personal issues had not developed over a long period of time. His problem was contained rather than generalized. In Laura's case, her problems were more global, affecting her self-perception and ability to cope and find solutions. She was much more fragile emotionally because her core constructs concerning her perceptions of self were easily threatened. Consequently, the counselling process needed to move more slowly.

By recognizing that Laura was struggling with the normal adolescent task of individuation and separation, the counsellor was able to use the counselling sessions as an arena in which Laura could practise making choices and being in control. In the first session, the counsellor made it clear to Laura that she had a choice about whether to disclose or not, and whether to come back for more counselling or not. In the second session, control issues were openly discussed, and ways in which Laura could have control during counselling were negotiated.

While proactively directing the counselling sessions by maintaining a focus on the primary counselling functions, the counsellor empowered Laura to find her own solutions. Counsellor self-disclosure was used to normalize Laura's anxieties regarding going to the dentist and memories of being sick. Throughout the counselling process, a variety of strategies and counselling skills from differing frameworks were opportunistically selected and combined to meet Laura's current needs. At different points in the process, the counsellor selectively used her inner adolescent or inner adult to communicate effectively.

References

Adams, G. R. and Marshall, S. K. (1996) 'A developmental social psychology of identity: understanding the person-in-context', *Journal of Adolescence*, 19: 429–42.

Alessi, N. (2000) 'Child and adolescent telepsychiatry: reliability studies needed', *CyberPsychology and Behavior*, 3 (6): 1009–15.

Alexander, A. and Kempe, R. (1984) 'The role of the lay therapist in long term treatment', *Child Abuse and Neglect*, 6: 329–34.

Alexander, F. (1965) 'Psychoanalytic contributions to short term psychotherapy', in L. R. Wolberg (ed.), *Short Term Psychotherapy*. New York: Grune & Stratton.

American Psychiatric Association (2013) *Diagnostic and Statistical Manual of Mental Disorders* (5th edn,). Washington, DC: American Psychiatric Association.

Anderson, D. A. (1993) 'Lesbian and gay adolescents: social and developmental considerations', *High School Journal*, 77: 13–19.

Angus, L. (1990) 'Metaphor and structure of meaning: the counselling client's subjective experience', First International Conference on Counselling Psychology (1988, Porto, Portugal), *Cadernos de Consulta Psicologica*, 6: 5–11.

Anthony, K. and Goss, S. (2009) *Guidelines for Online Counselling and Psychotherapy* (3rd edn). Lutterworth: British Association for Counselling & Psychotherapy.

Archer, R. P. (2005) *MMPI-A: Assessing Adolescent Psychopathology* (3rd edn). Mahwah, NJ: Lawrence Erlbaum.

Arnett, J. (1992) 'The soundtrack of recklessness: musical preferences and reckless behaviour among adolescents', *Journal of Adolescent Research*, 7: 313–31.

Arroyo, W. and Eth, S. (1985) 'Children traumatized by Central American warfare', in S. Eth and R. S. Pynoos (eds), *Post-traumatic Stress Disorder in Children*. Washington, DC: American Psychiatric Press. pp. 103–20.

Aseltine, R. H. (1996) 'Pathways linking parental divorce with adolescent depression', *Journal of Health and Social Behaviour*, 37: 133–48.

Asher, N. (2001) 'Checking the box: the label of "model minority"', in G. M. Hudak and P. Kihn (eds), *Labeling: Pedagogy and Politics*. London: Routledge Falmer. pp. 75–91.

Atlas, J., Weissman, K. and Liebowitz, S. (1997) 'Adolescent inpatients' history of abuse and dissociative identity disorder', *Psychological Reports*, 80: 1086–92.

Australian Psychological Society. (2011) *Guidelines for Providing Psychological Services and Products Using the Internet and Telecommunications Technologies*. Melbourne: Author.

Bagley, C., Bolitho, F. and Bertrand, L. (1997) 'Sexual assault in school, mental health and suicidal behaviours in adolescent women in Canada', *Adolescence*, 32: 341–66.

Baker, R. K. and White, K. M. (2011) 'In their own words: why teenagers don't use social networking sites', *CyberPsychology, Behavior & Social Networking*, 14 (6): 395–8.

Bambling, M., King, R., Reid, W. and Wegner, K. (2008) 'Online counselling: the experience of counsellors providing synchronous single-session counselling to young people', *Counselling & Psychotherapy Research*, 8 (2): 110–6.

Bandler, R. and Grinder, J. (1979) *Frogs into Princes*. Moab, UT: Real People Press.

Barak, A. and Dolev-Cohen, M. (2006) 'Does activity level in online support groups for distressed adolescents determine emotional relief', *Counselling & Psychotherapy Research*, 6 (3): 120–4.

Barker, P. (1990) *Clinical Interviews with Children and Adolescents*. New York: Norton.

Bartoszuk, K. and Pittman, J. F. (2010) 'Profiles of identity exploration and commitment across domains', *Journal of Child & Family Studies*, 19: 444–50.

Bauman, K. E. and Ennett, S. T. (1996) 'On the importance of peer influence for adolescent drug use: commonly neglected considerations', *Addiction*, 91: 185–98.

Baumeister, R. F. (1990) 'Suicide as escape from self', *Psychological Review*, 97: 90–113.

Baumrind, D. (1971) 'Current patterns of parental authority', *Developmental Psychology Monographs*, 4, no. 1, pt 2.

Baumrind, D. (1991a) 'Effective parenting during the early adolescent transition', in P. A. Cowan and E. M. Hetherington (eds), *Family Transitions*. Hillsdale, NJ: Lawrence Erlbaum. pp. 219–44.

Baumrind, D. (1991b) 'The influence of parenting style on adolescent competence and substance use', *Journal of Early Adolescence*, 11: 56–95.

Benitez, B. R. (2004) 'Confidentiality and its exceptions', *The Therapist*, 16 (4): 32–6.

Berndt, T. J. and Hanna, N. A. (1995) 'Intimacy and self-disclosure in friendships', in K. J. Rotenberg (ed.), *Disclosure Processes in Children and Adolescents*. Cambridge: Cambridge University Press.

Berne, E. (1964) *Games People Play: The Psychology of Human Relationships*. New York: Castle Books, in association with Grove Press.

Berne, E. (1996) *Games People Play: The Basic Handbook of Transactional Analysis*. New York: Ballantine Books.

Bernet, W. (1993) 'Humor in evaluating and treating children and adolescents', *Journal of Psychotherapy Practice and Research*, 2: 307–17.

Bers, M. U. (2006) 'The role of new technologies to foster positive youth development', *Applied Developmental Science*, 10 (4): 200–19.

Biederman, J. and Faraone, S. V. (2005) 'Attention-deficit hyperactivity disorder', *The Lancet*, 366: 237–48.

Billings, A. G. and Moos, R. H. (1981) 'The role of coping responses and social resources in attenuating stress of life events', *Journal of Behavioural Medicine*, 4: 139–57.

Biswas, A., Biswas, D. and Chattopadhyay, P. K. (1995) 'Cognitive behaviour therapy in generalised anxiety disorder', *Indian Journal of Clinical Psychology*, 22: 1–10.

Bjerregaard, B. and Smith, C. (1993) 'Gender differences in gang participation, delinquency, and substance abuse', *Journal of Quantitative Criminology*, 9: 329–55.

Block, A. M. and Greeno, C. G. (2011) 'Examining outpatient treatment dropout in adolescents: a literature review', *Child and Adolescent Social Work Journal*, 28: 393–420.

Bloom, D. (2010) 'Programs and policies to assist high school dropouts in the transition to adulthood', *The Future of Children*, 20 (1): 89–108.

Blos, P. (1979) *The Adolescent Passage: Developmental Issue.* New York: International Universities Press.

Bohart, A. C. and Tallman, K. (1996) 'The active client: therapy as self-help', *Journal of Humanistic Psychology*, 36: 7–30.

Boldero, J. and Fallon, B. (1995) 'Adolescent help-seeking: what do they get help for and from whom?', *Journal of Adolescence*, 18: 193–209.

Bonetti, L., Campbell, M. A. and Gilmore, L. (2010) 'The relationship of loneliness and social anxiety with children's and adolescents' online communication', *CyberPsychology, Behavior and Social Networking*, 13 (3): 279–85.

Bordin, E. S. (1994) 'Theory and research on the therapeutic working alliance: new directions', in A. O. Horvath and L. S. Greenberg (eds), *The Working Alliance: Theory, Research and Practice.* New York: Wiley.

Borrine, N. L., Handal, P. J., Brown, N. Y. and Searight, H. R. (1991) 'Family conflict and adolescent adjustment in intact, divorced and blended families', *Journal of Consulting and Clinical Psychology*, 59: 753–5.

Bowlby, J. (1969) *Attachment.* New York: Basic Books.

Boxer, P., Huesmann, L. R., Bushman, B. J., O'Brien, M. and Moceri, D. (2009) 'The role of violent media preference in cumulative developmental risk for violence and general aggression', *Journal of Youth and Adolescence*, 38: 417–28.

Bradley, L. J., Hendricks, B., Lock, R., Whiting, P. P. and Parr, G. (2011) 'E-mail communication: issues for mental health counselors', *Journal of Mental Health Counseling*, 33 (1): 67–79.

Brent, D., Perper, J., Maritz, G. and Allman, C. (1993) 'Bereavement or depression? The impact of the loss of a friend to suicide', *Journal of the American Academy of Child and Adolescent Psychiatry*, 32: 1189–97.

Brent, D. A., Poling, K. D. and Goldstein, T. R. (2011) *Treating Depressed and Suicidal Adolescents: A Clinician's Guide.* New York: The Guilford Press.

Briggs, J. (1992) 'Travelling indirect routes to enjoy the scenery: employing the metaphor in family therapy', *Journal of Family Psychotherapy*, 3: 39–52.

Briggs Myers, I., McCaulley, M. H., Quenk, N. L. and Hammer, A. L. (1998) *MBTI Manual (A Guide to the Development and Use of the Myers Briggs Type Indicator)* (3rd edn). Mountain View, CA: Consulting Psychologists Press.

British Association for Counselling and Psychotherapy (2010) *Ethical Framework for Good Practice in Counselling and Psychotherapy.* Lutterworth: Author.

British Psychological Society. (2013) *Ethics Guidelines for Internet-Mediated Research.* Leicester: Author.

Bronfenbrenner, U. (1977) 'Toward an experimental ecology of human development', *American Psychologist*, 32 (7): 513–31.

Bronzaft, A. L. and Dobrow, S. B. (1988) 'Noise and health: a warning to adolescents' (special issue on adolescence and the environment), *Children's Environments Quarterly*, 5: 40–5.

Brown, G. W., Summers, D., Coffman, B. and Riddell, R. (1996) 'The use of hypnotherapy with school age children: five case studies', *Psychotherapy in Private Practice*, 15: 53–65.

Browne, A. and Finkelhor, D. (1986) 'Impact of child sexual abuse: a review of the research', *Psychological Bulletin*, 99: 66–77.

Budman, S. H. and Gurman, A. S. (1992) 'A time sensitive model of brief therapy: the I–D–E approach', in S. H. Budman, M. F. Hoyt and S. Friedman (eds), *The First Session in Brief Therapy*. New York: Guilford Press. pp. 111–34.

Buhrmester, D. and Prager, K. (1995) 'Patterns and functions of self-disclosure during childhood and adolescence', in K. J. Rotenberg (ed.), *Disclosure Processes in Children and Adolescents*. Cambridge: Cambridge University Press.

Burge, D., Hammen, C., Davila, J. and Daley, S. (1997) 'Attachment cognitions and college and work functioning two years later in late adolescent women', *Journal of Youth and Adolescence*, 26: 285–301.

Calabrese, R. L. and Noboa, J. (1995) 'The choice for gang membership by Mexican-American adolescents', *High School Journal*, 78: 226–35.

Call, K. T., Riedel, A. A., Hein, K., McLoyd, V., Petersen, A. and Kipke, M. (2002) 'Adolescent health and well-being in the twenty-first century: a global perspective', *Journal of Research on Adolescence*, 12 (1): 69–98.

Carlbring, P. and Andersson, G. (2006) 'Internet and psychology treatment: how well can they be combined?', *Computers in Human Behavior*, 22: 545–53.

Casper, R. and Lyubomirsky, S. (1997) 'Individual psychopathology relative to reports of unwanted sexual experiences as predictor of a bulimic eating pattern', *International Journal of Eating Disorders*, 21: 229–36.

Champagne, M. P. and Walker-Hirsch, L. W. (1982) 'Circles: a self organisation system for teaching appropriate social/sexual behaviour to mentally retarded/developmentally disabled persons', *Sexuality and Disability*, 5: 172–4.

Chantler, K. (2005) 'From disconnection to connection: "race", gender and the politics of therapy', *British Journal of Guidance & Counselling*, 33 (2): 239–56.

Chapman, A. H. and Chapman-Santana, M. (1995) 'Humor as psychotherapeutic technique', *Arquivos de Neuro Psiquiatria*, 53: 153–6.

Chassin, L. and Barrera, M. (1993) 'Substance use escalation and substance use restraint among adolescent children of alcoholics', *Psychology of Addictive Behaviours*, 7: 3–20.

Chen, S.-Y. and Fu, Y.-C. (2009) 'Internet use and academic achievement: gender differences in early adolescence', *Adolescence*, 44 (176): 797–812.

Chester, A. and Glass, C. (2006) 'Online counselling: a descriptive analysis of therapy services on the Internet', *British Journal of Guidance and Counselling*, 34 (2): 145–60.

Christogiorgos, S., Vassilopoulou, V., Florou, A., Xydou, V., Douvou, M., Vgenopoulou, S. and Tsiantis, J. (2010) 'Telephone counselling with adolescents and countertransference phenomena: particularities and challenges', *British Journal of Guidance & Counselling*, 38 (3): 313–25.

Clark, A. J. (1995) 'Projective techniques in the counselling process', *Journal of Counselling and Development*, 73: 311–16.

Clarkson, P. (2013) *Gestalt Counselling in Action* (4th edn). London: Sage.

Clemens, E. V., Shipp, A. E. and Pisarik, C. T. (2008) 'MySpace as a tool for mental health professionals', *Child and Adolescent Mental Health*, 13: 97–8.

Colarusso, C. (1992) *Child and Adult Development: A Psychoanalytic Introduction for Clinicians*. New York: Plenum Press.

Coleman, M., Fine, M. A., Ganong, L. H., Downs, K. J. M. and Pauk, N. (2001) 'When you're not the Brady Bunch: identifying perceived conflicts and resolution strategies in step-families', *Personal Relationships*, 8: 55–73.

Comings, D. (1997) 'Genetic aspects of childhood behavioural disorders', *Child Psychology and Human Development*, 27: 139–50.

Compas, B. E., Malcarne, V. L. and Fondacaro, K. M. (1988) 'Coping with stressful events in older children and adolescents', *Journal of Consulting and Clinical Psychology*, 56: 405–11.

Connor, M. J. (1994) 'Peer relations and peer pressure', *Educational Psychology in Practice*, 9: 209–15.

Corey, G. (2013) *Theory and Practice of Counselling and Psychotherapy* (9th edn). Belmont, CA: Brooks/Cole, Cengage Learning.

Corey, G., Corey, M. S., Corey, C. and Callanan, P. (2011) *Issues and Ethics in Helping Professions* (9th edn). Belmont, CA: Brooks/Cole.

Cottrell, C., Drew, J., Gibson, J., Holroyd, K. and O'Donnell, F. (2007) 'Feasibility assessment of telephone-administered behavioral treatment for adolescent migraine', *Headache: The Journal of Head & Face Pain*, 47 (9): 1293–302.

Cox, A. D., Cox, D., Anderson, R. D. and Moschis, G. P. (1993) 'Social influences of adolescents' shoplifting: theory, evidence, implications for the retail industry', *Journal of Retailing*, 69: 234–46.

Crespi, T. D. and Generali, M. M. (1995) 'Constructivist developmental theory and therapy: implications for counselling adolescents', *Adolescence*, 30: 735–43.

Cross, D., Shaw, T., Hearn, L., Epstein, M., Monks, H., Lester, L. and Thomas, L. (2009) *Australian Covert Bullying Prevalence Study (ACBPS)*. Perth: Child Health Promotion Research Centre, Edith Cowan University.

Cruz, B. R., San Martin, A. H., Gutierrez, B. L. N., Farias, M. V. and Mora, I. S. (2001) 'Identifying young people's guidance needs through telephone counseling', *Adolescence*, 36 (141): 21–32.

Cutrona, C. E., Suhr, J. A. and Macfarlane, R. (1990) 'Interpersonal transactions and the psychological sense of support', in S. Duck (ed.), *Personal Relationships and Social Support*. London: Sage. pp. 30–45.

Dacey, J., Magolis, D. and Kenny, M. (2006) *Adolescent Development* (4th edn). Chicago, IL: Brown & Benchmark.

Dalai Lama and Cutler, H. C. (2000) *The Art of Happiness: Handbook for Living* (audio tapes). New York: Simon & Schuster.

Darke, S., Ross, J. and Hall, W. (1996) 'Overdose among heroin users in Sydney, Australia: responses to overdoses', *Addiction*, 91: 413–17.

Dattilio, F. R. (1998) *Case Studies in Couple and Family Therapy: Systemic and Cognitive Perspectives*. New York: Guilford.

DeGaston, J. F., Weed, S. and Jensen, L. (1996) 'Understanding gender differences in sexuality', *Adolescence*, 31: 217–31.

Dequine, E. and Pearson-Davis, S. (1983) 'Video-taped improvisational drama with emotionally disturbed adolescents: a pilot study', *Arts in Psychotherapy*, 10: 15–21.

Derlega, V. I., Metts, S., Petronio, S. and Margulis, S. T. (1993) *Self-disclosure*. Newbury Park, CA: Sage.

Desivilya, H. S., Gal, R. and Ayalon, O. (1996) 'Long term effects of trauma in adolescence: comparison between survivors of a terrorist attack and control counterparts', *Anxiety, Stress and Coping: An International Journal*, 9: 135–50.

DiGiuseppe, R., Linscott, J. and Jilton, R. (1996) 'Developing the therapeutic alliance in child–adolescent psychotherapy', *Applied and Preventative Psychology*, 5: 85–100.

Divinyi, J. E. (1995) 'Story telling: an enjoyable and effective therapeutic tool', *Contemporary Family Therapy: An International Journal*, 17: 27–37.

Downey, J. (2003) 'Psychological counselling of children and young people', in R. Woolfe, W. Dryden and S. Strawbridge (eds), *Handbook of Counselling Psychology*. London: Sage. pp. 322–42.

Downey, V. W. and Landry, R. G. (1997) 'Self reported sexual behaviours of high school juniors and seniors in North Dakota', *Psychological Reports*, 80: 1357–8.

Dryden, W., DiGiuseppe, R. and Neenan, M. (2010) *A Primer on Rational-Emotive Behavior Therapy* (3rd edn). Champaign, IL: Research Press.

Dunn, J., Davies, L. C., O'Connor, T. G. and Sturgess, W. (2000) 'Parents' and partners' life course and family experiences: links with parent-child relationships in different family settings', *Journal of Child Psychology and Psychiatry*, 41 (8): 955–68.

Dupre, D., Miller, N., Gold, M. and Rospenda, K. (1995) 'Initiation and progression of alcohol, marijuana and cocaine use among adolescent abusers', *American Journal on Addictions*, 4: 43–8.

Dusek, J. B. (1996) *Adolescent Development and Behavior*. Englewood Cliffs, NJ: Prentice-Hall.

Earls, F., Smith, E., Reich, W. and Jung, K. G. (1988) 'Investigating psychopathological consequences of a disaster in children: a pilot study incorporating a structured diagnostic interview', *Journal of the American Academy of Child and Adolescent Psychiatry*, 27: 90–5.

Ebata, A. T. and Moos, R. H. (1991) 'Coping and adjustment in distressed and healthy adolescents', *Journal of Applied Developmental Psychology*, 12: 33–54.

Eddowes, E. and Hranitz, J. (1989) 'Educating children of the homeless', *Childhood Education*, 65: 197–200.

Edwards-Hart, T. and Chester, A. (2010) 'Online mental health resources for adolescents: overview of research and theory', *Australian Psychologist*, 45 (3): 223–30.

Ehrhardt, A. A. (1996) 'Our view of adolescent sexuality: a focus on risk behavior without the developmental context', *American Journal of Public Health*, 86: 1523–5.

Elkind, D. (1967) 'Egocentrism in adolescence', *Child Development*, 38: 1025–34.

Elkind, D. (1980) 'The origins of religion in the child', in J. Tisdale (ed.), *Growing Edges in the Psychology of Religion*. Chicago, IL: Nelson-Hall.

Elliot, D. S., Wilson, W. J., Huizinga, D. and Sampson, R. J. (1996) 'The effects of neighbourhood disadvantage on adolescent development', *Journal of Research in Crime and Delinquency*, 33: 389–426.

Eltz, M. J., Shirk, S. R. and Sarlin, N. (1995) 'Alliance formation and treatment outcome among maltreated adolescents', *Child Abuse and Neglect*, 19: 419–31.

Epstein, J. and Bequette, A. W. (2013) 'Smart phone applications in clinical practice', *Journal of Mental Health Counseling*, 35 (4): 283–95.

Epstein, N. B., Bishop, D. S. and Levin, S. (1980) 'The McMaster model of family functioning', *Advances in Family Psychiatry*, 2: 73–89.

Erikson, E. (1968) *Identity: Youth and Crisis*. New York: Norton.

Erikson, E. (1987) *Childhood and Society*. London: Paladin.

Escobar-Chaves, S. L., Tortolero, S. R., Markham, C. M., Low, B. J., Eitel, P. and Thickstun, P. (2005) 'Impact of the media on adolescent sexual attitudes and behaviors', *Pediatrics*, 116: 303–26.

Eskilson, A. and Wiley, N. G. (1987) 'Parents, peers, perceived pressure and adolescent self-concept: is a daughter a daughter all of her life?', *Sociological Quarterly*, 28: 135–45.

Feindler, E. L. and Ecton, R. B. (1986) *Adolescent Anger Control: Cognitive-behavioral Techniques*. New York: Pergamon.

Fergusson, D. M., Horwood, L. J. and Lyndley, M. T. (1997a) 'The effects of unemployment on psychiatric illness during young adulthood', *Psychological Medicine*, 27: 371–81.

Fergusson, D. M., Lynskey, M. T. and Horwood, L. J. (1997b) 'The effects of unemployment on juvenile offending', *Criminal Behaviour and Mental Health*, 7: 49–68.

Finch, A. J., Nelson, W. M. and Ott, E. S. (1993) *Cognitive Behavioral Procedures with Children and Adolescents: A Practical Guide*. Boston, MA: Allyn & Bacon.

Fitzgerald, M. (1995) 'On the spot counselling with residential youth: opportunities for therapeutic intervention', *Journal of Child and Youth Care*, 10: 9–17.

Flavell, J. H., Miller, P. H., Miller, S. A. (2002) *Cognitive Development* (4th edn). Upper Saddle River, NJ: Prentice-Hall.

Fodor, I. G. (1992) *Adolescent Assertiveness and Social Skills Training: A Clinical Handbook*. San Francisco, CA: Springer.

Ford, M. (1992) *Motivating Humans: Goals, Emotions and Personal Agency Beliefs*. Thousand Oaks, CA: Sage.

Forman, S. G. (1993) *Coping Skills Interventions for Children and Adolescents*. San Francisco, CA: Jossey-Bass.

Fowler, J. (1981) *Stages of Faith*. Melbourne: Dove.

Frank, J. D. and Frank, J. B. (1991) *Persuasion and Healing: A Comparative Study of Psychotherapy* (3rd edn). Baltimore, MD: Johns Hopkins University Press.

Frankl, V. (1973) *Psychotherapy and Existentialism: Selected Papers on Logo Therapy*. Harmondsworth: Penguin.

Fransella, F. and Dalton, P. (2000) *Personal Construct Counselling in Action* (2nd edn). London: Sage.

Frauenglass, S., Routh, D. K., Pantin, H. M. and Mason, C. A. (1997) 'Family support decreases influence of deviant peers on Hispanic adolescents' substance use', *Journal of Clinical Child Psychology*, 26: 15–23.

Frederick, C. J. (1985) 'Children traumatized by catastrophic situations', in S. Eth and R. S. Pynoos (eds), *Post-traumatic Stress Disorder in Children*. Washington, DC: American Psychiatric Press. pp. 71–100.

Friedman, H. L. (1993) 'Adolescent social development: a global perspective – implications for health promotion across cultures', *Journal of Adolescent Health*, 14: 588–94.

Frydenberg, E. (1999) *Learning to Cope: Developing as a Person in Complex Societies*. Oxford: Oxford University Press.

Frydenberg, E. and Lewis, R. (1993) 'Boys play sport and girls turn to others: age, gender, and ethnicity as determinants of coping', *Journal of Adolescence*, 16: 253–66.

Fukkink, R. G. and Hermanns, J. M. A. (2009) 'Children's experiences with chat support and telephone support', *Journal of Child Psychology & Psychiatry*, 50 (6): 759–66.

Furman, L. (1990) 'Video therapy: an alternative for the treatment of adolescents', *Arts in Psychotherapy*, 17: 165–9.

Gaoni, B., Kronenberg, J. and Kaysar, N. (1994) 'Boundaries during adolescence', *Israeli Journal of Psychiatry and Related Sciences*, 31: 19–27.

Garcia, P. (1992) 'The family effect on adolescent drug use: environmental and genetic factors', *The American Psychological Association*, 13: 39–48.

Garnefski, M. and Diekstra, R. (1996) 'Child sexual abuse and emotional and behavior problems in adolescents: gender differences', *American Academy of Child and Adolescent Psychiatry*, 36: 323–9.

Garralda, N. E. (1992) 'A selective review of child psychiatric syndromes with a somatic presentation', *British Journal of Psychiatry*, 161: 759–73.

Geldard, K. (2009) *Practical Interventions for Young People at Risk*. London: Sage.

Geldard, K. and Geldard, D. (2005) *Practical Counselling Skills: An Integrative Approach*. Basingstoke: Palgrave Macmillan.

Geldard, K. and Geldard, D. (2009) *Relationship Counselling for Children, Young People and Families*. London: Sage.

Geldard, K. and Geldard, D. (2012a) *Basic Personal Counselling: A Training Manual for Counsellors* (7th edn). Frenchs Forest: Pearson Education Australia.

Geldard, K. and Geldard, D. (2012b) *Personal Counseling Skills: An Integrative Approach* (Rev. 1st edn). Springfield, IL: Charles C. Thomas.

Geldard, K., Geldard, D. and Yin Foo, R. (2013) *Counselling Children: A Practical Introduction* (4th edn). London: Sage.

Geldard, K., Yin Foo, R. and Shakespeare-Finch, J. (2009) 'How is a fruit tree like you? Using artistic metaphors to explore and develop emotional competence in children', *Australian Journal of Guidance and Counselling*, 19: 1–13.

Gerevich, J. and Bacskai, E. (1996) 'Protective and risk predictors in the development of drug abuse', *Journal of Drug Education*, 26: 25–38.

Gibson-Cline, J. (1996) *Adolescents: From Crisis to Coping – A Thirteen Nation Study*. Oxford: Butterworth-Heinemann.

Gilligan, C. (1983) 'New maps of developments: new visions of maturity', *Annual Progress in Child Psychiatry and Child Development*, 3: 98–115.

Gilvarry, E. and McArdie, P. (2007) 'Determinants of substance misuse in young people', *Developmental Medicine and Child Neurology*, 49; 636–40.

Gladding, S. T. (2012) *Groups: A Counseling Speciality* (6th edn). Upper Saddle River, NJ: Pearson.

Glasheen, K. and Campbell, M. (2009) 'The use of online counselling within an Australian secondary school setting: a practitioner's viewpoint', *Counselling Psychology Review*, 24 (2): 42–51.

Glasser, W. (2001) *Counseling with Choice Therapy: The New Reality Therapy*. New York: Quill.

Glod, C. and Teicher, M. (1996) 'Relationship between early abuse, post-traumatic stress disorder and activity levels in pre-pubertal children', *American Academy of Child and Adolescent Psychiatry*, 34: 1384–93.

Golish, T. D. (2003) 'Stepfamily communication strengths: understanding the ties that bind', *Human Communication Research*, 29 (1), 41–80.

Graham, R. (2011) 'Trends in anxiety during adolescence', *Healthcare Counselling & Psychotherapy Journal*, 11 (1): 14–8.

Greidanus, E. and Everall, R. D. (2010) 'Helper therapy in an online suicide prevention community', *British Journal of Guidance & Counselling*, 38 (2): 191–204.

Grigg, N., Bowman, J. and Redman, S. (1996) 'Disordered eating and unhealthy weight reduction practices among adolescent females', *Preventative Medicine*, 25: 748–56.

Grinder, J. and Bandler, R. (1976) *The Structure of Magic*, vol. 2. Palo Alto, CA: Science and Behavior Books.

Grossman, N. and Rowat, K. N. (1995) 'Parental relationships, coping strategies, received support, and wellbeing in adolescents of separated or divorced and married parents', *Research in Nursing and Health*, 18: 249–61.

Guerrero, L. K. and Afifi, W. A. (1995) 'What parents don't know: taboo topics and topic avoidance in parent–child relationships', in T. J. Socha and G. Stamp (eds), *Parents, Children, and Communication: Frontiers of Theory and Research*. Hillsdale, NJ: Lawrence Erlbaum. pp. 219–45.

Haan, N. (1977) *Coping and Defending: Processes of Self–Environment Organization*. New York: Academic Press.

Hall, R., Tice, L., Beresford, T., Willey, B. and Hall, A. (1989) 'Sexual abuse in patients with anorexia nervosa and bulimia', *Psychosomatics*, 30: 73–9.

Hallsworth, S. and Young, T. (2009) 'Working with gangs and other delinquent groups', in K. Geldard (ed.), *Practical Interventions for Young People at Risk*. London: Sage.

Hammarstrom, A. (1994) 'Health consequences of youth unemployment: review from a gender perspective', *Social Science and Medicine*, 38: 699–709.

Handford, H. A., Mayes, S. D., Mattison, R. E., Humphrey, F. J., Bagnato, S., Bixler, E. O. and Kales, J. D. (1986) 'Child and parent reaction to the Three Mile Island nuclear accident', *Journal of the American Academy of Child Psychiatry*, 25: 346–56.

Hanley, T. (2012) 'Understanding the online therapeutic alliance through the eyes of adolescent service users', *Counselling & Psychotherapy Research*, 12 (1): 35–43.

Harris, T. A. (1973) *I'm OK – You're OK*. London: Pan.

Havighurst, R. J. (1972) *Developmental Tasks and Education*. (3rd edn). New York: Longman.

Hawton, K., Saunders, K. E. A., and O'Connor, R. C. (2012) 'Self-harm and suicide in adolescents', *The Lancet*, 379: 2373–82.

Heubeck, B. G., Tausch, B. and Mayer, B. (1995) 'Models of responsibility and depression in unemployed young males and females', *Journal of Community and Applied Social Psychology*, 5: 291–309.

Hintikka, U., Laukanaen, E., Marttunen, M. and Lehtonen, J. (2006) 'Good working alliance and psychotherapy are associated with positive changes in cognitive performance among adolescent psychiatric inpatients', *Bulletin of the Menninger Clinic*, 70 (4): 316–35.

Hoffman, L. (1993) *Exchanging Voices: A Collaborative Approach to Family Therapy*. London: Karnac.

Hoffman, M. (1988) 'Moral development', in M. Bornstein and M. Lamb (eds), *Developmental Psychology: An Advanced Textbook*. Hillsdale, NJ: Lawrence Erlbaum. pp. 497–548.

Hoffmann, W. A. (2006) 'Telematic technologies in mental health caring: a web-based psy-choeducational program for adolescent suicide survivors', *Issues in Mental Health Nursing*, 27 (5): 461–74.

Holland, D. and Kipnis, A. (1994) 'Metaphors for embarrassment and stories of exposure: the not so egocentric self in American culture', *Ethos*, 22: 316–42.

Horvath, A. O. (2001) 'The therapeutic alliance: concepts, research and training', *Australian Psychologist*, 36: 170–6.

Horvath, A. O. and Symonds, B. D. (1991) 'Relation between the working alliance and out-come in psychotherapy: a meta-analysis', *Journal of Counseling Psychology*, 38: 139–49.

Hoste, R. R. and le Grange, D. (2009) 'Addressing eating problems', in K. Geldard (ed.), *Practical Interventions for Young People at Risk*. London: Sage.

Hu, F. B., Flak, B. R., Hedeker, D. and Syddiqui, O. (1995) 'The influence of friends and parental smoking on adolescent smoking behaviour: the effects of time and prior smok-ing', *Journal of Applied Social Psychology*, 25: 2018–47.

Hudak, G. M. (2001) 'On what is labeled "playing": locating the "true" in education', in G. M. Hudak and P. Kihn (eds), *Labeling: Pedagogy and Politics*. London: Routledge Falmer. pp. 9–26.

Hurrelman, K., Enel, U. and Wideman, J. C. (1992) 'Impacts of school pressure, conflict with parents, and career uncertainty on adolescent stress in the Federal Republic of Germany', *International Journal of Adolescents and Youth*, 4: 33–50.

Ianni, F. A. J. (1989) *The Search for Structure: A Report on American Youth Today*. New York: Free Press.

IMS Institute for Healthcare Informatics (2013) *Patient Apps for Improved Healthcare: From Novelty to Mainstream*. Parsippany: IMS Institute for Healthcare Informatics.

Irvine, L., Elliott, L., Wallace, H. and Crombie, I. K. (2006) 'A review of major influences on current public health policy in developed countries in the second half of the 20th cen-tury', *The Journal of the Royal Society for the Promotion of Health*, 126 (2): 73–8.

Ives, R. (1994) 'Stop sniffing in the states: approaches to solvent misuse prevention in the USA', *Drugs, Education, Prevention and Policy*, 1: 37–48.

Ives, R. (2009) 'Tacking the misuse of volatile substances', in K. Geldard (ed.), *Practical Interventions for Young People at Risk*. London: Sage.

Ivey, A. E., D'Andrea, M. J. and Ivey, M. B. (2012) *Theories of Counseling and Psychotherapy: A Multicultural Perspective* (7th edn). London: Sage.

Jackson, S. and Bosma, H. (1990) 'Coping and self in adolescence', in H. Bosma and S. Jackson (eds), *Coping and Self-concept in Adolescence*. Berlin: Springer-Verlag. pp. 203–21.

James, R. K. and Gilliland, B. E. (2013) *Crisis Intervention Strategies* (7th edn). Belmont, CA: Brooks/Cole.

Janis, I. and Mann, L. (1982) 'Counseling on personal positions', in I. Janis (ed.), *Counseling on Personal Decisions: Theory and Research on Short Term Helping Relationships*. New Haven, CT: Yale University Press.

Jenkins, J. E. (1996) 'The influence of peer affiliation and student activities on adolescent drug involvement', *Adolescence*, 31: 297–306.

Jensen, A. R., Cohn, S. J. and Cohn, C. M. (1989) 'Speed of information processing in aca-demically gifted youth', *Personality and Individual Differences*, 6: 621–9.

Jolley, R. and Thomas, G. (1994) 'The development of sensitivity to metaphorical expression of moods in abstract art', *Educational Psychology*, 14: 437–50.

Josselson, R. (1987) *Finding Herself: Pathways to Identity Development in Women*. San Francisco, CA: Jossey-Bass.

Jung, C. G. (1968) *Collected Works*, vol. 9, pt 1: *The Archetypes and a Collective Unconscious* (2nd edn, revised). Princeton, NJ: Princeton University Press.

Kaffman, M. (1995) 'Brief therapy in the Israel kibbutz', *Contemporary Family Therapy: An International Journal* (special issue on family therapy in Israel), 17: 449–68.

Kalff, D. M. (2004) *Sandplay: A Psychotherapeutic Approach to the Psyche*. Cloverdale, CA: Temenos.

Kaplan, S., Pelcovitz, D., Salzinger, S. and Mandel, F. (1997) 'Adolescent physical abuse and suicide attempts', *Journal of the American Academy of Child and Adolescent Psychiatry*, 36: 799–808.

Kazdin, A. E. (1985) *Treatment of Anti-social Behavior in Children and Adolescents*. Chicago, IL: Dorsey.

Kearney, C. A. and Silverman, W. K. (1995) 'Family environment of youngsters with school refusal behavior: a synopsis with implications for assessment and treatment', *The American Journal of Family Therapy*, 23: 124–32.

Keil, F. and Batterman, N. (1984) 'A characteristic-to-defining shift in the development of word meaning', *Journal of Verbal Learning and Verbal Behaviour*, 23: 221–36.

Kelly, G. A. (1955) *The Psychology of Personal Constructs*. New York: Norton.

Kendall, P. C. and Southam-Gerow, M. A. (1996) 'Long term follow up of cognitive behavioural therapy for anxiety disordered youth', *Journal of Consulting and Clinical Psychology*, 64: 724–30.

King, R., Bambling, M., Lloyd, C., Gomurra, R., Smith, S., Reid, W. and Wegner, K. (2006a) 'Online counselling: the motives and experiences of young people who choose the Internet instead of face to face or telephone counselling', *Counselling and Psychotherapy Research*, 6 (3): 169–74.

King, R., Bambling, M., Reid, W. and Thomas, I. (2006b) 'Telephone and online counselling for young people: a naturalistic comparison of session outcome, session impact and therapeutic alliance', *Counselling and Psychotherapy Research*, 6 (3): 175–81.

Kingsbury, S. J. (1994) 'Interacting within metaphors', *American Journal of Clinical Hypnosis*, 36: 241–427.

Knight, G., Dubro, A. and Chao, C. (1985) 'Information processing and the development of cooperative, competitive and individualistic social values', *Developmental Psychology*, 27: 37–45.

Knox, M., Lentini, J., Cummings, T. S., McGrady, A., Whearty, K. and Sancrant, L. (2011) 'Game-based biofeedback for paediatric anxiety and depression', *Mental Health in Family Medicine*, 8 (3): 195–203.

Kohlberg, L. (1968) 'The child as a moral philosopher', *Psychology Today*, 2: 25–30.

Kohlberg, L. (1984) *The Psychology of Moral Development: The Nature and Validity of Moral Stages*. San Francisco, CA: Harper & Row.

Koocher, G. P. and Keith-Spiegel, P. (2008) *Ethics in Psychology and the Mental Health Professions: Standards and Cases*. Oxford: Oxford University Press.

Kroger, J. (2005) *Identity in Adolescence: The Balance between Self and Other* (3rd edn). London: Routledge.

Kutcher, S. P. and Marton, P. (1990) 'Adolescent depression: a treatment review', in J. G. Simeon and B. Ferguson (eds), *Treatment Strategies in Child and Adolescent Psychiatry*. New York: Plenum Press. pp. 20–7.

Lamb, D. H. and Catanzaro, S. J. (1998) 'Sexual and nonsexual boundary violations involving psychologists, clients, supervisees, and students: implications for professional practice', *Professional Psychology: Research and Practice*, 29 (5): 498–503.

Lambie, I. (2009) 'Young people with sexual behaviour problems: towards positive and healthy relationships', in K. Geldard (ed.), *Practical Interventions for Young People at Risk*. London: Sage.

Larson, R. W. (2002) 'Globalization, societal change, and new technologies: what they mean for the future of adolescence', *Journal of Research on Adolescence*, 12 (1): 1–30.

Larson, R. W., Wilson, S., Brown, B. B., Furstenberg, J. F. F. and Verma, S. (2002) 'Changes in adolescents' interpersonal experiences: are they being prepared for adult relationships in the twenty-first century?', *Journal of Research on Adolescence*, 12 (1): 31–68.

Lawrence, G. and Kurpius, S. E. R. (2000) 'Legal and ethical issues involved when counseling minors in nonschool settings', *Journal of Counselling and Development*, 78 (2): 130–6.

Laye-Gindhu, A. and Schonert-Reichl, K. A. (2005) 'Nonsuicidal self-harm among community adolescents: understanding the "whats" and "whys" of self-harm', *Journal of Youth and Adolescence*, 34 (5): 447–57.

Lazarus, J. D. and Folkman, S. (1984) *Stress, Appraisal and Coping*. New York: Springer.

Leavitt, R. S. and Pill, C. J. (1995) 'Composing a self through writing: the ego and the ink', *Smith College Studies in Social Work*, 65: 137–49.

Leebert, H. (2006) 'Reflections on … the colour blindness of counselling', *Healthcare Counselling & Psychotherapy Journal*, 6 (4): 4–5.

Levingston, B. and Melrose, J. (2009) 'Alcohol and young people', in K. Geldard (ed.), *Practical Interventions for Young People at Risk*. London: Sage.

Lincoln, C. and McGorry, P. (1995) 'Who cares? Pathways to psychiatric care for young people experiencing a first episode of psychosis', *Psychiatric Services*, 46: 1166–71.

Lo, L. (1994) 'Exploring teenage shoplifting behavior: a choice and constraint approach', *Environment and Behavior*, 26: 613–39.

Lovat, T. J. (1991) *Childhood into Adolescence: Perspectives and Issues for Teachers*. Wentworth Fall, NSW: Social Science Press.

Lowenfeld, M. (1967) *Play in Childhood*. New York: John Wiley.

Luntz, B. and Widom, C. (1994) 'Anti-social personality disorder in abused and neglected children grown up', *American Journal of Psychiatry*, 151: 670–4.

Mabey, J. and Sorensen, B. (1995) *Counselling for Young People*. Buckingham: Open University Press.

Madanes, C. (1981) *Strategic Family Therapy*. San Francisco, CA: Jossey-Bass.

Madanes, C. (1984) *Behind the One-way Mirror: Advances in the Practice of Strategic Therapy*. San Francisco, CA: Jossey-Bass.

Madonna, J. and Caswell, P. (1991) 'The utilisation of flexible techniques in group therapy with delinquent adolescent boys', *Journal of Child and Adolescent Group Therapy*, 1: 147–57.

Malanchuk, M., Messersmith, E. E. and Eccles, J. S. (2010) 'The ontogeny of career identities in adolescence', *New Directions for Child and Adolescent Development*, 130: 97–110.

Manassis, K. (2012) *Problem Solving in Child and Adolescent Psychotherapy*. New York: The Guilford Press.

Manhal-Baugus, M. (2001) 'E-therapy: practical, ethical, and legal issues', *CyberPsychology & Behavior*, 4 (5): 551–563.

Mann, D. (1991) 'Humor in psychotherapy', *Psychoanalytic Psychotherapy*, 5: 161–70.

Martin, A. (1997) 'On teenagers and tattoos', *Journal of the American Academy of Child and Adolescent Psychiatry*, 36: 860–1.

Martinez, C. R. and Forgatch, M. S. (2002) 'Adjusting to change: linking family structure transitions with parenting and boys' adjustment', *Journal of Family Psychology*, 16 (2): 107–17.

Matthews, M., Doherty, G., Sharry, J. and Fitzpatrick, C. (2008) 'Mobile phone mood charting for adolescents', *British Journal of Guidance and Counselling*, 36 (2): 113–29.

Mazurek, M. O. and Kanne, S. M. (2010) 'Friendship and internalizing symptoms among children and adolescents with ASD', *Journal of Autism and Developmental Disorders*, 40: 1512–20.

Mazurova, A. and Rozin, M. (1991) 'Family conflicts of counter cultural youth of the USSR and possible psychotherapeutic approaches', *American Journal of Family Therapy*, 19: 47–53.

McBroom, J. R. (1994) 'Correlates of alcohol and marijuana use among junior high school students: family, peers, school problems, and psychosocial concerns', *Youth and Society*, 26: 54–68.

McClellan, J., McCurry, C., Ronnei, M. and Adams, J. (1997) 'Relationship between sexual abuse, gender and sexually inappropriate behaviors in seriously mentally ill youth', *Journal of the American Academy of Child and Adolescent Psychiatry*, 367: 959–65.

McEvoy, A. and Erickson, E. (1990) *Youth and Exploitation*. Holmes Beach, FL: Learning Publications.

McGee, R., Wolfe, D. and Wilson, S. (1997) 'Multiple maltreatment experiences and adolescent behaviour problems: adolescent perspectives', *Development and Psychopathology*, 9: 131–49.

Mead, M. (1975) *Coming of Age in Samoa*. New York: Morrow.

Meeus, W., Dekobic, M. and Iedema, J. (1997) 'Unemployment and identity in adolescence: a social comparison perspective', *Career Development Quarterly*, 45: 369–80.

Mehta, S. and Chalhoub, N. (2006) 'An e-mail for your thoughts', *Child and Adolescent Mental Health*, 11 (3): 168–70.

Meier, S. T. and Davis, S. R. (2011) *The Elements of Counseling* (7th edn). Pacific Grove, CA: Brooks/Cole.

Meshot, C. and Leitner, L. (1993) 'Adolescent mourning and parental death', *Amiga Journal of Death and Dying*, 26: 287–99.

Michell, L. and West, P. (1996) 'Peer pressure to smoke: the means depends on the method', *Health Education and Research*, 11: 39–49.

Miller, S. M. (ed.) (1983) *Counseling and Psychotherapy with Children and Adolescents*. Tampa, FL: Mariner.

Molidor, C. E. (1996) 'Female gang members: a profile of aggression and victimisation', *Social Work*, 41: 251–7.

Monsour, M. (1992) 'Meanings of intimacy in cross-and same-sex friendships', *Journal of Social and Personal Relationships*, 9: 277–95.

Moore, S. (2009) 'Sexual health related interventions', in K. Geldard (ed.), *Practical Interventions for Young People at Risk*. London: Sage.

Morra, S., Caloni, B. and d'Amico, M. (1994) 'Working memory and the intentional depiction of emotions', *Archives of Psychology*, 62: 71–87.

Mortlock, J. (1995) 'Chloe: "Who cares for me" counselling with a disturbed and disturbing teenager', *Therapeutic Care and Education*, 4: 10–13.

Moula, A., Timpka, T. and Puddephatt, A. J. (2009) 'Adult–adolescent interaction and adolescents' brain development: integrating pragmatism/interactionism and neuroscience to develop a platform for research on adolescents' life regulation', *Sociology Compass*, 3 (1): 118–36.

Naar-King, S. (2011) 'Motivational interviewing in adolescent treatment', *Canadian Journal of Psychiatry*, 56 (11): 651–57.

Nader, K., Pynoos, R. S., Fairbanks, L. and Frederick, C. (1990) 'Children's PTSD reactions one year after a sniper attack at their school', *American Journal of Psychiatry*, 147: 1526–30.

Nelson, E.-L. and Bui, T. (2010) 'Rural telepsychology services for children and adolescents', *Journal of Clinical Psychology*, 66 (5): 490–501.

Nelson, R. C. (1992) *On the Crest: Growing through Effective Choices*. Minneapolis, MN: Educational Media Corporation.

Neumark-Sztainer, D., Story, M., French, S. and Resnick, N. (1997) 'Psycho-social correlates of health compromising behaviours among adolescents', *Health Education Research*, 12: 37–52.

O' Connell, B. (2012) *Solution Focused Therapy* (3rd edn). London: Sage.

O'Keefe, M. (1996) 'The differential effects of family violence on adolescent adjustment', *Child and Adolescent Social Work Journal*, 13: 51–68.

O'Koon, J. (1997) 'Attachment to parents and peers in adolescence and their relationship with self image', *Journal of Adolescence*, 32: 471–82.

Oh, E., Jorm, A. F. and Wright, A. (2009) 'Perceived helpfulness of websites for mental health information', *Social Psychiatry & Psychiatric Epidemiology*, 44 (4): 293–99.

Oppenheimer, R., Howels, K., Palmer, R. and Chalomer, D. (1985) 'Adverse sexual experiences in childhood and clinical eating disorders: preliminary description', *Journal of Psychiatric Research*, 19: 357–61.

Ougrin, D., Tranah, T., Leigh, E., Taylor, L. and Asarnow, J. R. (2012) 'Practitioner review: self-harm in adolescents', *Journal of Child Psychology and Psychiatry*, 53 (4): 337–350.

Palazzoli, S. N., Boscolo, L., Cecchin, F. G. and Prata, G. (1980) 'Hypothesising circularity neutrality: three guidelines for the conductor of the session', *Family Process*, 19: 3–12.

Parks, M. R. and Floyd, K. (1996) 'Meanings for closeness and intimacy in friendship', *Journal of Social and Personal Relationships*, 13: 85–107.

Patton, G. C., Bond, L., Carlin, J. B., Thomas, L., Butler, H., Glover, S., Catalano, R. and Bowes, G. (2006) 'Promoting social inclusion in schools: a group-randomized trial of effects on student health risk behavior and well-being', *American Journal of Public Health*, 96 (9): 1582–7.

Patton, W. and Noller, P. (1990) 'Adolescent self-concept: effects of being employed, unemployed or returning to school', *Australian Journal of Psychology*, 42: 247–59.

Perry, M. J. and Mandell, W. (1995) 'Psychosocial factors associated with the initiation of cocaine use among marijuana users', *Psychology of Addictive Behaviours*, 9: 99–100.

Peters, M. and Weller, E. (1994) 'Resolved: several weeks of depressive symptoms after exposure to a friend's suicide is "major depressive disorder: negative"', *Journal of the American Academy of Child and Adolescent Psychiatry*, 33: 584–6.

Peters, T. C. (1990) 'Student graffiti and social class: clues for counsellors', *School Counsellor*, 38: 123–32.

Peterson, R. W. (1994) 'The adrenalin metaphor: narrative mind and practice in child and youth care', *Journal of Child and Youth Care*, 9: 107–21.

Piaget, J. (1948/1966) *Psychology of Intelligence*. New York: Harcourt.

Pierce, R. A., Nichols, M. P. and Du Brin, J. R. (1983) *Emotional Expression in Psychotherapy*. New York: Amereon.

Pierce, W., Lemke, E. and Smith, R. (1988) 'Critical thinking and moral development in secondary students', *High School Journal*, 71: 120–6.

Prabhakar, E. (2013) 'E-therapy: ethical considerations of a changing healthcare communication environment', *Pastoral Psychology*, 62 (2): 211–18.

Prochaska, J. O. (1999) 'How do people change, and how can we change to help many more people', in M. Hubble, B. Duncan and S. Miller (eds), *Heart and Soul of Change: What Works in Therapy*. Washington, DC: American Psychological Association.

Radkowski, M. and Siegel, L. J. (1997) 'The gay adolescent: stresses, adaptations, and psychosocial interventions', *Clinical Psychology Review*, 17: 191–216.

Raich, R. N., Rosen, J. C., Deus, J. and Perez, O. (1992) 'Eating disorder symptoms among adolescents in the United States and Spain: a comparative study', *International Journal of Eating Disorders*, 11: 63–72.

Raviv, A. and Maddy-Weitzman, E. (1992) 'Parents of adolescents: help seeking intentions as a function of help sources and parenting issues', *Journal of Adolescence*, 15: 115–21.

Readdick, C. A. (1997) 'Adolescents and adults at the mall: diadic interactions', *Adolescence*, 32: 313–22.

Reamer, F. G. (2013) 'Social work in a digital age: ethical and risk management challenges', *Social Work*, 58 (2): 163–72.

Reddy, P. (2006) 'Cultural diversity and professional practice', in S. Morrissey and P. Reddy (eds), *Ethics and Professional Practice for Psychologists*. Thompson: Melbourne.

Reinecke, M. A., Dattilio, F. M. and Freeman, A. (2006) *Cognitive Therapy with Children and Adolescents: A Casebook for Clinical Practice* (2nd edn). New York: Guilford Press.

Reyes, B. (1994) 'Cultural symbols and images in the counselling process', *Pastoral Psychology*, 42: 277–84.

Riemer-Reiss, M. L. (2000) 'Utilizing distance technology for mental health counseling', *Journal of Mental Health Counseling*, 22 (3): 189–203.

Robin, S. S. and Johnson, E. O. (1996) 'Attitude and peer cross pressure: adolescent drug and alcohol use', *Journal of Drug Education*, 26: 69–99.

Rochlen, A. B., Zack, J. S. and Speyer, C. (2004) 'Online therapy: review of relevant definitions, debates, and current empirical support', *Journal of Clinical Psychology*, 60: 269–83.

Rogers, C. R. (1955) *Client-Centered Therapy*. Boston, MA: Houghton–Mifflin.

Rogers, C. R. (1965) *Client-Centered Therapy: Its Current Practice, Implications and Theory*. Boston, MA: Houghton–Mifflin.

Rosenbaum, R. (1994) 'Single session therapies: intrinsic integration?', *Journal of Psychotherapy Integration*, 4: 229–52.

Rosengren, D. B. (2009) *Building Motivational Interviewing Skills: A Practitioner Workbook*. New York: The Guilford Press.

Rotenberg, K. J. (1995) *Disclosure Processes in Children and Adolescents*. Cambridge: Cambridge University Press.

Rutter, V. (1995) 'Adolescence: whose hell is it?', *Psychology Today*, 28: 54–65.

Ryce-Menuhin, J. (1992) *Jungian Sand Play: The Wonderful Therapy*. New York: Routledge, Chapman & Hall.

Ryder, R. G. and Bartle, S. (1991) 'Boundaries as distance regulators in personal relationships', *Family Process*, 30: 393–406.

Safran, D. J. and Muran, J. C. (2000) *Negotiating the Therapeutic Alliance: A Relational Treatment Guide*. New York: Guilford Press.

Safran, D. J., Muran, J. C., Eubanks-Carter, C. (2011) 'Repairing alliance ruptures', in J. C. Norcross (ed.), *Psychotherapy Relationships That Work* (2nd edn). New York: Oxford University Press.

Safyer, A. W., Leahy, B. H. and Colan, N. B. (1995) 'The impact of work on adolescent development', *Families in Society*, 76: 38–45.

Salzman, J. (1997) 'Ambivalent attachment in female adolescents: association with affective instability and eating disorders', *International Journal of Eating Disorders*, 21: 251–9.

Sanders, B. and Giolas, M. (1991) 'Dissociation and childhood trauma in psychologically disturbed adolescents', *American Journal of Psychiatry*, 148: 50–4.

Sandler, I. N., Wolchik, S. A., MacKinon, D., Ayers, T. and Roosa, M. W. (1997) 'Developing linkages between theory and intervention in stress and coping processes', in A. Walchik and I. Sandler (eds), *Handbook of Children's Coping: Linking Theory and Intervention*. New York: Plenum Press. pp. 3–40.

Santrock, J. W. (1993) *Adolescence*. Madison, WI: Brown & Benchmark.

Sattler, J. M. (2014) *Foundations of Behavioral, Social, and Clinical Assessment of Children* (6th edn). La Mesa, CA: Jerome M. Sattler, Publisher.

Schaeffer, C., Chang, R. and Henggeler, S. W. (2009) 'Responding to the use of illicit drugs', in K. Geldard (ed.), *Practical Interventions for Young People at Risk*. London: Sage.

Schlossberg, N. K. (1989) 'Marginality and mattering: key issues in building community', *New Directions for Children's Services*, 48: 5–15.

Schmidt, M. (1991) 'Problems of child abuse with adolescents in chemically dependent families', *Journal of Adolescent Chemical Dependency*, 1: 9–24.

Schonert-Reichl, K. A. and Muller, J. R. (1996) 'Correlates of help seeking in adolescents', *Journal of Youth and Adolescence*, 25: 705–31.

Schrof, J. (1995) 'Unhappy girls and boys', *US News and World Report*, 119: 86–8.

Searight, H. R., Thomas, S. L., Manley, C. M. and Ketterson, T. U. (1995) 'Self-disclosure in adolescents: a family systems perspective', in K. J. Rotenberg (ed.), *Disclosure Processes in Children and Adolescents*. Cambridge: Cambridge University Press. pp. 204–25.

Seiffge-Krenke, I. (1995) *Stress, Coping, and Relationships in Adolescence*. Hillsdale, NJ: Lawrence Erlbaum.

Shanahan, M. J., Mortimer, J. T. and Kruger, H. (2002) 'Adolescence and adult work in the twenty-first century', *Journal of Research on Adolescence*, 12 (1): 99–120.

Sharp, D. L., Cole, R. E., Kourofsky, C. E. and Blaakman, S. W. (2009) 'Intervening with youth who engage in fire-lighting', in K. Geldard (ed.), *Practical Interventions for Young People at Risk*. London: Sage.

Shave, D. and Shave, B. (1989) *Early Adolescence and the Search for Self: A Developmental Perspective*. New York: Praeger.

Shim, S., Serido, J. and Barber, B. L. (2011) 'A consumer way of thinking: linking consumer socialization and consumption motivation perspectives to adolescent development', *Journal of Research on Adolescence*, 21 (1): 290–9.

Shiner, A. (2008) 'Self-harm in adolescence', *InnovAiT*, 1 (11): 750–8.

Shulman, S., Seiffge-Krenke, I., Levy-Shiff, R. and Fabian, B. (1995) 'Peer group and family relationships in early adolescence', *International Journal of Psychology*, 30: 573–90.

Sigler, R. T. (1995) 'Gang violence', *Journal of Health Care for the Poor and Underserved*, 6: 198–203.

Simeonsson, R. J. (1994) *Risk, Resilience and Prevention: Promoting the Well Being of All Children*. Baltimore, MD: Brookes.

Singer, M. I., Anglin, T. M., Song, L. Y. and Lunghofer, L. (1995) 'Adolescents' exposure to violence and associated symptoms of psychological trauma', *Journal of the American Medical Association*, 273: 477–82.

Skegg, K. (2005) 'Self-harm', *The Lancet*, 366: 1471–83.

Slavin, J. H. (1996) 'Readiness for psychoanalytic treatment in late adolescents: developmental and adaptive considerations', *Psychoanalytic Psychology*, 13: 35–51.

Smith, C. (1997) 'Factors associated with early sexual activity among urban adolescents', *Social Work Journal*, 42: 334–46.

Sommers-Flanagan, J. and Sommers-Flanagan, R. (1996) 'The Wizard of Oz metaphor in hypnosis with treatment resistant children', *American Journal of Clinical Hypnosis*, 39: 105–14.

Spinelli, E. (2003) 'The existential-phenomenological paradigm', in R. Woolfe and W. Dryden (eds), *Handbook of Counselling Psychology* (2nd edn). London: Sage. pp. 180–98.

Spirito, A., Stark, L., Grace, N. and Stamoulis, D. (1991) 'Common problems and coping strategies reported in childhood and early adolescence', *Journal of Youth and Adolescence*, 20: 531–44.

Stedmon, J. and Dallos, R. (eds) (2009) *Reflective Practice in Psychotherapy and Counselling*. Berkshire: Open University Press.

Steinberg, L. (1990) 'Autonomy, conflict, and harmony in the family relationship', in S. S. Feldman and G. R. Elliot (eds), *At the Threshold: The Developing Adolescent*. Cambridge, MA: Harvard University Press. pp. 255–76.

Steinberg, L. and Steinberg, W. (1994) *Crossing Paths: How Your Child's Adolescence Triggers Your Own Crisis*. New York: Simon & Schuster.

Steiner, H., Garcia, I. and Matthews, Z. (1997) 'Post-traumatic stress disorder in incarcerated juvenile delinquents', *American Academy of Child and Adolescent Psychiatry*, 36: 357–65.

Stewart, I. (2007) *Transactional Analysis Counselling in Action* (3rd edn). London: Sage.

Stoddard, F. J., Norman, D. K. and Murphy, J. M. (1989) 'A diagnostic outcome study of children and adolescents with severe burns', *Journal of Trauma*, 29: 471–7.

Story, N., French, S. A., Resnick, N. D. and Blum, R. W. (1995) 'Ethnic/racial and socioeconomic differences in dieting behaviours and body image perceptions in adolescence', *International Journal of Eating Disorders*, 18: 173–9.

Sude, M. E. (2013) 'Text messaging and private practice: ethical challenges and guidelines for developing personal best practices', *Journal of Mental Health Counseling*, 35 (3): 211–27.

Sussman, T. and Duffy, M. (1996) 'Are we forgetting about gay male adolescents in AIDS related research and prevention?', *Youth and Society*, 27: 379–93.

Swanson, M. S. (1991) *At Risk Students in Elementary Education: Effective Schools for Disadvantaged Learners*. Springfield, IL: Thomas.

Taanila, A., Laitinen, E., Moilanen, I. and Jarvelin, M.-R. (2002) 'Effects of family interaction on the child's behavior in single-parent or reconstructed families', *Family Process*, 41 (4): 693–708.

Takizawa, R., Maughan, B. and Arseneault, L. (2014) 'Adult health outcomes of childhood bullying victimization: evidence from a five-decade longitudinal British birth cohort', *American Journal of Psychiatry*, 171 (7): 777–84.

Talmon, M. (1990) *Single Session Therapy: Maximizing the Effect of the First (and Often Only) Therapeutic Encounter*. San Francisco, CA: Jossey-Bass.

Tedeschi, G. J., Zhu, S.-H., Anderson, C. M., Cummins, S. and Ribner, N. G. (2005) 'Putting it on the line: telephone counseling for adolescent smokers', *Journal of Counseling & Development*, 83 (4): 416–24.

Tervalon, M. and Murray-Garcia, J. (1998) 'Cultural humility versus cultural competence: a critical distinction in defining physician training outcomes in multicultural education', *Journal of Health Care for the Poor and Underserved*, 9 (2): 117–25.

Tharp, R. (1991) 'Cultural diversity and the treatment of children', *Journal of Consulting and Clinical Psychology*, 59: 799–812.

Tomori, M. (1994) 'Personality characteristics of adolescents with alcoholic parents', *Adolescence*, 29: 949–59.

Tubman, J. G., Windle, M. and Windle, R. C. (1996) 'Cumulative sexual intercourse patterns among middle adolescents: problem behavior precursors and concurrent health risk behaviors', *Journal of Adolescent Health*, 18: 182–91.

Tucker, R. (1989) 'Teen Satanism', paper presented at the Conference on Ritual Abuse: Fact or Fiction, The Institute for the Prevention of Child Abuse, Ontario.

Turner, G. (1999) 'Peer support and young people's health', *Journal of Adolescence*, 22: 567–72.

Tyler, M. (1978) *Advisory and Counselling Services for Young People*, DHSS Research Report no. 1. London: HMSO. *USA Today Magazine* (1997) 125 (2622): 8.

Underwood, M. K., Ehrenreich, S. E., More, D., Solis, J. S. and Brinkley, D. Y. (2013) 'The BlackBerry Project: the hidden world of adolescents' text messaging and relations with internalizing symptoms', *Journal of Research on Adolescence*, 1–17.

Uno, M., Mortimer, J. T., Kim, M. and Vuolo, M. (2010) '"Holding on" or "coming to terms" with educational underachievement: a longitudinal study of ambition and attainment', *New Directions for Child and Adolescent Development*, 130: 41–56.

Valkenburg, P. M. and Jochen, P. (2009) 'Social consequences of the Internet for adolescents: a decade of research', *Current Directions in Psychological Science*, 18 (1): 1–5.

Valliant, P. and Antonowicz, D. H. (1991) 'Cognitive behaviour therapy and social skills training improves personality and cognition in incarcerated offenders', *Psychological Reports*, 68: 27–33.

VanderMay, B. and Meff, R. (1982) 'Adult–child incest: a review of research and treatment', *Adolescence*, 17: 717–35.

Vernon, A. (2009) *Counseling Children and Adolescents* (4th edn). Denver, CO: Love.

Villani, D., Gatti, E., Confalonieri, E. and Riva, G. (2012) 'Am I my avatar? A tool to investigate virtual body image representation in adolescence', *CyberPsychology, Behavior and Social Networking*, 15 (8): 435–40.

Volman, M. and ten Dam, G. (2007) 'Learning and the development of social identities in the subjects Care and Technology', *British Educational Research Journal*, 33 (6): 845–66.

Vondracek, F. W. and Corneal, S. (1995) *Strategies for Resolving Individual and Family Problems*. Pacific Grove, CA: Brooks/Cole.

Waiswol, N. (1995) 'Projective techniques as psychotherapy', *American Journal of Psychotherapy*, 49: 244–59.

Wampold, B. E. (2001) *The Great Psychotherapy Debate: Models, Methods, and Findings*. Mahwah, NJ: Erlbaum.

Wang, A. Y. (1994) 'Pride and prejudice in high school gang members', *Adolescence*, 29: 279–91.

Wang, M. Q., Fitzheugh, E. C., Eddy, J. M. and Fu, Q. (1997) 'Social influences on adolescents' smoking progress: a longitudinal analysis', *American Journal of Health Behavior*, 21: 111–17.

Wardle, J., Bindra, R., Fairclough, B. and Westcombe, A. (1993) 'Culture and body image: body perception and weight concern in young Asian and Caucasian British women', *Journal of Community and Applied Social Psychology*, 3: 173–81.

Warner, R. E. (1996) 'Comparison of client and counsellor satisfaction with treatment duration', *Journal of College Students Psychotherapy*, 10: 73–88.

Warren, J. M. (2012) 'Mobile mind mapping: using mobile technology to enhance Rational Emotive Behavior Therapy', *Journal of Mental Health Counseling*, 34 (1): 72–81.

Warren, S., Huston, L., Edgeland, B. and Sroufe, L. (1997) 'Child and adolescent anxiety disorders and early attachment', *Journal of the American Academy of Child and Adolescent Psychiatry*, 36: 637–44.

Warshak, R. A. (2000) 'Remarriage as a trigger of parental alienation syndrome', *The American Journal of Family Therapy*, 28: 229–41.

Waterman, A. (1984) *The Psychology of Individualism*. New York: Praeger.

Waterman, A. S. (1992) 'Identity as an aspect of optimal psychological functioning', in R. Adams, T. P. Gulotta and R. Montemoyr (eds), *Adolescent Identity Formation*. Thousand Oaks, CA: Sage. pp. 50–72.

Webster, R. A., Hunter, M. and Keats, J. A. (1994) 'Peer and parental influences on adolescents' substance abuse: a path analysis', *International Journal of the Addictions*, 29: 647–57.

Weinhold, B. K. (1987) 'Altered states of consciousness: an explorer's guide to inner space', *Counselling and Human Development*, 20: 1–12.

Welch, S., Doll, H. and Fairburn, C. (1997) 'Life events and the onset of bulimia nervosa: a controlled study', *Psychological Medicine*, 27: 515–22.

Werner-Wilson, R. J., Fitzharris, J. L. and Morrissey, K. M. (2004) 'Adolescent and parent perceptions of media influence on adolescent sexuality', *Adolescence*, 39 (154): 303–13.

West, D. J. (1982) *Delinquency: Its Roots, Careers and Prospects*. Cambridge, MA: Harvard University Press.

West, M. O. and Prinz, R. J. (1988) 'Parental alcoholism and childhood psychopathology', in S. Chess, A. Thomas and M. E. Hertzig (eds), *Annual Progress in Child Psychiatry and Child Development*. New York: Brunner/Mazel. pp. 278–314.

White, F. A. (1996) 'Parent, adolescent communication and adolescent decision making', *Journal of Family Studies*, 2: 41–56.

White, M. (2007) *Maps of Narrative Practice*. New York: Norton.

Widon, C. S. (1994) 'Childhood victimization and adolescent problem behaviors', in R. B. Kettellinus and N. E. Land (eds), *Adolescent Problem Behaviors*. Hillsdale, NJ: Lawrence Erlbaum. pp. 127–64.

Wilkes, T. C., Belsher, G., Rush, A. J. and Frank, E. (1994) *Cognitive Therapy for Depressed Adolescents*. New York: Guilford Press.

Williams, R., Bambling, M., King, R. and Abbott, Q. (2009) 'In-session processes in online counselling with young people: an exploratory approach', *Counselling & Psychotherapy Research*, 9 (2): 93–100.

Wills, T. A., Pierce, J. T. and Evans, R. I. (1996) 'Large scale environmental risk factors for substance abuse', *American Behavioral Scientist*, 39: 808–22.

Wilson, C. J. and Deane, F. P. (2001) 'Adolescent opinions about reducing help-seeking barriers and increasing appropriate help engagement', *Journal of Educational and Psychological Consultation*, 12 (4): 345–64.

Winefield, A. H. and Tiggemann, M. (1990) 'Employment status and psychological well-being: a longitudinal study', *Journal of Applied Psychology*, 75: 455–9.

Winter, D. A. (2003) 'The constructivist paradigm', in R. Woolfe and W. Dryden (eds), *Handbook of Counselling Psychology* (2nd edn). London: Sage. pp. 241–59.

Word, W. (1996) 'Mortality awareness and risk taking in late adolescence', *Death Studies*, 20: 133–48.

World Health Organization (1994) *ICD-10 Classification of Mental and Behavioural Disorders: Clinical Descriptions and Diagnostic Guidelines*. Geneva: World Health Organization.

World Health Organization, Collaborating Centre for Mental Health and Substance Abuse (1997) *Treatment Protocol Project Management of Mental Disorders*. Sydney: World Health Organization.

Yarnold, B. M. and Patterson, V. (1995) 'Factors correlated with adolescent use of crack in public schools', *Psychological Reports*, 76: 467–74.

Young, R. A., Antal, S., Bassett, M. E., Post, A., DeVries, N. and Valach, L. (1999) 'The joint actions of adolescents in peer conversations about career', *Journal of Adolescence*, 22: 527–38.

Youniss, J. and Smollar, J. (1985) *Adolescent Relations with Mothers, Fathers and Friends*. Chicago, IL: University of Chicago Press.

Index